BLOOMSBURY
DICTIONARY OF DEDICATIONS

BLOOMSBURY

DICTIONARY
OF
DEDICATIONS

———

ADRIAN ROOM

BLOOMSBURY

First published 1990
by Bloomsbury Publishing Limited, 2 Soho Square, London W1V 5DE

Copyright © 1990 Adrian Room

British Library Cataloguing in Publication Data

A CIP catalogue record for this book
is available from the British Library

ISBN 0 7475 0521 7

1 3 5 7 9 10 8 6 4 2

Designed by Geoff Green

Typeset by Discript, London

Printed in Great Britain by Butler and Tanner, Frome, Somerset

For dear Ursie, who understands perfectly what 'dedication' means.

ACKNOWLEDGMENTS

I am indebted to a number of people for information and advice regarding specific dedicators and dedicatees in this book.

First and foremost I would like to express my warm thanks to Elizabeth Murray, who from her enviable domestic base near the British Library, London, searched with diligence and enthusiasm for relevant titles, texts, and related information and who in the process fell an involuntary victim to the lure of dedications. Her generous feedback and personal involvement were greatly appreciated.

Second, I owe grateful thanks to those who kindly guided me as best they could towards information regarding particular authors and books. For help of this kind regarding John Buchan and *The Three Hostages* I express my thanks to the Hon. William Buchan, Janet Adam Smith, Russell Paterson and P.R. Quarrie in their respective capacities as JB's son, his biographer, the Hon. Secretary of the John Buchan Society, and the College Librarian and Keeper of the College Collections at Eton College.

For similar assistance in the deciphering of the Dedication to Vita Sackville-West's *Challenge* I am more than grateful to John Phillips, her executor, as well as to Suzanne Stroh, Nigel Nicolson and Victoria Glendinning.

My thanks are further due to Andrew Pares for information on his father's translation from the Russian of Krylov's *Fables*; to William Mayne for the background to the dedications in two of his novels, *Sand* and *The Incline*, and for permission to reproduce them; to Robert Leake, Secretary of the Dracula Society, for revealing the identity of Bram Stoker's dedicatee (long a mystery); to J.A. Simpson, co-editor of the *Oxford English Dictionary*, for the background to the various dedications to the *OED* and its *Supplement*, and equally to the Oxford University Press, by whose kind permission they are reproduced; to D.L.L. Howells, Head of the Slavonic Section, Taylor Institution Library, Oxford University, for copies of the original dedications to selected Russian works; to the Librarian of the Institut Français du Royaume-Uni, London, for similar French texts; and to John Grigg for his initial encouragement for the venture as a whole.

For information regarding the current policy of dedications to the Queen I am indebted to Dickie Arbiter, Assistant Press Secretary, Buckingham Palace.

Dedications from the following works are reprinted by permission of the publishers or agents stated: Jonathan Cape Ltd from A.E. Housman, *More Poems* and T.E. Lawrence, *The Seven Pillars of Wisdom*; Faber & Faber Ltd from Arnold

Silcock, *Verse and Worse*, T.S. Eliot, *The Elder Statesman* and W.H. Auden, *Collected Poems*; Feinman & Krasilovsky from Robert Service, *Songs of a Sun-Lover*; John Johnson Ltd from Forrest Reid, *Private Road*. The dedication from *The House at Pooh Corner* is copyright A.A. Milne under the Berne Convention and is reproduced by permission of Curtis Brown, London.

INTRODUCTION

The opening pages of a book, containing what in Britain is known as the preliminary matter ('prelims') and in the United States as the front matter, should not be overlooked, for they can offer the reader a bonus or two.

Apart from the Title-Page, naming the book and its author, there will often be found further items, of varying length, which can both aid and advise the reader and make the production as a whole much more valuable. They can include a Preface (usually by the author), or a Foreword (usually not), an Introduction (like this one that you, dear reader, are now perusing), possibly some Acknowledgments (where appropriate or deserved) and very likely a Table of Contents, as the 'menu' for the meal about to be served.

And quite frequently, too, there will be a Dedication. This will usually be a personal thing, often quite irrelevant to the subject of the book, and addressed to an intimate member of the author's family (wife, husband, mother, father) or to a close friend. Or to a colleague. Or to a famous person. Or to anyone or anything.

If the compliment is a personal one, it may well be paid to someone no longer living. It is one effective way of commemorating the dead.

In some instances, and more frequently the further back one goes in time, the Dedication will be in the form of a letter. In it, the author will perhaps tell the dedicatee why he or she has been the chosen one for that particular book. Similarly, the author may like to say an informal word about the book itself, especially if it is a novel, or a work that would not otherwise have a Preface or Introduction.

But in Elizabethan times, in the sixteenth century, many books contained not simply a Dedication but a 'Dedicatory Epistle' of precise intent. It was really a commercial affair, which was usually arranged on the following terms: a would-be author selected a worthy or noted patron, not necessarily even known to him, and then offered to sing his praises in his book if he (the patron) would pay for this privilege. The author thus offered a eulogy, and received financial recognition for it. The patron, in turn, was personally promoted in (usually) glowing terms to all who read the book.

For this reason, Elizabethan dedications are among the most fulsome and lengthy that we have. But however verbose they may seem to us today, they are of considerable interest, giving an insight into the motives that prompted the writing of a particular book, or that reveal the author's personal circumstances or opinions. In those days, there was much that was acutely controversial, particularly in religion and politics, and many writers used their dedications to polemicise for or against a particular cause, criticising this or that fellow author, or else refuting (or supporting) a topical argument or philosophical viewpoint.

At the same time, from a purely personal angle, the Elizabethan Dedication gives us a first-hand picture of the aristocracy of the day, for most Dedicatory Epistles were addressed either to royalty or to a specific member of the gentry, whether lord or lady.

But of course dedications go back much further than the Elizabethan period. Nor are they restricted to English writers or those of any other single nationality.

Dedications addressed to patrons can be found in ancient times in classical authors. Among others, Horace, Virgil, Cicero and Lucretius all dedicated their writings to a particular patron. Catullus dedicated his poems to Cornelius Nepos, for instance, while Horace dedicated his *Odes* to Maecenas, as Virgil did his *Georgics*. (Maecenas, who lived in the first century BC, was a noted patron of letters. Hence the quite common mention of his name in later dedications as that of an archetypical dedicatee.) The motivations for such dedications were virtually the same as they are today, and involved the status of the writer, his circumstances at the time, and simply the fancy or whim that prompted the Dedication in the first place. There was little that was systematic about it, and where one writer liked to include a Dedication in his work, another may equally have chosen not to do so.

Then as now, too, a whole work could be a virtual Dedication in itself. In more recent times, poets have frequently used a poem in this way. Hence all those poems entitled 'To X', often as not the name of a loved one.

Here, however, we are concerned with the Dedication pure and simple, as the distinctive piece of prose or verse that is found printed at the beginning of a book. (Of course, words *written* by the author of a book in a copy that he or she presents to a friend are also a dedication, inasmuch as they are a personal address. I have a copy of *Some of These Days*, the autobiography of the American entertainer Sophie Tucker, in which she has written: 'To Barry O'Brien (with love from Sophie Tucker) (and *no commission*). July 1948'. Such books, known as 'signed copies' in the book trade, usually sell at a premium. But inscriptions of this type, however attractive and interesting, are not what *this* book is about.)

A Dedication may, incidentally, be written by someone other than the author: Samuel Johnson was a great composer and contributor of dedications, for example, to the first edition of Percy's *Reliques* (1765).

Although most of the dedications quoted in this book have an accompanying 'gloss' or comment, the identity of the dedicatee will not always be given, if only because frequently it is not known. The main criterion for the inclusion of a given Dedication is that its wording should be interesting or original, even where little or nothing is known about either dedicator or dedicatee. In many instances, of course, something *is* known, and will be stated accordingly. But where a 'neat' Dedication is given, without comment, it will have qualified for entry on the grounds given, and should be worth the reading.

Because of this criterion, brief dedications of the 'To Jane' variety, simply naming the dedicatee, are virtual non-starters. Nor, incidentally, are apparent dedications included which are actually addresses 'To the reader' on the part of the author.

Today, many dedications have 'For' as the word that precedes the name of the dedicatee. Formerly, this word was usually 'To'. What is the difference, and why the change? It is almost certainly a matter of approach and intent. 'To' suggests that the work, with its Dedication, is being sent or addressed to someone, rather in the manner of a letter or parcel. 'For' implies that the work was actually *written* for a particular person, so that it is a personally created gift.

In previous years, there were other words besides 'dedicate' that were used to refer to the act of dedication. One was 'inscribe'; another, though much less common, was 'consecrate'. But 'dedicate' is far and away the most frequently found. The word itself, perhaps unexpectedly, does not derive from a Latin root meaning 'give', despite Latin *dare* in this sense, with past tense *dedi*, 'I have given'. It comes from a form of Latin *dicere*, 'to say', 'to speak', from which 'diction' also derives. (And also 'dictionary', making the title of this book a literal tautology, as a 'collection of spoken words containing words spoken'.)

A quick glance at the entries will show that not all dedications are to individual persons. There are thus dedications to groups of people (Louisa M. Alcott, *Eight Cousins*), to abstract qualities (James Lane Allen, *The Heroine in Bronze*), to animals (Hermione Baddeley, *The Unsinkable Hermione Baddeley*), to buildings (Desmond Bagley, *The Vivero Letter*), to God (Philip James Bailey, *Festus*), to places (Margaret Campbell Barnes, *Mary of Carisbrooke*), to the sea (Charles Berlitz, *The Bermuda Triangle*), to a canoe (Poultney Bigelow, *History of the German Struggle for Liberty*), to a bird (John Burroughs, *Bird and Bough*), to a country (Arthur C. Clarke, *Rendezvous with Rama*), and to an occasion (Fanny Cradock, *The Defence of Castle Rising*), among others. Some writers dedicate their works to themselves (Charlotte Charke, *Narrative of the Life of Mrs Charlotte Charke*), others to no one in particular (John Clarmont, *Did I Do That?*). In among all this variety, too, the reader will find dedications that are amusing as well as those that are serious, ones that are hackneyed ('To X, without whom ...') and ones that border on the embarrassing or even the bizarre.

Since Elizabethan times, dedications to reigning monarchs have become increasingly rare, so that today, in the new Elizabethan age, dedications to the Queen are seldom found, and occur only in prestigious works such as the second edition of the great *Oxford English Dictionary* (see under its co-editor, J.A. Simpson) and the seventh edition of *The Times Atlas of the World* (see under its publisher, John Bartholomew & Son Ltd.). In principle, in fact, the Queen does not really accept dedications at all, unlike her royal forebears.

A word should be said about the actual presentation of the dedications in this anthology. Inevitably, some of the earlier dedications, such as the Elizabethan ones, were simply too lengthy to quote in full. Where they have been cut, the aim has been to omit as far as possible the 'impersonal' content of the address, and to retain all that is personal in the relationship between dedicator and dedicatee. Any such excisions from the text are indicated by three dots in square brackets. It is hoped that readers will not flinch from the original contemporary English that has been retained for the majority of such dedications, as well as for some of later vintage. This is not simply to give a period flavour to the text, but to preserve a greater authenticity. Few words will give even small difficulty, and where they are ambiguous, will in most cases have been glossed in modern English. Indeed, readers may acquire quite a taste for Elizabethan spellings and turns of phrase, and find our modern twentieth-century English flat and colourless by comparison!

There is a small representation of dedications in non-English languages. With minor exceptions for some of the shorter dedications, these have not been quoted in the original, but have been translated, either by myself ('AR') or by the named translator. Where no translator is named, none was named in the source from which the already translated text was taken. For such dedications, however, the original foreign-language title of the work is quoted, if only because its English version may differ from the original, or not be readily recognised.

As mentioned, most dedications have an accompanying commentary. The aim is primarily to identify the dedicator and, even more, the dedicatee, where known. But there are also comments on style, content and general background which may prove of interest and use. Where no identity is given for the dedicatee, it should not be automatically assumed that no attempt was made to trace it. Efforts were made in a number of cases that proved fruitless, even for some of the better-known writers. A typical abortive search was the following. John Buchan's *The Three Hostages* (1924) has a dedicatory letter addressed to 'A Young Gentleman of Eton College'. Who was he? It would obviously be interesting to discover, since an examination of the author's autobiographical writings gives no clue. Yet despite appeals to the Archivist of Eton College, to the Secretary of the John Buchan Society, to Janet Adam Smith, Buchan's biographer, and even to his son, the Hon. William Buchan, who in turn consulted his elder brother, Sir John Buchan, Baron Tweedsmuir, himself an Old Etonian, the identity of the youthful dedicatee remains, alas, elusive.

If any reader *can* identify an unidentified dedicatee, it would be most helpful and welcome if such identity, ideally with supporting evidence, could be sent to me care of the publishers, for inclusion (and due acknowledgment) in any new edition of the book.

Some quite well-known writers will certainly be looked for in vain in the book. This is very likely because they chose only rarely, or even not at all, to dedicate their works. Bernard Shaw, for example, was more interested in introducing his plays with vivid lengthy prefaces than with personal dedications, and H.G. Wells only rarely dedicated his novels. Or it may be that there *are* dedications, but only of the minimal sort. Angus Wilson's short stories *A Bit Off the Map* (1957) are simply 'For Francis and Honoria', and C.P. Snow's novel *The Conscience of the Rich* (1958) is dedicated *tout court* 'To Pamela Hansford Johnson', otherwise to his wife, whom he had married eight years earlier. But of course it should not be assumed that the absence of a literary name means that the writer in question never dedicated any books. He or she may simply have escaped the net when I was trawling for entries for the book. To this end I spent many full weeks in libraries, both public and 'private', and in new and second-hand bookshops, both borrowing and even buying for the purpose. A coincidental consequence of the exercise resulted in my actually reading whole books that I might otherwise never have even opened, from Fanny Burney's wonderful *Evelina* (1778) to John Miller's both repulsive yet compulsive *Former Soldier Seeks Employment* (1989). And I don't think I have mugged up Molière so intensively since schooldays. It was a pleasant and rewarding experience.

To compensate for absences, since obviously any anthology has to be finite, I have endeavoured to give a fuller representation of dedications for certain writers who customarily dedicated their writings. Such dedications are not only readable and interesting in themselves, but together give a good all-round picture of the writer as he or she gradually progressed through the literary world and life in general. So fairly extensive dedicatory runs will therefore be found for the following differing writers: Jane Austen, Robert Browning, John Buchan, Edward Bulwer Lytton, Byron, Lewis Carroll, Agatha Christie, John Dryden, Gerald Durrell, T.S. Eliot, Graham Greene, Charles Kingsley, George Macdonald, A.A. Milne, Molière, Thomas Moore, Eric Partridge, Arthur Quiller-Couch, Walter Scott, William Shakespeare, Edmund Spenser, R.L. Stevenson, Alfred, Lord Tennyson, Mark Twain, Dennis Wheatley. In some instances, a writer will alter a Dedication for a later edition of a book, or even drop it altogether. Thus Graham Greene dedicated the first edition of *Journey Without Maps* (1934) to his wife, but the 1978 edition to his cousin, and omitted the original Dedication to *It's a Battlefield* (1934) from subsequent editions.

Anyone who has read a Dedication in the original will know that, often as not, the text is often displayed in an original or artistic manner, often with a whole page to itself. From Elizabethan times, too, the dedicatory art frequently involved different kinds of contrasting typeface, with much use of upper case (capital) letters for the opening word or words. This technique still exists today, so that the dedication to L.P. Hartley's *Facial Justice* (1960), for instance, appears in the book as follows:

DEDICATED
with homage, acknowledgments and
apologies to the memory of
Nathaniel Hawthorne

In Victorian times, too, many dedications were not only artistically displayed like this, usually symmetrically, but printed entirely in upper case letters, even when the text is extensive. (Charles Kingsley's *Westward Ho!*, published in 1855, is of this type, with a text of over a hundred words.)

For reasons of space, however, it has not been possible to reproduce such layouts here in their original form, so that dedications appear as continuous linear text. Nonetheless, punctuation has been preserved, although where a pause in the text was indicated in the original by a break to a fresh line of print, it has now been denoted by the addition of a comma. However, verse dedications have been reproduced in their original form.

In presenting this collection of literary dedications to the reader, it would of course be wrong to overlook the existence of other types of dedication. Several famous films, for example, have had their dedications, so that *The Great Escape* was dedicated to 'the fifty', the prisoners of war whose tragic story is the subject of the 1963 movie. Musical compositions, too, have often been dedicated. Beethoven's Bagatelle in A minor for piano, composed in 1810, has even come to be popularly known by the two opening words of its Dedication, 'Für Elise', although the identity of the dedicatee is still uncertain. And every church called 'St Martin's' or 'Holy Trinity' has been formally dedicated to the named saint or deity.

Normally, though, 'dedication' means 'literary dedication', and it is this type that is the sole subject of the present book.

So, resisting the temptation to write a whole tome on the subject by way of this Introduction, I invite the reader to browse through the pages and savour the dedicatory delights. I hope he or she will soon find a favourite or two, as I have done in the enjoyable if time-consumimg task of compiling the selection with all its associated literary and biographical research. And suggestions for interesting dedications not included here will be welcome for any new edition of the book.

Adrian Room

❧ A ❧

Edwin A. Abbott, *St Thomas of Canterbury: His Death and Miracles*, 1898
~ To the memory of Thomas, once Archbishop of Canterbury, now venerated by some as saint and martyr, by others admired as a hero, by some vilified as a narrow ecclesiastic, but deserving to be studied by all, whether friends, critics, or enemies, as a conspicuous proof that the spirit may be then first manifested in its full power when defeat and corruption have triumphed over the flesh.

A biography dedicated to its subject is a logical step not followed by many biographers. Abbott was headmaster of the City of London School when this was published; he otherwise generally made his name as a clergyman who was an authority on Shakespeare, Bacon and various literary subjects.

Ernest Hamlin Abbott, *On the Training of Parents*, 1908
~ No man has the right to dedicate to another what is not his own. All that is mine in this little book is its infelicities. These I dedicate to oblivion. The rest belongs to those two women from whom I, as son and as husband, have learned all that I know of the training of parents.

Edmond About, *The Nose of a Lawyer*, 1862
~ To Monsieur Alexandre Bixio. Allow me, Sir, to inscribe at the beginning of this little book the dear and honoured name of a man who has devoted his whole life to the cause of progress, the name of a father who has offered his two sons to the deliverance of Italy, and of a friend who was among the first to come to give me proof of his sympathy on the day after 'Gaetana'.

Translated from the French by AR; original title: *Le Nez d'un notaire*. Jacques Alexandre Bixio was a French publicist and politician who took part in the 1830 Revolution and who supported the reformist movement that culminated in the 1848 Revolution, when the French monarchy was overthrown. 'Gaetana' was 13 February 1861, when the Italian port of Gaeta capitulated to the Italians, thus ending the Bourbon Kingdom of the Two Sicilies.

Edmond About, *The Man with the Broken Ear*, 1862

TO THE COMTESSE DE NAJAC
This little book is sheltered by your wing,

~ 1 ~

Oh, for good times and good friendship's laugh!
With days filled full, too short by half!
Indeed, your Brittany's a beauteous thing.

I saw it, too, when Fougas came to print:
The memories then fled far from off my page,
Like captive finches flying from their cage;
I thought of it – but did not read one hint.

What grand and wondrous form the ocean had!
And how the sun made all so bright and glad.
All dressed in white, with tearful mocker's art!

Who shall return those stolen hours to me,
Those happy talks, those pancakes crisp for tea,
Those waltzes gay, that peace once more at heart?

Translated from the French by AR; original title: *L'Homme à l'oreille cassée*. A dedication that is perhaps more verse than poetry. The American publisher and writer Henry Holt brought out his own English translation of the novel in 1867 with the following dedication: 'Dear Leypoldt: You have not forgotten that nearly two years ago, before our business connection was thought of, this identical translation was "respectfully declined" by you with that same courtesy, the exercise of which in frequent similar cases each one of us now tries so hard to shove on the other's shoulders. I hope that your surprise on reading this note of dedication will not interfere with your forgiving the pertinacity with which, through it, I still strive to make the book *yours*. H.H.'.

Andrew Leith **Adams**, MD, *Wanderings of a Naturalist in India, The Western Himalayas, and Cashmere*, 1867

~ I dedicate this volume to the memory of Francis Adams, A.M., M.D., LL.D., as a small token of filial devotion, and in grateful remembrance of that training in early life by which he directed my mind to an appreciation of the works of nature, and a love for all intellectual and improving studies.

A doctor son's tribute to his doctor father, who was an army surgeon first and a naturalist second.

Thomas **Adams**, *Sermons*, 1629

~ To the Right Honourable and Truly Noble William, Earl of Pembroke, &c.; Lord High Steward of His Majesty's Household; of His Majesty's Most Honourable Privy Council; Chancellor of the University of Oxford; and Knight of the Most Noble Order of the Garter. My Lord, Your honourable name hath stood long, like a happy star, in the orb of divine volumes; a sanctuary of protection to the labours and persons of students; and if I have presumed to flee thither also for refuge, I am taught the way by more worthy precedents. It cannot but be for your honour that your patronage is so generally sought for, not only by private ministers, but even by whole universities. In the vouchsafing whereof, you have daily as many prayers as the earth hath saints. I am bold also to present my poor offering, as one loath to be hindmost in that acknowledgment which is so nobly deserved, and so joyfully rendered, of all tongues. Divers of these sermons did presume on the help of your noble wing, when they first adventured to fly abroad. In their retrief, or second flight, being now sprung up again in greater number, they humbly beg the same favour. They all speak the same language, and desire so to be understood. Yet for fear of misinterpretation, I beseech your Lordship to give them all your pass; and, lest they should grow poor with contempt, your legacy of approbation. So I doubt not but that for your noble name's sake, (not their own merit,) wheresoever they light, they shall find respective entertainment, and do yet some more good to the church of God. Which success, together with your Honour's true happiness, both of this and a better life, is still prayed for, by your Lordship's humbly devoted, and ready to be commanded, THO. ADAMS.

William Herbert, 3rd Earl of Pembroke, was one of the most generous literary patrons of his day, as this dedication indicates. Many such dedications were jointly inscribed to William and his brother Philip, the 4th Earl, among the most famous being that of the first folio of Shakespeare's works, where they are referred to as 'the most noble and incomparable paire of brethren'. (See the last of SHAKESPEARE's dedications below for the full text.) A powerful and popular preacher, Thomas Adams was himself noted for his many 'epistles dedicatory', including ones to Sir Thomas Egerton, Lord Ellesmere and Sir Henry Montague, Lord Chief Justice of England, to whom he was appointed 'observant chaplain'. In his dedication above, 'respective' means 'respectful'. The spelling is modernised.

Joy **Adamson**, *The Searching Spirit*, 1978

~ To Oma and Elsa.

The author dedicated her autobiography to 'Oma', her nickname for her maternal grandmother, and to the lioness who became the famous subject of the book (and film) *Born Free*.

Joseph **Addison**, *Works*, 1721

~ To the Right Honourable James Craggs, Esquire, his Majesty's principal secretary of State. Dear Sir, I cannot wish that any of my writings should last longer than the memory of our friendship, and therefore I thus publicly bequeath them to you, in return for the many valuable instances of your affection. That they may come to you with as little disadvantage as possible, I have left the care of them to one, whom, by the experience of some years, I know well qualified to answer my intentions. He has already the honour and happiness of being under your protection; and, as he will very much stand in need of it, I cannot wish him better, than that he may continue to deserve the favour and countenance of such a patron. [...] May the frankness and generosity of your spirit continue to soften and subdue your enemies, and gain you many friends, if possible, as sincere as yourself. When you have found such, they cannot wish you more true happiness than I, who am, with the greatest zeal, Dear Sir, your most entirely affectionate Friend, and faithful obedient Servant, J. Addison.

Addison died in 1719, leaving the publication of his collected works to his protégé ('well qualified to answer my intentions'), the poet Thomas Tickell. Tickell is now mostly or entirely forgotten, except perhaps for his Epitaph on Addison's death, with the lines 'There taught us how to live; and (oh! too high / The price of knowledge) taught us how to die'.

Sir William **Addison**, *Understanding English Place-Names*, 1978
~ To the memory of P.H. Reaney, who encouraged me to believe that although I might never find the right answers I might one day become capable of asking the right questions.

Reaney made his name with scholarly but popular books on place-names and surnames, but especially with *A Dictionary of British Surnames* (1958), still regarded as a definitive work. Addison's own companion volume to the above, *Understanding English Surnames* (1978), has no dedication.

Thomas **Ady**, *A Candle in the Dark*, 1656
~ To the Prince of the Kings of the Earth.

As frequently in seventeenth-century works, the substance of the book is indicated in its subtitle, which was: 'A Treatise concerning the Nature of Witches and Witchcraft: Being Advice to Judges, Sheriffes, Justices of the Peace, and Grand Jury Men, what to do before they passe sentence on such as are arraigned for their lives as Witches'. The dedication is followed by an entreaty that the Holy Spirit may possess the understanding of whoever opens the book, and the title-page itself has an illustration of an arm coming out of the clouds, holding a lighted candle.

Grace **Aguilar**, *Home Influence*, 1847
~ To Mrs. Herbert Townshend Bowen: My dear friend, – Independent of the personal feelings which urged the dedication of this unpretending volume to you, I know few to whom a story illustrative of a mother's solemn responsibilities, intense anxiety to fulfil them, and deep sense of the Influence of Home could, with more justice, be tendered. Simple as is the actual narrative, the sentiments it seeks to illustrate are so associated with you, – have been so strengthened from the happy hours of unrestrained intercourse I have enjoyed with you, – that, though I ought, perhaps, to have waited until I could have offered a work of far superior merit to a mind like yours, I felt as if no story of mine could more completely belong to you. Will you, then, pardon the *unintentional* errors which I fear you, as an earnest Protestant, *may* discern, and accept this little work as a slight tribute of the warm affection and sincere esteem with which you have been so long regarded by, Your truly attached Friend, Grace Aguilar.

A somewhat convoluted epistle. The book was an 'improving' one, with the subtitle 'A Tale for Mothers and Daughters'. Grace Aguilar was an English novelist of Spanish–Jewish parents. She wrote on Jewish subjects, and her delicate health was not improved by her literary exertions, which largely contributed to her early death, at the age of thirty-one, only a few weeks after this book appeared. Her parenthetical comment here would be best phrased otherwise today, one feels.

Anna **Akhmatova**, *A Poem without a Hero*, 1940–62
~ I dedicate this poem to the memory of its first hearers – my friends and fellow citizens, who perished in Leningrad during the siege.

Translated from the Russian by AR; original title: *Poema bez geroya*. For many years officially ostracised by the Soviet authorities, and banished from the Soviet Writers' Union, Akhmatova was accorded recognition again near the end of her life, when, after a break of several years, she resumed her writing. She died in 1966 at the age of seventy-eight. This poem, a 'triptych' on the suffering endured by Russians in the Second World War, and especially in the Siege of Leningrad (1941–4), has the above dedication as part of its preface (headed 'By way of an introduction'), as well as three further verse dedications, dated respectively 1940, 1945 and 1956.

Louisa M. **Alcott**, *Eight Cousins; or, The Aunt-Hill*, 1875
~ To the many boys and girls whose letters it has been impossible to answer, this book is dedicated as a peace-offering by their friend, L.M.A.

A book that appeared seven years after the famous *Little Women*, but eleven years before that novel's sequel, *Jo's Boys*.

Brian **Aldiss**, *New Arrivals, Old Encounters*, 1979
~ For Harold Boyes, who taught me all I know and much I still don't know.

Brian **Aldiss**, *Life in the West*, 1980
~ *Life in the West* is dedicated to the other Distinguished Persons, Chen, David, Iris, Maysie, and Michael, by no means forgetting Felix, Elena, Derek, and Janet, to show them what one of their number was up to before we sampled life in the East and walked the Great Wall together.

New Arrivals (above) is a collection of twelve short stories on science fiction themes; *Life in the West*, despite the factual dedication, is a (non science-fiction) novel, although like its predecessors, *The Hand-Reared Boy* and *A Soldier Erect*, based on the author's own experiences.

Sir William **Alexander**, *Aurora*, 1604
~ To the Right Honorable and Vertuous Lady, the Lady Agnes Dowglas, Countesse of Argyle. Madame, when I remember the manie obligations which I owe to your manifold merits, I oftentimes accuse my selfe to my self of forgetfulnes, and yet I am to be excused: for how can I satisfie so infinit a debt, since whilst I go to disengage my self in some measure by giving you the patronage of these unpolished lines (which indeed for their manie errors, had need of a respected Sanctuary) I but engage my self further, while as you take the patronage of so

unpolished lines. Yet this shal not discourage me, for alwayes I carie this advantage, that as they were the fruits of beautie, so shal they be sacrificed as oblations to beautie. And to a beautie, though of it selfe most happie, yet more happie in this, that it is thought worthie (and can be no more then worthy) to be the outward cover of so many inward perfections. So assuring my selfe, that as no darknesse can abide before the Sunne, so no deformitie can be found in those papers, over which your eyes have once shined, I rest, Your Honors most humbly devoted, William Alexander.

Sir William, Earl of Stirling, and a noted Scottish poet and courtier, was offering the lady a collection of songs and sonnets, as doubtless the title suggests, and as the dedication itself implies ('oblations to beautie'); 'then' is modern 'than', as elsewhere in dedications of this period.

Ted **Allbeury**, *The Girl from Addis*, 1984
~ This book is dedicated to all those men and women, past and present, of BBC Drama, who have entertained us all so well. Long may they go on doing so – this book is for them – with love.

Ted Allbeury established his name as a novelist in the early 1970s.

James Lane **Allen**, *The Heroine in Bronze*, 1912
~ To Youth – its Kingdoms and Ideals.

Allen was an American novelist who had taught school and college for thirteen years from 1872.

William **Allen**, *Killing Noe Murder Briefly Discourst in Three Quæstions*, 1657
~ To his Highnesse OLIVER CROMWELL, May it please your Highnesse, – How I have spent some howers of the leasure your Highnes hath been pleased to give me, this following Paper will give your Highnes an accompt. How you will please to interpret it I can not tell, but I can with confidence say my intention in it is, to procure your Highnes that justice no body yet does you, and to let the people see the longer they deferr it the greater injury they doe both themselves and you: To your Highnes justly belongs the honour of dying for the people, and it cannot choose but be an unspeakable consolation to you in the last moments of your life to consider, with how much benefit to the world you are like to leave it. 'Tis then onely (my Lord) the titles you now usurpe will be truly yours; you wil then be indeed the deliverer of your country and free it from a bondage little inferiour to that from which Moyses delivered his. You will then be that true Reformer, which you would now be thought. Religion shalbe then restored, Liberty asserted and Parliaments have those priviledges they have sought for. We shall then hope that other Lawes will have place besides those of the sword, and that justice shal be otherwise defind then the will and pleasure of the strongest, and we shalthen hope men wil keep oathes again, and not have the necessitie of being false, and perfidious to preserve themselves and be like their Rulers: all this we hope from your Highnes

happie expiration who are the true father of your countrie, for while you live we can call nothing ours, and as it is from your death that we hope for our inheritances. [...] But amongst all that put in their requests and supplications for your Highnesses speedy deliverance from all earthly troubles none is more assiduous nor more fervent than he, that with the rest of the nation hath the honour to be, May it please your Highnesse, Your Highnesse present slave and vassall, W.A.

A famous ironic dedication that has been imitated many times since, but rarely equalled. The writer who so boldly advocates Cromwell's assassination appeared as 'William Allen' on the title-page of the pamphlet, but was actually the Leveller, Edward Sexby. William Allen was the real name of one of Cromwell's former Ironsides.

A.M., *The Work Table and Embroidery Frame Companion*, 1843
~ To her most gracious Majesty the Queen. Madam, This manual of all the accomplishments dependent upon the needle, is most humbly and most respect-fully dedicated to your Majesty, by one, who feels conscientiously urged thereto, in consequence of the scarcely paralleled popularity of a former work, entitled 'Woman as Virgin, Wife, and Mother;' in which an elevated morality, extension of industry, refinement of manner, and improved taste, were warmly advocated, and because it is presumed that the same qualities form a conspicuous feature in the present work. As a gift of love or friendship, in the hands of a Father, a Brother, or one who is on the point of marriage, this little work possesses peculiar appropriateness; and, in all Families and Schools it would be the index to economy of time, and the cultivation of the most elegant as well as useful Female Accomplishments. It is in this singleness of purpose, that the Authoress ventures on the present Dedication; and also in a profound conviction of the high advantages which have been diffused among her Sex by your Majesty's august example. In conclusion, she will ever remain, Madam, your Majesty's most dutiful, most loyal, and devoted subject.

One of scores of earnest dedications made to Queen Victoria. This particular work was subtitled 'A Manual of all the Accomplishments Dependent upon the Needle'. The writer modestly names herself only by her initials.

Jeffery Amhurst, *Wandering Abroad*, 1976
~ Dedicated, firstly to the memory of Winifred Clemence Dane, who originally talked me into venturing on the slippery slopes of autobiography, and secondly to David Farrer, who with his encouraging persistence cajoled me into finishing it.

Winifred Clemence Dane was 'Clemence Dane', the popular playwright and novelist whose real name was Winifred Ashton (died 1965); David Farrer was the director of Secker & Warburg, the firm that published Amhurst's book.

John **Amis**, *Amiscellany: My Life, My Music*, 1985

~ 'To my friends pictured within' and some who are not: in particular, Michael Rose.

The quoted words will certainly represent an earlier stock dedication.

Roald **Amundsen**, *The South Pole*, 1912

~ To my comrades, the brave little band that promised in Funchal Roads to stand by me in the struggle for the South Pole, I dedicate this book.

The book, written in Norwegian, appeared the year after Amundsen had successfuly reached the South Pole with four companions and fifty-two dogs.

Marie Philomene **Anderson**, *Model*, 1988

~ This book is dedicated to my special guides and teachers: Marcelle Poirier Anderson and Bruce Anderson, Jr, William Russell Gray, Pera Marshall Odishoo, Lawrence Lee Close, Stanley Edward Malinowski, Jr, Jane Marie Stewart, Donna Surges-Tatum, Christopher Owen, Matthew Louis Amato, J. Cortland Boyd, and most of all to God! Without His strength and guidance this book would not have been possible.

The book is a practical guide to modelling as a career, with the author duly acknowledging her debt to her Maker. There is good biblical precedent for linking the divine with the delightful, of course, for example 'He hath made every thing beautiful' (Ecclesiastes 3:11).

Poul **Anderson**, *The Avatar*, 1978

~ To Bubbles. Go raibh maith agat, mo chroi.

The popular American fantasy and science fiction writer words his brief dedication (to his wife?) with an Irish sentence which translates as 'Thank you, my love'.

Sherwood **Anderson**, *Winesburg, Ohio*, 1919

~ To the memory of my mother, Emma Smith Anderson, whose keen observations on the life about her first awoke in me the hunger to see beneath the surface of lives, this book is dedicated.

This was the volume of stories that established the reputation of the American writer.

Anonymous, *Amusements Serious and Comical; or A New Collection of Bons-Mots, Keen-Jests, Ingenious Thoughts, Pleasant Tales, and Comical Adventures*, 1719

~ To John Merrill Junior, Esqr. Your Father having instructed me with the Direction of your first Studies, I thought it became me to discharge my Duty in such a manner as might both instruct, and divert you. That is the scope of these Amusements, which I take the freedom to dedicate to you, and which are purposely designed to assist you in that part of your Education, the learning of the French tongue. This trust incumbent upon me can but be an agreeable Occupation to me, since it is so scarce to find in any gentleman of eight Years of Age the quickness of Apprehension, and the eagerness to learn so conspicuous in you. An happy omen of your future advancement. As you are related to the most illustrious Persons among our Nobility, and assisted with such a Genius as you are Master of, what may not be justly expected of you? Those rare Examples of Uprightness, and Virtue, shining every day so bright upon You, in the Persons of Your Parents, cannot but carry you towards what is excellent. Happy, Sir, who, besides that tendency to Good, have before your eyes in Mr. MERRILL's Person a Pattern to frame Your self by, in whom are found united all those so uncommon Accomplishments that equally constitute a sound Christian, a zealous Patriot, and an ingenious and compleat Gentleman. That You may one day imitate his Virtues, is the most ardent wish of him who is, with all possible passion and esteem, Sir, Your most humble, and obedient Servant.

It is difficult to establish the precise identity of the precocious eight-year-old dedicatee, or his undoubtedly virtuous father. Perhaps they were among those English Merrills who were the forerunners of the many American families of the name. The book itself is in both English and French, including the title and dedication, and is intended, according to the subtitle, 'For the Use of such as design to learn either French, or English'. It is strange, and rather frustrating, that such an enterprising work should be anonymous.

John **Arden**, *Silence Among the Weapons*, 1982
~ To the Subject peoples – subjected, that is to say, to their own rules, to someone else's, to ours, to *us* …

The book is a picaresque novel on the colonial ambitions of the Roman Empire, set in the 1st century BC.

Thomas **Armstrong**, *King Cotton*, 1947
~ For those people of Lancashire without whose sacrifices the United States of America might not exist as we know it to-day, whose 'sublime Christian heroism', in the words of Abraham Lincoln, is not to be found commonly recorded in the history books of his mighty country across the sea.

The book tells the story of destitution in the Lancashire mills in the mid nineteenth century.

Sir Edwin **Arnold**, *The Secret of Death*, 1884
TO MY DAUGHTER
Because I know my verse shall henceforth live
    On lips to be, on hearts as yet unbeating;
Because the East and West will some day give –
    When Faith and Doubt are friends, at some far meeting –
Late praise to him that dreamed it, – therefore here,
    As one that carves upon a growing willow
The word it is to keep for many a year;
    As one that paints, before she breasts the billow,
A dear name on his vessel's prow, as one

> That finishing a fane, makes dedication
> With golden letters on the polished stone,
>   Crowning his toil by loving celebration, –
> Here, while these last, our love I celebrate,
> For thy sake and thy mother's, – writing 'Kate'.

Sir Edwin, poet, journalist and orientalist, went with his daughter Katharine Lilian on a lengthy tour of the Pacific coast and Japan four years after this work was published. Earlier, he had made his name with a blank-verse epic on the life and teachings of the Buddha, *The Light of Asia* (1879). But his verse hardly lingers on the lips today.

Roger **Ascham**, *The Scholemaster*, 1570

~ To the honorable Sir William Cecill Knight, principall Secretarie to the Quenes most excellent Majestie. Sondry & reasonable be the causes why learned men have used to offer and dedicate such workes as they put abrode to some such personage as they thinke fittest, either in respect of abilitie of defense, or skill for jugement, or private regard of kindenesse and dutie. Every one of those considerations, Syr, move me of right to offer this my late husbands M. Aschams worke unto you. For well remembryng how much all good learnyng oweth unto you for defense therof, as the Universitie of Cambrige, of which my said late husband was a member, have in chosing you their worthy Chaunceller acknowledged, and how happily you have spent your time in such studies & caried the use therof to the right ende, to the good service of the Quenes Majestie and your contrey to all our benefites, thyrdly how much my sayd husband was many wayes bound unto you, and how gladly and confortably he used in hys lyfe to recognise and report your goodnesse toward hym, leavyng with me then hys poore widow and a great sort of orphanes a good comfort in the hope of your good continuance, which I have truly found to me and myne, and therfore do duely and dayly pray for you and yours: I could not finde any man for whose name this booke was more agreable for hope [of] protection, more mete for submission to judgement, nor more due for respect of worthynesse of your part and thankefulnesse of my husbandes and myne. Good I trust it shall do, as I am put in great hope by many very well learned that can well judge therof. Mete therefore I compt it that such good as my husband was able to do and leave to the common weale, it should be received under your name, and that the world should owe thanke therof to you to whom my husband the authour of it was for good receyved of you, most dutiefully bounden. And so besechyng you, to take on you the defense of this booke, to avaunce the good that may come of it by your allowance and furtherance to publike use and benefite, and to accept the thankefull recognition of me and my poore children, trustyng of the continuance of your good memorie of M. Ascham and his, and dayly commendyng the prosperous estate of you and yours to God whom you serve and whoes you are, I rest to trouble you. Your humble Margaret Ascham.

Ascham, a classical scholar and teacher, and tutor to the royal children of Henry VIII, had died two years earlier, leaving his widow to compose this poignant dedication to his former wealthy patron. Her text is interesting for the light it casts on the duty of patron and author at that time, and on the actual role of the dedication. Ascham was educated at St John's College, Cambridge, and was associated with both college and university for most of his life. The work itself was a treatise on education.

Jean-Charles **Aschero**, *The Sole Witness*, 1987

~ To Véronique Pitois, my future fellow-writer, who will recognise (herself?), in at least three pages, the little schoolteacher of the 'highway'. Wishing that she will follow (in the real or figurative sense) just the byways, more slowly but more surely, and lined with flowering trees and birdsong.

Translated from the French by AR; original title: *L'Unique Témoin*. The novel is a crime story involving the author's police investigator, Inspector Joubert, the book being the first of a series.

Arthur **Ashe** with Neil Amdue, *Off the Courts*, 1982

~ To that nameless slave girl off H.M.S. *Doddington*, and her daughter Lucy, her granddaughter Peggy, her great-granddaughter Peggy, and her great-great-grandson Hammett, all of whom were born, lived and died as slaves.

The autobiography of the famous black American tennis player (born 1943), tracing his ancestry back to slave origins.

Joe **Ashton**, *Grass Roots*, 1977

~ For Maggie my wife, who has suffered so much for me and my job.

The Labour politician's first novel, about the doings of a right-wing Labour MP in 'Gritnall', a 'typical Yorkshire town'. He himself is a Yorkshireman, born in Sheffield in 1933.

Isaac **Asimov**, *View From A Height*, 1964

~ To Natalie Greenberg, Miss Efficiency.

Isaac **Asimov**, *Extraterrestrial Civilizations*, 1980

~ To the memory of Paul Nadan (1929–1978), for whom I should have started this book sooner.

Louis **Auchinloss**, *The Book Class*, 1984

~ For My Good Friend James W. Tuttleton, with my deep appreciation of his illuminating criticism of my work.

The dedication seems sincere enough. The novel itself is set in Manhattan.

W.H. Auden, *Collected Poems*, 1976
~ For Christopher Isherwood and Chester Kallman.
> Although you be, as I am, one of those
> Who feels a Christian ought to write in prose,
> For poetry is magic: born in sin, you
> May read it to exorcise the Gentile in you.

Note the punning reference ('one of those') to the fact that Auden, Isherwood and Kallman were/are not only poets but homosexuals. Kallman was long Auden's lover.

Aunt Fanny, *Night Caps*, nd (*c.* 1880)
> To my
> Rusty, fusty, crusty, gusty,
> Kind, good-hearted, generous, trusty
> Bachelor Brother
> And no other
> (Who will maintain, were't his last word,
> That children should be seen, not heard),
> This book of many a childish trait
> And talk, which he pretends to hate,
> Most lovingly I dedicate.

Aunt Fanny, an American children's writer, was in reality a Mrs Barrow (1822–94), and also the author of *Aunt Fanny's Christmas Stories*.

Jane Austen, *Love and Freindship*, 1790
~ To Madame La Comtesse De Feuillide This Novel is inscribed by Her obliged Humble Servant The Author.

Jane Austen, *The History of England*, 1791
~ To Miss Austen elder daughter of the Revd George Austen, this Work is inscribed with all due respect by The Author.

Jane Austen, *Lesley Castle*, 1792
~ To Henry Thomas Austen Esqre. Sir, I am now availing myself of the Liberty you have frequently honoured me with of dedicating one of my Novels to you. That it is unfinished, I greive; yet fear that from me, it will always remain so; that as far as it is carried, it Should be so trifling and so unworthy of you, is another concern to your obliged humble Servant, The Author.

Jane Austen, *A Collection of Letters*, 1792
~ To Miss Cooper. Cousin, Conscious of the Charming Character which in every Country, & every Clime in Christendom is Cried, Concerning you, with Caution & Care I Commend to your Charitable Criticism this Clever Collection of Curious

Comments, which have been Carefully Culled, Collected & Classed by your Comical Cousin, The Author.

Jane **Austen**, *The Three Sisters*, 1792
~ To Edward Austen Esqre The following unfinished Novel is respectfully inscribed by His obedient humle servt, The Author.

Jane **Austen**, *Emma*, 1816
~ To His Royal Highness The Prince Regent this work is, by His Royal Highness's permission, most respectfully dedicated, by His Royal Highness's dutiful and obedient servant, The Author.

The first five works above are juvenilia, written when the author was still in her teens, and dedicated fairly whimsically to various friends and family members. Jane Austen was the youngest of seven children; George Austen was her father, Henry and Edward her brothers, Cassandra ('Miss Austen elder daughter') her sister, and Miss Cooper a childhood friend who married in the year of writing. Something of the childhood humour and wit remains in the dedication to her mature novel, *Emma*, addressed to the Prince Regent and deliberately coolly correct. The Prince was a keen admirer of Jane Austen's novels, keeping a set in each of his houses. Austen, for her part, was no admirer of his by way of returning the compliment. Her wording does not reveal the fact that the dedication had been written at the Prince's suggestion, rather than by his permission, since the initiative was his, and his wish had been passed to her through his librarian.

Jane **Austen**, *The Watsons*, 1928
~ To my father John Hubback, to remind him of the time when we wrote 'Jane Austen's Sailor Brothers' together. E.B.

The novel is a completion of Jane Austen's unfinished original by Edith Brown, Austen's great-grand-niece, and her husband Francis Brown.

Alfred **Austin**, *The Garden That I Love*, 1894
~ To Madeleine and Dorothy Stanley. Dear Madeleine and Dorothy, Do you remember how, when first you saw the Garden That I Love, inexorable clouds, as though of opinion your presence was sunshine enough, came drifting from the south, and fitful showers drenched border and flower-bed? [...] You therefore, I know, will tend your own flowers, even as already in some degree, you tend them at your dear Arlington. [...] That is why, more even than for the friendship, you and yours have shown me, I ask you to accept the dedication of this little volume. Believe me always, Yours affectionately, Alfred Austin.

Austin was first and foremost a poet, although this was a popular prose work. Two years later he became Poet Laureate, an appointment that caused considerable public mockery. The poet's talents were in general popularly received, but not highly rated by those 'who knew', and the unfortunate man was frequently parodied.

Florence **Ayscough**, *A Chinese Mirror*, 1925

~ To Amy Lowell, whose writing-brush is full of life's movement, from Florence Ayscough. Since I wrote the Dedication to this book the sun has risen from out of a sea mist, has climbed to its zenith, and has sunk in the long grass at the edge of the horizon twenty-three times; and yesterday at the hour when her room, high under the eaves, is filled with its slant shining, Amy Lowell laid down her writing-brush for ever.

Amy Lowell, born 1874, died (as the dedication relates) 1925, was a 'self-liberated' American woman who was a stout (in more senses than one) champion of modern poetry. She and Florence Ayscough closely collaborated in their lives and work, and together produced free verse renderings of Chinese poems in *Fir-Flower Tablets* (1922). Their correspondence about translations from the Chinese was published in 1946, four years after Ayscough's own death.

❦ B ❦

Richard **Bach**, *Jonathan Livingston Seagull*, 1970
~ To the real Jonathan Seagull, who lives within us all.

The American writer's brief but popular bestseller, an allegorical tale about a bird who longs to fly free. 'Flying free', in the literal and spiritual sense, is a theme that runs through most of the former US Air Force pilot's stories. Compare his title below.

Richard **Bach**, *The Bridge Across Forever*, 1985
~ For Leslie, who taught me to fly.

The author of *Jonathan Livingston Seagull* (see above) and *Illusions* (1977) continued his search for love in a less mystical vein in this, his eighth novel. The dedication here is to his wife, Leslie Parrish-Bach.

Alice Mabel **Bacon**, *Japanese Girls and Women*, 1902
~ To Stematz, the Countess Oyama, in the name of our girlhood's friendship, unchanged and unshaken by the changes and separations of our maturer years, this volume is affectionately dedicated.

Francis **Bacon**, *Essayes*, 1597
~ To M. Anthony Bacon, his deare Brother. Loving and beloved Brother, I do nowe like some that have an Orcharde ill neighbored, that gather their fruit before it is ripe, to prevent stealing. These fragments of my conceites were going to print. To labour the staie of them had bin troublesome, and subject to interpretation; to let them passe had beene to adventure the wrong they mought receive by untrue Coppies, or by some garnishment, which it mought please any that shold set them forth to bestow upon them. Therefore I helde it best discreation to publish them my selfe as they passed long agoe from my pen, without any further disgrace, then the weakenesse of the Author. And as, I did ever hold, there mought be as great a vanitie in retiring and withdrawing mens conceites (except they bee of some nature) from the world, as in obtruding them; so in these particulars I have played my selfe the Inquisitor, and find nothing to my understanding in them contrarie, or infectious to the state of Religion, or manners, but rather (as I suppose) medicinable. Only I disliked now to put them out because they will bee like the

late newe halfe-pence, which though the Silver were good, yet the peeces were small. But since they would not stay with their Master, but would needes travaile abroade, I have preferred them to you, that are next myselfe, Dedicating them, such as they are, to our love, in the depth whereof (I assure you) I sometimes wish your infirmities translated upon my selfe, that her Majestie mought have the service of so active and able a mind, & I mought be with excuse confined to these contemplations & studies for which I am fittest, so commende I you to the preservation of the divine Majestie. From my Chamber at Graies Inne, this 30. of Januarie, 1597. Your entire Loving brother. Fran. Bacon.

As he states here, Bacon published the first edition of his essays himself, fearing that an unauthorised version was about to be printed. His elder brother Anthony, a diplomat, had been in delicate health from infancy and was lame all his life. Until 1594 he lived with his brother Francis, either at Gray's Inn or at his home, Twickenham Park, by the Thames.

Francis **Bacon**, *The Proficience and Advancement of Learning. The First Book*, 1605

~ To the King. There were under the Lawe (excellent King) both dayly Sacrifices, and free will Offerings; the one proceeding upon ordinarie observance; the other uppon a devout cheerefulnesse. In like manner, there belongeth to Kings from their Servants, both Tribute of dutie and presents of affection. In the former of these, I hope I shal not live to be wanting, according to my most humble dutie, and the good pleasure of your Majesties employments: for the later, I thought it more respective to make choyce of some oblation, which might rather referre to the proprietie and excellencie of your individuall person, than to the business of your Crowne and State. [...] Therefore I did conclude with myself, that I could not make unto your Majesty a better oblation, then of some treatise tending to that end, whereof the summe will consist of these two partes: the former concerning the excellencie of learning and knowledge, and the excellencie of the merit and true glory, in the Augmentation and Propagation thereof; the latter, what the particular actes and workes are, which have been embraced and undertaken for the advancement of learning: and againe what defects and undervalewes I finde in such particuler actes: to the end, that though I cannot positively or affirmativelie advise your Majestie, or propound unto you framed particulers; yet I may excite your princely Cogitations to visit the excellent treasure of your owne mind, and thence to extract particulers for this purpose, agreeing to your magnanimitie and wiesdome.

These are the first and last paragraphs only of a lengthy dedication to James I, the rest being in essence a eulogy to the King's wisdom and learning. Bacon's work was the first stage in his radical programme of intellectual and scientific reform that in the event was never fully realised.

Hermione **Baddeley**, *The Unsinkable Hermione Baddeley*, 1984
~ For George, my wonderful French bulldog.

One of a select category of dedications made to the writer's pet animal. The actress's dog was named after Sister George in Frank Marcus's play *The Killing of Sister George*, a taxing role played by Baddeley.

Desmond **Bagley**, *Landslide*, 1967
~ For Philip Joseph and all good booksellers.

Desmond **Bagley**, *The Vivero Letter*, 1968
~ To that stalwart institution the British pub, particularly the Kingsbridge Inn, Totnes, and the Cott Inn, Dartington.

Desmond Bagley was a much-travelled and widely experienced thriller writer who did not begin writing novels until he was forty, when he became an instant bestseller with *The Golden Keel*. These two dedications show that he had his priorities right. He died in 1983, aged fifty-nine.

Philip James **Bailey**, *Festus*, 1839

My Father! unto Thee to whom I owe
All that I am, all that I have and can;
Who madest me in Thyself the sum of man
In all its generous aims and powers to know,
These first-fruits bring I; nor do Thou forego
Marking when I the boyish feat began,
Which numbers now three years from its plan,
Not twenty summers had embrowned my brow:
Like is at blood-heat every page doth prove:
Bear with it. Nature means necessity.
If there be aught that Thou canst love, it springs
Out of the hope that I may earn that love,
More unto me than immortality,
Or to have strung my harp with golden strings.

The author's self-conscious dedication to God. As Bailey more than a touch turgidly explains, he had begun the work at the age of twenty, and completed it three years later. *Festus* is a lengthy poem which tells the story of Faust, and is based on Goethe's work. 'Embrowned' is Baileyese for 'sun-tanned'. Today he is not only unread, but virtually unreadable.

Beryl **Bainbridge**, *Young Adolf*, 1978
~ For luvely Don Mackinlay.

Bainbridge's novel is a fictional account of the early years of Hitler.

J. Dyer **Ball**, *Things Chinese: Being Notes on Various Subjects Connected with China*, 1900
~ To HER whose help the Author has missed in passing this Third Edition through the Press.

Presumably this is a tribute to the author's late wife, and is a kind of epitaph to her.

John Kendrick **Bangs,** *The Pursuit of the House-Boat, being Some Further Account of the Divers Doings of the Associated Shades, under the leadership of Sherlock Holmes, Esq.,* 1899

~ To A. Conan Doyle, Esq., with the author's sincerest regards, and thanks for the untimely demise of his great detective, which made these things possible.

Conan Doyle had 'killed off' Holmes in 1894, when the great hero fell from a precipice in a life-and-death tussle with a master criminal. Immediately, devotees and aspiring crime writers jumped on the bandwagon to continue his adventures, as Bangs did here. Doyle brought Holmes back in 1902, though, in *The Hound of the Baskervilles* and in further stories.

Lynne Reid **Banks,** *Defy the Wilderness,* 1981

~ For those who will not be angry.

Charles Wareing **Bardsley,** *A Dictionary of English and Welsh Surnames,* 1901

~ To William McKinley, President of the United States of America, this dictionary of English and Welsh surnames with special American instances is by express permission gratefully dedicated.

Although written almost a century ago, and long superseded by recent scholarly dictionaries of surnames, Bardsley's book is still of value.

Margaret Campbell **Barnes,** *Mary of Carisbrooke,* 1956

~ To the beauty and unspoiled courtesy of the Wight.

The book tells the tale of Charles I's captivity in Carisbrooke Castle, Isle of Wight.

Richard **Barnfield,** *Cynthia,* 1595

~ To the Right Honourable, and most noble-minded Lorde, William Stanley, Earle of Darby, &c. Right Honorable, the dutifull affection I beare to your manie vertues, is cause, that to manifest my love to your Lordship, I am constrained to shew my simplenes to the world. Many are they that admire your worth, of the which number, I (though the meanest in abilitie, yet with the foremost in affection) am one that most desire to serve your Honour. Small is the gift, but great is my good-will; the which, by how much the lesse I am able to expresse it, by so much the more it is infinite. Live long; and inherit your Predecessors vertues, as you do their dignitie and estate. This is my wish: the which your honorable excellent giftes doe promise me to obtaine: and whereof these few rude and unpollished lines, are a true (though an undeserving) testimony. If my ability were better, the signes should be greater; but being as it is, your honour must take me as I am, not as I should be. My yeares being so young, my perfection cannot be great. But howsoever it is, yours it is; and I my selfe am yours; in all humble service, most readily to be commaunded. Richard Barnefeilde.

Barnfield, a lyrically gifted pastoral poet, wrote this classical allegory with direct reference to Queen Elizabeth. He was just twenty-one at the time. His humility and affection for his patron are almost certainly genuine.

Walter **Barrett**, *The Old Merchants of New York City*, 1885

~ To the memory of John Jacob Astor, one of the first and most prosperous merchants of New York City, this volume is dedicated.

Astor was the famous German-born millionaire after whom hotels and other public buildings called 'Astoria' are named. Walter Barrett's real name was Joseph A. Scoville.

John **Bartholomew** & Son Ltd, *The Times Atlas of the World*, 7th edn, 1985

~ To Her Majesty Queen Elizabeth II THE TIMES ATLAS OF THE WORLD is with her most gracious permission respectfully dedicated by Her Majesty's Cartographers John Bartholomew & Son Limited.

This 'Comprehensive' edition of the well-known atlas was published jointly by Times Books and John Bartholomew to commemorate the 200th anniversary of *The Times*, which first appeared (as *The Daily Universal Register*) on New Year's Day, 1785.

Tryphosa B. **Batcheller**, *Glimpses of Italian Court Life*, 1906

~ Dedicated by special permission to Her Most Gracious Majesty, Queen Elena of Italy.

Elena, the daughter of Prince (later King) Nicholas of Montenegro, was the wife of Victor Emmanuel III, King of Italy from 1900.

Charles **Baudelaire**, *The Flowers of Evil*, 1857

~ To the impeccable poet, to the perfect Magician of French Arts, to my most dear and most respected Master and Friend, Théophile Gautier, with sentiments of the profoundest humility, I dedicate these maladive flowers. C.B.

Translated from the French by AR; original title: *Les Fleurs du mal*. Baudelaire's penultimate word in the original, *maladives*, today used to mean 'sickly', 'morbid', puns on the title. Two draft verse dedications, one incomplete, also exist for the work, a volume of poetry in which the author seeks beauty or good in the perverse and grotesque, otherwise in the morbid.

Richard **Baxter**, *The Saint's Everlasting Rest*, 1650

~ To my beloved Friends, the Inhabitants of the Burrough and Forreign of Kederminster, both Magistrates and People [...].

Richard Baxter was a popular Presbyterian preacher closely associated with Kidderminster. He wrote much of his book while staying with his friends Sir Thomas and Lady Jane Rous, at the village of Rous Lench, north of Evesham, and the two are also included in his dedication. Today Baxter is perhaps best remembered for his popular hymn, 'Ye holy angels bright'.

Sir Wyke **Bayliss**, *Rex Regum: The Likeness of Christ*, 1898
~ By Command: This Tribute to the King of Kings is dedicated to her Most Gracious Majesty, Victoria, Queen Empress, by the Author.

This is Bayliss's best known work, a detailed study of the traditional portraits of Christ. He was himself an artist of note, with churches and cathedrals predominant among his subjects.

Edward L. **Beach**, *Cold is the Sea*, 1978
~ There are some that go down to the sea in ships, and some who go under the sea. The causes of catastrophe can be subtle as well as manifold, but fortunately only a few fail to come back to port. To them and to their valiant memory, this story is dedicated.

The book is a novel centring on submarine warfare in the United States Navy.

Frederick **Beachner**, *Godric*, 1980
~ In memoriam patris mei et ad maiorem Dei gloriam atque sancti Godrici.

The author's tenth novel has an appropriate Latin dedication to its subject, the famous English twelfth-century hermit, St Godric of Durham. An English version would read: 'In memory of my country and to the greater glory of God and St Godric'.

Greg **Bear**, *The Serpent Mage*, 1986
~ This book, finally, is for Kristine – unbeknownst to herself, a kind of Beatrice, 1951–1971.

Greg **Bear**, *The Forge of God*, 1987
~ For Alan Brennert, who gave me hell on TV.

The Serpent Mage and *The Forge of God* are science fiction novels, both set in the future, the former in Los Angeles.

Dan **Beard**, *Dan Beard's Animal Book*, 1907
~ To my son, Daniel Bartlett Beard, the most enjoyable pet and interesting specimen I have ever been fortunate enough to possess.

Daniel C. Beard was an American painter and illustrator who organised the Boy Scout movement in the United States in 1910 and who wrote many practical books on camping, woodcraft and related outdoor activities. Mount Bear, near Mount McKinley, is named after him.

Lady Suzanne **Beauclerk**, Duchess of St Albans, *The Road to Bordeaux*, 1976

~ Once more it is entirely due to the continual encouragement (not to say downright pressurising) of my noble spouse that this book was written. All blame is to be firmly laid at his door.

The book is an autobiography. The author's 'noble spouse' is Charles Beauclerk, 13th Duke of St Albans, whom she married (as his second wife) in 1947.

Francis **Beaumont**, *The Masque of the Inner-Temple & Gray's Inn*, 1612

~ To the Worthie Sir Francis Bacon, His Majesties Sollicitor Generall, and the grave and learned Bench of the anciently allied houses of Grayes Inne, and the Inner Temple, the Inner Temple, and Grayes Inne. Yee that spared no time nor travell, in the setting forth, ordering, & furnishing of this Masque, being the first fruits of honor in this kinde, which these two societies have offered to his Majestie, will not thinke much now to looke backe upon the effects of your owne care and worke: for that whereof the successe was then doubtfull, is now happily performed and gratiously accepted and that which you were then to thinke of in straites of time, you may now peruse at leysure. And you, Sir Francis Bacon, especially, as you did then by your countenance and loving affection advance it, so let your good word grace it and defend it, which is able to adde value to the greatest, and least matters.

This was Beaumont's only masque, dedicated to Francis Bacon, who duly 'countenanced and advanced' it, otherwise approved and financed it. Beaumont had been entered as a barrister at the Inner Temple, while Bacon was at Gray's Inn. Hence the cooperation in entertainment between the two Inns of Court.

Robert **Beckman**, *The Downwave*, 1983

~ This book is dedicated to those persons whose actions are deflected by thought along with the few remaining people of intelligence who are still able to read and who do sometimes purchase books. From this nucleus will come the harbingers of the glorious twenty first century.

Beckman's book had forecast a sensational crash in the world stock market, a prediction that in the event was only partially realised.

Venerable **Bede**, *A History of the English Church and People*, 731

~ To the Most Glorious King Ceolwulf, Bede the Priest and Servant of Christ. Some while ago, at Your Majesty's request, I gladly sent you the history of the English Church and People which I had recently completed, in order that you might read it and give it your approval. I now send it once again to be transcribed, so that Your Majesty may consider it at greater leisure. I warmly welcome the diligent zeal and sincerity with which you study the words of Holy Scripture and your eager desire to know something of the doings and sayings of men of the past, and of famous men of our own nation in particular. [...]

Translated from the Latin by Leo Sherley-Price, 1955; original title: *Historia Ecclesiastica Gentis Anglorum*. Bede's important work was a record of the early history of Britain. He dedicated it to Ceolwulf, King of the Northumbrians, who died in 764. The Latin original begins: 'Gloriosissimo regi Ceoluuolpho ...'.

Mark **Bego**, *Sade*, 1986

~ To my partner in crime ... David Salidor: 'When *are* we going to make a living?'

The book is a biography of the famous pop singer, not the infamous Marquis!

Aphra **Behn**, *Feign'd Curtizans*, 1679

~ [...] So excellent and perfect a creature as yourself differs only from the divine powers in this: the offerings made to you ought to be worthy of you, whilst they accept the will alone. [...] Who can doubt them power of that illustrious beauty, the charms of that tongue, and the greatnesse of that minde, who has subdu'd the most powerfull and glorious monarch of the world; and so well you bear the honours you were born for, with a greatness so unaffected, an affability so easie, an Humor so soft, so far from pride or vanity, that the most envious, and most disaffected, can finde no cause or reason to wish you less. [...]

Who is this paragon? None other than 'Mrs. Ellen Guin', as the eulogy names her, otherwise Nell Gwyn, mistress of Charles II. This lady was the recipient of a number of dedications. For others, see THOMAS DUFFETT and WILLIAM WYCHERLEY. Aphra Behn is usually regarded as the first professional English woman writer, although many of her plays were based on those of earlier writers.

Lilian **Bell**, *The Instinct of Stepfatherhood*, 1898

~ To My Lovely Mother: Whose descent not only from the Pilgrim Fathers but from Plymouth Rock, enables her to withstand my frantic appeal when she is minded too ruthlessly to clip the wings of the fledglings of my heart and brain. Nevertheless, to her extraordinary critical faculty do I owe much of the gentle criticism of the public, and to her unfailing tenderness and patience do I hereby publicly bear witness.

Bell was an American fiction writer who wrote such books as *Love Affairs of an Old Maid* (1893) and *Why Men Remain Bachelors, and Other Luxuries* (1906). One gets the drift.

Hilaire **Belloc**, *The Girondin*, 1912

~ To the Horses Pacte and Basilique, now with their father Jove.

Hilaire **Belloc**, *The Four Men*, 1912

~ To Mrs. Wright-Biddulph, of Burton in the county of Sussex, under whose roof so much of this book was written.

Hilaire **Belloc**, *The Green Overcoat*, 1912

~ My dear Maurice, You wrote something called *The Green Elephant*, and I have

written something called *The Green Overcoat*. It is on this account that I dedicate
to you my work *The Green Overcoat*, although (and I take this opportunity of
reproaching you for the same) you did not dedicate to me your work *The Green
Elephant*. [...] My endeavour was to copy you, and to have a title which would
get people mixed up, so that the great hordes of cultivated men and women desiring
to see your play should talk by mistake of *The Green Overcoat*. And then their
aunts, or perhaps a prig-visitor, would say: 'Oh, no, that is the *book*!' In this way
the book would be boomed. That was my game. If people had done this sort of
thing before it would not work now; but they haven't. Now, Maurice, I end this
preface, for I cannot think of anything more to write. H. BELLOC.

A small selection of dedications from the many writings of Belloc, novelist, poet, biographer,
travel-writer, historian and a good deal more, although now little read. The first title above
is a historical novel, the second is an account of a walk with three companions from one
end of his beloved Sussex to the other. The dedicatee in the last book was Belloc's close
friend, the writer and Russophile, Maurice Baring.

Saul **Bellow**, *Herzog*, 1961
~ To Pat Covici, a great editor, and better yet, a generous friend, this book is
affectionately dedicated.

Compare STEINBECK's tribute, below.

Douglas **Bence** and Clive **Branson**, *Roy Jenkins: A Question of Principle?*, 1982
~ To the wind of change in British politics.

Roy Jenkins, a first-rank Labour politician, had co-founded the Social Democratic Party
in 1981, and became its first leader in the year this study of him was published.

Arnold **Bennett**, *A Great Man*, 1904
~ To my dear friend, Frederick Marriott, and the imperishable memory of old
times.

Arnold **Bennett**, *Buried Alive*, 1908
~ To John Frederick Farrar, M.R.C.S., L.R.C.P., my collaborator in this and
many other books, a grateful expression of old-established regard.

Arnold **Bennett**, *Anna of the Five Towns*, 1912
~ I dedicate this book with affection and admiration to Herbert Sharpe, an artist
whose individuality and achievement have continually inspired me.

Arnold Bennett frequently collaborated with others in his writings: the second title here,
originally a novel, appeared as the play *The Great Adventure* in 1913 and brought him great
popularity.

Daphne **Bennett**, *Queen Victoria's Children*, 1980
~ Dedicated by gracious permission to Her Majesty Queen Helen of Roumania, great-granddaughter of Queen Victoria and granddaughter of Queen Victoria's eldest child.

Queen Helen, who died in 1982, was the wife of King Carol of Roumania and the third child of Princess Sophia, herself the sixth child of Princess Victoria, Queen Victoria's eldest child.

A.C. **Benson**, *The Leaves of the Tree*, 1911
~ To Reginald John Smith, once my fagmaster, now my publisher, I dedicate this book.

Smith had been Benson's fagmaster (senior boy disciplinarian) at Eton, and had then become a barrister before joining the publishers Smith, Elder & Co. in 1894, taking over the firm only five years later. Benson had himself gone on to be a housemaster at his old public school before becoming Master of Magdalene College, Cambridge, in 1915.

E.F. **Benson**, *The Vintage: A Romance of the Greek War of Independence*, 1898
~ This Romance dealing with the regeneration of her people is dedicated by permission to her Majesty, Olga, Queen of the Hellenes.

E.F. **Benson**, *The Freaks of Mayfair*, 1916
~ Dedicated to frank eyes and kindly ears.

This Benson was the younger brother of A.C. BENSON, and a prolific writer. Of his total of ninety-three books, these are just two reasonably representative dedications.

Michael **Bentine**, *The Condor and the Cross*, 1987
~ For 'Fusty', our daughter, whose spirit soars like a condor.

Bentine's book is a history of the naval conquest of Peru. The popular actor and comedian had two daughters by his second wife, former ballet dancer Clementina Stuart.

E.C. **Bentley**, *Trent's Last Case*, 1913
~ My dear Gilbert, I dedicate this story to you. First: because the only really noble motive I had in writing it was the hope that you would enjoy it. Second: because I owe you a book in return for *The Man Who Was Thursday*. Third: because I said I would when I unfolded the plan of it to you, surrounded by Frenchmen, two years ago. Fourth: because I remember the past.

Bentley dedicated his famous novel, the prototype of the modern detective story, to G.K. Chesterton, who had earlier dedicated his own fantasy, *The Man Who Was Thursday*, to *him*, prefacing it with a longish poem beginning: 'A cloud was on the mind of men, and wailing was the weather, / Yea, a sick cloud upon the soul when we were boys together'. Both men had been 'boys together' at St Paul's School, London.

Evelyn **Berckmann**, *The Blessed Plot*, 1976
~ For Kenneth Timings of the Public Record Office with admiration and affection, and special thanks for suggesting the title of the book.

The book is a historical novel, for which, as often, historical research is needed.

Maurice **Beresford**, *The Lost Villages of England*, 1954
~ To my friends, who have walked and dug with me.

Maurice **Beresford**, *History on the Ground*, 1957
~ To my Mother, who packed the sandwiches.

Maurice **Beresford**, *Walks Round Red Brick*, 1980
~ To the memory of Lulu, companion in these walks during 1977 and 1978, whose four feet were usually there first.

Beresford, now Professor of Economic History at Leeds University, has been a pioneer in literal roadwork and fieldwork as a necessary adjunct to studies in English social history. This third book deals with the architecture of Leeds.

Charles **Berlitz**, *The Bermuda Triangle*, 1975
~ To the sea and its mysteries – whose solution may tell us more about ourselves ...

Berlitz's book did much to popularise the history of ships and aircraft that had disappeared in the Bermuda Triangle, although he did not invent the phrase.

Eric **Berne**, *Games People Play*, 1964
~ To my patients and students who taught me more and more and are still teaching me about games and the meaning of life.

The bestseller, subtitled 'The Psychology of Human Relationships', by the Canadian-born American psychologist and psychiatrist. The theory is that all human activity involves the playing of games, such as 'life games', 'marital games', 'party games', 'sexual games', 'underworld games' and so on.

John **Betjeman**, 'The Wykehamist' in *Mount Zion*, 1932
~ To Randolph Churchill, but not about him.

The poem is about a 'keen ecclesiologist' and lover of Norman church fonts who is described as 'a rather dirty Wykehamist'. However, neither Betjeman nor Churchill had been to Winchester, but to Marlborough and Eton respectively.

John **Betjeman**, *A Nip in the Air*, 1974
~ To my Grandchildren, Lucy, Imogen and Endellion.

Of the three dedicatees, the third girl must have been named after St Endellion, the Cornish village that Betjeman knew so well and wrote about ('Saint Endellion! Saint Endellion! The name is like a ring of bells'). He died in 1984 at Trebetherick, only four miles away.

The **Bible,** Authorised Version, 1611

~ To the most high and mightie Prince, James by the grace of God King of Great Britaine, France and Ireland, Defender of the Faith, &c. The Translators of the Bible, wish Grace, Mercie, and Peace, through Jesus Christ our Lord. Great and manifold were the blessings (most dread Soveraigne) which Almighty God, the Father of all Mercies, bestowed upon us the people of England, when first he sent your Majesties Royall person to rule and raigne over us. For whereas it was the expectation of many, who wished not well unto our Sion, that upon the setting of that bright *Occidentall Starre* Queene Elizabeth of most happy memory, some thicke and palpable cloudes of darkenesse would so have overshadowed this land, that men should have bene in doubt which way they were to walke, and that it should hardly be knowen, who was to direct the unsetled State. The appearance of your Majestie, as of the *Sunne* in his strength, instantly dispelled those supposed and surmised mists, and gave unto all that were well affected, exceeding cause of comfort; especially when we beheld the government established in your Highnesse and your hopefull Seed, by an undoubted Title, and this also accompanied with Peace and tranquillitie, at home and abroad. [...] There are infinite arguments of this right Christian and Religious affection in your Majestie: but none is more forcible to declare it to others, then the vehement and perpetuated desire of the accomplishing and publishing of this Worke which now with all humilitie we present unto your Majestie. [...] And now at last, by the Mercy of God, and the continuance of our Labours, it being brought unto such a conclusion, as that we have great hope that the Church of *England* shall reape good fruit thereby, we hold it our duety to offer it to your Majestie, not onely as to our King and Soveraigne, but as to the principall moover and Author of the Worke. Humbly craving of your most Sacred Majestie, that since things of this quality have ever bene subject to the censures of ill meaning and discontented persons, it may receive approbation and Patronage from so learned and judicious a Prince as your Highnesse is, whose allowance and acceptance of our Labours, shall more honour and incourage us, then all the calumniations and hard interpretations of other men shall dismay us. [...]

One of the best-known of all dedications in English, but also, it has to be said, one of the most obsequious, almost as if addressed to God himself, rather than to James I, who had commissioned the translation. The work was carried out by fifty-four scholars, divided into six groups. It was not a translation from the original, however, but relied heavily on the Geneva Bible of 1560 (dedicated to Queen Elizabeth) and Tyndale's even earlier translation from the Greek of the New Testament in 1526.

Poultney **Bigelow,** *History of the German Struggle for Liberty,* 1903

~ To Caribee, my Cruising Canoe: In her have I slept by night and sailed by day for weeks and months at a time, exploring the beautiful waterways of the German Fatherland. She has made me friends with every kind of man, – the bargee, the raftsman, the wood-chopper, the weaver, the gendarme, the parish parson, the miller, the tax-collector, – and many more of the types that make life interesting to the contemplative traveler. By the aid of Caribee I learned to feel how Germans feel. Without her this book would not have been written.

Bigelow was an American traveller, journalist and author who was not only a Germanophile but a personal friend of the Kaiser, Wilhelm II.

Isabella **Bird**, *A Lady's Life in the Rocky Mountains*, 1879

~ To my sister, to whom these letters were originally written, they are now affectionately dedicated.

During her travels, Isabella Bird wrote regular letters to her sister Henrietta. She published this selection of them when she was forty-seven.

George A. **Birmingham**, *Spanish Gold*, 1908

~ To Theodosia and Althea, who asked me to write a story about treasure buried on an island.

And here is the book that the author's daughters requested, set on an island off the west coast of Ireland, his native land. ('George A. Birmingham' was his pen name, his real name being James Owen Hannay.) See also his next dedication below.

George A. **Birmingham**, *Fed Up*, 1931

~ My dear Lady Horner, I have long wished to dedicate one of my stories to you. I hesitated to ask permission because I felt that it might strain your side of a friendship, very precious to me, if your name were connected in any way with writing so foolishly flippant as mine. You might very well feel aggrieved if one of them had your name on that additional title page which carries what is called the dedication. Now at last I feel that the friendship – your side of it, mine is in no doubt – is strong enough to survive the offering to you of the very most foolish and flippant story I have ever written, even if it is about so serious a subject as English politics. I am affectionately yours, James O. Hannay (George A. Birmingham).

See above.

Sheila **Black**, *The Reluctant Money-Minder*, 1980

~ To the men in my life who taught me to understand and to spend money, starting with my husband and ending with ...?

The book is a practical guide to doing just what the writer was taught to do.

J.M. **Blake**, ed., *Joy of Tyrol*, nd (*c.* 1900)

~ Dedicated by order of the Lady to all such as be hindered from the Joy of Tyrol.

The book has the subtitle: 'A Human Revelation, with 111 original Illustrations, Drawn by the Lady'. The latter was presumably the author's wife.

Thomas **Block,** *Airship Nine*, 1984

~ To all those who have, with sometimes no more than a few words or a quick glance, given me things to write about – not the least of whom are Ryan, Steven, Kim and the perennial EFB.

No doubt a family dedication, with the last named the writer's wife. The author is a pilot, and the book itself is a futurist novel about World War III.

Wilfrid **Blunt,** *Married to a Single Life: An Autobiography 1901–1938*, 1983

~ To the memory of Clifford Canning and Rupert Goodall, who jointly did much to make my five years of imprisonment at Marlborough tolerable, even at times enjoyable.

Wilfrid Blunt, writer on art, travel, gardening and handwriting, was eighty-two when this was published. Canning had been his housemaster at Marlborough College, and Goodall his contemporary and friend. Anthony Blunt, who advised the Queen on her pictures and drawings, and who died in 1983, was the author's younger brother.

Evelyn **Board,** *The Right Way To His Heart*, 1952

~ To the Guinea Pigs: my dear husband, who under all circumstances, doggedly declares 'I *prefer* it like this'; and to my son, without whose good appetite, and mercifully cast-iron digestion, these recipes could never have been fully tested.

The cookbook, published in the Elliott 'Right Way' series (hence its title), is subtitled 'New Ideas in Everyday Cooking'.

John **Bodenham,** *England's Helicon*, 1600

~ To his very loving friends, M. Nicholas Wanton and M. George Faucet. Though many miles (but more occasions) doo sunder us (kinde Gentlemen) yet a promise at parting dooth in justice claime performance, and assurance of gentle acceptance, would mightilie condemne me if I should neglect it. *Helicon*, though not as I could wish, yet in such good sort as time would permit, having past the pikes of the Presse, comes now to *Yorke* to salute her rightfull patrone first, and next (as his deere friends and kindsmen) to offer you her kinde service. If shee speede well there, it is all shee requires; if they frowne at her heere, she greatly not cares: for the wise (shee knowes) will never be other then them selves: as for such then as would seeme so, but neither are, nor ever will be, she holds this as a maine principle; that their malice neede as little be feared, as their favour or friendship is to be desired. So hoping you will not forget us there, as we continuallie shall be mindefull of you heere, I leave you to the delight of *Englands Helicon*. Yours in all he may, A.B.

This famous collection of pastoral poems was probably arranged by Bodenham, who would thus be the 'rightfull Patrone' mentioned in the dedication by 'A.B.'. But if Bodenham was the compiler, he may well not have been the actual editor, and this may have been Nicholas Ling, a well-known publisher of the time.

Rolf **Boldrewood**, *Robbery Under Arms*, 1888

~ I dedicate this 'ower true tale' of the wilder aspects of Australian life to my old comrade R. Murray Smith, late Agent-General for the colony of Victoria, with hearty thanks for the time and trouble he has devoted to its publication [...]

'Rolf Boldrewood' was the pseudonym of the Australian novelist Thomas Alexander Browne. This was his best-known novel, first published in serial form in the *Sydney Mail* in 1881.

Joseph **Bonanno** with Sergio Lalli, *A Man of Honour: The Autobiography of a Godfather*, 1983

~ With profound esteem and memories of love, to my humble, loyal and devoted wife, Fay – With infinite affection, to my children, Salvatore, Catherine and Joseph – With pride in our name and hope for a better future, to all my grandchildren – I love you all.

Martin **Bookspan**, *101 Masterpieces of Music and Their Composers*, 1972

~ [...] Finally, my wife, Janet, and our three children have been most under-standing and indulgent of the many hours over the years when I have retreated into my own little 'Basic Rep' world in order to listen to dozens of different recorded performances of the same music. That they have emerged from the ordeal with an undiminished love for the staples of our musical culture is a tribute to their fortitude. It is to them – Janet and the three B's (Rachel, David and Deborah) – that I dedicate this book with thanks and love.

This is the final paragraph of the Introduction to the book. The 'three B's' must be so called with reference to their family name.

James **Boswell**, *The Life of Samuel Johnson, Ll.D.*, 1791

~ My dear Sir, Every liberal motive that can actuate an Authour in the dedication of his labours, concurs in directing me to you, as the person to whom the following work should be inscribed. [...] If a work should be inscribed to one who is a master of the subject of it, and whose approbation, therefore, must ensure it credit and success, the life of Dr. Johnson is, with the greatest propriety, dedicated to Sir Joshua Reynolds, who was the intimate and beloved friend of that gentleman. [...] You, my dear Sir, studied him, and knew him well: you venerated and admired him. Yet, luminous as he was upon the whole, you perceived all the shades which mingled in the grand composition; all the little peculiarities and slight blemishes which marked the literary Colossus. [...] I am, My dear Sir, Your much obliged friend, and faithful humble servant, James Boswell.

A discreet and artistically worded address to the dedicatee, the painter Joshua Reynolds who, as Boswell says, knew Johnson well.

Beriah **Botfield**, *Journal of a Tour through the Highlands of Scotland*, 1830

~ To the Best and Loveliest of her Sex this volume is dedicated: She for whom it is intended will accept and appreciate the compliment; Those for whom it is not intended will do the same.

This dedication is clearly based on the one in DISRAELI's *Vivian Grey*, published four years previously. For the original, see this below. Botfield's dedication could not have been to his wife, as he did not marry until 1858, when he was fifty-one, although it could of course have been to the lady who *became* his wife.

Marjorie **Bowen**, *Dickon*, 1929

~ This romance of King Richard III is dedicated to Tom Heslewood, whose knowledge of the characters and period of the fifteenth century may make him sympathetic towards this attempt at a portrait of the last Plantagenet king.

'Majorie Bowen' was one of the pseudonyms of the English novelist, playwright and biographer (as here) whose real name was Gabrielle Margaret Vere Long, née Campbell. She died in 1952 at the age of sixty-four.

John Clarke **Bowman**, *Pocahontas*, 1973

~ For Lynn, my own particular star still shining bright.

A biography of the American Indian princess who died in England in 1617, dedicated by the author to his wife.

Robert **Bowring**, *Specimens of the Russian Poets*, 1823

~ To His Imperial Majesty Alexander I, autocrat of all the Russia, etc., etc. The flattering mark of your approbation with which you were pleased to honour the former volume of the Russian anthology, induces me to inscribe the name of your Majesty upon the dedication page of this. [...] The destiny of millions is in your Majesty's hands. Under your auspices, your empire has made gigantic strides in knowledge and in power. The future is formed by the present. O, be it your most imperial ambition to make that knowledge and that power the source of virtue and of liberty! Such are the wishes, and such the hopes of one to whom your reputation is dearer than to a thousand flatterers, and who is in all sincerity, Your Majesty's most obedient, and devoted humble servant, John Bowring.

Bowring had been travelling through Europe for commercial purposes and compiled this selection on his return from Russia in 1820. Alexander had earlier given him a diamond ring for his *Russian Anthology* (1820–23), mentioned here, which was similarly dedicated to the tsar. Compare the somewhat similar dedication to the same ruler by KARAMZIN, below.

Jimmy **Boyle**, *A Sense of Freedom*, 1977

~ [...] There are a number of people that I owe my survival to; and many that have reached out and touched me. [...] It is to them that I am tempted to dedicate this book, but won't. Instead, I dedicate it to my two children, not because I am their father, but more importantly they are the symbols of the future. A future that is in *our* hands.

The autobiography of a murderer, serving a life sentence from 1967 in Barlinnie Prison, Glasgow.

David **Bradberry**, *Tetelestai: The Final Close: A Poem*, 1794

~ To the most Sublime, most High and Mighty, most Puissant, most Sacred, most Faithful, most Gracious, most Catholic, most Sincere, most Reverend, and most Righteous Majesty, Jehovah Emmanuel, by indefeasible right Sovereign of the Universe and Prince of the Kings of the Earth, Governor-General of the World, Chief Shepherd or Archbishop of Souls, Chief Justice of Final Appeal, Judge of the Last Assize, Father of Mercies and Friend of Man, This Poem (a feeble testimony of his obligation and hopes) is gratefully and humbly presented by His Majesty's highly favoured but very unworthy subject and servant The Author.

This is just part of the lengthy and eccentric dedication to God, which includes several other titles in the same vein, and which became almost as well known as the work itself. The poem is a description of Judgment Day from an evangelical viewpoint, its Greek title translating as 'They shall be completed'.

Malcolm **Bradbury**, *The History Man*, 1975

~ This fiction is for Beamish, whom, while en route for some conference or other, I last saw at Frankfurt airport, enquiring from desk to desk about his luggage, unhappily not loaded onto the same plane as he. It is a total invention with delusory approximations to historical reality, just as is history itself. [...] As for the characters, [...] they are pure inventions, as is the plot in which they more than participate. Nor did I fly to a conference the other day; and if I did, there was no one on the plane named Beamish, who certainly did not lose his luggage. The rest of course, is true.

These are the opening and closing sentences of an 'Author's Note', so are distinct from the dedication proper, which (although omitted from the paperback reprint of the novel) is 'to Matthew and Dominic', the author's two sons. Beamish is not a character in the novel itself.

Maria Zimmer **Bradley**, *The Catch Tray*, 1979

~ To Kerry, without whom I would probably never have begun this book, and to Walter, without whom I would certainly never have finished it.

A fairly stock type of dual dedication, based on the familiar 'without whom ...' formula.

Caryl **Brahms**, *Gilbert and Sullivan: Lost Chords and Discords*, 1975

~ To Margaret Daniel and Shirley Mowbray, who have stayed with this book through a wilderness of sentences, hailstorms of commas and colons, and, of course, thin and thick.

Richard **Brathwaite**, *A Strappado for the Divell*, 1615

~ To all usurers, broakers, and promoters, sergeants, catch-poles, and regraters, ushers, panders, suburbes traders, cockneies that have manie fathers; ladies, monkies, parachitoes, marmosites, and catomitoes, falls, high-tires and rebatoes, false-haires, periwigges, monchatoes, grave gregories and shee-painters – send I greeting at adventures, and to all such as be evill, my *Strappado for the Divell*.

A colourful inventory of the various kinds of people, together with their fashionable additions, at whom this satirical work is directed. A good dictionary may supply individual meanings; the animal names are used figuratively, so that a 'marmosite' is an 'ape', a ridiculous follower of fashion.

Nicholas **Breton**, *The Pilgrimage to Paradise*, 1592

~ Right noble Lady, whose rare vertues the wise no lesse honour, then the learned admire, and the honest serve: how shall I, the abject of fortune, unto the object of honour presume to offer so simple a present, as the poeticall discourse of a poore pilgrimes travaile? I know not how but, with falling at the feete of your favour, to crave pardon for my imperfection. Who hath redde of the Duchess of Urbina, may saie, the Italians wrote wel: but who knows the Countesse of Penbrooke, I thinke hath cause to write better. [...]

Mary Herbert, Duchess of Pembroke, was the recipient of many dedications in her time, and a generous patroness. For two other famous dedications to her, see SPENSER's *Ruines of Time* and the fine one by her brother, SIR PHILIP SIDNEY, in his *Arcadia*. Nicholas Breton also dedicated his *Auspicante Jehoua, Marie's Exercise* (1597), to the Duchess, with an apology for having remained so long silent in her praises ('my long forgetfullnesse of your favoure') in the intervening six years.

Mary **Bringle**, *Death of an Unknown Man*, 1987

~ This book is dedicated to Andrew 'Scobie' Drummond, who will not feel the need to read it.

André **Brink**, *A Dry White Season*, 1979

~ For Alta, who sustained me in the dry season.

The novel, by a South African author, is set in Johannesburg after the Soweto riots of 1976.

Vera **Brittain**, *Born 1925*, 1948

~ To Paul Berry, and his contemporaries who survived the Second World War, with love.

The novel, on youth in war, was a sequel to the author's better-known *Testament to Youth*, whose action ended in 1925, when the hero of this sequel, Adrian Carbury, was born.

A.M. **Broadley**, *Dr Johnson and Mrs Thrale*, 1909

~ To my loyal friend, James Penderel-Brodhurst, a Staffordshire man both by birth and affection, a lineal descendant of Humphrey Penderel of Boscobel and a kinsman of one of Samuel Johnson's early friends and contemporaries, this volume is inscribed.

Alexander Meyrick Broadley was an English barrister and writer (and collector of Napoleana). The five Penderel brothers, Richard, Humphrey, William, John and George, had helped Charles II to escape after the Battle of Worcester (1651) by offering him refuge at Boscobel, where William was the tenant.

Charlotte **Brontë**, *Jane Eyre*, 1847

~ To W.M. Thackeray, Esq., this work is respectfully inscribed by the author.

In the Preface to the second edition of her famous novel, Charlotte Brontë (then still writing as Currer Bell) explained that she had dedicated the book to Thackeray, 'if he will accept the tribute of a total stranger'.

Sylvia **Brooke**, *Queen of the Head Hunters*, 1970

~ I dedicate this book to the memory of my husband – the man who was my greatest friend, who never let me down, and who made me laugh more than anyone I have ever known.

Sylvia Brooke was the wife of Sir Charles Vyner Brooke, the third (and last) member of the Brooke family to be Rajah of Sarawak. Sir Charles, who died in 1963, ceded Sarawak to Britain in 1946.

Ewart **Brookes**, *The Glass Years*, 1957

~ To all those who went over during the heat and burden of the day and never reached the Glass Years, and, above all, to a lovable Irishman who once came back to help me in the dark of the night, so that I am here to write. The eyes of the gods were turned away the day I tried to repay, but I steadfastly believe he knows that, and understands, the Darlin' Man.

Brookes was a naval reserve officer in the Second World War. His first book was *Proud Waters* (1954), about the lives of people caught up in the war, and *The Glass Years* was a sequel, with the same characters. The 'glass years' (a phrase from Swinburne) were the bitter, brittle ones after the war.

Dale **Brown**, *Flight of the Old Dog*, 1987

~ This book is dedicated to the thousands of men and women of the United States Air Force Strategic Air Command who assure the quality of our nation's strategic deterrent force. [...] To all the bomber pukies, tanker toads, missile weenies, sky cops, knuckle-busters, and BB stackers of the Strategic Air Command – this one's for you.

A selection of mock-derogatory slang terms for various airforce trades and duties.

John **Brown**, *Our Dogs*, 1862
~ To Sir Walter and Lady Trevelyan's glum and faithful 'Peter' (a dog) with much regard.

See below.

John **Brown**, *Spare Hours*, 1866
~ The author dedicates this volume to the memory of Abraham Lincoln, 'Who through faith subdues kingdoms and wrought righteousness'.

Dr John Brown, the author of both these books, was the Scottish physicist and essayist now best remembered for his dog story *Rab and His Friends*. Sir Walter Trevelyan was an English naturalist and geologist who went to Scotland in 1820 to continue the scientific studies he had begun in Oxford. Lady Trevelyan, his first wife, née Paulina Jermyn, died in 1866.

John Crosby **Brown**, *A Hundred Years of Merchant Banking: A History of Brown Brothers & Company, Brown Shipley & Company, and the Allied Firms*, 1909
~ TO MY PARTNERS, that a study of the traditions of the past and of the example of the founders may stimulate them to transmit to their descendants and successors the high ideals of their predecessors and to maintain the good name of the old firm with credit unimpaired. TO MY SONS, that they may appreciate the rich legacy of Christian character and high commercial integrity which is their inheritance. TO MY WIFE, without whose suggestion this work would never have been begun and without whose encouragement it would never have been finished.

The 'Edwardian ethic' at work, and a significant order of priorities!

Mary Elizabeth **Brown** and William Adams Brown, *Musical Instruments and their Homes*, 1888
~ To the One: Who has not only given the true keynote to our home, but whose firm yet gentle touch has resolved all its transient discords into harmony, this book is affectionately dedicated by his wife and eldest son.

That is, to the John Crosby Brown who was the father of the American theologian William Adams Brown, his eldest son.

William **Browne**, *The Inner Temple Masque*, 1614
~ To the honorable society of the Inner Temple. Gentlemen. I give you but your owne. If you refuse to foster it, I knowe not who will. By your meanes it may live. If it degenerate in kinde from those other our society hath produced, blame your selves for not seekinge to a happier muse. I knowe it is not without faultes, yet such as your loves, or at least Poetic Licentia (the common salve) will make tollerable. What is good in it, that is yours; what bad, myne; what indifferent, both; & that will suffice, since it was done to please ourselves in private by him that is all yours, W. Browne.

Browne, a noted pastoral poet, wrote this masque for the entertainment of his fellow members of the Inner Temple, London, as one of the four Inns of Court, or legal societies.

Elizabeth Barrett **Browning**, *Poems*, 1844

~ DEDICATION TO MY FATHER. When your eyes fall upon this page of dedication, and you start to see to whom it is inscribed, your first thought will be of the time far off when I was a child and wrote verses, and when I dedicated them to you, who were my public and my critic. [...] Somewhat more faint-hearted than I used to be, it is my fancy thus to seem to return to a visible personal dependence on you, as if indeed I were a child again; to conjure your beloved image between myself and the public, so as to be sure of one smile, – and to satisfy my heart while I sanctify my ambition, by associating with the great pursuit of my life, its tenderest and noblest affections.

This was written two years before the poet's marriage to Robert Browning, so that 'E.B.B.' here does not stand for 'Elizabeth Barrett Browning' but 'Elizabeth Barrett Barrett', her full maiden names. Her father, who had assumed the name Barrett (instead of his original name, Moulton) on succeeding to an estate in Jamaica, had forbidden all twelve of his adult sons and daughters to marry. When Elizabeth did so – at age forty, as the eldest – this led to a permanent rift between the two.

Elizabeth Barrett **Browning**, *Aurora Leigh*, 1857

~ The words 'cousin' and 'friend' are constantly recurring in this poem, the last pages of which have been finished under the hospitality of your roof, my own dearest cousin and friend; – cousin and friend, in a sense of less equality and greater disinterestedness than Romney's. Ending, therefore, and preparing once more to quit England, I venture to leave in your hands this book, the most mature of my works, and the one into which my highest convictions upon Life and Art have entered; that as, through my various efforts in literature and steps in life, you have believed in me, borne with me, and been generous to me, far beyond the common uses of mere relationship or sympathy of mind, so you may kindly accept, in sight of the public, this poor sign of esteem, gratitude, and affection, from, Your unforgetting E.B.B.

John Kenyon, who died only a few weeks after this was written, was a poet and philanthropist who had been a close friend of the Brownings, and whose Somerset house, where Elizabeth had written the work, had been their home. Robert Browning had dedicated his own *Dramatic Romances and Lyrics* to Kenyon, and Kenyon had not only given the Brownings £100 to live on but left Robert Browning £6,500 in his will, and Elizabeth £4,500, substantial sums for those days. But if Elizabeth and John Kenyon were indeed cousins, the relationship was only a remote one. The 'Romney' referred to is one of the central characters of the poem, and the cousin of the heroine, Aurora Leigh.

Robert **Browning**, *Pippa Passes*, 1841

~ Two or three years ago I wrote a play, about which the chief matter I much care to recollect at present is, that a Pitfull of good-natured people applauded it:

ever since, I have been desirous of doing something in the same way that should better reward their attention. What follows, I mean for the first of a series of Dramatical Pieces, to come out at intervals; and I amuse myself by fancying that the cheap mode in which they appear, will for once help me to a sort of Pit-audience again. Of course such a work must go on no longer than it is liked; and to provide against a too certain but too possible contingency, let me hasten to say now – what, if I were sure of success, I would try to say circumstantially enough at the close – that I dedicate my best intentions most admiringly to the Author of *Ion* – most affectionately to Sergeant Talfourd. Robert Browning.

Sir Thomas Talfourd wrote worthy but incredibly uninspired tragedies in colourless blank verse, including the one singled out here by Browning. But he was good-natured and won many friends, and thus was the recipient of several dedications, including not only this one but the one by Dickens to *Pickwick Papers*, when first published, in monthly instalments, in 1836–7. Browning's work here was published as No. 1 in the series entitled *Bells and Pomegranates*.

Robert **Browning**, *Colombe's Birthday*, 1844
~ No one loves and honours Barry Cornwall more than does Robert Browning; who, having nothing better than this play to give him in proof of it, must say so.

'Barry Cornwall' was the pseudonym of the poet Bryan Waller Procter, a prolific author of volumes of lyrics and songs. Browning's dedication to him is attractively brief and nicely balanced.

Robert **Browning**, *Luria*, 1846
~ I dedicate this last attempt for the present at Dramatic Poetry to a Great Dramatic Poet; 'Wishing what I write may be read by his light'; if a phrase originally addressed, by not the least worthy of his contemporaries, to Shakespeare, may be applied here, by one whose sole privilege is in a grateful admiration, to Walter Savage Landor.

Landor, a colourful poet and essayist, was renowned for his apparently ungovernable temper, and in his irascible old age was looked after by Browning in Florence, where he had lived on and off for several years.

Robert **Browning**, *Fifty Men and Women*, 1855
TO E.B.B.
There they are, my fifty men and women
Naming me the fifty poems finished.
Take them, Love, the book and me together:
Where the heart lies, let the brain lie also. [...]

The first four lines of many stanzas of 'One Word More', an address by Browning to his wife at the end of this collection of (actually) fifty-one poems on a great range of subjects. 'One Word More' was a private phrase first picked up in the couple's correspondence ten years earlier.

Robert **Browning**, *Sordello*, 1863

~ To J. Milsand, of Dijon. Dear Friend, – Let the next poem be introduced by your name, therefore remembered along with the deepest of my affections, and so repay all trouble it ever cost me. I wrote it twenty-five years ago for only a few, counting even in these on somewhat more care about its subject than they really had. My own faults of expression were many; but with care for a man or book such would be surmounted, and without it what avails the faultlessness of either? I blame nobody, least of all myself, who did my best then and since; for I lately gave time and pains to turn my work into what the many might – instead of the few must – like; but after all, I imagined another thing at first, and therefore leave as I find it. The historical decoration was purposely of no more importance than a background requires and my stress lay on the incidents in the development of a soul: little else is worth study. I, at least always thought so, – you, with many known and unknown to me, think so, – others may one day think so; and whether my attempt remain for them or not, I trust, though away and past it, to continue ever yours. R.B.

Browning wrote this dedication for a reprint. Joseph Milsand had written favourably on Browning in 1851 in the *Revue des deux mondes*, and this had led to a lasting friendship between them. The work, originally published in 1840, described the 'development of the soul' of the twelfth-century troubadour Sordello.

Robert **Browning**, *Balaustion's Adventure*, 1871

~ [...] If I mention the simple truth: that this poem absolutely owes its existence to you, – who not only suggested, but imposed on me as a task, what has proved the most delightful of May-month amusements – I shall seem honest, indeed, but hardly prudent; for, how good and beautiful ought such a poem to be! Euripides might fear little; but I also, have an interest in the performance: and what wonder if I beg you to suffer that it make, in another and far easier sense, its nearest possible approach to those Greek qualities of goodness and beauty, by laying itself gratefully at your feet? R.B.

The dedicatee here was Countess Cowper, wife of the 7th Earl Cowper. The poem itself, based on an episode from Plutarch, was one of a great number of later works that Browning produced in his sixties.

Robert **Browning**, *Asolando*, 1889

~ To Mrs Arthur Bronson. To whom but you, dear friend, should I dedicate verses – some few written, all of them supervised, in the comfort of your presence, and with yet another experience of the gracious hospitality now bestowed on me since so many a year, – adding a charm even to my residences at Venice, and leaving me little regret for the surprise and delight at my visits to Asolo in bygone days. I unite, you will see, the disconnected poems by a title-name popularly ascribed to the inventiveness of the ancient Secretary of Queen Cornaro whose palace-tower still overlooks us! *Asolare* – 'to disport in the open air, amuse oneself at random'. The objection that such a word nowhere occurs in the works of the Cardinal is hardly important. [...] I use it for love of the place, and in requital of your pleasant assurance that an early poem of mine first attracted you thither – where and elsewhere, at La Mura as Ca Alcisi, may all happiness attend you. Gratefully and affectionately yours, R.B.

This was Browning's last volume of poems, dedicated to the wife of Arthur Bronson, a lady who ran a literary salon in Venice where Browning and his sister spent the winters from 1883. The dedication is dated 15 October, and the work itself appeared on the day of Browning's death, 12 December 1889. Asolo is a small town north of Venice.

J. **Bryan** III, *Hodgepodge: A Commonplace Book*, 1986
~ For my ouaffe, from her ossban.

The writer's compliment to his French wife.

Arthur **Bryant**, *The Turn of the Tide*, 1957
~ For Alanbrooke, whose war diaries are the jewel for which this book is the setting.

The book itself has the subtitle: 'A Study based on the Diaries and Autobiographical Notes of Field Marshal the Viscount Alanbrooke, K.G., O.M.'.

Arthur **Bryant**, *Spirit of England*, 1982
~ To Wilfrid House, the dear friend of my Oxford youth, who in 1918, an acting Brigade Major of twenty-three, held against odds a vital gap in the British line and so helped to halt the German drive on the Channel ports.

Jacob **Bryant**, *Observations and Inquiries Relating to Various Parts of Ancient History*, 1767
~ To His Grace the Duke of Marlborough. My Lord, I would not presume to introduce the ensuing Treatises to Your Grace's notice, were I not well acquainted with Your love of truth, and Your zeal to obtain it through the most severe investigation. A mind so devoted is the best judge of evidence in every degree, being influenced by a more exquisite taste and discernment, and enriched with superiour knowledge. It is from this principle, my Lord, that You have been rendered so happy in every rational attainment, and led to an union with virtues the most similar to Your own. Hence it is, that I am emboldened to lay before Your Grace the following Dissertations, which contain matter of dark and remote enquiry; and are the fruits of that ease and retirement, with which, under Providence, I am blest by your benevolence and favour. [...] Permit me to subscribe myself with the highest sense of duty and esteem, My Lord, Your Grace's most faithful and most obliged humble servant, Jacob Bryant.

Bryant was a classical scholar and ardent bibliophile. This was his first work, attacking the opinions of various writers and thinkers. He had been appointed secretary to the Duke of Marlborough in 1756, in his early forties, and the Marlborough family had given him rooms at Blenheim Palace, the use of the library there, and a handsome allowance (for those days) of £1,000 a year.

John **Buchan**, *John Burnet of Barns*, 1898
~ To the memory of my sister Violet Katherine Stuart.

John **Buchan**, *The Thirty-Nine Steps*, 1915
~ To Thomas Arthur Nelson (Lothian and Border Horse). My dear Tommy, You and I have long cherished an affection for that elementary type of tale which Americans call the 'dime novel' and which we know as the 'shocker' – the romance where the incidents defy the probabilities, and march just inside the borders of the possible. During an illness last winter I exhausted my store of those aids to cheerfulness, and was driven to write one for myself. This little volume is the result, and I should like to put your name on it in memory of our long friendship, in the days when the wildest fictions are so much less improbable than the facts. J.B.

The first of Buchan's thrillers featuring Richard Hannay, and probably his best known novel (although already his twenty-seventh book).

John **Buchan**, *Huntingtower*, 1922
~ To W.P. Ker. If the Professor of Poetry in the University of Oxford has not forgotten the rock whence he was hewn, this simple story may give him an hour of entertainment. I offer it to you because I think you have met my friend Dickson McCunn, and I dare to hope that you may even in your many sojournings in the Westlands have encountered one or other of the Gorbals Die-Hards. [...] Such as it is, I dedicate the story to you, and ask for no better verdict on it than that of that profound critic of life and literature, Mr Huckleberry Finn, who observed of the *Pilgrim's Progress* that he 'considered the statements interesting, but steep'. J.B.

William Paton Ker, who died the following year, aged sixty-eight, was a Scots critic and noted authority on medieval literature who after a number of academic appointments was elected Professor of Poetry at Oxford in 1920.

John **Buchan**, *Midwinter*, 1923
TO VERNON WATNEY
We two confess twin loyalties –
Wychwood beneath the April skies
Is yours, and many a scented road
That winds in June by Evenlode.
Not less when autumn fires the brake,
Yours the deep heath by Fannich's lake,
The corries where the dun deer roar
And eagles wheel above Sgurr Mór.

> So I, who love with equal mind
> The southern sun, the northern wind,
> The lilied lowland water-mead
> And the grey hills that cradle Tweed,
> Bring you this tale which haply tries
> To intertwine our loyalties.

Not only a 'marriage of minds' but a bond between north and south here: Wychwood and the Evenlode are in Oxfordshire.

John **Buchan**, *The Three Hostages*, 1924

> To A Young Gentleman of Eton College.
> Honoured Sir, On your last birthday a well-meaning godfather presented you with a volume of mine, since you had been heard on occasion to express approval of my works. The book dealt with a somewhat arid branch of historical research, and it did not please you. You wrote to me, I remember, complaining that I had 'let you down', and summoning me, as I valued your respect, to 'pull myself together'. In particular you demanded to hear more of the doings of Richard Hannay, a gentleman for whom you professed a liking. [...] He was so good as to tell me the tale of an unpleasant business in which he had recently been engaged, and to give me permission to retell it for your benefit. [...] So I herewith present it to you, in the hope that in the eyes of you and your friends it may atone for certain other writings of mine with which you have been afflicted by those in authority. J.B.

Despite extensive enquiries, it has – to date – proved impossible to discover the identity of the 'Young Gentleman' who felt so let down in this way. The historical book referred to by Buchan may have been one of the twenty-four volumes of his *Nelson's History of the War* (1915–19), or, more probably, *The History of the South African Forces in France* (1920).

Colonel Angus **Buchanan**, *Sahara*, 1926

~ To Feri n'Gashi, Only a camel, But steel-true and Great of heart.

Robert **Buchanan**, *Undertones*, 1863

~ To whom can I more appropriately dedicate these *Undertones* than to the man whose friendship has been a comfort to me during four years of the bitterest struggle and disappointment, and whose voice has whispered 'courage!' when I seemed faltering down the easy descent to Acheron? The world knows least of your noble soul. High-minded, gracious-hearted, possessed of the true instinct of an artist, you have laid me under a debt of affection which I can never repay; yet take the Book, as a token that I love and honour you. [...]

The dedicatee was the dramatic poet and critic John Westland Marston, whose London home was a meeting place for many noted literary figures of the day. Buchanan had come to London from Scotland in 1860, at the age of nineteen, and was struggling to make a living as a writer and contributor.

Robert **Buchanan**, *London Poems*, 1866

~ My dear Dixon, This book is inscribed to you; and lest you should ask wherefore, I will refresh your memory. Seven years ago, when I was an ambitious lad in Scotland, and when the north-easter was blowing coldly on me, you sent me such good words as cheered and warmed me. You were one of two (the gentle, true, and far-seeing George Henry Lewes was the other) who first believed that I was fitted for noble efforts. Since then you have known me better, and abode by your first hope. [...] Accept these poems, given under a genuine impulse, and not merely in compliment. [...]

The dedicatee here was William Hepworth Dixon, traveller and historian, and a contributor to the *Athenaeum* and the *Daily News*. George Henry Lewes is best remembered as the 'husband' and encourager of George Eliot (real name Mary Ann Evans).

Robert **Buchanan**, *God and the Man, a Romance*, 1881

> I would have snatch'd a bay-leaf from thy brow,
>> Wronging the chaplet on an honoured head;
> In peace and tenderness I bring thee *now*
>> A lily-flower instead.
>
> Pure as thy purpose, blameless as thy song,
>> Sweet as thy spirit, may this offering be;
> Forget the bitter blame that did thee wrong,
>> And take the gift from me!

A 'let's be friends again' plea to Dante Gabriel Rossetti, whom Buchanan had attacked, as well as other Pre-Raphaelite poets (the 'Fleshly School of Poetry'), in the *Contemporary Review* ten years earlier, under the pseudonym of 'Thomas Maitland'. After Rossetti's death in 1882, Buchanan recanted, and confessed publicly that 'Mr Rossetti, I freely admit now, was never a Fleshly Poet at all' (*The Academy*, 1 July 1882). A second edition of this novel had two further dedicatory verses:

> Calmly, thy royal robe of Death around thee,
>> Thou sleepest, and weeping Brethren round thee stand;
> Gently they placed, ere yet God's angel crown'd thee,
>> My lily in thy hand!
>
> I never knew thee living, O my brother!
>> But on thy breast my lily of love now lies;
> And by that token we *shall* know each other
>> When God's voice saith, 'Arise!'

These samples of Buchanan's work coincidentally illustrate why he is now mostly unread.

Henry Thomas **Buckle**, *The History of Civilisation in England*, vol. I, 1857

~ To my Mother I dedicate this first volume of my first work.

Buckle adored his mother, and confided almost everything to her. 'Almost', as this dedication was the only part of the book he had not discussed with her, and she was agitated on discovering what he had intended as a pleasant surprise. The second volume was dedicated to her memory.

Richard **Buckle**, ed., *U and Non-U Revisited*, 1978

~ To Holly. One night in New York last May I was told dinner would be late because the English television serial *Upstairs, Downstairs*, was showing. This was introduced by Alistair Cooke, who had the hard task of explaining why English servants had not murdered their masters long before the latter were killed in the 1914–18 War. I told my host that I was fed up with this serial because every time I dined with Felicity, my nearest Wiltshire neighbour, it always seemed to be on the night of *Upstairs, Downstairs*, and she too changed all the household arrangements because she could not bear to miss a moment of it. I added that Felicity's former husband Anthony was married to Pauline the daughter of Hermione, whose sister Angela (now dead) played the part of the cook in the popular serial. Furthermore, I told him, the girl-friend of Anthony's and Felicity's son Henry, i.e. you, was the stepdaughter of Alistair Cooke. [...] When Brookie [...] asked me to edit this collection of essays, I thought he must have been overwhelmed by my genius. Not at all: he was simply inviting me on your recommendation. That is why I dedicate this book, with my love, to you. Dicky.

Much name-dropping here, as might be expected in a book whose subject is the difference between upper-class and lower-class speech and vocabulary. Buckle is better-known as a writer on ballet. Felicity was the former wife of Sir Anthony Rumbold, whose second wife was Mrs Pauline Graham, daughter of the Hon. David Tennant and Hermione Baddeley, the actress and sister of Angela Baddeley (who played the cook). Henry is now Sir Henry Rumbold, the husband of Frances, née Hawkes, herself formerly married to Julian Berry. Alistair Cooke's second wife was Jane White, née Hawkes. Brookie is H.B. Brooks-Baker, then managing director of *Debrett's Peerage*, who published the book.

James M. **Buckley**, *The Wrong and Peril of Woman Suffrage*, 1909

~ To men and women who look before they leap.

Buckley was an American Methodist Episcopal clergyman, at the time editor of the *Christian Advocate*. This was the heyday of the suffrage movement, with much strong feeling and polemic on either side. Buckley nails his colours firmly to the mast in his title.

William F. **Buckley**, Jr, *See You Later Alligator*, 1985

~ For my nieces and nephews.

All forty-nine are listed by family.

Augustus C. **Buell**, *History of Andrew Jackson*, 1904

~ To the embodiment in our times of the Jacksonian spirit, Theodore Roosevelt, the author respectfully dedicates these volumes.

Andrew Jackson was of course the great American hero and seventh President. Roosevelt, cast here in his image, was the twenty-sixth President.

Edward **Bulwer Lytton**, *Eugene Aram*, 1832

~ To Sir Walter Scott, Bart., etc. etc. Sir, It has long been my ambition to add some humble tribute to the offerings laid upon the shrine of your genius. At each succeeding book that I have given the world, I have paused to consider if it were worthy to be inscribed with your great name, and at each I have played the procrastinator, and hoped for that morrow of better desert which never came. But *defluat annis*, the time runs on – and I am tired of waiting for the ford which the tides refuse. I seize, then, the present opportunity, not as the best, but as the only one I can be sure of commanding, to express that affectionate admiration with which you have inspired me in common with all your contemporaries, and which a French writer has not ungracefully termed 'the happiest prerogative of genius'. […] You, I feel assured, will not deem it presumptuous in one, who, to that bright and undying flame which now streams from the grey hills of Scotland, – the last halo with which you have crowned her literary glories, – has turned from his first childhood with a deep and unrelaxing devotion: you, I feel assured, will not deem it presumptuous in him to inscribe an idle work with your illustrious name: – a work which, however worthless in itself, assumes something of value in his eyes when thus rendered a tribute of respect to you. The Author of 'Eugene Aram'.

The novel is the story of a schoolmaster driven to crime by poverty.

Edward **Bulwer Lytton**, *Rienzi, The Last of the Tribunes*, 1835

~ To Alessandro Manzoni, as to the genius of the place, are dedicated these fruits gathered on the soil of Italian fiction.

Manzoni was a noted Italian novelist and poet, well known for his novel *I Promessi Sposi* (1825–6), a historical study of seventeenth-century Italy. Bulwer Lytton's novel is also historical, with its central character the fourteenth-century Italian patriot, 'last of the Romans', Rienzi (real name Niccolò Gabrini), who led a revolt in Rome and who was murdered in a riot.

Edward **Bulwer Lytton**, *Ernest Maltravers*, 1837

~ To the great German people, a race of thinkers and of critics, a foreign but familiar audience, profound in judgment, candid in reproof, generous in appreciation, this work is dedicated by an English author.

Edward **Bulwer Lytton**, *Pilgrims of the Rhine*, 1840

~ To Henry Lytton Bulwer. Allow me, my dear Brother, to dedicate this work to you. The greater part of it (viz., the tales which vary and relieve the voyages of Gertrude and Trevelyan) was written in the pleasant excursion we made together some years ago. Among the associations – some sad, and some pleasing – connected with the general design, none are so agreeable to me as those that remind me of the friendship subsisting between us, and which, unlike that of near relations in general, has grown stronger and more intimate as our footsteps have receded farther from the fields where we played together in our childhood. I dedicate this

Work to you with the more pleasure, not only when I remember that it has always been a favourite with yourself, but when I think that it is one of my writings most liked in foreign countries; and I may possibly, therefore, have found a record destined to endure the affectionate esteem which this Dedication is intended to convey. Yours etc., E.L.B.

The book had been first published in 1834. Bulwer Lytton's brother was William Henry Lytton Earle Bulwer, Baron Dalling and Bulwer, better known as Sir Henry Bulwer. In 1822 he published a small book of poems dedicated to his younger brother.

Edward **Bulwer Lytton**, *Collected Works*, 1840

~ My dear Mother, In inscribing with your beloved and honoured name this Collection of my Works, I could wish that the fruits of my manhood were worthier of the tender and anxious pains bestowed upon my education in youth. [...] From your graceful and accomplished taste, I early learned that affection for literature which has exercised so large an influence over the pursuits of my life; and you were my first guide, were my earliest critic. [...] Never more than at this moment did I wish that my writings were possessed of a merit which might outlive my time, so that at least these lines might remain a record of the excellence of the Mother, and the gratitude of the Son. E.L.B.

Bulwer Lytton's mother was Elizabeth Barbara Lytton, who married Colonel Bulwer in 1798. He was born in 1803, and his childhood and upbringing were largely dependent on his mother alone, as his father died when he was only four. It was when his mother died, in 1843, that the original Edward Bulwer expanded his surname, in her honour, to Bulwer Lytton, although 'Lytton' was already one of his own Christian names. After 1866, when raised to the peerage, he was usually known more unambiguously as simply Lord Lytton.

R.W. **Burchfield**, ed., *A Supplement to the Oxford English Dictionary*, 1972–86

~ This Supplement to the Oxford English Dictionary is respectfully dedicated to HER MAJESTY THE QUEEN by her gracious permission.

One of the few works dedicated to Queen Elizabeth II. The *Supplement* was published in four volumes, respectively in 1972, 1976, 1982 and 1986, and this dedication appears in volumes 2 and 4 only. Compare the dedication in the *Oxford English Dictionary* itself (under the name of its chief editor, DR. JAMES MURRAY).

Gelett **Burgess**, *The Lively City O'Ligg*, 1899

~ To Arnold's sensitive taste and Robin's adventurous spirit, these headlong fancies are fearfully dedicated.

Thornton W. **Burgess**, *Mother West Wind's Children*, 1911

~ To all the little friends of Johnny Chuck and Reddy Fox, and to all who love the green meadows and the smiling pool, the laughing brook, and the merry little breezes, this little book is dedicated.

Burgess was an American author who the previous year had written *Old Mother West Wind*, a series of whimsical tales about Johnny Chuck, Reddy Fox, Peter Rabbit, Grandfather Frog and other animals, as a sort of blend of Kenneth Grahame's *Wind in the Willows*, the Beatrix Potter stories, and the *Uncle Remus* tales of JOEL CHANDLER HARRIS.

Brian **Burland**, *A Fall from Aloft*, 1968
~ For Edwina Ann, my love, and a lot of friends – most of whom seemed to be named John.

F.C. **Burnand**, *A New History of Sandford and Merton*, 1872
~ My two elder sons, C.H.B. and H.C.B. My dear Charles Hubert and Harry Cecil, This book is for your instruction – negatively. Your pastors and masters will teach you what to *do*, but the New History of Sandford and Merton will, I trust, teach you what to *don't*. Beware, too, of Mr Barlow, an immortal humbug. Avoid, in a general way, the examples set by all the characters in this volume, without exception. Be good – be virtuous, and save up your pocket-money in order to provide for your father in his old age. Thus you will ensure for yourselves many Merry Christmases and Happy New Years; and that you may enjoy a very merry holiday is the sincere wish, not only of Mr Sambourne who has profusely illustrated this work, but also of Your Affectionate Father, F.C. Burnand.

The children's book is a parody of Thomas Day's collection of stories for children, *The History of Sandford and Merton* (1783–9). GEORGE GROSSMITH and WEEDON GROSSMITH dedicated *The Diary of a Nobody* to Burnand.

Charles **Burney**, *A General History of Music*, 2nd edn, 1789
~ To the Queen. Madam, – The condescension with which your Majesty has been pleased to permit your name to stand before the following History, may justly reconcile the Author to his favourite study, and convince him, that whatever may be said by the professors of severer wisdom, the hours which he has bestowed upon Music have been neither dishonourably nor unprofitably spent. [...] To those who know that Music is among your Majesty's recreations, it is not necessary to display its purity or assert its dignity. May it long amuse your leisure, not as a relief from evil, but as an augmentation of good; not as a diversion from care, but as a variation of felicity. Such, Madam, is my sincerest wish, in which I can however boast no peculiarity of reverence or zeal; for the virtues of your Majesty are universally confessed; and however the inhabitants of the British empire may differ in their opinions upon other questions, they all behold your excellencies with the same eye, and celebrate them with the same voice; and to that name which one nation is echoing to another, nothing can be added by the respectful admiration and humble gratitude of, Madam, Your Majesty's most obedient and most devoted servant, Charles Burney.

This extract represents about half the overall original dedication, which was written not by Charles Burney, however, but by Dr Johnson, who on more than one occasion provided dedications for the works of his friends. James Boswell, Johnson's biographer, collected books to which his friend had contributed in this way and had a direct comment to make on the matter: 'What an expense, Sir, do you put us to in buying books, to which you have written Prefaces or Dedications' (*Life of Samuel Johnson*, 1791). The queen in the dedication here is Charlotte Sophia, wife of George III.

Fanny **Burney**, *Evelina*, 1778

~ To the Authors of the Monthly and Critical Reviews. Gentlemen, The liberty which I take in addressing to you the trifling production of a few idle hours, will doubtless move your wonder, and probably your contempt. I will not, however, with the futility of apologies, intrude upon your time, but briefly acknowledge the motives of my temerity; lest, by a premature exercise of that patience which I hope, will befriend me, I should lessen its benevolence, and be accessory to my own condemnation. Without name, without recommendation, and unknown alike to success and disgrace, to whom can I so properly apply for patronage, as to those who publicly profess themselves Inspectors of all literary performances? [...] The language of adulation, and the incense of flattery, through the natural inheritance, and constant resource, from time immemorial, of the Dedicator, to me offer nothing but the wistful regret that I dare not invoke their aid. [...] In addressing you jointly, I mean but to mark the generous sentiments by which liberal criticism, to the utter annihilation of envy, jealousy, and all selfish views, ought to be distinguished. I have the honour to be, Gentlemen, Your most obedient Humble Servant, *** ****.

Fanny Burney originally published this epistolary novel anonymously, at the age of twenty-five, and it was well received by the *Monthly Review*, to which her father, CHARLES BURNEY (see previous dedication above), regularly contributed. It was equally well noticed by the *Critical Review*, founded in opposition to the *Monthly Review* as a Tory and Church journal. The author has some shrewd comments to make on dedications (and dedicators) in general here. Her book also had an original inscription, addressed 'To *****', actually to her father. It was in five stanzas, as an additional dedication or 'offering', with the first and last as follows:

> Oh, Author of my being! – far more dear
> To me than light, than nourishment, or rest,
> Hygeia's blessings, Rapture's burning tear,
> Or the life-blood that mantles in my breast! [...]
>
> Oh! of my life at once the source and joy!
> If e'er thy eyes these feeble lines survey,
> Let not their folly their intent destroy;
> Accept the tribute – but forget the lay.

From 1793, when she married, Fanny Burney was known equally by her (French) husband's name, as Madame d'Arblay.

John **Burroughs,** *Bird and Bough,* 1906
~ To the kinglet that sang in my evergreens in October and made me think it was May.

The author was an American naturalist and friend of Walt Whitman. A 'kinglet' is a gold-crested wren.

Octavia **Butler,** *Adulthood Rites (Xenogenesis: 2),* 1988
~ To Lynn – write!

Michael **Butterworth,** *The Man in the Sopwith Camel,* 1974
~ To my friends among bank managers.

Lord **Byron,** *Hours of Idleness,* 1808
~ To the Right Honourable Frederick, Earl of Carlisle, Knight of the Garter, etc., etc., the second edition of these poems is inscribed, by his obliged ward and affectionate kinsman, The Author.

In 1798 Frederick Howard, 5th Earl of Carlisle, had been appointed the legal guardian of Byron, who was his first cousin once removed. Byron did not long remain his 'affectionate kinsman', however, and in *English Bards and Scotch Reviewers*, published the following year, he indicated the cause of the rift in a note: 'It may be asked why I have censured the Earl of Carlisle, my guardian and relative, to whom I dedicated a volume of puerile poems [...]. The guardianship was nominal, at least so far as I have been able to discover; the relationship I cannot help, and am very sorry for it; but as his lordship seemed to forget it, on a very essential occasion to me, I shall not burden my memory with the recollection.' The first edition of the volume appeared in 1807.

Lord **Byron,** *Childe Harold's Pilgrimage,* Canto I, 1812
TO IANTHE

The first canto of the famous work is dedicated thus with an accompanying five-stanza poem, addressed to, and lovingly describing, a 'Young Peri of the West' half the age of Byron himself ('My years already doubly number thine'). The dedicatee, disguised under this name, was actually eleven-year-old Lady Charlotte Mary Harley, the second daughter of Edward Harley, 5th Earl of Oxford, who later married a Captain Antony Bacon and became Lady Charlotte Bacon. Byron was thus twenty-two at this time. For the dedication to the fourth canto of this work, see below, and for a similar age comparison, see that for LEWIS CARROLL's *Through the Looking-Glass.*

Lord **Byron,** *The Giaour,* 1813
~ To Samuel Rogers, Esq., as a slight but most sincere token of admiration for his genius, respect for his character, and gratitude for his friendship, this production is inscribed, by his obliged and affectionate servant, Byron.

Rogers was a poet admired by Byron.

Lord **Byron**, *The Bride of Abydos*, 1813

~ To the Right Hon. Lord Holland, this tale is inscribed, with every sentiment of regard and respect, by his gratefully obliged and sincere friend, Byron.

Byron had first spoken in the House of Lords the previous year, and Lord Holland had helped him with his speeches.

Lord **Byron**, *The Corsair*, 1814

~ To Thomas Moore, Esq. My dear Moore, I dedicate to you the last production with which I shall trespass on public patience, and your indulgence, for some years; and I own that I feel anxious to avail myself of this latest and only opportunity of adorning my pages with a name, consecrated by unshaken public principle, and the most undoubted and various talents. [...] It might be of some service to me, that the man who is alike the delight of his readers and his friends, the poet of all circles, and the idol of his own, permits me here and elsewhere to subscribe myself, Most truly, and affectionately, his obedient servant, Byron.

The first and last sentences of a longish letter to the famous Irish poet, with Byron expressing his views on poetry and on the portrayal of his characters. Byron and Moore had been friends since 1811, and on his death Byron left the manuscript of his 'Memoirs' to Moore, who used material from it to compile his *Letters and Journals of Lord Byron, with Notices of His Life* (1830). See MOORE's own dedications, below.

Lord **Byron**, *Parisina*, 1816

~ To Scrope Beardmore Davies, Esq., the following poem is inscribed, by one who has long admired his talents, and valued his friendship.

Lord **Byron**, *Childe Harold's Pilgrimage*, Canto IV, 1818

~ To one whom I have known long and accompanied far, whom I have found wakeful over my sickness and kind in my sorrow, glad in my prosperity and firm in my adversity, true in counsel and trusty in peril – to a friend often tried and never found wanting – to yourself. [...] In dedicating to you its complete, or at least concluded state, a poetical work which is the longest, the most thoughtful and comprehensive of my compositions, I wish to do honour to myself by the record of many years' intimacy with a man of learning, of talent, of steadiness, and of honour. [...]

A brief extract from Byron's long address to his close friend, John Cam Hobhouse, later Lord Broughton, a politician who travelled through Europe with Byron and who was adviser to John Murray, the publisher of much of Byron's work. Byron had originally intended to dedicate *Childe Harold* to the Rev. William Harness, his contemporary at Harrow, but was dissuaded from doing so for fear of harming his professional status as a schoolmaster. But see MARY RUSSELL MITFORD's dedication to this same man.

Lord **Byron**, *Don Juan*, 1819–24

> Bob Southey! You're a poet – Poet-laureate,

And representative of all the race; [...]
Meantime, Sir Laureate, I proceed to dedicate,
In honest simple verse, this song to you.

The first two and last two lines of the seventeen stanzas dedicating Byron's famous work to the poet (and then Poet Laureate) Robert Southey. The whole dedication is intended ironically, for there was no love lost between the two poets, and they spent much time and ink vilifying and attacking each other. This particular dedication was suppressed at first, but was later reinstated. It still does its writer little credit, and the mocking references to Southey and other famous poets (Coleridge and Wordsworth among them) in the work itself are really enough to express Byron's feelings on the matter. The literary quarrel with Southey had begun in 1819, when the older poet had written a hostile article on Byron in *Blackwood's Magazine*.

Lord **Byron**, *The Prophecy of Dante*, 1821

Lady! if for the cold and cloudy clime
  Where I was born, but where I would not die,
  Of the great Poet-sire of Italy
I dare to build the imitative rhyme,
Harsh Runic copy of the South's sublime,
  Thou art the cause; and howsoever I
  Fall short of his immortal harmony,
Thy gentle heart will pardon me the crime. [...]

The first of two stanzas addressed to Teresa, Countess Guiccioli, a young married woman of nineteen (herself married to a wealthy but eccentric man three times her age) with whom Byron had fallen deeply in love, and who later became his mistress. She described her relationship with him in *My Recollections of Lord Byron*, published in French in 1868.

Lord **Byron**, *Sardanapalus*, 1821

~ To the illustrious Goethe, a stranger presumes to offer the homage of a literary vassal to his liege lord, the first of existing writers, who has created the literature of his own country, and illustrated that of Europe. The unworthy production which the author ventures to inscribe to him is entitled, *Sardanapalus*.

Byron had been pleased to have Goethe's praise of *Manfred* (1817). Later, Goethe wrote of this dedication: 'Well knowing myself and my labours, in my old age, I could not but reflect with gratitude and diffidence on the expressions contained in this dedication, not interpret them but as the generous tribute of a superior genius, no less original in the choice than inexhaustible in the materials of his subjects'.

Lord **Byron**, *Cain*, 1821

~ To Sir Walter Scott, Bart., this mystery of Cain is inscribed, by his obliged friend and faithful servant, The Author.

Lord **Byron,** *Werner; or, The Inheritance,* 1823
~ To the illustrious Goethe, by one of his humblest admirers, this tragedy is dedicated.

An appropriate dedicatee for a poetic drama based on a German story.

❧ C ❧

'Caesar', *Where's Master?*, 1910
~ To Master's Queen – and mine; To the beautiful Lady who found room in her poor broken heart for the sorrow of the King's little dog Cæsar.

A sentimental yet touching 'autobiography' of Edward VII's dog Caesar, his beloved fox terrier, who grieved unconsolably after his master's death in 1910 until nursed back to normality by the late King's Consort, Queen Alexandra. She is thus the dedicatee. The actual author of the book was Sir Ernest Hodder-Williams, chairman of the firm of Hodder & Stoughton, who published it.

Hall **Caine**, *The Bondman*, 1890
~ To my son, 'Little Sunlocks'.

This is also the nickname of the small son in the story, born to Stephen Orry and his wife Liza Killey, 'a bonny, sunny boy': 'He had christened it Michael, but because its long wavy hair grew to be of the colour of the sun he called it, after the manner of his people, Sunlocks'.

John **Caius**, *Of Englishe Dogges*, 1576
~ To the most learned man, and his especial patron, E. Perne, most worthy Dean of Ely Cathedral church, Abraham Fleming dedicates. Not many years ago (O best of patrons) a man most advised in every branch of life; one who has deserved well of the company of the learned; bound by the ties of family to yourself; a most shining light of the University of Cambridge; its jewel and glory, John Caius, wrote not without elegance to Conrad Gesner, a man exceedingly skilled and sagacious in the investigation of recondite matters; [...] the same man wrote an epitome concerning British dogs, not so concise as elegant and useful; [...] a book which when by chance I had met with it, and was covered with delight at the novelty of its appearance, I attempted to translate into English. After I had finished my task, a sudden conceit arose in me touching the dedication of the pamphlet. [...] By these inducements conquered, I proposed free interpretation into English of the treatise on British dogs, and have dedicated it to you rather than to anyone else as my one patron, and unique Mæcenas. [...] O most erudite Sir, I beseech you to command, that under your patronage, it may boldly go forth into all parts of our country, and I solemnly pray to you to receive from me this book bearing a humble and obscure inscription, but embracing an argument new and as yet

unheard of; as well as entirely free from any Sybaritic obscenity. The most bounden to your service, (signed) ABRAHAM FLEMING.

The original of this book, one of the earliest in English on dogs to be published, had a title-page that ran as follows: 'Of English Dogges, the diuersities, the names, the natures, and the properties. A Short Treatise written in latine by Iohannes Caius of late memorie, Doctor of Phisicke in the Universitie of Cambridge, And newly drawne into Englishe by Abraham Fleming Student [...].' The author of the Latin treatise was none other than the noted physician and humanist who enlarged and refounded his old Cambridge college as Gonville and Caius College in 1557. Abraham Fleming, who translated it, was an antiquary and poet who took holy orders after studying at Cambridge and became chaplain to the Countess of Nottingham. His real passion, however, was the translation and publication of contemporary popular scientific works, such as this one. His own dedication to the work was also in Latin, and the translation of it excerpted here his as well. 'E. Perne', who was 'D. Perne' in the Latin dedication, was actually Andrew Perne, Dean of Ely, as mentioned, but also Master of Peterhouse, the college where Fleming studied.

Brian **Callison**, *The Textant*, 1981
~ To my wife, Phyllis, who reminds me – in the nicest possible way – of one of the characters in this novel.

Albert F. **Calvert**, *Spanish Arms and Armour*, 1907
~ Dedicated with profound respect and esteem to her Majesty, Queen Maria Cristina of Spain, who so worthily and so long maintained those glorious traditions of Spanish greatness, which are symbolised in the treasures of the Royal Armoury.

Queen Maria was the mother of Alfonso XIII of Spain, for whom she acted as regent until 1902.

Albert F. **Calvert**, *Toledo, An Historical and Descriptive Account of the City of Generations*, 1907
~ To S.A. Infanta Maria Teresa, in whose sympathy the ancient grandeur is linked with the future greatness of Spain, this volume, with an assurance of sincere esteem, is dedicated.

Maria Teresa was the sister of Alfonso XIII of Spain; see the dedication above.

William **Camden**, *Remains Concerning Britain*, 1674
~ To the High and Mighty Prince, Charles Lodowick, By the Grace of God, Prince Elector, Arch-Dapifer and Vicar of the Sacred Empire, Count Palatine of the ancient Principality of the Rhene, Duke of Bavare, and Knight of the most Illustrious Order of the Garter. Sir, It hath pleased your Highness to acknowledg to have received much contentment in reading the description of Great Britain, made by William Camden, Esquire, Clarenceux, King of Arms. And this Book, being the remains of that greater work, was collected by him, and being now (with some Additions of mine) to be printed, it most humbly craves Patronage from

your Highness. The Author was worthily admired for his great Learning, Wisdom, and Vertue through the Christian world. [...] And standing thus deeply obliged, I shall ever pray, that successful and perpetual felicity may crown your Highness, and that in your Princely Clemency you will afford a gracious acceptance to the humble endeavours of Your Highnesses thrice humble and most faithful servant, Jo. Philipot, Somerset Herald.

This was the seventh edition of the *Remains*, edited by Philipot, who knew Camden personally and greatly admired him. The dedicatee is Charles Louis (Karl Ludwig), Elector Palatine, the son of Frederick V. The first edition of the *Remains* (1605) had been dedicated to 'The right worshipful worthy and learned Sir Robert Cotton', and the second edition (1614) to the same man, with these words: 'Pardon me, Right Worthy Baronet, if at the Printer's request I address these Remaines, with some supplement, to you againe in the same wordes I did ten years since'. Camden's original great work, *Britannia*, published in Latin in 1586, was itself dedicated to Lord Burghley, the Lord Treasurer.

Ramsey **Campbell**, *Obsession*, 1985
~ For Richard and Jean, with love (it's all a bit like life, really).

Thomas **Campion**, *Observations in the Art of English Poesy*, 1602
~ To the Right Noble and worthily honourd, the Lord Buckhurst, Lord High Treasurer of England. In two things (right honorable) it is generally agreed that man excels all other creatures, in reason and speech: and in them by how much one man surpasseth an other, by so much the neerer he aspires to a celestiall essence. Poesy in all kind of speaking is the chiefe beginner, and maintayner of eloquence, not only helping the eare with the acquaintance of sweet numbers, but also raysing the minde to a more high and lofty conceite. For this end I have studied to induce a truer forme of versefying into our language: for the vulgar and unarteficiall custome of riming hath, I know, deter'd many excellent wits from the exercise of English Poesy. The observations which I have gathered for this purpose I humbly present to your Lordship, as to the noblest judge of Poesy, and the most honorable protector of all industrious learning; which if your Honour shall vouchsafe to receive, who both in your publick and private Poemes have so devinely crowned your fame, what man will dare to repine or not strive to imitate them? Wherefore, with all humility I subject my selfe and them to your gratious favour, beseeching you in the noblenes of your mind to take in worth so simple a present, which by some worke drawne from my more serious studies, I will hereafter endevour to excuse. Your Lordships humbly devoted, Thomas Campion.

Unusually, Campion was here advocating classical metres as against 'the vulgar and unarteficiall custome of riming'. The dedicatee here, Baron Buckhurst, is better known as Thomas Sackville, the poet and diplomat, who collaborated with Thomas Norton to write the *Tragedy of Gorboduc* (1561), the earliest English tragedy, and who, in his political capacity, less happily, announced her death sentence to Mary, Queen of Scots in 1586.

Thomas **Campion**, *A New Waye of Making Fowre Partes in Counterpoint*, 1610
~ To the Flowre of Princes, Charles, Prince of Great Brittaine. The first inventor
of Musicke (most sacred Prince,) was by olde records Apollo, a King, who, for
the benefit which Mortalls received from his so divine invention, was by them
made a God. David, a Prophet, and a King, excelled all men in the same excellent
Art. What then can more adorne the greatnesse of a Prince, then the knowledge
thereof? But why should I, being by profession a Physition, offer a worke of
Musicke to his Highnesse? Galene either first, or next the first of Physitions,
became so expert a Musition, that he could not containe himselfe, but needed he
must apply all the proportions of Musicke to the uncertaine motions of the pulse.
Such far-fetcht Doctrine dare not I attempt, contenting my selfe onely with a
poore, and easie invention; yet new and certaine; by which the skill of Musicke
shall be redeemed from much darknesse, wherein envious antiquitie of purpose
did involve it. To your gratious hands most humbly I present it, which if your
Clemency will vouchsafe favourably to behold, I have then attained to the full
estimate of all my labour. Be all your daies ever musicall (most mighty Prince)
and a sweet harmony guide the events of all your royall actions. So zealously
wisheth Your Highnesse most humble servant, Tho: Campion.

Campion was not only a 'Physition' but a poet and composer, and this textbook on
counterpoint long remained a standard work for students of music. The dedicatee was the
ten-year-old prince and son of James VI of Scotland who fifteen years later would become
Charles I, King of Great Britain and Ireland. He was a patron of the arts, but in the event
was not noticeably musical. Nor were his 'daies ever musicall', as Campion had wished
him, for his troubled life ended in death on the scaffold when he was still not yet fifty.

Neville **Cardus**, *Full Score*, 1970
~ To David Ascoli, who has conducted this book and maintained the right tempo.

Cardus was both a music critic and cricketer. Hence the punning references and, best of
all, the nicely ambiguous title.

Gary **Carey**, *All the Stars in Heaven: Louis B. Meyer's M-G-M*, 1982
~ For Carol Estelle Koshinskie Carey, my own kapusta swieza na kwasno.

The Polish endearment translates literally as 'my own fresh sour cabbage', but clearly means
something much sweeter.

Ian **Carmichael**, *Will the Real Ian Carmichael ...*, 1979
~ In memory of Lucy – and for Samantha, Kate, Christian, Rupert, and any
others who may follow in the same line. Also for Pym – who undoubtedly deserved
a medal.

The famous stage and TV actor's autobiography. Pym, short for Pyman, a family name,
was his wife (who died in 1983).

Dale Carnegie, *How to Win Friends and Influence People,* 1937
~ This Book is Dedicated to a Man Who Doesn't Need to Read It: My Cherished Friend HOMER CROY.

A dedication that has become almost as much a catch phrase as the title of the best-selling book by the American teacher of public speaking, and that has been utilised elsewhere by more than a few dedicators.

Pedro Carolino, *The New Guide of the Conversation in Portuguese and English,* 1869
~ [...] We expect then, who the little book (for the care what we wrote him, and for her typographical correction) that may be worth the acceptation of the studious persons, and especialy of the Youth, at which we dedicate him particularly.

This is the original English version – as the final paragraph of the Preface – of the much-quoted dedication in the book that later became popularly known as *English As She Is Spoke*. It occurs in a version of a bilingual (Portuguese–English) book that was published in Paris in 1855 under the title of *O Novo Guia da Conversação em Portuguez e Inglez*, by José da Fonseca and Pedro Carolino, with this in turn a reworking of an original book, entitled *O Novo Guia da Conversação em frances e portuguez*, by José da Fonseca alone, published in Paris in 1836 as a French–Portuguese phrasebook.

Nathaneal Carpenter, *Geographie Delineated Forth in Two Books,* 2nd edn, 1635
~ To the Right Honourable William Earle of Pembroke, Lord Chamberlaine to the King's most excellent Maiesty, Knight of the Most Noble Order of the Garter and Chancellour of the University of Oxford. Right Honourable: This poore Infant of mine, which I now offer to Your Honourable acceptance, was consecrated Yours in the first conception: if the hasty desire I had to present it makes it (as an abortive brat) seem unworthy my first wishes, Your favourable Patronage impute it (I beseech You) not to selfe-will but duty: which would rather show yourselfe too officious, then negligent. What I now dedicate rather to Your Honour, then mine owne ambition, I desire no farther to bee accepted Mine, then Your generous approbation: wishing it no other fate then either to die with Your Dislike or live with Your Name and Memory. [...] Your Honour's in all duty and service to be commanded, Nathaneal Carpenter.

The dedicatee is believed by many to have been the 'Mr W.H.' (i.e. William Herbert) to whom SHAKESPEARE dedicated his *Sonnets* (1609) (see below). Both Carpenter and the Earl had Oxford connections: Carpenter was a student at Exeter College and Sir William was not only Chancellor of the university but gave the name of Pembroke College (1624). The first edition of this book was published in 1625. 'Then', as usual, means 'than' here.

J.L. Carr, *The Battle of Pollocks Crossing,* 1985
~ For C.M. in his basement. R.I.P.

J.L. **Carr**, *What Hetty Did*, 1988

~ To John Baskerville of Birmingham, freethinker, who designed a type-fount and lost money cheerfully on particular books which he published.

A sense of fellow-feeling here: J.L. Carr published this novel himself, and lost money in the process. (He gave an account of his experience in *The Sunday Times*, 4 December 1988.) It was Baskerville (died 1775) who gave his name to the type-face that he invented, now used in many books as standard, e.g. *The Concise Oxford Dictionary*.

Lewis **Carroll**, *The Rectory Magazine*, 1850

~ To the Inhabitants of the Rectory, Croft, and especially to the younger members of that house, this Magazine, their own united labour and produce, is respectfully Dedicated by The Editor.

This was a children's magazine for 'home consumption' edited by Carroll as a teenager. The 'younger members' of the house (in the village of Croft, just south of Darlington, Yorkshire) were his brothers and sisters: he himself was the third eldest of his parents' eleven children, seven of whom were girls.

Lewis **Carroll**, *Alice's Adventures in Wonderland*, 1865

> [...] Alice! A childish story take,
> And with a gentle hand
> Lay it where Childhood's dreams are twined
> In memory's mystic band,
> Like pilgrim's withered wreath of flowers
> Pluck'd in a far-off land.

This is the final stanza of the prefatory verses to the famous book, beginning 'All in the golden afternoon', and recalling the day in 1862 when Carroll and a clergyman friend took the three young Liddell sisters on a boating trip up the Thames at Oxford. The second oldest of the three was the original Alice, then aged ten, who inspired the book. See also the dedications below.

Lewis **Carroll**, *Through the Looking-Glass*, 1871

> Child of the pure unclouded brow
> And dreaming eyes of wonder!
> Though time be fleet, and I and thou
> Are half a life asunder,
> Thy loving smile will surely hail
> The love-gift of a fairy-tale. [...]

The dedication, of which this is the first of six stanzas, was also to Alice Liddell (see above), although the story itself was directly inspired by another Alice, Alice Raikes, the daughter of a local MP and family friend. A further reference to the original Alice comes in the last line of the final stanza, 'The pleasance of our fairy-tale': Alice Liddell's middle name was Pleasance. 'Half a life asunder' refers to Carroll's age compared with Alice's: he was then thirty-nine, and she nineteen. For a similar reference, see the dedication to 'Ianthe' for BYRON's *Childe Harold's Pilgrimage*.

Lewis **Carroll**, *The Hunting of the Snark*, 1876

> Girt with a boyish garb for boyish task,
>   Eager she wields her spade: yet loves as well
> Rest on a friendly knee, intent to ask
>   The tale he loves to tell.
>
> Rude spirits of the seething outer strife,
>   Unmeet to read her pure and simple spright,
> Deem, if you list, such hours a waste of life,
>   Empty of all delight!
>
> Chat on, Sweet Maid, and rescue from annoy,
>   Hearts that by wiser talk are unbeguiled.
> Ah, happy he who owns that tenderest joy,
>   The heart-love of a child.
>
> Away fond thought, and vex my soul no more!
>   Work claims my wakeful nights, my busy days, –
> Albeit bright memories of that sunlit shore
>   Yet haunt my dreaming gaze!

The name of the dedicatee here is indicated cryptically, in typical Carrollian fashion, as a double acrostic: the initial letters of each line, as well as the first words of each verse, spell out 'Gertrude Chataway', the little eight-year-old who was Carroll's favourite at the time. (He first met her when on holiday in the Isle of Wight.) A similar acrostic, although not a dedication, spells out the name 'Alice Pleasance Liddell', his first love, in the poem that appears at the end of *Through the Looking-Glass*, beginning 'A boat, beneath a sunny sky'. Compare, too, the dedication below. Later children's writers have also used the dedicatory device. See, for example, the one by WILLIAM MAYNE below for his novel *The Incline*.

Lewis **Carroll**, *Sylvie and Bruno*, 1889

> Is all our Life, then, but a dream
> Seen faintly in the golden gleam,
> Athwart Time's dark resistless stream?
>
> Bowed to the earth with bitter woe,
> Or laughing at some raree-show,
> We flutter idly to and fro.
>
> Man's little Day in haste we spend,
> And, from its merry noontide, send
> No glance to meet the silent end.

A brief but rather fine verse dedication which uses exactly the same devices as that of *The Hunting of the Snark*, above. The initial letters of each line, as well as the first three letters of each stanza, spell out the name of another of Carroll's child friends, Isa Bowman. And given that her name was pronounced as in 'Isabel', Carroll also appears to have consciously echoed the syllables of her name in the rhyme at the end of each line, so that 'Isa' goes with 'dream', 'Bow' with 'woe', and 'Man' with 'spend'. He must have been pleased at the neatness of her name for poetic purposes, and the ease with which the syllables convert to standard words.

Charles E. **Carryl**, *Davy and the Goblins*, 1884

TO GUY

Dear little boy, upon these pages find
The tangled fancies of thy Father's mind,
Born of the hours when thou, a little child,
Throned on his knee, in breathless rapture smiled,
Hearing entranced the marvels that were told
Of Fay and Goblin in the days of old.
Would that the glamour of those cloudless days
Might cheer thee still, what time the toilsome maze
Of riper years hath banished fairy lore –
And blithesome youth had fled to come no more!

Charles E. Carryl was a New York stockbroker and railroad company director who was inspired by his near namesake, LEWIS CARROLL (see above), to write Alice-style fantasies for his children and those of his friends. This was the first.

Rachel **Carson**, *The Edge of the Sea*, 1952
~ To Dorothy and Stanley Freeman, who have gone down with me into the low-tide world and have felt its beauty and its mystery.

A study of the natural life of the seashore, in the same spirit as most of Carson's books.

Angela **Carter**, *The Infernal Desire Machines of Doctor Hoffman*, 1972
~ For the family, wherever they are, reluctantly including Ivan who thought he was Alyosha.

Ashley **Carter**, *Miz Lucretia of Falconhurst*, 1985
~ Affectionately dedicated to Suzanne and Donald Cantrell, who love Miz Lucretia Borgia almost as much as I do ...

The named character is the 'Amazon black beauty' who is an overseer of slaves in this and related stories.

Brian **Carter**, *Jack*, 1986
~ To all the horses that did not find their green pastures.

The novel deals with an Irish boy and a roan mare and their adventures.

Emma Smuller **Carter**, *Lays of the Lake*, 1910

~ To my Sister. You have often asked me to gather into a little book some of the verses that have come to me from time to time, many of them written at your suggestion. I have tried to do it, but they seem for the most part so simple, springing up as they have done along the pathway of everyday life, – just the common wayside flowers, – possibly few besides ourselves may care to look among the leaves for our vagrant blossoms. However, here they are for you, dear, the daisies, the sweet briar, the heal-all and the heartsease, the ragweed and the jewel weed, plucked along the way, such a bunch as you and I have often carried home together. Yours, E.

The author wrote this when at Lincoln University, Pennsylvania.

Agnes and Egerton **Castle**, *Love Gilds the Scene*, 1911

~ TO THE BARON KANZLER. If, dear friend, you will examine its illustrated title page, you will perhaps understand why we ventured to inscribe this little book to you. It is not to the learned *Archæologist*, not to the curator of so many of the priceless historic treasures of the *Vatican*, not to the *Musician* world-renowned for his deep lore in ancient and sacred music, that we would presume to dedicate a volume of mere stories. No, it is to the lover of the eighteenth century, that age so alluring to the cultured mind, the spirit of which you have delightfully assimilated, till it seems to us sometimes as if it actually lived in you – The '*Goldoni*' period your countrymen fondly call it; the '*Powder and Patch*' days, as we in England often say. Now, in this design you will discern many of the attributes popularly associated with the special romance of those time, *at least in England*. [...]

And we may discern many of the Italian dedicatee's attributes by the description of him. The husband-and-wife writers produced several popular novels in the early years of the twentieth century, several of which were dramatised. The illustration on the title page that they refer to shows, among other things, a wayside inn, a handsome horseman, a signpost (London to Bath road), and various relevant objects such as a punch bowl, a walking sword, and a pair of traveller's pistols.

Willa **Cather**, *O Pioneers!*, 1913

~ To the memory of Sarah Orne Jewett, in whose beautiful and delicate work there is the perfection that endures.

See below.

Willa **Cather**, *My Ántonia*, 1918

~ To Carrie and Irene Miner. In memory of affections old and true.

Willa Cather was a highly popular American novelist in the first half of the twentieth century, who wrote many studies of women in the Midwest. She was influenced by Sarah Orne Jewett (see above), a writer of 'local colour' studies and sketches of New England life.

Peter Cave, *Foxbat*, 1978

~ For Jack Kerouac, who lit the fire, Mike Moorcock, who added the first fuel, and Margaret, who blew the embers into flame again.

The initial inspirer here was the 'Beat Generation' writer who achieved international fame with his part-autobiographical *On the Road*, 1957.

William Caxton, *The Game and Playe of the Chesse*, 1475

~ To the right noble, right excellent, and vertuous prince George duc of Clarence, Erle of Warwyk and of Salisburye, great chamberlayn of England and leutenant of Irelond, oldest broder of kynge Edward by the grace of god kynge of England and of Fraunce. [...]

The dedicatee was George, Duke of Clarence, son of Richard, Duke of York, who only four years after this would be charged with treason and seeking the throne, and executed at the Tower of London, aged twenty-nine. Caxton had translated the French version (itself translated by Jean de Vignay from the Latin) of the *Ludus Scaccorum* by JACQUES DE CESSOLES, which see below.

William Caxton, *Godeffrey of Bologne, or the Siege and Conqueste of Jerusalem*, 1481

~ [...] Thenne to hym, my moost drad naturel and soverayn lord, I adresse this symple and rude booke, besechyng his moost bounteous and haboundant grace to receyve it of me, his indigne and humble subgette, William Caxton. And to pardonne me so presumynge; besechyng almyghty God that this sayd book may encourage, moeve, and enflamme the hertes of soome noble men, that by the same the mescreauntes maye be resisted and putte to rebuke, Cristen fayth encreaced and enhaunced, and the holy lande, with the blessyd cyte of Iherusalem, recoverd, and may come agayn in to cristen mens hondes.

This work, translated by Caxton from the French, was dedicated to Edward IV. The 'mescreauntes' were the heathen Turks.

William Caxton, *The History of Blanchardin and Eglantine*, 1489

~ [To] the right noble puyssaunt and excellent pryncesse my redoubted lady my lady Margarete duchesse of Somercete, moder unto our naturel and soverayn lord and most crysten Kynge henry ye seuenth.

That is, to Margaret Beaufort, Duchess of Somerset, known as 'Lady Margaret' and the mother of Henry VII. She was a noted patron, and gave her name to Lady Margaret Hall, Oxford.

William Caxton, *Eneydos*, 1490

~ [To] the hye born, my tocomynge naturell & soverayn lord, Arthur, by the grace of God, Prynce of Walys, Duc of Cornewayll, & Erle of Chester [etc].

Caxton had translated a French romance (*Liure des Eneydes*, 1483) that was itself based on the Latin of Virgil's *Aeneid* and Boccaccio's *De casibus virorum illustrium* ('The Fall of Princes'). He dedicated his translation to the young Prince Arthur, then only four years old (hence 'tocomynge', or future) and due to succeed his father Henry VII to the throne. However, he died in 1502, aged just sixteen, having married Catherine of Aragon the previous year, and never having reigned.

David **Cecil**, *The Cecils of Hatfield House*, 1973
~ This book by a Cecil of Hatfield is dedicated to the illustrious memory of Queen Elizabeth I in homage and gratitude.

William Cecil, Lord Burghley, and his son Robert, 1st Earl of Salisbury, were chief ministers to Elizabeth I, and were respectively founders of the senior branch of the family, the earls and marquises of Exeter, and the junior branch, the earls and marquises of Salisbury. The author of this book was Lord David Cecil, the younger son of the 4th Marquess of Salisbury, who died in 1986.

Bennett **Cerf**, *Out on a Limerick*, 1961
> There is a young lady from Fife
> Whom I never have seen in my life.
>> So the devil with her;
>> Instead I prefer
> To dedicate this to my wife.

The American writer and humorist's book, with the limerick as its subject, has a limerick as its dedication.

Jacques de **Cessoles**, *Ludus scaccorum*, 1360
~ To the right noble and excellent prince John of France, Duke of Normandy and Auvergne, son of Philip by the grace of God King of France, Friar John of Vignay, your humble monk, along with the rest of your servants, wishes you peace, holy joy, and victory over your foes. Beloved and redoubtable Lord, in as much as I have heard and am convinced that you gladly see and hear things profitable and honourable and which may tend to the establishment of good manners, I have done into French from the Latin a little book which came recently into my hand, where divers testimonies and sayings of doctors and philosophers and poets and ancient sages are recounted and applied to the morality of nobles and commons in accordance with the game of chess, which book, most puissant and most redoubtable Lord, I have done in the name and under the shadow of yourself, for the which thing, beloved Sir, I beseech and beg you, out of the goodness of your heart, that you deign to receive this book in good part, as from a greater master than myself, for my fond endeavour to do what I can to the best of my ability ought to be imputed to me for the deed. [...]

Translated from the French. Jean de Vignay was no mere 'humble monk', as he modestly says, but a gifted theologian, moralist and translator. He dedicates his translation here to King John (Jean II le Bon) of France, the son and successor of Philip VI, who would later be conquered by the Black Prince and who died in London in 1364. The title of the Latin work translates as 'The Game of Chess': compare the dedication to CHAUCER's *Game and Playe of the Chesse* above, directly derived from this same work via Cesseroles' version.

Paul Du **Chaillu,** *Ivar the Viking,* 1893

~ To George W. Childs. My dear Childs: Years of our unbroken friendship, going back more than a quarter of a century, have passed away, and the recollection of all your kindness during that time comes vividly before my mind. Many a time your home in Philadelphia, at the sea-side, or at Wootton has been my home, and many of the happy days of my life have been spent with you and your kind wife. Three years ago, I lay on a sick-bed at your house, and all that tender nursing, the skill of the physician, and loving hands could do that winter was done for me, and for all that I am indebted to you and to Mrs. Childs. Now a twenty miles' walk day after day does not fatigue. *Ivar the Viking* was partly written after my recovery, under the shade of Wootton and in the midst of the perfume of its flowers. To you, my dear old friend, I dedicate the book as a token of the esteem and high regard I have for your noble character, and in grateful remembrance of all you have done for me. Paul Du Chaillu.

Du Chaillu was a French-born American writer and explorer of Africa (after one visit he brought back with him the first gorillas ever seen in America). Childs was an American publisher.

Wilbur J. **Chamberlin,** *Ordered to China,* 1904

~ To the vast army of men unnamed who serve their country with pen and brain no less truly and with no smaller share of heroism than they who bear the country's colors into battle, and especially to the memory of THREE BROTHERS who early spent themselves, and who, in great crises, laid down their lives in loyalty to duty, this volume is dedicated in token of deepest appreciation.

In other words, to war correspondents, of whom Chamberlin was one. The book was published posthumously, two years after Chamberlin's death on his way back from China. The descriptive subtitle of the book runs: 'Letters of Wilbur J. Chamberlin, written from China while under commission from the New York *Sun* during the Boxer uprising of 1900 and the international complications which followed'.

Edgar **Chambers,** *Roadtown,* 1910

~ This book is dedicated to J. Pierpont Morgan, a straight player of a crooked game, who, it is said, played his usual role in the Wall Street Manipulations of the Central Railroad of George Securities, which adroitly and legally absorbed the small savings and happiness of many unsophisticated investors – an action which, in my case at least, proved to be a blessing in disguise, for it made me suffer first and then made me think. Hence the gratitude and consequent dedication to Mr. Morgan for starting the train of Roadtown, a plan for side-stepping the crooked game as now played so that henceforth whosoever will may become a straight player of a straight game.

John Pierpont Morgan was the American banker and financier who, among other things, reorganised many important railroads, as well as founding his own house of J.P. Morgan & Co. (1895) and the internationally known United States Steel Corporation (1901).

A. Bertram **Chandler**, *The Rim of Space*, 1958
~ For Susan, whose blend of saintliness and cynicism is peculiar to the Rim.

A science fiction tale in which the 'Rimrunners' patrol the outer edge of the galaxy.

Joy **Chant**, *When Voiha Wakes*, 1983
~ For Jack, who heard it through and saw me through.

George **Chapman**, *Homer's Iliad, translated from the Greek*, 1598–1611
~ To Anne, Queen of England, &ca., Sacred Fountaine of Princes, Sole Empresse of Beawtie and Vertve. To the Right Gracious and Worthy, the duke of Lennox. To the most Grave and honored temperer of Law and Equity, the Lord Chancelor, &ca. To the most Worthie Earle, Lord Treasurer & Treasurer of Our Country, the Earle of Salisbury, &ca. To the most honored Restorer of Ancient Nobility, both in bloud & vertue, the Earle of Suffolke, &ca. To the most Noble and learned earle, the Earle of Northampton, &ca. To the most Noble, my singular good Lord, the Earle of Arundell. To the learned and most noble Patron of learning, the Earle of Pembroke, &ca. To the Right Gracious Illustrator of Vertue, and worthy of the favour Royall, the Earle of Montgomerie. To the most learned and noble Conductor of the Warres, Arte, and the Muses, the Lord Lisle, &ca. To the Great and Vertuous, the Countesse of Montgomerie. To the Happy Starre Discovered in our Sydneian Asterisme, comfort of learning, Sphere of all the vertues, the Lady Wrothe. To the Right Noble Patronesse and Grace of Vertue, the Countesse of Bedford. To the Right Valorous and Vertuous Lord, the Earle of South-Hampton, &ca. To my exceeding good Lord, the Earle of Sussex, with duty alwaies remembered to his honour'd Countesse. To the right Noble and Heroicall, my singular good Lord, the Lord of Walden, &ca. To the most truely noble and vertue-gracing Knight, Sir Thomas Howard. Ever most humbly and faithfully devoted to you, and all the rare Patrons of divine Homer. Geo. Chapman.

An impressive multiple dedication to a whole pleiad of lords and ladies at the court of King James I of England (James VI of Scotland), but even so one that is shorter than the original, which for example included a tribute to 'our English Athenia, chaste arbitress of vertue and learning, the Lady Arabella', otherwise Lady Arabella Stuart, first cousin of James VI and next in succession to him, after Queen Elizabeth, to both the Scottish and English thrones. But she was involved in intrigues aimed at eliminating James VI as Elizabeth's successor, and in 1615 died, insane, a prisoner in the Tower of London. Her name was thus understandably withdrawn from the dedication. The work itself, which took several years to write, was subsequently made famous by Keats's poem devoted to it, 'On First Looking into Chapman's Homer'.

George **Chapman**, *The Widdowes Teares*, 1612

~ To the right Vertuous and truly noble Gentleman, Mr. Jo. Reed of Mitton, in the Countie of Glocester, Esquire. Sir, if any worke of this nature be worth the presenting to Friends Worthie, and Noble; I presume this will not want much of that value. Other Countrie men have thought the like worthie of Dukes and Princes acceptations; *Injusti Sdegnij; Il Pentamento Amorose; Calisthe, Pastor Fido, &c.* (all being but plaies) were all dedicate to Princes of Italie. And, therefore, only discourse to shew my love to your right vertuous and noble disposition, this poor Comedie (of many desired to see printed) I thought not utterly unworthie that affectionate designe in me. Well knowing that your free judgement weighs nothing by the Name, or Forme; or any vaine estimation of the vulgar; but will accept acceptable matter, as well in Plaies; as in many lesse materialls, masking in more serious Titles. And so, till some worke more worthie I can select, and perfect, out of my other Studies, that may better expresse me; and more fit the gravitie of your ripe inclination, I rest, Yours at all parts most truly affected, Geo. Chapman.

A confident dedication by Chapman for his witty comedy.

George **Chapman**, *The Revenge of Bussy D'Ambois*, 1613

~ To the right Vertuous and truely noble Knight, Sr Thomas Howard. Sir, Since Workes of this kinde have beene lately esteemed worthy of the patronage of some of our worthiest nobles I have made no doubt to preferre this of mine to your undoubted vertue, and exceeding true noblesse: as contayning matter no lesse deserving your reading, and excitation to Heroycall life, then any such late Dedication. Nor have the great Princes of Italie and other Countries conceived it any least diminution to their greatnesse, to have their names wing'd with these tragicke plumes, and disperst by way of Patronage, through the most noble notices of Europe.

Another tribute to the same patron is included in the dedication to CHAPMAN's *Homer's Iliad*. See above.

Guy **Chapman**, *A Passionate Prodigality*, 1933

~ To the memory of certain soldiers, who have now become a small quantity of Christian dust, this faint reanimation, and for R.A. Smith.

The book is a description of life in the trenches in the First World War.

Charlotte **Charke**, *Narrative of the Life of Mrs. Charlotte Charke, Written by Herself*, 1775

~ The Author to Herself. Madam, Tho' flattery is universally known to be the spring from which Dedications frequently flow, I hope I shall escape that odium so justly thrown on poetical petitioners, notwithstanding my attempt to illustrate those wonderful qualifications by which you have so eminently distinguish'd yourself, and gives you a just claim to the title of a nonpareil of the age. [...] Your two friends, Prudence and Reflection, I am inform'd, have lately ventur'd to pay you a visit; for which I heartily congratulate you, as nothing can possibly be more joyous to the heart than the return of absent friends, after a long and painful peregrination. Permit me, madam, to subscribe myself for the future what I ought to have been some years ago, your real friend and humble servant, Charlotte Charke.

Mrs Charke was the youngest daughter of the famous, if eccentric, playwright, Colley Cibber. She had married young, her husband perhaps being a violinist, and pursued a variety of occupations, from selling sausages to performing as a strolling player, preferring male roles in this (and also frequently cross-dressing as a man in everyday life). This work, dedicated to herself, describes her family background and colourful life. It was published posthumously, however, as she had died in about 1760, probably aged forty-seven.

Leslie **Charteris**, *The Saint Plays With Fire*, 1938

~ To Bartlett Cormack. My dear Bart: Once upon a time, when a chance letter of yours dragged me for my dizzy whirl on to the madman's merry-go-round called Hollywood, I decided to write a book called *The Saint in Hollywood*, and I knew then that it must be dedicated to you. But the years have ambled on, and somehow or other that story still hasn't been started, and I'm ashamed to keep you waiting any longer for what I meant to give you so long ago. So will you take this instead, with the same affection and gratitude as I should have dedicated that unwritten adventure? Always, Leslie Charteris.

One of the many stories featuring the gentleman adventurer Simon Templar, known as 'The Saint', who dealt with crime by criminal means, together with a reference to a 'Saint' adventure that never materialised.

Jerome **Charyn**, *Paradise Man*, 1987

~ For Elia Kazan, Norman Mailer, and Arthur Penn, who taught me about the wicked witch of drama during the writing of this book.

A tribute to three key figures in contemporary American arts, with an influential novelist and journalist in between two leading film directors.

Geoffrey **Chaucer**, *A Treatise on the Astrolabe*, 1391

~ Litel Lowis my sone, I have perceived wel by certeyne evidences thyn abilite to lerne sciencez touchinge noumbres and proporciouns; and as wel considered I thy bisy preyere in special to lerne the Tretis of the Astrolabie. Than, for as mechel as a philosofre seith, 'he wrappeth him in his frend, that condescendeth to the rightful preyers of his frend', ther-for have I geven thee a suffisaunt Astrolabie as for oure orizonte, compowned after the latitude of Oxenford; upon which, by mediacion of this litel tretis. I purpose to teche thee a certein nombre of conclusions appertening to the same instrument.

To Chaucer's younger son, Lewis, then probably aged ten. The work is a complex one, describing the use of the astrolabe, an early astronomical (and astrological) instrument that measured the altitude of stars and planets. A few words and phrases may need explaining in modern English: *bisy preyere* = 'earnest request'; *for as mechel as* = 'forasmuch as'; *compowned* = 'constructed'; *mediacion* = 'means'. Although the work was calculated for readings taken in Oxford, Chaucer and his family lived most of his life in Kent, not there.

Ednah D. **Cheney**, ed., *Life, Letters and Journals of Louisa M. Alcott*, 1889
~ To Mrs. Anna B. Pratt: The sole surviving sister of Louisa M. Alcott, and her never failing help, comforter, and friend from birth to death, this memoir is respectfully and tenderly dedicated by Ednah D. Cheney.

A tribute published the year following the death of the famous author of *Little Women*. See her own dedication to *Eight Cousins*, 1875, above.

G.K. **Chesterton**, *What's Wrong with the World*, 1910
~ To C.F.G. Masterman, M.D. My dear Charles: – I originally called this book 'WHAT IS WRONG', and it would have satisfied your sardonic temper to note the number of social misunderstandings that arose from the use of the title. Many a mild lady visitor opened her eyes when I remarked casually, 'I have been doing What is Wrong all the morning'. And one minister of religion moved quite sharply in his chair when I told him (as he understood it) that I had to run upstairs to do what was wrong, but would be down again in a minute. Exactly of what occult vice they silently accused me I cannot conjecture, but I know of what I accuse myself; and that is, of having written a very shapeless and inadequate book, and one quite unworthy to be dedicated to you. As far as literature goes, this book is wrong, and no mistake. [...] Why then should I trouble you with a book which, even if it achieves its object (which is monstrously unlikely) can be only a thundering gallop of theory? [...] I offer it to you because there exists not only comradeship, but a very different thing, called friendship; an agreement under all the arguments and a thread which, please God, will never break. Yours always, G.K. Chesterton.

Masterman was a Liberal politician, author and journalist who was acutely aware of, and afraid of, social change. Five years earlier he had published his own book on the subject, *Perils of Change*.

Maurice **Chevalier**, *I Remember It Well*, 1971
~ To all my American friends. Having been liked for such a long time in America is the pride of my life.

This is the dedication to the British edition of the autobiography of the famous French entertainer, who died the following year, aged eighty-four. The French original, published in 1969, was entitled *Môme à cheveux blancs*, 'Kid with White Hair'.

Agatha **Christie**, *The Mysterious Affair at Styles*, 1920
~ To my mother.

The famous crime novelist's first novel, published when she was thirty.

Agatha **Christie**, *The Secret Adversary*, 1922
~ To ALL THOSE WHO LEAD MONOTONOUS LIVES in the hope that they may experience at second hand the delights and dangers of adventure.

Agatha Christie's second novel.

Agatha **Christie**, *The Mysterious Mr Quin*, 1930
~ To Harlequin the invisible.

A collection of twelve stories, in the first of which a character appears 'dressed in every colour of the rainbow', and introduces himself with the words, 'By the way, my name is Quin – Harley Quin'. In 1972 a pop singer, Harley Quinne, entered the British charts with a song called 'New Orleans' – but he is hardly the subject of this dedication.

Agatha **Christie**, *Giants' Bread*, 1930
~ To the memory of my best and truest friend, my mother.

Compare the first Christie dedication above. This is not a crime novel, but a romantic story, originally published under the author's pseudonym of 'Mary Westmacott'.

Agatha **Christie**, *Peril at End House*, 1932
~ To Eden Phillpotts, to whom I shall always be grateful for his friendship and the encouragement he gave me many years ago.

Eden Phillpotts, aged seventy at the time of this dedication, was a prolific author of historical novels and of stories set in his native Devonshire.

Agatha **Christie**, *Murder in Mesopotamia*, 1936
~ To my many archaeological friends in Iraq and Syria.

A crime novel with a plot based on an archaeological dig in Iraq, with the archaeologist's wife as the murder victim. Agatha Christie had been on just such an expedition with her husband earlier that year.

Agatha **Christie**, *Dumb Witness*, 1937
~ To Dear Peter, most faithful of friends and dearest of companions. A dog in a thousand.

To Agatha Christie's own dog, a wire-haired terrier. The 'dumb witness' of the story was a dog of the same breed named Bob.

Agatha **Christie**, *Death on the Nile*, 1937
~ To Sybil Burnett, who also loves wandering about the world.

Agatha **Christie**, *Hercule Poirot's Christmas*, 1938
~ My dear James, You have always been one of the most faithful and kindly of my readers, and I was therefore seriously perturbed when I received from you a

word of criticism. You complained that my murders were getting too refined – anaemic, in fact. You yearned for a 'good violent murder with lots of blood'. A murder where there was no doubt about its being murder! So this is your special story – written for you. I hope it may please. Your affectionate sister-in-law, Agatha.

Dedicated to James Mallowan, the younger brother of Agatha Christie's husband, Sir Max Mallowan.

Agatha **Christie**, *Towards Zero*, 1944

~ To Robert Graves. Dear Robert, Since you are kind enough to say you like my stories, I venture to dedicate this book to you. All I ask is that you should sternly restrain your critical faculties (doubtless sharpened by your recent excesses in that line!) when reading it. This is a story for your pleasure and *not* a candidate for Mr Graves's literary pillory! Your friend, Agatha Christie.

To the formidable and prolific poet, novelist, critic and classical scholar and translator, who died in 1985.

Agatha **Christie**, *Death Comes as the End*, 1944

~ To Professor S.R.K. Glanville. Dear Stephen, It was you who originally suggested to me the idea of a detective story set in Ancient Egypt, and but for your active help and encouragement this book would never have been written. I want to say here how much I have enjoyed all the interesting literature you have lent me and to thank you once more for the patience with which you have answered my questions and for the time and trouble you have expended. The pleasure and interest which the writing of this book has brought to me you already know. Your affectionate and grateful friend, Agatha Christie.

The plot of the story centres on a murder in Egypt over 4,000 years ago. Stephen Glanville, who died in 1956, was an Egyptologist friend of Agatha Christie and her husband. Not only had he encouraged her to write the book, but had made detailed comments on it from a professional angle, chapter by chapter, as it was written.

Agatha **Christie**, *Come, Tell Me How You Live*, 1946

~ To my husband, Max Mallowan; to the Colonel, Bumps, Mac and Guilford, this meandering chronicle is affectionately dedicated.

Not a crime novel but a memoir of an archaeological expedition in Syria in the 1930s, with the dedication made to members of the expedition. ('Mac', for example, was an architect, Robin Macartney.) Agatha Christie published this book under the name of Agatha Christie Mallowan.

Agatha **Christie**, *The Hollow*, 1946

~ For Larry and Danae, with apologies for using their swimming pool as the scene of a murder.

The reference is to the house in Haslemere, Surrey, that was the home of the actor Francis L. Sullivan (Larry), and his wife Danae.

Agatha **Christie**, *They Do It With Mirrors*, 1952
~ To Peter Saunders, in gratitude for his kindness to authors.

Peter Saunders was Agatha Christie's theatre manager, and producer of her famous play *The Mousetrap*, first staged in 1952 and still running even now.

Agatha **Christie**, *The Mirror Crack'd from Side to Side*, 1962
~ To Margaret Rutherford, in admiration.

The well-known actress Margaret Rutherford had achieved popularity in her role as Miss Marple, the elderly spinster detective in the films based on Agatha Christie's novels, beginning with *Murder, She Said* (1961), the screen version of *4.50 from Paddington* (1952).

Agatha **Christie**, *By the Pricking of my Thumbs*, 1968
~ This book is dedicated to the many readers in this and other countries who write to me asking: 'What has happened to Tommy and Tuppence? What are they doing now?' My best wishes to you all, and I hope you will enjoy meeting Tommy and Tuppence again, years older, but with spirit unquenched! Agatha Christie.

'Tommy and Tuppence' are a husband-and-wife detective team in several Agatha Christie novels, their full names being Lieutenant Thomas Beresford and Prudence Beresford, née Cowley.

Agatha **Christie**, *Hallowe'en Party*, 1969
~ To P.G. Wodehouse, whose books and stories have brightened my life for many years. Also, to show my pleasure in his having been kind enough to tell me that he enjoys *my* books.

A tribute to the famous humorist. It is rather odd, however, that Agatha Christie should choose to boast of being read and praised by a fellow writer at this stage, when she was nearly eighty and more than popularly established.

Agatha **Christie**, *Postern of Fate*, 1973
~ To Hannibal and his master.

Dedicated to the dog detective in the book, who was himself based on Agatha Christie's black Manchester terrier Bingo, whose photo appeared on the novel's back cover.

Richard **Church**, *The Porch*, 1937
~ To the administrative and the executive of our Civil Service, who together comprise a treasury of good fellows.

The novel tells of the first year of a junior clerk in the Customs and Excise Department of the Civil Service.

Richard **Church**, *The Room Within*, 1940

~ One of the figures in the background of this story is drawn from life, with the knowledge and affection of a friendship that lasted twenty years, until 4th January 1940, when Humbert Wolfe died, a month before the book was finished. I can therefore offer it only as a memorial to him.

The third novel of a trilogy, of which *The Porch* (above) was the first and *The Stronghold* (1939) the second. Humbert Wolfe was an Italian-born British poet and critic.

Winston **Churchill**, *Savrola*, 1900

~ This book is inscribed to the officers of the IVth (Queen's Own) Hussars, in whose company the author lived for four happy years.

The British prime minister's only novel. Churchill had served in the Hussars from 1895 to 1899.

Winston **Churchill**, *My Early Life*, 1930

~ To a new generation.

A simple but meaningful dedication, typical of Churchill and the early thirties, when the world was still struggling to rebuild itself after the devastation of the First World War.

Thomas **Churchyard**, *A Pleasant Conceite*, 1593–4

~ To the Queenes most excellent Majestie. May it please your Majestie, so long as breath is in my breast, life in the hart, and spirit in the heade, I cannot hold the hand from penning of some acceptable device to your Majestie, not to compare (in mine own over weening) with the rare Poets of our florishing age, but rather counterfeyting to sette foorth the workes of an extraordinarie Painter, that hath drawne in a pleasant conceite, divers flowers, fruites, and famous Townes: which pleasant conceite I have presumed (this Newe-yeeres day) to present to your Majestie, in signe and token that your gracious goodnesse towardes me oftentimes (and cheefely now for my pencyon) shal never goe out of my remembrance, with all dutifull services, belonging to a loyall subject. So under your princely favour & protection, praying for your prosperous preservation and Royall estate, I proceede to my purposed matter. Your Majesties humble Servaunt, Thomas Churchyard.

'Conceit' was a favourite word and concept with sixteenth-century writers. They used it to denote a literary work or device that required some kind of intellectual or fanciful interpretation on the part of the reader or audience. Many such 'conceits', like this one, dedicated to Queen Elizabeth, were simply witty entertainments. Churchyard had been granted a pension by the Queen, and at the time of writing was about seventy-three.

Arthur C. **Clarke**, *Report on Planet Three and other Speculations*, 1972

~ In accordance with the terms of the Clarke–Asimov Treaty, the second-best science writer dedicates this book to the second-best science fiction writer.

So that the best is the other in each case! Both Isaac Asimov and Arthur C. Clarke have done much to win enormous popularity both for science fiction and popular scientific subjects generally. The two men are virtual contemporaries, born within three years of each other.

Arthur C. **Clarke**, *Rendezvous with Rama*, 1973
~ To Sri Lanka, where I climbed the Stairway of the Gods.

Clarke has lived in Sri Lanka since the 1950s, when it was still known as Ceylon.

Eliot C. **Clarke**, *Astronomy from a Dipper*, 1910
~ Dedicated to my grand-daughter, Alice de Vermandois Ware, a Nova, who first graced the celestial universe with her presence on the day that this monumental astronomical work was accepted by its publishers.

The American work's title page has a picture of a sleeping baby, with the caption: 'NOVA BOSTONIAE. From observation 24 hours after first appearance'.

James Stanier **Clarke** and John M'Arthur, *Life and Services of Horatio Viscount Nelson*, 1840
~ To Sir Thomas Masterman Hardy, Bt. G.C.B., Vice-Admiral of the Blue; and Governor of Greenwich Hospital. Sir, The World will at once understand the propriety of prefacing your name to a LIFE OF NELSON: as it was almost the last word he uttered when passing into a glorious immortality, so will it be the first in the recollection of every Briton, in association with his heroic history. It is therefore, Sir, a source of the highest gratification, to be permitted the honour of dedicating to YOU this authentic memoir of your illustrious Companion: and, praying that you may, during many added years, enjoy the proud reflection of having been the chosen Friend of him whose name is England's pride, whose example her shield and strength, We remain, Sir, Your obliged and faithful servants, The Publishers.

This is the second edition of the historic record, published even so only thirty-five years after the Battle of Trafalgar and death of Nelson. Nelson's flag captain is associated so closely with his fellow officer and friend ('Kiss me, Hardy') that his subsequent career is usually ignored. But this dedication gives a clue to his later life. He died in 1839.

John **Clarmont**, *Did I Do That?*, 1987
~ To no one in particular.

Robert **Cleaver**, *A Godlie Forme of Householde Governement*, 1598
~ To the Right Worshipful Maister Robert Burgaine, of Roxall, One of her Maiesti's Iustices of peace, in the Countie of Warwicke: to the Right Worshipfull Maister Jone Dine, of Ridlington Parke, in the Countie of Rutland: and to the Worshipfull Maister Edmund Temple, of Templehall, in the Countie of Leicester, Esquires, as also to their religious and virtuous wives, R.C. wisheth with heart

and mind grace from God the Father by Iesus Christ, and constancie in the trueth of the Gospell, to the end, and in the end.

A fairly long 'Epistle Dedicatorie' to these same gentry follows. The work is subtitled, in part: 'for the Ordering of Private Families according to the Direction of God's Word'. 'Roxall' is the village of Wroxall, near Warwick.

Roger Cleeve, *Daughters of Jerusalem*, 1985
~ Dedicated to the hope for peace and friendship between Arabs and Jews in Palestine.

A novel centring on the lives of four women, two Arab and two Jewish.

Sir Hugh Clifford, *The Downfall of the Gods*, 1911
~ To Betty, This, the first book that I have written, is inscribed.

Two stanzas by Swinburne ('This is my Lady's praise ...') follow. Hugh Clifford was a noted colonial official, who the year after this was published was appointed Governor of the Gold Coast. The dedicatee was his second wife, Elizabeth Bonham, a widow, formerly the wife of Henry de la Pasture, and a novelist in her own right. A daughter by her earlier marriage was the much better-known novelist 'E.M. Delafield', real name Elizabeth Monica Dashwood, née de la Pasture.

John Clive, *The Last Liberator*, 1980
~ This book is dedicated to The Movie-Makers, who filled my head with Hollywood and gave my imagination an education.

A wartime novel on the exploits of a United States aircraft, a B-24 Liberator.

Colonel Sir Charles Close, *The Map of England*, 1932
~ This little book is dedicated to all those walkers, cyclists, and motorists who take Ordnance Maps with them on their journeys about the country.

Sir Charles Frederick Close, who changed his name to Arden-Close in 1938, was the geographer and mapmaker who became Director-General of the Ordnance Survey in 1911.

Sebastian Coe with David Miller, *Running Free*, 1981
~ For Peter ... or was it Percy?

The famous athlete's autobiography.

Anthea Cohen, *Fallen Angel*, 1984
~ To Emily, small, nervous, and much loved: whom, in the end, the author hopes she helped a little.

Sir Aston Cokayne, *The Tragedy of Ovid*, 1662
~ To my most highly honoured cousin, Charles Cotton, Esquire. [...] I should accuse myself of much ingratitude did I not dedicate it to you, and entreat your

favour that it might visit the world under the secure patronage of your name. I beseech you therefore to afford it so much grace, and to give it leave to lie in your parlour window, since you have been pleased to signalise it with two excellent epigrams.

Aston Cokayne was a poet of some repute in his time, but is now not only unread but hardly even heard of. He did sing the praises of his cousin Charles Cotton, however, as in this dedication, and the latter can perhaps be judged a better and a more durable poet by present standards. His 'Ode to Winter' was a favourite with Wordsworth, and Coleridge thought highly of him. These lines of Cotton's still appear in collections and anthologies, three hundred years on:

> The shadows now so long do grow,
> That brambles like tall cedars show,
> Molehills seem mountains, and the ant
> Appears a monstrous elephant.

Grenville A.J. Cole, *Open-Air Studies*, 1895

~ To Richard Whately Dickinson. This little book was in my mind all the time that we were studying together. So I dedicate it to you and to all those who like seeing things for themselves in the open air.

A simple but affectingly 'unstuffy' dedication, whoever the dedicator and dedicatee were.

Stuart Dodgson Collingwood, *The Life and Letters of Lewis Carroll*, 1898

~ To the child friends of Lewis Carroll and to all who love his writings this book is dedicated.

And all who love acrostic verse dedications should see those by CARROLL himself, above. Collingwood was Carroll's nephew, and with commendable speed and efficiency produced this important biographical record literally within months of his uncle's death.

Wilkie Collins, *The Woman in White*, 1860

~ To Bryan Waller Procter, from one of his younger brethren in literature, who sincerely values his friendship and who gratefully remembers many happy hours spent in his house.

Bryan Waller Procter was better known under his pseudonym of 'Barry Cornwall', as whom he produced a quantity of poems and songs. His daughter, Adelaide Anne Procter, is still remembered as the author of several hymns and of the poem 'The Lost Chord' ('Seated one day at the organ ...'), set to suitably saccharinic music by Sullivan.

Lydia Kingsmill Commander, *The American Idea*, 1907

~ This book – a sincere study of a grave social problem – is dedicated to Theodore Roosevelt, who first aroused the Nation to the danger of 'race suicide', and who has been the only American President to recognize officially the supreme importance of those questions that directly concern the family and the home.

Richard **Condon**, *The Manchurian Candidate*, 1960

~ To Max Youngstein, and not only for reasons of affection and admiration, this book is warmly dedicated.

William **Congreve**, *The Old Bachelor*, 1693

~ To the Right Honourable Charles, Lord Clifford, of Lanesborough, &c. My Lord. It is with a great deal of Pleasure, that I lay hold on this first Occasion, which, the Accidents of my Life have given me of writing to your Lordship: for since at the same time, I write to all the World, it will be a means of publishing (what I would have every Body know) the Respect and Duty which I owe and pay to you. I have so much inclination to be yours, that I need no other Engagement: But the particular Ties, by which I am bound to your Lordship and Family, have put it out of my Power to make you any Compliment; since all Offers of my self, will amount to no more than an honest Acknowledgment, and only shew a willingness in me to be grateful. [...] It is impossible for me to come near your Lordship, in any kind, and not receive some Favour; and while in appearance I am only making an Acknowledgment (with the usual under-hand dealing of the World) I am at the same time, insinuating my Bill of my own Privileges. [...] It is a sort of Poetical Logick, which, at this Time I would make use of, to argue your Lordship into a Protection of this Play. It is the first Offence I have committed in this kind, or indeed in any kind of Poetry, tho' not in the first made publick; and, therefore, I hope will the more easily be pardoned: But had it been Acted, when it was first written, more might have been said in its behalf; Ignorance of the Town and Stage, would then have been excuses in a young Writer. [...] Thus I may live in hopes (some time or other) of making the Town amends; but, you, my Lord, I never can, tho' I am ever Your Lordship's most Obedient, and most Humble Servant, Will. Congreve.

This, Congreve's first play, was dedicated to Charles Boyle, of the elder branch of the family, which held the barony of Clifford of Lanesborough as well as the earldoms of Cork and Burlington. Congreve approaches his potential patron with all due circumspection!

William **Congreve**, *The Double Dealer*, 1694

~ To the Right Honourable Charles Montague, One of the Lords of the Treasury. Sir, I heartily wish this Play were as perfect as I intended it, that it might be more worthy your Acceptance; and that my Dedication of it to you, might be more becoming that Honour and Esteem which I, with every Body, who is so fortunate as to know you, have for you. It had your Countenance when yet unknown; and now it is made publick, it wants your Protection. [...] I must now, Sir, declare to the World, how kind you have been to my Endeavours; for in regard of what was well meant, you have excus'd what was ill perform'd. I beg you would continue the same Method in your Acceptance of this Dedication. I know no other way of making a Return to that Humanity you shew'd, in protecting an Infant, but by enrolling it in your Service, now that it is of Age and come into the World.

Therefore be pleas'd to accept of this as an Acknowledgement of the Favour you have shewn me, and an Earnest of the real Service and Gratitude of, Sir, Your Most Obliged Humble Servant, William Congreve.

Charles Montague, later 1st Earl of Halifax and prime minister, was a noted wit and patron of literature, and himself the co-author, with Matthew Prior, of *The City Mouse and the Country Mouse*, a parody on Dryden's *The Hind and the Panther*.

William **Congreve**, *Love for Love*, 1695

~ To the Right Honourable Charles, Earl of Dorset and Middlesex, Lord Chamberlain of His Majesty's Houshold, and Knight of the Most Noble Order of the Garter, &c. My Lord, A Young Poet, is liable to the same Vanity and Indiscretion with a Young Lover; and the Great Man who smiles upon one, and the Fine Woman who looks kindly on t'other, are both of 'em in Danger of having the Favour publish'd with the first Opportunity. But there may be a different Motive, which will a little distinguish the Offenders. For tho' one shou'd have a Vanity in ruining another's Reputation, yet the other may only have an Ambition to advance his own. And I beg leave, my Lord, that I may plead the latter, both as the Cause and Excuse of this Dedication. [...] I am not ignorant of the Common Form of Poetical Dedications, which are generally made up of Panegyricks, where the Authors endeavour to distinguish their Patrons, by the shining Characters they give them, above other Men. But that, my Lord, is not my Business at this time, nor is Your Lordship *now* to be distinguish'd. I am contented with the Honour I do my self in this Epistle; without the Vanity of attempting to add to, or explain Your Lordship's Character. [...] This Reflection of Prolixity, (a Fault, for which scarce any one Beauty will atone) warns me not to be tedious now, and detain Your Lord[s]hip any longer with the Trifles of, My Lord, Your Lordship's Most Obedient and Most Humble Servant, William Congreve.

A dedication with some pertinent observations on the dedicatory epistles of the day, made here to Charles Sackville, 6th Earl of Dorset and Earl of Middlesex, who as Lord Chamberlain was instrumental in licensing the Lincoln's Inn Fields theatre, which opened its career with this play by Congreve.

William **Congreve**, *The Way of the World*, 1700

~ To the Right Honourable Ralph, Earl of Mountague, &c. My Lord, Whether the World will arraign me of Vanity, or not, that I have presum'd to Dedicate this Comedy to Your Lordship, I am yet in Doubt: Tho' it may be it is some degree of Vanity even to doubt of it. [...] Whatever value may be wanting to this Play while it is yet mine, will be sufficiently made up to it, when it is once become Your Lordship's; and it is my Security, that I cannot have overrated it more by my Dedication, than Your Lordship will dignifie it by Your Patronage. [...] But I could wish, at this time, that this Address were exempted from the common Pretence of all Dedications; and that as I can distinguish Your Lordship even among the most Deserving, so this Offering might become remarkable by some particular Instance of Respect, which should assure Your Lordship, that I am, with all due sense of Your extream Worthiness and Humanity, My Lord, Your Lordship's most Obedient and most Oblig'd Humble Servant, Will. Congreve.

Ralph Montagu, later Duke of Montagu, was a noted patron of the arts, and the recipient of dedications from a number of other famous writers. His London residence, Montagu House, Bloomsbury, was demolished in the nineteenth century to give land for the new British Museum.

Ralph **Connor**, *Gwen: An Idyll of the Canyon*, 1899
~ To all who question the *why* of human pain.

The story, originally appearing in the Canadian magazine *Sky Pilot*, is a moral and 'improving' one of a 'Foothill country' girl hurt in a riding accident, and her subsequent feats of endurance, thanks to her religious faith.

Ralph **Connor**, *The Man from Glengarry*, 1901
~ To the Men of Glengarry, who in patience, in courage, and in the fear of God, are helping to build the empire of the Canadian West, this book is humbly dedicated.

'Ralph Connor' was the pseudonym of Charles William Gordon, a Canadian Presbyterian clergyman and novelist, born in Glengarry, Ontario, and after missionary work among miners and lumberjacks in the Canadian Northwest, a pastor in Winnipeg. This is just one of his novels about life in the Canadian Northwest: one sequel was *The Girl from Glengarry* (1933). Gordon meant to adopt the pen name 'Cannor', from the abbreviated title of his missionary organisation, 'Brit. Can. Nor. West Mission', but his editor changed this to 'Connor' and added 'Ralph'.

William **Connor**, *Cassandra's Cats*, 1958
~ Forty years back and afar and very asunder, I learnt Latin and I had to decline a lot of nouns including the noun *Felis*. *Felis* is the Latin for a cat. I will now decline (which doesn't mean refuse) the plural of the noun *Felis*. Here we go: '*Feles; Feles; Feles; Felium; Felibus; Felibus*.' Know what that means? I'll tell you. 'Cats; O Cats; Cats; Of Cats; To, or for Cats; With, by or from Cats'. I dedicate this book to them.

William Connor was not only a cat-lover, but, as 'Cassandra', an influential columnist (from 1935) in the *Daily Mirror*.

Joseph **Conrad**, *Lord Jim*, 1900
~ To Mr and Mrs G.F.W. Hope, with grateful affection after many years of friendship.

Joseph **Conrad**, *The Mirror of the Sea*, 1906
~ To Mrs Katherine Sanderson, whose warm welcome and gracious hospitality,

extended to the friend of her son, cheered the first dark days of my parting with the sea, these pages are affectionately inscribed.

Joseph **Conrad**, *The Secret Agent*, 1907
~ To H.G. Wells, the chronicler of Mr Lewisham's love, the biographer of Kipps, the historian of the ages to come, this simple tale of the XIX century is affectionately dedicated.

Conrad dedicated a number of his books to fellow authors. Here he expresses his admiration of H.G. Wells by referring to three of that writer's books: *Love and Mr Lewisham* (1900), *Kipps* (1905), and *A Modern Utopia* (1905), in the last of which he predicts the possible future of the human race.

Joseph **Conrad**, *Under Western Eyes*, 1911
~ To Agnes Tobin, who brought to our door her genius for friendship from the uttermost shore of the west.

Joseph **Conrad**, *The Rescue*, 1920
~ To Frederic Courland Penfield, last Ambassador of the United States of America to the last Austrian Empire, this old-time tale is gratefully inscribed in memory of the rescue of certain distressed travellers effected by him in the world's great storm of the year 1914.

E. **Thornton Cook**, *Sir Walter's Dogs*, 1931
~ Dedicated to all dogs, and also to those humans who have 'given their hearts to a dog to tear'.

A book on the dogs owned by Sir Walter Scott. The quoted words are from Kipling's *The Power of the Dog* (1900).

Jean **Cooke**, *Song Without Music*, 1935
~ To Madge, dearest of eldest sisters, who has nobly given of her interests to the progress of Charlotte from her creation to her final form, I now dedicate this book, with love and very high regard.

Charlotte Fenwick is the young girl who is the book's central character, aged fourteen at its outset, and a married woman at the end. The author's first novel was *Now Rests That Unquiet Heart*, a historical romance.

John Byrne **Cooke**, *The Snowblind Moon*, 1984
~ For my father, who helped to instill in me a love of books, which was easy, and of history, which took somewhat longer.

The book here is a 'novel of the West'.

Catherine **Cookson**, *Maggie Rowan*, 1954

~ To Peter and Michael Lavelle, my two cousins, without whose technical help and guidance this book would certainly not have been written; and to Peter for leading me to the coal face and answering my endless questions; to Michael for supplying me with most valuable data; and to Jimmy Tiplady whose descriptive reminiscences lent colour to my thinking: and to those miners whom I saw working in the bowels of the earth and who evoked so much of my admiration that my fear became lost under it.

Catherine **Cookson**, *The Cinder Path*, 1978

~ To the one and only to whom I owe so much.

Susan **Coolidge**, *What Katy Did*, 1872

TO FIVE

Six of us once, my darlings, played together
    Beneath green boughs, which faded long ago,
Made merry in the golden summer weather,
    Pelted each other with new-fallen snow. [...]

So, darlings, take this childish story,
    In which some gleams of the old sunshine play,
And, as with careless hands you turn the pages,
    Look back and smile, as here I smile to-day.

The first and last of an eight-stanza dedication to this children's classic by its American author. The six children referred to were the author herself (real name, Sarah Chauncy Woolsey), represented by Katy Carr in the book, together with the 'five': her younger sisters Jane, Elizabeth and Theodora (Katy's sisters Clover, Elsie and Joanna in the novel), her brother William (Phil), and an orphaned cousin Theodorus (Dorry). Compare the next dedication below.

Susan **Coolidge**, *A Round Dozen*, 1904

TO VVVVV

Five little buds grouped round the parent stem,
Growing in sweet airs, beneath gracious skies,
Watched tenderly from sunrise to sunrise,
Lest blight, or chill, or evil menace them. [...]

The first four lines of twelve. The five ('vvvvv') referred to are the author's childhood siblings: see above for their identities.

James Fenimore **Cooper**, *The Pilot*, 1823

~ To William Branford Shubrick, Esq., U.S. Navy. My dear Shubrick: Each year brings some new and melancholy chasm in what is now the brief list of my naval friends and former associates. War, disease, and the casualties of a hazardous profession, have made fearful inroads in the limited number; while the places of the dead are supplied by names that to me are those of strangers. With the consequences of these sad changes before me, I cherish the recollection of those with whom I once lived in close familiarity, with peculiar interest, and feel a triumph in their growing reputations, that is but little short of of their own honest pride. But neither time nor separation has shaken our intimacy; and I know that in dedicating to you this volume, I tell you nothing new, when I add, that it is a tribute paid to an enduring friendship, by your old Messmate, The Author.

Shubrick, an American naval officer, went on to command the Pacific squadron in the Mexican War of 1847–8. James Fenimore Cooper had served at sea with him before this, first as a foremast hand, then as a midshipman. He resigned in 1811, however, when still only twenty-one, to live the life of a country gentleman. His first novel, prompted by his wife, then appeared in 1820, when he was thirty, and was followed by the many more with which he made his name.

Robert **Coover**, *The Public Burning*, 1977
~ For Justice William I. Douglas, who exchanged a greeting with me while out walking on the old canal towpath one day not long after these events …

A fictional account involving the (real) American spies, Julius and Ethel Rosenberg, whom it is planned to burn publicly in New York's Times Square.

Marie **Corelli**, *Ziska*, 1897
~ To The Present Living Re-Incarnation of Araxes.

Whoever he is here, in classical mythology Araxes was a river name, that of the present Turkish river Aras.

Victoria **Coren**, *Love 16*, 1989
~ This book is dedicated to SPGS Class of 1990 (with lots of affection).

An account of schoolgirl love by 'one who knows', the author being the sixteen-year-old daughter of Alan Coren, former editor of *Punch*. Victoria wrote the book while at St Paul's Girls School ('SPGS'), London, with 1990 the year that she and her classmates take their 'A' levels and enter the big wide world. The book itself is based on her articles in the *Daily Telegraph*.

Edwin **Corley**, *Air Force One*, 1978
~ This story is totally fictional. But the achievements made by the real people, who inspired it, are very real. Dedicated, loyal, highly qualified, they are a credit to the Air Force and to this nation. Therefore, I dedicate *Air Force One* to: The men and women of the 19th Military Airlift Wing at Andrews AFB, Maryland.

Edwin **Corley**, *The Genesis Rock*, 1980
~ This one is for all the lovely Lisas in my life!

Pierre **Corneille**, *Polyeuctus*, 1642

~ TO THE QUEEN REGENT. MADAME, Whatever awareness I may have of my weakness, whatever deep respect YOUR MAJESTY may impress on the souls of those who approach you, I confess that I throw myself at your feet without timidity and without diffidence, and that I hold myself certain of pleasing you because I am certain of talking to you about what you best love. It is only a play that I present to you, but one that will converse with you of God: the dignity of the theatre is so great, that the impotence of the craftsmen cannot demean it, and your royal soul takes too much pleasure in this kind of converse to be offended by the faults of a work in which you will encounter the delights of your heart. It is by that, MADAME, that I hope to obtain YOUR MAJESTY's pardon for the long time that I have taken to pay you this sort of homage. Every time that I have set moral or political virtues on our stage, I have always regarded the scenes as unworthy to appear before you, and when I have considered with what care I might select them from history, and with what ornaments I might adorn them, you would only see greater examples in yourself. To show things proportionately, it was necessary to go to the highest of its kind, and not to undertake to offer anything of this nature to a very Christian queen, who is even more so by her deeds than by her title, unless I could offer her a portrait of Christian virtues in which the love and glory of God could shape the finest lines, and which could offer her the pleasures that she could take as rightfully to exercise her piety as to calm her spirit. It is to this extraordinary and admirable piety, MADAME, that France is beholden for the blessings that have been bestowed upon her from the first campaigns of her king; the happy successes that they have obtained are acts of brilliant retribution and strokes of divine fortune, which abundantly bestrew the whole kingdom with the rewards and graces that YOUR MAJESTY has deserved. [...] God does not leave his works imperfect: he will complete them, MADAME, and will render not only the regency of YOUR MAJESTY but her whole life a continuous succession of prosperity. Those are the wishes of all France, and those are they that with the greatest zeal are made, MADAME, by YOUR MAJESTY's most humble, obedient and faithful servant and subject, Corneille.

Translated from the French by AR; original title: *Polyeucte*. The royal dedicatee is Anne of Austria, consort of Louis XIII, who had just become Queen Regent for her son Louis XIV (who was only five years old when he succeeded to the throne) and who would remain so for the next eight years. Corneille appeals to the Queen's well-known piety as patron for his play, which was a tragedy based on the life and martyrdom of St Polyeuctus in the third century. When the dramatist says that the Queen is more Christian 'by her deeds than by her title' he is referring to the fact that the kings of France bore the title of 'Most Christian' (*Très Chrétien*). For another dedication to Queen Anne, see MOLIÈRE's *Criticism of the School for Wives* below.

Philip **Cornford**, *The Outcast*, 1988

~ To those who knew, and who must forever remain silent.

A nuclear spy story set in Australia.

Thomas **Coryate**, *Crudities*, 1611

~ To the High and Mighty Prince Henry, Prince of Wales, Duke of Cornwall and Rothsay, Earle of Chester, Knight of the most noble Order of the Garter, &c. Though I am very confidently perswaded (most gracious Prince, the Orient Pearle of the Christian world) that I shall expose my selfe to the severe censure at the least, if not the scandalous calumniations of divers carping criticks, for presuming to dedicate to your Highnesse the greene fruits of my short travels, especially as I am no schollar, but a man altogether unworthy to be dignified with so laudable a title. [...] Wherefore most humbly beseeching your Highnesse to pardon my presumption, I recommend your Highnesse to the mercifull clientele of him whose throne is the heaven, and whose foote-stoole is the earth. By him that travelleth no less in all humble and dutifull observance to your Highnesse then he did to Venice and the parts above mentioned, Your Highnesse poore Observer, THOMAS CORYATE, Peregrine of Odcombe.

The full title of this work, a hodgepodge account of the author's travels and experiences in various European countries, is *Coryats Crudities, Hastily Gobbled Up In Five Months Travels*. It is still readable today as a sort of scrapbook of contemporary curiosities. If he had a sense of humour or imagination, which he undoubtedly had, the future Henry VIII would have enjoyed the collection, and doubtless the dedication, of which this is necessarily a very brief extract. (The original is roughly six times as long.) The end title after Coryate's name refers to the parish of Odcombe, near Yeovil, Somerset, where his father was the rector. JOHN TAYLOR, the 'Water Poet', dedicated his *Three Weekes* to Coryate. See below.

Kate **Coscarelli**, *Pretty Women*, 1989

~ This book is dedicated with love to Don, my traveling companion from one end of the world to the other, through this life to the next ... and to all the pretty women who stand beside their men in uniform.

A novel about officers of the United States Air Force and their wives, based on personal experience.

Patrick **Cosgrave**, *Adventure of State*, 1984

~ I wrote the early parts of this book in hospital. I was encouraged to do so by my doctor, who came to see me each day. He was bullying and kindly by turns and became my friend. So this story is for JOHN HUNT.

Arthur **Cotterell**, *A Dictionary of World Mythology*, 1979

~ In memory of my father Percy Cotterell, who in his own way knew.

Norman **Cousins**, *Human Options*, 1981

~ For Bill Hitzig, lifelong friend, who has gone more extra miles for more people than even the poets dreamed possible.

Philip **Coventry**, *Tiger, Tiger*, 1984
~ Marion Burns, Robbie Robinson. Good friends both, sadly missed. This book is for them.

William **Cowper**, *Tirocinium, or a Review of Schools*, 1785
~ To the Rev. William Cawthorne Unwin, rector of Stock in Essex, the following Poem, recommending private tuition in preference to an education at School, is inscribed, by his affectionate friend, William Cowper.

Cowper's poem is actually a fierce attack on public schools ('Public schools 'tis public folly feeds', line 250), and takes its title from the Latin word meaning 'body of young recruits', 'first trial', itself derived from *tiro* (modern English 'tyro').

Fanny **Cradock**, *The Lormes of Castle Rising*, 1975
~ To Johnnie, because we can both echo Justin Aynthorp's *'vale'* ... *'je t'aime et je ne regrette rien'*. Jill.

The novel is one of a series about a fictional family descended from Justin, Lord Aynthorp.

Fanny **Cradock**, *Shadows over Castle Rising*, 1976
~ To Dea Vi (Lort-Phillips), who understands, remembers and echoes with regret *'où sont les neiges d'antan'*.

Fanny **Cradock**, *Uneasy Peace of Castle Rising*, 1979
~ To Simon Buck, who corrected my historical references accurately when he was only ten. With love, Fanny.

A frank admission by an established writer of historical romances!

Fanny **Cradock**, *The Defence of Castle Rising*, 1984
~ To the memory of a night on the Isle of Dogs and those who were with us.

Alexander **Craig**, *The Amorose Songes, Sonets, and Elegies*, 1606
~ To the most godly, vertuous, beautifull, and accomplished Princesse, meritoriously dignified with all the Titles Religion, Vertue, Honor, Beautie can receive, challange, afforde, or deserve; Anna, by divine Providence, of Great Britane, France, and Ireland, Queene; Alexander Craige wisheth all health, wealth, and royall felicitie. [...] I am bold (divine Ladie) to borrow thy blessed name, to beautifie my blotted Booke. [...] Happie beyonde the measure of my merit shall I bee, if I can purchase this portion of your Princely approbation, as to accept and entertaine these triviall toys (where once your Grace shall smell Flowers to refresh, Hearbs to cure, and Weedes to be avoyded in the lowest degree of least favour). But, howsoever, wishing your Highness as many happie yeares as there are words in my Verses and Verses in my worthless Volume: I am Your Majestie's most obsequious Orator, Alexander Craige.

A flowery tribute to Anne of Denmark, wife of James I, who was crowned at Windsor in 1603. She always spelled her name 'Anna'. A generous tribute, too: there must be around 20,000 words in Craig's verses!

Mary Craig, *Were He a Stranger*, 1979
~ To Corc, whose mountain overlooks this sea.

F. Marion Crawford, *The Children of the King*, 1893
~ To the Middy, the Laddie, the Mate, and the Men, the Skipper of the old 'Leone' dedicates this story.

F. Marion Crawford, *Francesca da Rimini*, 1902
~ To Madame Sarah Bernhardt, who by her magic creation has after six hundred years reincarnated the Soul of Francesca, 'Che piange e dice'.

This is one of the best known plays by the American romantic novelist and playwright, Francis Marion Crawford, written specially for Sarah Bernhardt. Francesca da Rimini was a thirteenth-century adultress slain by her husband, and the subject of hundreds of artistic and literary works. The Italian phrase here means 'Who weeps and tells'.

David Creaton, *Beasts and Babies*, 1978
~ To my wife. She always insisted her diaries would come in useful one day.

A farmer's autobiography.

Harry Crews, *A Feast of Snakes*, 1977
~ This book is for Johnny Feiber: in good times and bad I've never raised a glass with a better friend.

Edmund Crispin, *Swan Song*, 1947
~ TO GODFREY SAMPSON. My dear Godfrey, You're not, I fancy, an habitual reader of such murderous tales as this, and in the ordinary way I should be decidedly shy of dedicating one of them to you. But a book with a background of *Die Meistersinger* – well, what else could I do? It was you who first introduced me to that noble work (in the days when the sum of my musical activity consisted in trying to evade piano lessons), and our mutual admiration of it is not the least of many bonds of friendship between us. Accept the story, then, for the sake of its setting, and as a foretaste of the day when Wagner's masterpiece returns to Covent Garden – without, let us hope, any of the dismal impediments which beset it in the following pages. Yours as ever, E.C.

'Edmund Crispin', the crime novelist, was the pseudonymous alter ego of Bruce Montgomery, composer, especially of film music. The dedication is followed by a very brief musical extract, barely a single bar, from *Die Meistersinger*, and is a reminder that German composers were in many instances *personae non gratae*, and so unheard, in the Second World War.

Samuel Rutherford **Crockett**, *Sweetheart Travellers*, 1896
~ Dedicated to all who have sweethearts of their own, and to those others who only wish they had.

Crockett, a thirty-six-year-old Scot, had abandoned the Free Church ministry the previous year to devote his life to writing sentimental novels about 'small town' Scottish life.

William S. **Crockett**, *The Scott Originals*, 1912
~ To Daniel Aitkenhead, schoolmaster-emeritus of Earlston.

A five-stanza poem follows, with the first running: 'Dear Maister – From the ABC / To Greek and grand Latinity / You drave the lessons into me'.

Aleister **Crowley**, *Diary of a Drug Fiend*, 1922
~ To ALOSTRAEL, Virgin Guardian of the Sangraal in the Abbey of Thelema in 'Telepylus', and to ASTARTE LULU PANTHEA, its youngest member, I dedicate this story of its Herculean labours towards releasing Mankind from every form of bondage.

Crowley was a notorious practitioner of, and writer on, black magic and the occult. A gloss to his dedication explains that Alostrael was in reality Leah Hirsig, that 'Telepylus' was actually Cefalu, in Sicily, and that Astarte Lulu Panthea was Crowley's daughter by Ninette Fraux, born at the Abbey in 1920. Crowley wrote the book in twenty-eight days to cure himself of heroin addiction.

John **Crowne**, *The Destruction of Jerusalem*, 1677
~ [...] I fix then your Grace's Image at this Jewish Temple gate to render the buildings sacred, nor can the Jews be angry with so beautiful a profanation; and in guiding them to you, they are conducted like their ancestors to repose and happiness, in the most fair and delightful part of the world.

Part of a dedication to the Duchess of Portsmouth, a popular patroness of literary works. See, for example, OTWAY's address to her in *Venice Preserv'd*.

Jonathan **Crowther**, ed., *The Azed Book of Crosswords*, 1975
~ For Ali, with glue and scissors.

Crowther, the professional crossword compiler 'Azed' (a reversal of the name of the Spanish inquisitor Don Diego de Deza, as well as implying 'A–Z'), dedicated his collection to his wife, choosing an apt wording that, presumably deliberately, suggests 'with love and kisses'.

Alexander **Cruden**, *A Complete Concordance to the Holy Scriptures*, 1st edn, 1737
~ To the Queen. Madam, This Concordance, the work of several years, was begun with a design to promote the study of the holy Scriptures; and, in pursuance thereof, is now published with many improvements beyond any kind of book in the English language. Long before this Work was ready for the press, I designed humbly to offer it to your Majesty, and to beg leave to publish it under your royal

protection. Your Majesty's illustrious qualities and example and the great scenes of your valuable life, encourage me humbly to beg your countenance to a well-meant attempt for prompting the knowledge of our holy Religion. Whatever may be wanting either in the Work or the Author, is abundantly supplied by the dignity of the subject; which consideration chiefly encourages me to presume to offer it to your Majesty, whom God hath exalted to the most eminent station, and blessed with extraordinary endowments of mind, and with a benevolent and beneficent disposition. To whom then can I more properly offer this Work than to your Majesty, who is celebrated both for your inclination and capacity to do good? [...] May it please your Majesty, Your Majesty's most dutiful, and Most obedient Servant, Alexander Cruden.

The opening sentences and close of a more than obsequious dedicatory epistle to Queen Caroline, the wife of George II, whose palate may have soon become cloyed with the rich tributes, however deserving. (The address continues in the same vein, with mentions of the Queen's beauty, the 'fine accomplishments' of her mind, her 'fine taste in the elegant arts', her 'royal and numerous progeny', 'skill in several modern languages' and so forth.) Cruden presented his now famous *Concordance* to Queen Caroline in person, as he himself recorded ('She smiled upon the author, and said she was mightily obliged to him'). This was on 3 November 1737. A week later, however, the Queen fell ill, and died on the 20th of the same month, aged fifty-five, so that any promised patronage never materialised. See below for the continuation of the matter!

Alexander **Cruden**, *A Complete Concordance to the Holy Scriptures*, 2nd edn, 1761

~ To the King. Sire, This Concordance was begun with a design to promote the study and knowledge of the holy Scriptures, and the method taken therein is deemed by competent judges to be the best towards a complete Concordance that hath hitherto appeared in our language. [...] Therefore to whom can this new Edition be more properly offered than to your Majesty, now in the beginning of your reign, having already manifested a great regard to Religion, and an earnest concern for promoting it among your subjects? [...] I doubt not but your Majesty will pardon my forbearing to enter upon your valuable personal Accomplishments: I shall only add that, when it pleased GOD, the sovereign Lord of life and death, to deprive us of the blessing of your Royal Grandfather KING GEORGE THE SECOND, the Protector of our Religion and Liberties for many years, it was esteemed a national blessing that GOD had favoured Great Britain with a Prince born and educated among us, who makes the happiness of his people the rule of his government; and without Religion there can be no real happiness for Prince or People. [...] May it please your Majesty, Your Majesty's most dutiful, And most obedient Subject and Servant, Alexander Cruden.

Although George III, to whom Cruden dedicated the second edition of his *Concordance*, was indeed born in London, he was hardly more properly 'British' than his German-born father and grandfather. He had been on the throne for only a year at the time of this dedication.

Richard **Curle**, *Women: An Analytical Study*, 1947
~ To my women friends on both sides of the Atlantic, whether they agree with me or not.

The book now reads oddly as a 'Guide for Men' to women in thirty-two chapters, with such headings as 'Women in Love', 'Women without Men', 'Feminine Ruthlessness', 'Why Women Tell Lies', and so on. Curle declared his study to be 'not anti-feminine, even if it does tend to be pro-man', but he might well have had to reword his dedication if the book had appeared forty years on – and if any publisher would take it on in this form, that is.

George William **Curtis**, *Prue and I*, 1856
~ To Mrs Henry W. Longfellow, in memory of the happy hours at our castle in Spain.

The book consists of a series of 'sketches', representing the reveries of an old clerk living in New York who tours the world with romantic memories of his beloved Prue. Longfellow's wife was his second, Frances Appleton, who invited many literary contemporaries to her hospitable home, Craigie Castle, at Harvard. The 'castle in Spain' thus refers both concretely to this and to the old fellow's daydreams.

Clive **Cussler**, *Cyclops*, 1986
~ To the eight hundred American men who were lost with the *Leopoldville* Christmas Eve 1944 near Cherbourg, France. Forgotten by many, remembered by few.

❦ D ❦

Curtis B. **Dall**, *FDR: My Exploited Father-in-Law*, 1967

~ Dedicated to young Americans – May you benefit from observing how certain shadowy forces contrive to ruthlessly advance their own financial and ideological objectives at your expense. They select, they groom, and ultimately control many of our highest government officials. [...] Hence, I say, young Americans, be alerted – be more effective than my unsuspecting and bemused generation. Sally-forth, defend and preserve for yourself and those who follow you our great heritage of freedom and liberty. The Author.

Dall was the husband of Anna Roosevelt, daughter of Franklin D. Roosevelt, and as a 'Christian Crusader' and ardent conservative strove in his book to highlight the duplicity and underhand machinations and manipulations associated with the Roosevelt presidency.

Samuel **Daniel**, *Delia*, 1592

~ To the Right Honourable the Ladie Mary, Countesse of Pembroke. Right honorable, although I rather desired to keep in the private passions of my youth from the multitude as things uttered to my selfe and consecrated to silence, yet seeing I was betraide by the indiscretion of a greedie Printer and had some of my secrets bewraide to the world uncorrected, doubting the like of the rest, I am forced to publish that which I never ment. [...] And for my selfe, seeing that I am thrust out into the worlde, and that my unboldned Muse is forced to appeare so rawly in publique, I desire onely to bee graced by the countenance of your protection. [...] Samuel Danyell.

Daniel dedicated his *Cleopatra* (1594) and *The Civile Wars between the Houses of Lancaster and York* (1609) also to the popular Countess of Pembroke, the recipient of many dedications of the day.

Samuel **Daniel**, *Historie of England*, 1617

~ To the Majesty of Anne of Denmarke, Queene of England, Scotland, France and Ireland. Queenes, the Mothers of our Kings, by whom is continued the blessing of succession that preserves the Kingdome, having their parts running in the times wherein they live, are likewise interressed in the Histories theoreof, which containe their memories and all that is left of them, when they have left to be in this world. And therefore to you, great Queene of England [...] doe I your humblest servant addresse this peece of our History; which, as it is a worke of mine, appertaines of right to your Majestie, being for the most parte done under your Roofe, during my attendance upon your sacred person: and if ever it shall come to bee an intire worke, and merit any acceptation in the world, it must remaine among the memorials of you, and your time, as brought forth under the splendor of your goodnes. [...] And though at high Altares, none but Priests ought to sacrifize, yet vouchsafe mighty Queene, to accept this poore oblation from the hand of your Majesties Humblest servant, Samuel Danyel.

A better poet and writer of masques than historian, Daniel had gained the favour of Queen Anne, who herself danced in one of his masques at Hampton Court, and the historical work here was fostered, as he tells us, under her patronage.

John **Daniell**, *Ava Gardner*, 1982

~ To the memory of my Grandmother, Ellen Martha, 1893–1977. With thanks for all those childhood afternoon matinées.

A necessarily cinematic biography.

Dante Alighieri, *The Divine Comedy*, 1502

~ To the Worthy Lady Victoria Colonna, most illustrious Marchioness of Pescara Andrea di Asola. Having newly reprinted, oh most illustrious lady, the divine poet Dante, inferior to none of other writers, ancient or modern that have lived [...]: Under a name more noble than that of yours is, I do not think I could send it forth, – and it is not only my ancient subservience that has directed me toward your Most Noble House, but even more, the enduring fame of the immortals and the divine beauties which from day to day keep increasing and advancing as they do with a handsome woman. [...] Honesty, demureness, discretion, modesty, courtesy, purity, grace, chastity, magnificence & eloquence as great as could be desired in a noble lady, all are in thee and plentifully are they given thee: Therefore, because dowered with so many and so great divine gifts, this, my gift, do I dedicate and consecrate your honour: for whose sweet thanks bowing I kiss thy hands.

Translated from the Italian. Dante's great work was originally completed in 1321. The dedication here is thus by Aldus Manutius, the Italian printer and classical scholar who founded the Aldine Press (named after him). The last three words of the opening sentence form the name of Aldus's father-in-law, which always appeared with his own in imprints after 1505, when he married. And the paragon of a dedicatee was Vittoria Colonna, now aged nineteen, who married the Marquis of Pescara in 1509, but who was subsequently gradually estranged from him. She was the admired object of attention of other writers, including Michelangelo, who wrote sonnets to her, and Ariosto, and she herself was a poet of considerable charm. For a visual memorial to this goddess, here praised so fulsomely, see Veronese's painting *The Marriage at Cana* (original now in the Louvre, Paris), where she is the lady with the toothpick.

Iris Rainer **Dart**, *Beaches*, 1985

~ For Stephen Dart, because his wisdom, integrity, and fire inspire everything I do. And for Gregory Michael Wolf, because his sensitivity, warmth, and maturity are a loving lesson to everyone who knows him.

The two dedications appear on consecutive pages of the book, not together.

Charles **Daubeny**, *The Atomic Theory*, 1850

~ To the memory of John Dalton, F.R.S., Late President of the Literary and Philosophical Society of Manchester, Corresponding Member of the Academy of Sciences of the Royal Institute of France, and Honorary D.C.L. of the University of Oxford, the framer of a theory with respect to the mode of combination between bodies, which stands foremost among the discoveries of the present age, for the universality of its applications, and the importance of its practical results; [...] this essay, which in a less mature form was honored by his approval, is now inscribed, as a slight tribute to his posthumous reputation by his former friend and devoted admirer, the Author.

Daubeny had written *An Introduction to the Atomic Theory* in 1831, when Professor of Chemistry at Oxford, and this present book was its second edition. Dalton, the famous chemist, gave the first clear statement of the atomic theory in 1803. He died in 1840.

Diana **Davenport**, *The Power Eaters*, 1979

~ For Dorson Liss, who was there at all times, in all ways, who gave me the courage to believe in this book. It is dedicated with love and gratitude.

A love story. The name of the dedicatee seems rather contrived, but may of course be genuine.

Lester **David** and Irene David, *The Shirley Temple Story*, 1984

~ To the 'old' movies, which, imperfect though they were, helped lift the spirits of a more imperfect world.

Max **Davidson**, *Hugger Mugger*, 1986

~ For North and South, at a different bridge table.

The story of a married couple.

E. **Davies**, *Other Men's Minds*, nd [*c.* 1875]

~ As genuine worth ought always to be recognised and published to the world, not for the sake of ostentation, but to provoke to imitation, the opportunity is seized of dedicating this volume – the fruit of several years' mental labour – to H.G.G. LUDLOW, ESQ., J.P., D.L., of Heywood House, not merely as an expression of deep thankfulness for many personal kindnesses received from him, but as a token of admiration for his unwearied benevolence to the poor, his profound interest in the young, and his decided sympathy with acknowledged evangelical truth and personal religion. To him, and to his truly devoted wife, the parishioners of Heywood are unspeakably indebted both for the beautiful Church in which they worship God, and the numerous Christian advantages they now happily possess.

The book has a descriptive subtitle: 'Seven thousand choice extracts on history, science, philosophy, religion, etc., selected from the standard authorship of ancient and modern times, and classified in alphabetical order', so is in essence an anthology of quotations. It opens with a brief selection of nine dedications ('To the Deity', 'To a Divine', 'To a Mother', etc.), of which this, for the book itself, is one ('To an Esquire').

Jefferson **Davis**, *The Rise and Fall of the Confederate Government*, 1878–81

~ To the Women of the Confederacy, – whose pious ministrations to your wounded soldiers soothed the last hours of those who died far from the objects of their tenderest love; whose domestic labors contributed much to supply the wants of our defenders in the field; whose zealous faith in our cause shone a guiding star undimmed by the darkest clouds of war; whose fortitude sustained them under all privations to which they were subjected; whose annual tribute expresses their enduring grief, love, and reverence for our sacred dead; and whose patriotism will teach their children to emulate the deeds of our revolutionary sires; – these pages are dedicated by their countryman Jefferson Davis.

Davis was President of the Confederate States of America during the Civil War (1861–5).

Joe **Davis**, *The Breaks Came My Way*, 1976

~ Dedicated to my many fans, who gave me much encouragement in writing this book.

The autobiography of the champion billiards and snooker player, regarded as the father of modern snooker, who died in 1978.

Peter **Davis**, *Where is Nicaragua?*, 1987

~ For Victor Nowasky, who first suggested I go to Nicaragua, and for Roberta Lichtman, who stayed at the end when I no longer could.

Sir Humphrey **Davy**, *Elements of Chemical Philosophy*, 1812

~ [...] There is no individual to whom I can with so much propriety or so much pleasure dedicate this work as to you. The interest you have taken in the progress of it, has been a constant motive for my exertions, and it was begun and finished in a period of my life, which owing to you has been the happiest. Regard it as a pledge that I shall continue to pursue Science with unabated ardour. Receive it as a proof of my ardent affection, which must be unalterable, for it is founded upon the admiration of your moral and intellectual qualities. [...]

A correct, but none the less genuine token of gratitude expressed by the famous chemist to his wife, the former Mrs Apreece, whom he had married only a few months earlier.

John William **Dawson**, *The Origin of the World*, 1877

~ To his excellency, the Right Honourable, the Earl of Dufferin, K.P., K.C.B., etc., Governor-General of Canada; this work is respectfully dedicated, as a slight tribute of esteem to one who graces the highest position in the dominion of Canada by his eminent personal qualities, his reputation as a statesman and an author, and his kind and enlightened patronage of education, literature, and science.

The Earl of Dufferin was Frederick Temple Hamilton-Temple Blackwood, 1st Marquis of Dufferin and Ava, who was appointed Governor-General for Canada in 1872, and went on to be ambassador to several foreign countries.

Daniel **Defoe**, *The Military Memoirs of Captain George Carleton*, 1728

~ To the Right Honourable Spencer, Lord Compton, Baron of Wilmington, Knight of the Bath, and one of his Majesty's most Honourable Privy Council. It was my fortune, my Lord, in my juvenile years, *Musas cum marte commutare*; and truly I have reason to blush, when I consider the small advantage I have reaped from that change. But lest it should be imputed to want of merit, I have wrote these Memoirs, and leave the world to judge of my deserts. [...] To you, therefore, my Lord, I present them; to you who have so eminently distinguished yourself, and whose wisdom has been so conspicuous to the late representatives of Great Britain, that each revolving age will speak in your praise; and if you vouchsafe to be the Maecenas of these memoirs, your name will give them sufficient sanction. [...] My Lord, your lordship's most obedient, and most devoted humble servant, G. Carleton.

The entire book was long believed to have been the work of the 'old soldier' who wrote its dedication, but it is now almost certain that Defoe was the author, using the innocent-seeming dedication to mask his purpose. The key Latin phrase means 'to exchange the Muses for war'.

J.B. **De Freval**, *The History of the Heavens*, 1752

~ To His Royal Highness Prince George: Sir, the homage I here take the liberty to offer, has no other motive than my true zeal for Your Royal Highness, and a passionate desire of evidencing that zeal. And, indeed, Sir, who would not be animated by those sentiments for a young prince born of the Two most illustrious Personages in Europe? We already discern their virtues in your looks, and shall soon see You, copying from those accomplish'd models, become, what They truly are, the delight of every Briton, and the admiration of the whole world. The book I now presume to offer to Your Royal Highness, is no more than a translation of a work from the French, whose author had made, and is still making, himself famous by many excellent and useful productions. [...] Your Royal Highness, whose noble aspect, though at an age remote from puberty, gives presages both of genius and greatness of mind to every beholder, will in a short time comprehend the purport and relish the beauties of this history, the reading whereof cannot fail of affording Your Royal Highness much pleasure and delight. [...] Your Royal Highness's Most obedient and Most devoted servant, J.B. De Freval.

The work's full title and subtitle reads impressively as: 'The History of the Heavens, Considered according to the Notions of the Poets and Philosophers, Compared with the Doctrines of Moses. Being an Inquiry into the Origine of Idolatry, and the Mistakes of Philosophers upon the Formation and Influences of the Celestial Bodies. Translated from the French of the Abbé Pluche, by J.B. De Freval, Esq.' The dedicatee was the future George III, who in the year of publication would have been fourteen, and thus hardly 'at an age remote from puberty'. But no doubt the dedication was written some years earlier. His parents were Frederick Louis, Prince of Wales, and Princess Augusta of Saxe-Gotha. The Abbé Pluche, a contemporary, was a populariser of scientific knowledge, best known for his *Spectacle de la nature* (1732).

Thomas **Dekker**, *Newes from Hell*, 1606

~ To my most respected, loving, and Juditious friend Mr. John Sturman Gentleman. Sir, the begetting of Bookes, is as common as the begetting of Children; onely heerein they differ, that Bookes speaks so soone as they come into the world, and give the best wordes they can to al men, yet are they driven to seek abroad for a father. That hard fortune follows al & fals now upon THIS of mine. It gladly comes to you upon that errand, and if you vouchsafe to receive it lovingly, I shall account my selfe and It, very happie. [...] Accept it therefore, and if hereafter I may be a voyager to any happyer coast, the Fruits (of that as now of this) shall be most affectionately consecrated to you. From him that wishes he could be a deserver of you. Tho. Dekker.

A prolific playwright and writer generally, Dekker boldly selected for his patron here a person quite unknown to him.

Thomas **Dekker**, *The Gull's Horn-Book*, 1609

~ To all Gulls in general, Wealth and Liberty: Whom can I choose, my most worthy Mæcen-asses, to be patrons to this labour of mine fitter than ourselves? [...] Who is more liberal than you? Who, but only citizens, are more free? Blame me not, therefore, if I pick you out from the bunch of booktakers, to consecrate these fruits of my brain, which shall never die, only to you. O know that most of you, O admirable Gulls! can neither read nor write. A Horn-book have I invented, because I would have you well schooled. Paul's is your walk, but this is your guide: if it lead you right, thank me; if astray, men will bear with your errors, because you are Gulls. Farewell, T.D.

A 'gull' was an ignorant poseur, an attitude-striking fop. Dekker's ironical dedication was designed to make such people even more objectionable than they were already, and his 'hornbook' (properly a kind of spelling guide for beginners) included practical behaviour tips, for example, to 'rise with a screwed and discontented face from your stool to be gone' in the middle of a play, whether good or bad, in order to show up the playwright for any reason.

Thomas **Dekker**, *The Ravens Almanacke*, 1609

~ To the Lyons of the Wood (the young Courtiers), to the wild Buckes of the Forest (the Gallants and younger Brothers), to the Harts of the Field, and to all the whole countrey, that are brought up wisely, yet prove Gulls; and are born riche, yet die beggars: the New English Astrologer dedicateth his Ravens Almanacke.

This quite brief dedication is followed by a lengthy satirical address beginning 'O you Lyons of the Wood! (you young courtiers) that are kept warme under the wings of princes and kings of Christendom ...' For 'gulls', see the dedication above. Dekker saw himself as a 'raven', or bird of prophecy, foretelling the judgment that will surely be passed on all these grand and privileged young people, the 'yuppies' of their day, for their wanton ways and wiles.

R.F. **Delderfield**, *The Green Gauntlet*, 1968

~ My dear Olive and Cyril, In the brave old days of the three-decker novel authors wrote their dedication in the form of an amiable, rambling letter. This is old-fashioned but then so am I, so I make no apology for reverting to the practice. [...] This book is an expression of my thanks to you both for all the years of encouragement you have contributed, not only to me personally, but to our way of life 'downalong'. Affectionately, R.F.D.

R.F. **Delderfield**, *God is an Englishman*, 1970

~ For My Wife, May, without whose affection, oceans of coffee, and classical records, this would never have been finished.

R.F. **Delderfield**, *Theirs Was the Kingdom*, 1971

~ For my old friend and colleague Eric McKenzie, as enterprising as any Swann. Salesman and cheer-leader extraordinary.

The novel, set in the late nineteenth century, is the second part of a saga in which Adam Swann and other Swanns are involved. Ronald F. Delderfield, who died in 1972, aged sixty, is best remembered as a playwright (especially his comedy *Worm's Eye View*, first staged in 1945, about life in the RAF) and writer of 'nostalgic' novels and historical romances.

Charles **Derennes**, *Emile and the Others*, 1924

~ To Claude Farrère, because of Cat Like That, and to Paul Léautaud, because of Chati, Little Coffee, Minne, Riquet, Bibi, Pitou ... and Golo and Emile ... and the others.

Translated from the French by AR; original title, *Emile et les autres*. The book is the third on animals in the author's series called *The Sentimental Bestiary*. Emile was his cat, as the reader will have already gathered, named after his friend and fellow poet, Emile Despax.

Kevin Desmond, *The Harwin Chronology of Inventions, Innovations, Discoveries,* 1987
~ This chronology is dedicated to GOD Creator of all things.

Sir Aubrey De Vere, *Songs of Faith, Devout Exercises, and Sonnets,* 1842
~ To WILLIAM WORDSWORTH, Esq. My dear Sir, – To know that you have perused many of the following Poems with pleasure and did not hesitate to reward them with your praise, has been to me cause of unmingled happiness. In accepting the Dedication of this volume you permit me to link my name – which I have hitherto done so little to illustrate – with yours, the noblest of modern literature. I may at least hope to be named hereafter as one among the friends of WORDSWORTH. As such I trust you will ever regard your faithful AUBREY DE VERE.

Aubrey De Vere was a voluminous Irish poet, and a personal friend of Tennyson, Browning and Ruskin. But he is hardly read at all today.

Justin de Villeneuve, *An Affectionate Punch,* 1986
~ This book is dessicated to Bunny Roger whom I first blimpoed ball and chalking it down Bondo Strada. From the top of his holy roller to the tips of his St Louis, he was a tonsorial, sartorial wonder. To say he was my inspirano is an undercarriage.

The autobiography of the famous Cockney impresario (real name Nigel Davies), best known as the manager of Twiggy. The dedication and much of the book erupts, rather self-consciously, into Cockney slang, but is always glossed, so that the above translates as follows: 'This book is dedicated to Bunny Roger whom I first glimpsed walking down Bond Street. From the top of his bowler hat to the tips of his shoes he was a tonsorial, sartorial wonder. To say he was my inspiration is an understatement'.

Thomas Dick, *The Philosophy of a Future State,* 1831
~ To Thomas Chalmers, D.D., Professor of Moral Philosophy in the University of St. Andrews. Sir, In Dedicating to you this volume, which has for its object to exhibit a popular view of the Philosophy of a Future State, as deduced from the light of science and revelation, – a consideration of a far higher nature than the formal and customary honour of addressing a man of literary and scientific attainments, induced me to shelter it under your patronage. [...] Your kind indulgence to me, on the slight acquaintance I have of you personally, and your approbation of some of my labours, in endeavouring to connect Science and Religion, induce me to hope, that, if the views taken of the present subject, in any measure correspond with your own, you will countenance my humble attempt to dispel the prejudices which many well meaning Christians may entertain, as to the beneficial tendency of exhibiting the sciences of a *present*, as applicable to the circumstances and relations of a *future* world. That you may long be spared as the advocate of vital Christianity – as a blessing and ornament to your country – and as a zealous instructor of those who are destined to promote its best interests; and

that you may enjoy, without interruption, the pleasures arising from a consciousness of the esteem and approbation of the wise and the pious, is the sincere prayer
of, Sir, Your much obliged, and humble Servant, Thomas Dick.

Thomas Dick was a Scottish scientific writer who did much to popularise the philosophical
overlap – today we might call it the 'interface' – that was believed to exist between science
and religion. The recipient of his dedication here was a fellow Scot, who had gained a
reputation as a theologian and preacher, and who broke away from the Church of Scotland
to found the Free Church of Scotland in 1841, becoming its first moderator.

Thomas **Dick**, *The Christian Philosopher*, 8th edn, 1842

~ To Sir David Brewster, LL.D., Fellow of the Royal Society of London;
Secretary to the Royal Society of Edinburgh; Honorary Member of the Royal
Irish Academy; Member of the Royal Swedish Academy of Sciences; Honorary
Associate of the Royal Academy of Sciences at Lyons, etc.; This volume, intended
to illustrate the connexion of science and philosophy with religion, and with the
moral improvement of mankind, is inscribed, as a testimony of respect for the
acquisitions which science has derived from his philosophical discoveries and
literary labours, by his most obedient and humble servant, The Author.

This was Dick's first major work, originally published in 1823, when he was still a
schoolteacher in Perth (see above for more about him). It enabled him to give up teaching
and turn to a literary life, making his base a small cottage on the banks of the Tay fitted
with an astronomical observatory and a library, thus combining the scientific with the
cerebral. David Brewster's academic accreditations are largely set out here, but as a scientist
he was best known for his studies of optics and polarised light and for inventing that lovely
toy, the kaleidoscope. By the time of this dedication, too, he was Principal of St Andrews
University.

Charles **Dickens**, *Master Humphrey's Clock*, 1840

~ My dear Sir, – Let me have *my* pleasures of memory in connection with this
book, by dedicating it to a poet whose writings all the world knows are replete
with generous and earnest feeling, and to a man whose daily life (as all the world
does not know) is one of active sympathy with the poor and humblest of his kind.

The dedicatee was the then popular poet Samuel Rogers, author of *The Pleasures of Memory*
(1792), hence Dickens' reference to '*my* pleasures'. Dickens' own work served as the basis
for *The Old Curiosity Shop*.

Charles **Dickens**, *American Notes*, 1842

~ I dedicate this book to those friends of mine in America who, giving me a
welcome I must ever gratefully and proudly remember, left my judgment free,
and who, loving their country, can bear the truth, when it is told good-humouredly,
and in a kind spirit.

Dickens had originally been highly impressed by America, when he and his wife first went
there in 1842, but his delight was soon succeeded by disillusion, and this was reflected in

this book, which unsurprisingly caused considerable offence to his former friends there, as did the American episodes and stereotypes in *Martin Chuzzlewit* (1844).

Charles **Dickens**, *Bleak House*, 1852–3

~ Dedicated as a remembrance of our friendly union to my companions in the Guild of Literature and Art.

The Guild, which Dickens, Bulwer Lytton and others had founded in 1851, provided a fund to benefit impoverished authors and artists. It failed a few years later, however.

Benjamin **Disraeli**, *Vivian Grey*, 1826

~ To the Best and Greatest of Men, I dedicate these volumes. He, for whom it is intended, will accept and appreciate the compliment; Those, for whom it is not intended, will – Do the same.

This was Disraeli's first novel, published anonymously. The dedicatee was actually his father, Isaac D'Israeli, who features in the book as the kindly, scholarly Mr Grey, the father of the eponymous central character. Compare BERIAH BOTFIELD's dedication, above.

Benjamin **Disraeli**, *Henrietta Temple: A Love Story*, 1837

~ To the Count Alfred D'Orsay, these volumes are inscribed by his affectionate friend.

Disraeli had begun the novel three years earlier, during his open love affair with Lady Henrietta Sykes. Count D'Orsay was a Frenchman who had come to London and gained social fame as a wit and artist.

Benjamin **Disraeli**, *Venetia*, 1837

~ To Lord Lyndhurst. In happier hours, when I first mentioned to you the idea of this Work, it was my intention, while inscribing it with your name, to have entered into some details as to the principles which had guided me in its composition, and the feelings with which I had attempted to shadow forth, though as 'in a glass darkly', two of the most renowned and refined spirits that have adorned these our latter days. But now I will only express a hope that the time may come when, in these pages, you may find some relaxation from the cares, and some distraction from the sorrows, of existence, and that you will then receive this dedication as a record of my respect and my affection.

John Singleton Copley, Baron Lyndhurst, was the American-born Lord Chancellor of England at this time. Four years earlier he had suffered a deep personal loss in the death of his wife, hence Disraeli's tactful wording. The two 'renowned and refined spirits' that he refers to were the poets Byron and Shelley, on whom two of the novel's characters, Plantagenet Carducis and Marmion Herbert, are loosely based.

Benjamin **Disraeli**, *Coningsby*, 1844

~ To Henry Hope. It is not because these volumes were conceived and partly executed amid the glades and galleries of the DEEPDENE, that I have inscribed them with your name. Nor merely because I was desirous to avail myself of the most graceful privilege of an author, and dedicate my work to the friend, whose talents I have always appreciated and whose virtues I have ever admired. But because in these pages I have endeavoured to picture something of that development of the new and, as I believe, better mind of England, that has often been the subject of our converse and speculation. In these volumes you will find many a thought illustrated and many a principle attempted to be established that we have often together partially discussed and canvassed. Doubtless you may encounter some opinions with which you may not agree, and some conclusions the accuracy of which you may find cause to question. But if I have generally succeeded in my object: to scatter some suggestions that may tend to elevate the tone of public life; ascertain the true character of political parties; and induce us for the future more carefully to distinguish between facts and phrases, realities and phantoms; I believe that I shall gain your sympathy, for I shall find a reflex to their efforts in your own generous spirit and enlightened mind. Δ.

This is one of the best known novels by the future British Conservative prime minister, together with *Sybil* (see below) and *Tancred* (1847).

Benjamin **Disraeli**, *Sybil; or, The Two Nations*, 1845
~ I would inscribe these volumes to one whose noble spirit and gentle nature ever prompt her to sympathise with the suffering; to one whose sweet voice has often encouraged, and whose taste and judgment have ever guided, their pages; the most severe of critics, but – a perfect wife!

Disraeli had married Mrs Wyndham Lewis (née Mary Anne Evans), a colleague's widow, in 1839.

Isaac **D'Israeli**, *Curiosities of Literature*, 1791–1834
~ To Francis Douce, Esq., these volumes of some literary researches are inscribed; as a grateful acknowledgment to a lover of literature, by his friend, I. D'Israeli.

Francis Douce was an antiquarian who had visited Oxford with D'Israeli in 1830 and who left his fine collection of books to the Bodleian Library there. D'Israeli was the father of BENJAMIN DISRAELI, and his work here, which went through several editions, was a curiosity in itself as a sort of gallimaufry of literary gleanings and anecdotes, including a section on literary dedications.

Beulah Marie **Dix**, *Merrylips*, 1910
~ To every little girl who has wished for an hour to be a little boy, this story is dedicated by her friend the Author.

Dix was an American novelist, born in 1876, who in the year this was published married George H. Flebbe and thereafter called herself by her husband's surname.

Austin **Dobson**, *Poems on Several Occasions*, 1889
To you I sing, whom towns immure,

And bonds of toil hold fast and sure; –
  To you across whose aching sight
  Come woodlands bathed in April light,
And dreams of pastime premature.

And you, O Sad, who still endure
Some wound that only Time can cure, –
  To you, in watches of the night,
  To you I sing!

But most to you with eyelids pure,
Scarce witting yet of love or lure; –
  To you with birdlike glances bright,
  Half paused to speak, half-poised in flight,
O English Girl, divine, demure,
  To *you* I sing!

Good Victorian sentiment, but with rather more subtlety than at first sight appears: Dobson, a noted biographer, as well as a poet, dedicates his collection of verse to the toilweary and grieving, and to the innocent young maiden, but implies that his poems are *for* the former, whom he seeks to comfort, but *about* the latter, whom he wishes to 'sing' or portray, in idealised or even individualised form.

Charles F. **Dole**, *The American Citizen*, 1891

~ To American citizenship after the type of Washington, the Adamses, and Lincoln, noble, devoted, disinterested, magnanimous, fearless, reverent, this book is dedicated.

Dole was an American Unitarian clergyman who wrote several books of this type. Others include *The Citizen and the Neighbor* (1884) and *The Golden Rule in Business* (1895).

John **Donne**, *Obsequies to the Lord Harrington*, 1614

~ To the Countesse of Bedford. Madame, I have learn'd by those lawes wherein I am a little conversant, that hee which bestowes any cost upon the dead, obliges him which is dead, but not the heire; I do not therefore send this paper to your Ladyship, that you should thanke mee for it, or thinke that I thanke you in it; your favours and benefits to mee are so much above my merits, that they are even above my gratitude, if that were to be judged by words which must expresse it. But, Madame, since your noble brothers fortune being yours, the evidences also concerning it are yours, so his vertue being yours, the evidences concerning it, belong also to you, of which by your acceptance this may be one peece, in which quality I humbly present it, and as a testimony how intirely your familie possesseth, Your Ladiships most humble and thankfull servant, John Donne.

One of many tributes to the popular patron, the Countesse of Bedford, in this case more appropriate than most, since the subject of Donne's work is her recently deceased elder brother, John Harrington, who had saved the young Princess Elizabeth from the Gunpowder

Plot conspirators in 1605 and had accompanied her to Germany in 1613 on her marriage to Frederick V, the Elector Palatine, at the age of sixteen. He died on the return journey, however, in circumstances not without suspicion of foul play.

Val **Doonican**, *Walking Tall*, 1986

~ I can't think of a better dedication than the one I used in my first book – To both my families, old and new, and to the entire cast of this book.

The popular singer's autobiographical sequel to *The Special Years* (1980).

Roland **Dorgelès**, *The Castle of Fogs*, 1932

~ I dedicate this book to my comrades of twenty years who on 2 August 1914 left the Butte singing and never came back.

Translated from the French by AR; original title: *Le Château des brouillards*. Dorgelès, whose real name was Roland Lécavelé, and who died in 1973, led a Bohemian life in Montmartre, Paris, before the First World War, which he evoked in this and other novels. He volunteered for military service in the war, and wrote simply and movingly about life in the trenches in his best-known book, *The Wooden Crosses* (1919). In later life he was President of the Goncourt Academy, having been a member from 1929. The 'Butte' ('hill') is a synonym for Montmartre itself, the colourful artists' quarter of Paris.

Lloyd **Douglas**, *The Robe*, 1942

~ Dedicated with appreciation to Hazel McCann, who wondered what became of The Robe.

Douglas, an American Congregational clergyman and novelist, achieved near worldwide fame with this and similar fictional accounts of biblical themes, the 'robe' in this case being that of Jesus.

Norman **Douglas**, *Siren Land*, 1911

~ To my friend of long standing, Kenneth Macpherson, once a mere visitor to Siren Land and now something infinitely better (with many thanks for the admirable map). And please don't forget that this book was written in 1900–1909.

It was this book, essentially an account of travel in Italy and elsewhere, that first brought Douglas to the notice of the public. The title refers to Capri and the Sorrento Peninsula, 'where Sirens sang'.

O. **Douglas**, *The House That is Our Own*, 1940

~ To you, J.B., who, with little liking for mild domestic fiction, read patiently my works, blue-pencilling when you had to, praising when you could, encouraging always, I dedicate this story, which you are not here to read, of places you knew and loved.

'O. Douglas' (Olive Douglas) was the pseudonym of Anna Buchan, sister of the novelist JOHN BUCHAN, the 'J.B.' of this dedication. She wrote many novels about Fife and the Scottish border country, such as this one. She died in 1943.

John **Dowland,** *The First Book of Songs or Airs,* 1597

~ To the Right Honourable Sir George Carey, of the Most Honorable Order of the Garter Knight: Baron of Hunsdon, Captaine of her Majesties gentlemen Pensioners, Governor of the Isle of Wight, Lieutenant of the countie of South. Lord Chamberlaine of her Majesties most Royall house, and of her Highnes most honourable Privie Counsell. [...] This small booke containing the consent of speaking harmony, joyned with the most musicall instrument, the Lute, being my first labour, I have presumed to dedicate to your Lordship: who, for your vertue & nobility, are best able to protect it: and for your honourable favors towards me, best deserving my duety and service. [...] Neither in these your honours, may I let passe the dutifull remembrance of your vertuous Lady, my honourable mistris, whose singular graces towards me have added spirit to my unfortunate labours. What time and diligence I have bestowed in the search of Musicke, what travel in forren countries, what successe and estimation, even among strangers, I have found, I leave to the report of others. Yet all this in vaine, were it not that your honorable hands have vouchsaft to uphold my poore fortunes: which I now wholy recommend to your gratious protection, with these my first endevors, humbly beseeching you to accept and cherish them with your continued favours. Your Lordships most humble servant, John Dowland.

Dowland was not only a fine Elizabethan composer but a highly competent lutenist himself, and was appointed in this post to James I of England. George Carey, 2nd Lord Hunsdon, held a number of influential posts and royal positions, as the dedication indicates, and came to be closely associated with the Isle of Wight, where he appointed himself 'Governor' and did much to build up the island's defences against possible attack by the Spanish Armada. The 'countie of South' is Hampshire, which was originally 'Southampton-shire'.

Arthur Conan **Doyle,** *The White Company,* 1891

~ To the hope of the future, the reunion of the English-speaking races, this little chronicle of our common ancestry is inscribed.

One of Doyle's historical tales, set in England and France in the fourteenth century, and now only painfully readable, although the optimistic dedication remains valid.

Arthur Conan **Doyle,** *A Duel,* 1899

~ To Mrs. Maude Crosse. Dear Maude: All the little two-oared boats into the great ocean have need of some chart which will show them how to lay their course. Each starts full of happiness and confidence, and yet we know how many founder, for it is no easy voyage, and there are rocks and sandbanks upon the way. So I give a few pages of your own private log, which tell of days of peace and days of storm, – such storms as seem very petty from the deck of a high ship, but are serious for the two-oared boats. If your peace should help another to peace or, your storm console another who is storm-tossed, then I know that you will feel repaid for this intrusion upon your privacy. May all your voyage be like the outset, and when at last the oars fall from your hands, and those of Frank, may other loving ones be ready to take their turn of toil – and so, *Bon voyage!* Ever your friend, The Author.

A sustained but in the end rather contrived metaphor for Doyle's dedication to one of his lesser works.

Arthur Conan **Doyle**, *The Hound of the Baskervilles*, 1902

~ My dear Robinson: It was your account of a West Country legend which first suggested the idea of this little tale to my mind. For this and for the help which you gave me in its evolution all thanks. Yours most truly, A. Conan Doyle.

A novel featuring the famous detective Sherlock Holmes, whom Doyle had in fact 'killed off' in a story of 1894 in an attempt to rid himself of his creation, since he regarded him as a threat to his serious work as a doctor. The story was thus presented as an early case for Holmes to solve. However, Doyle was subsequently obliged to resurrect him for genuine new adventures. The dedicatee was Doyle's journalist friend Fletcher Robinson, himself a Devonshire man born on the edge of Dartmoor. The two men would often go for long walks over the moors, and it may well have been in the course of one of these that Robinson recounted the legend to his friend.

Michael **Drayton**, *Poly-olbion, The First Part*, 1612

~ To the High and Mightie, Henrie, Prince of Wales. The first part of my intended Poeme I consecrate to your Highnes: in whom (beside my particuler zeale) there is a naturall interest in my Worke as the hopefull Heyre of the kingdoms of this Great Britaine: whose Delicacies, Chorographicall description, and Historie, be my subject. My Soule, which hath seen the extremitie of Time and Fortune, cannot yet despaire. The influence of so glorious and fortunate a Starre may also reflect upon me: which hath power to give me new life, or leave me to die more willingly and contented. My Poeme is genuine, and first in this kinde. It cannot want envie: for, even in the Birth, it alreadie finds that. Your Gracious acceptance, mighty Prince, will lessen it. May I breath to arrive at the Orcades (whither in this kind I intend my course, if the Muse fail me not) I shall leave your whole British Empire, as this first and southerne part, delineated: To your HIGHNES, The most humbly devoted, Michael Drayton.

See below.

Michael **Drayton**, *Poly-olbion, The Second Part*, 1622

~ To the High and Mightie, Charles, Prince of Wales. The First Part of this Poeme (most Illustrious Prince) I dedicated to your deceased Brother of most famous Memorie, whose princely Bountie, and usage of mee, gave me much encouragement to goe on with this second Part, or Continuance thereof; which now, as his Successor, I owe to your Highnesse. If meanes and time fail me not, being now arrived at Scotland, I trust you shall see mee crowne her with no worse Flowers, then I have done her two Sisters, England and Wales: and without any partialitie, as I dare bee bold, to make the Poets of that Kingdom my Judges therin. If I arive at the Orcades, without sinking in my flight, your Highnesse cannot but say, that I had no ill Perspective that gave me things so cleerely, when I stood so farre off. To your Highnesse most humbly devoted, Michael Drayton.

Drayton's major work, a vast poem in the form of a 'chorographical description' of England and Wales – what would now be regarded as a combined historical and geographical gazetteer in verse form – appeared in two parts as stated here. The first part was dedicated to Prince Henry, the eldest son of James VI of Scotland (James I of England), whom he was due to succeed to the throne. He died, however, aged eighteen, in the year the work appeared, although not before giving the author £10 for his tribute. Drayton thus dedicated the second part of the work to Henry's younger brother, Prince Charles, then aged twenty-two and the future Charles I. Drayton had dedicated earlier works to James VI (I), but had been poorly favoured by him. The 'Orcades' are the Orkney Islands. The first part had a portrait of Prince Henry, with lines opposite beginning as follows:

> Britaine, behold here portray'd to thy sight,
> Henry, thy best hope and the world's delight;
> Ordain'd to make thy eight great Henries, nine:
> Who, by that vertue in the Trebble Trine,
> To his owne goodnesse (in his Being) brings
> These several Glories of th' eight English Kings.

But, as mentioned, Britain was not to crown a king Henry IX, despite the 'lucky number' potential ('Trebble Trine').

John **Drinkwater**, *Oliver Cromwell*, 1921
~ To Bernard Shaw, with homage to the master dramatist of his age, and with the gratitude that is his due from every younger writer for the English theatre.

See below.

John **Drinkwater**, *Robinson of England*, 1937
~ To the Right Honourable J. Ramsay MacDonald, M.P. Dear Ramsay MacDonald, In dedicating this book about England to a Scotsman who more than any other has helped to make the history of our time, I do so with a sense of the many kindnesses that you have never allowed the cares of office to withhold from those whom you have honoured with your friendship. […] In return for an inspiration that I have shared with so many of my countrymen on both sides of the Border, I offer you this story with esteem, and may I say, affection. John Drinkwater.

Drinkwater is remembered today – even if he is rarely read – for his many volumes of verse and his historical plays, of which the above is an example. *Robinson of England*, however, is a straightforward novel, sentimental in tone, but 'honest', and dedicated to the leading Labour politician who was twice Britain's Prime Minister.

John **Dryden**, *Annus Mirabilis*, 1667
~ To the Metropolis of Great Britain, the most Renowned and late Flourishing City of London, in its Representatives The Lord Mayor and Court of Aldermen,

the Sherifs and Common Council of it. As perhaps I am the first who ever presented a work of this nature to the Metropolis of any Nation, so it is likewise consonant to Justice, that he who was to give the first Example of such a Dedication should begin it with that City, which has set a pattern to all others of tru Loyalty, invincible Courage and unshaken Constancy. Other Cities have been prais'd for the same Virtues, but I am much deceiv'd if any have so dearly purchas'd their reputation; their fame has been won them by cheaper trials then an expensive, though necessary, War, a consuming Pestilence, and a more consuming Fire. [...] To you therefore this Year of Wonders is justly dedicated, because you have made it so: You who are to stand a wonder to all Years and Ages, and who have built your selves an immortal Monument on your own ruines. [...] I am therefore to conclude, that your sufferings are at an end; and that one part of my Poem has not been more an History of your destruction, then the other a Prophecy of your restoration. The accomplishment of which happiness, as it is the wish of all true Englishmen, so is by none more passionately desired then by The greatest of your Admirers, and most humble of your Servants, John Dryden.

The subjects of Dryden's poem are the Dutch War of 1665–6 and the Great Fire of London, in September 1666, both of which, together with the Great Plague of 1664 ('a consuming Pestilence'), he mentions in the dedication itself.

John **Dryden**, *The State of Innocence and Fall of Man*, 1674

~ To Mary of Este, Duchess of York. [...] Greatness is, indeed, communicated to some few of both sexes; but beauty is confined to a more narrow compass. 'Tis only in your sex, 'tis not shared by many, and its supreme perfection is in you alone. And here, Madam, I am proud that I cannot flatter. [...] You are never seen but you are blest: And I am sure you bless all those who see you. We think not the day is long enough when we behold you: and you are so much the business of our souls, that while you are in sight, we can neither look nor think on any else. There are no eyes for other beauties: you only are present, and the rest of your sex are but the unregarded parts that fill your triumph. [...]

Part, only, of the lengthy 'hymn of praise' sung by Dryden to the charms of his dedicatee, who was then only fifteen: Mary Este, the daughter of Anne Hyde, Duchess of York, and James, Duke of York, the future James II. Dr Johnson liked the dedication, calling it an 'attempt to mingle earth and heaven, by praising human excellence in the language of religion', but the critic Joseph Wharton thought otherwise, describing it as 'a piece of the grossest and most abject adulation that ever disgraced true genius'. The wording is cloying to the modern taste, although it is easy to overstate, rather than understate, when describing a 'young lovely', as this pretty little rich girl undoubtedly was. The work itself was described by Dryden as 'An Opera', and, bizarrely, was a musical adaptation of Milton's *Paradise Lost*. It was never performed.

John **Dryden**, *All for Love*, 1678

~ To the Right Honourable Thomas, Earl of Danby, Viscount Latimer, and Baron Osborne of Kiveton, in Yorkshire; Lord High Treasurer of England, one of His

Majesty's Most Honourable Privy Council, and Knight of the Most Noble Order of the Garter. My Lord, – The gratitude of poets is so troublesome a virtue to great men, that you are often in danger of your own benefits: for you are threatened with some epistle, and not suffered to do good in quiet, or to compound for their silence whom you have obliged. Yet, I confess, I neither am nor ought to be surprised at this indulgence; for your lordship has the same right to favour poetry, which the great and noble have ever had. [...] I have put off my own business, which was my dedication, till it is so late, that I am now ashamed to begin it; and therefore I will say nothing of the poem, which I present to you, because I know not if you are like to have an hour, which, with a good conscience, you may throw away in perusing it; and for the author, I have only to beg the continuance of your protection to him, who is, my lord, your lordship's most obliged, most humble, and most obedient servant, John Dryden.

This was Dryden's first drama in blank verse, dedicated to Thomas Osborne, 1st Earl of Danby, appointed Lord High Treasurer in 1673, but subsequently engaged in corrupt politics and imprisoned in the Tower of London until 1684, after which he gained rehabilitation and became virtual prime minister. Dryden is so carried away about the role of patrons and the poets they patronise that he leaves the actual dedication to the very end of his long epistle.

John **Dryden**, *Eleanora*, 1692

~ Dedicated to the Memory of the Late Countess of Abingdon. To the Right Honourable The Earl of Abingdon, &c. My Lord, The Commands, with which You honour'd me some Months ago, are now perform'd: They had been sooner, but betwixt ill health, some business, and many troubles, I was forc'd to deferr them till this time. [...] I therefore chose rather to obey You late, than ill: if at least I am capable of writing any thing, at any time, which is worthy Your Perusal and Your Patronage. [...] But I think it the peculiar happiness of the Countess of Abingdon, to have been so truly lov'd by you, while she was living, and so gratefully honour'd, after she was dead. [...] Be pleas'd to accept of these my Unworthy Labours; this Paper Monument; and let her Pious Memory, which I am sure is Sacred to You, not only plead the Pardon of my many Faults, but gain me Your Protection, which is ambitiously sought by, My Lord, Your Lordship's Most Obedient Servant, John Dryden.

Dryden's poem was almost certainly written to order: hence his apology for not 'delivering' earlier. He appears not to have been personally known to the Earl or his late wife. Dryden had been hoping to gain the patronage of James II, but the Revolution of 1688 put paid to that.

John **Dryden**, *Fables, Ancient and Modern*, 1700

~ To His Grace The Duke of Ormond. My Lord, Some Estates are held in England, by paying a fine at the change of every Lord: I have enjoy'd the Patronage of your Family, from the time of your excellent Grandfather to this present Day. I have dedicated the Lives of Plutarch to the first Duke; and have celebrated the

Memory of your Heroick Father. Tho' I am very short of the Age of Nestor, yet I have liv'd to a third Generation of your House; and by your Grace's Favour am admitted still to hold from you by the same Tenure. I am not vain enough to boast that I have deserv'd the value of so Illustrious a Line; but my Fortune is the greater, that for three Descents they have been pleas'd to distinguish my Poems from those of other Men; and have accordingly made me their peculiar Care. May it be permitted me to say, That as your Grandfather and Father were cherish'd and adorn'd with Honours by two successive Monarchs, so I have been esteem'd, and patronis'd, by the Grandfather, the Father, and the Son, descended from one of the most Ancient, most Conspicuous, and most Deserving Families in Europe. 'Tis true, that by delaying the Payment of my last Fine, when it was due by your Grace's Accession to the Titles, and Patrimonies of your House, I may seem in rigour of Law to have made forfeiture of my Claim, yet my Heart has always been graciously pleas'd, by your permission of this Address, to accept the tender of my Duty, 'tis not yet too late to lay these Poems at your Feet. [...] Your Grace's most humble, most oblig'd, and most obedient Servant, John Dryden.

To take the three generations in order mentioned here: the 1st Duke of Ormond was James Butler, who died in 1688. He was succeeded by his grandson, the 2nd Duke, also James Butler, the dedicatee of this present work. The 1st Duke's son, meanwhile, was Thomas Butler, Earl of Ossory, who died in 1680. In the year in which this work was published, Dryden died, aged sixty-nine. He compares himself unfavourably to Nestor, the Greek king of Pylos who lived to a great age, according to Homer outliving two generations. The actual *Fables* begin with lines addressed 'To Her Grace the Dutchess of Ormond', with some lines from Chaucer, and with concluding lines by Dryden expressing the wish that she would soon bear a son to continue the ducal line. But in the event the only male child she bore died in infancy, the other children being five daughters. This meant that the Ormond title lapsed in 1758 with the death of the 2nd Duke's brother, Charles. Thus in the event Dryden's last major work was dedicated to the last of the Ormonds (although the title was subsequently revived in 1825).

David **Dubal**, *The World of the Concert Pianist*, 1985
~ For Margaret Mercer and also my parents, who on one fine day bought me a piano.

Elizabeth Neil **Dubus**, *To Love and to Dream*, 1986
~ This novel is dedicated to Roger Scholl, whose editorial skills are matched only by his compassionate humanity; to Sallie Gouverneur, who is a rare combination of business acumen and gentle wisdom; and to Claudette Price, who entered my life as a book-buyer par excellence and stayed to become a friend.

Thomas **Duffett**, *The Spanish Rogue*, 1674
~ [...] Since a play in print, without an epistle dedicatory, is now like a modeste gallant without a mistriss, or a papist without a tutelar saint, I resolv'd to obey custom in making a dedication, and my own free inclination in the choice of your

excellent self, at whose feet I humbly lay this. Not contented to be safe in the barren praise of doing no ill, but so readily and so frequently doing good, as if it were not your nature, but your business, that next to your beauty these virtues are the greatest miracle of the age. If I am the first that has taken the boldness to tell you this in print, 'tis because I am more ambitious that all others, to be known by the title of, Madam, Your admirer and humblest servant, T.D.

The chosen lady was none other than Nell Gwyn, Charles II's mistress, then aged twenty-four, with Duffett taking the credit for being the first to tell her publicly how wonderful she was. For another dedication to her, see APHRA BEHN and compare also that of WILLIAM WYCHERLEY.

Maureen **Duffy**, *Housespy*, 1978
~ For Ted Willis, who insisted it should be written.

Ted Willis (Lord Willis) is the prolific stage and screen playwright and novelist whose filmscript for *The Blue Lamp* went on to generate the television *Dixon of Dock Green* series about everyday incidents in the life of a policeman.

Daphne **du Maurier**, *The King's General*, 1946
~ To My Husband, also a general, but, I trust, a more discreet one.

The famous novelist's husband was Lieutenant-General Sir Frederick Browning, who died in 1965.

Daphne **du Maurier**, *The Parasites*, 1949
~ For Whom the Caps fit.

Daphne **du Maurier**, *The Glass-Blowers*, 1963
~ To my forebears, the master glass-blowers of la Brulonnerie, Cherigny, La Pierre and le Chesne-Bidault.

As her name implies, Daphne du Maurier was of French descent, and was educated in Paris. Her grandfather was the novelist and artist George du Maurier, who himself was born in Paris as the grandson of refugees from the French Revolution.

Jane **Duncan**, *My Friend Martha's Aunt*, 1962
~ This book, which is all about selfishness, is for the least selfish person I have ever met – Iain.

The sixth novel in the author's Reachfar series, with titles beginning 'My Friend ...'.

Norman **Duncan**, *Billy Topsail and Company*, 1910
~ To Chauncey Lewis and to 'Buster', good friends both, sometimes to recall them to places and occasions at Mike Man's: Dead Man's Point, Rolling Ridge, the Canoe Landing, the swift and wilful waters of the West Branch, Squaw Mountain, the rail to Dead Stream, the raft on Horseshoe, the Big Fish, the

gracious kindness of the L.L. of E.O. (as well as her sandwiches), and the never-to-be-forgotten flapjacks that 'didn't look it', but were indeed 'all there'.

As the evocative place-names suggest, Duncan was a Canadian writer. 'L.L.' perhaps stands for 'landlady'.

Robert L. Duncan, *Temple Dogs*, 1978
~ To James Henry Holmes, of New York and Holdenville, dear friend, a man with a keen eye, an articulate rage, and an abundant heart.

Sara Jeanette Duncan, *A Social Departure*, 1890
~ This volume, as a slight tribute to the unimportance of her opinion and a humble mark of profoundest esteem, is respectfully dedicated to Mrs. Grundy.

That is, to the legendary lady who personifies strict, grim propriety. Duncan was a Canadian novelist, the wife of Everard Cotes, an English journalist who was later the London correspondent of the *Christian Science Monitor* in India, where many of her stories were set. Her novel here, subtitled 'How Orthodocia and I Went Round the World by Ourselves', and written just before her marriage, is one of her best known.

Joseph Dupuis, *Journal of a Residence in Ashantee*, 1824
~ To the King's Most Excellent Majesty, George the Fourth, &c., &c., &c. Sire, In conformity with the permission which I have received, I now place under the patronage of your Majesty's august name, a volume exhibiting the intimate and political feelings of the Sovereign of Ashantee, demonstrative of a friendly regard, as well towards your Royal person as to the commercial prosperity of the British Colonies on the Gold Coast; the contents of which I stood pledged to make known to your Majesty. With sentiments of the purest attachment to your Majesty's service, and to the honour and interest of the crown, I remain, With the profoundest veneration, Sire, Your Majesty's most faithful Subject, and dutiful Servant, Joseph Dupuis.

Dupuis was the British envoy in Ashanti, which waged four wars with the British from 1824 (when coincidentally his diary was published) and was claimed as a British protectorate in 1894. It is now a region of central Ghana.

Gerald Durrell, *My Family and Other Animals*, 1956
~ To my Mother.

Gerald Durrell, *Encounters with Animals*, 1958
~ For Eileen Molony, in memory of late scripts, deep sighs and over-long announcements.

Gerald Durrell, *A Zoo in my Luggage*, 1960
~ For Sophie, In memory of Tio Pepe, Wiener Schnitzel and dancing kleek to kleek.

Gerald **Durrell**, *The Whispering Land*, 1961

~ This is for Bebita, who, by leaving Argentina, has deprived me of my best reason for returning.

Gerald **Durrell**, *Beasts in My Belfry*, 1973

~ For Bianca and Grandy, in memory of three-quarters of a gorilla and many other things.

Gerald **Durrell**, *Golden Bats and Pink Pigeons*, 1977

~ This is for Farida and Wahab whose kindness and hospitality sum up the whole charm of Mauritius.

Gerald **Durrell**, *The Garden of the Gods*, 1978

~ This book is for Ann Peters, at one time my secretary and always my friend, because she loves Corfu and probably knows it better than I do.

Gerald **Durrell**, with Lee Durrell, *The Amateur Naturalist*, 1982

~ This book is for Theo (Dr Theodore Stephanides), my mentor and friend, without whose guidance I would have achieved nothing, and for Pa (Wilson James Northcross Sr), Lee's grandfather, who encouraged her early interest in wildlife, especially by building palatial homes for her animals.

The world-ranging, gregarious life of the famous travel writer and natural historian is well mirrored in this selection of dedications from his many books, the last-named of which was written together with his wife, Lee (christened Jacqueline), although their fruitfully cooperative marriage was actually dissolved in 1979.

Lawrence **Durrell**, *Mountolive*, 1958

~ A Claude *tò 'ónoma toû 'ágathon diámonos*.

The Greek translates as 'the name of the good and only one'. Other novels are similarly dedicated, including *Tunc* (1968) ('For Claude-Marie Vincendon') and *Nunquam* (1970) ('A Claude Vincendon'). Lawrence Durrell is the elder brother of GERALD DURRELL.

❦ E ❦

Alice Morse **Earle,** *Sun-Dials and Roses of Yesterday*, 1902
~ To my daughter Mary Earle Moore, to commemorate her first summer with her own garden and sundial. May the motto of her dial be that of her life: I MARK ONLY SUNNY HOURS.

Alice M. Earle, who died in 1911, was an American writer who wrote several books about the nostalgic past, others for example being *Customs and Fashions in Old New England* (1893) and *Two Centuries of Costume in America* (1903).

Georg **Ebers,** *The Sisters*, 1880
~ To Herr Edward von Hallberger: Allow me, my dear friend, to dedicate these pages to you. I present them to you at the close of a period of twenty years during which a warm and fast friendship has subsisted between us, unbroken by any disagreement. Four of my works have first seen the light under your care and have wandered all over the world under the protection of your name. This, my fifth book, I desire to make especially your own; it was partly written in your beautiful home at Tutzing, under your hospitable roof, and I desire to prove to you by some visible token, that I know how to value your affection and friendship and the many happy hours we have passed together, refreshing and encouraging each other by a full and perfect interchange of thought and sentiment. Faithfully your friend, Georg Ebers.

Translated from the German by Clara Bell; original title: *Die Schwestern*. Ebers was a German Egyptologist and novelist who lectured at the universities of both Jena and Leipzig and who in 1873 acquired the famous sixteenth-century BC Egyptian medical papyrus now known as the 'Ebers Papyrus'. His novels were mainly on historical themes and set in Egypt, as one might expect, although not this one.

Wessel **Ebersohn,** *Divide the Night*, 1981
~ For Elizabeth, who expects much from life and seems likely to have her expectations realised.

Lord **Eccles,** *Half-Way to Faith*, 1966
~ To my father who from his youth up had an unshaken belief in the Creator.

And to my mother who showed me that the knowledge and love of God would be very difficult, and probably impossible, to attain.

The book is part autobiography, part personal philosophy of religion and education, of the politician who was twice Minister of Education in the 1950s and 1960s.

Gillian **Edwards**, *Uncumber and Pantaloon*, 1968
~ To the Ratepayers of Cambridge in Gratitude for the Books I Consulted and the Library where I Worked.

The book is a discursive consideration of various English words and their meanings and origins. Presumably the author studied in the Cambridge City Library, rather than the University Library.

Robert **Elegant**, *Mandarin*, 1983
~ For Richard Hughes, who, I sometimes believe, was present.

The novel is the second of three giving a fictional account of the historic relationship between China and the West. This one covers the period 1854 to 1875.

T.S. **Eliot**, *The Waste Land*, 1922
~ For Ezra Pound, *il miglior fabbro*.

The Italian phrase, translating as 'the best maker', is Eliot's compliment to his fellow poet, friend and counsellor. Could there also be a punning reference to his publishers, Faber & Faber (then Faber & Gwyer), of whom he became a director (see below) three years later?

T.S. **Eliot**, *Old Possum's Book of Practical Cats*, 1939
~ This book is respectfully dedicated to those friends who have assisted its composition by their encouragement, criticism and suggestions: and in particular to Mr. T.E. Faber, Miss Alison Tandy, Miss Susan Wolcott, Miss Susanne Morley, and the Man in White Spats.

Eliot's famous children's book is appropriately dedicated to the children of various acquaintances, including his own godson, Tom Faber, the son of Geoffrey Faber of Faber & Faber, the firm that published the book and of which Eliot himself was a director. 'The Man in White Spats', however, was not a cat, but Eliot's friend, the critic and bibliophile John Hayward, with whom Eliot would share a house in Chelsea for eleven years from 1946. The nickname 'Old Possum' was given Eliot by Ezra Pound (see above), and Eliot sometimes signed himself 'T.P.' (Tom Possum) when writing to friends.

T.S. **Eliot**, *Defence of the Islands*, 1941
~ *Defence of the Islands* cannot pretend to be verse, but its date – just after the evacuation from Dunkirk – and occasion have for me a significance which makes me wish to preserve it. McKnight Kauffer was then working for the Ministry of Information. At his request I wrote these lines to accompany an exhibition in New York of photographs illustrating the war effort of Britain. [...] I now dedicate them to the memory of Edward McKnight Kauffer.

T.S. **Eliot,** *To the Indians who Died in Africa,* 1943

~ *To the Indians who Died in Africa* was written at the request of Miss Cornelia Sorabji for *Queen Mary's Book for India* (Harrap & Co. Ltd., 1943). I dedicate it now to Bonamy Dobree, because he liked it and urged me to preserve it.

Bonamy Dobree, who died in 1974, was Professor of English Literature at Leeds University and a noted 'man of letters'.

T.S. **Eliot,** *The Elder Statesman,* 1958

TO MY WIFE

To whom I owe the leaping delight
That quickens my sense in our wakingtime
And the rhythm that governs the repose of our sleepingtime,
    The breathing in unison

Of lovers ...
Who think the same thoughts without need of speech
And babble the same speech without need of meaning:

To you I dedicate this book, to return as best I can
With words a little part of what you have given me.
The words mean what they say, but some have a further meaning
    For you and me only.

These stanzas are very similar to those of Eliot's poem 'A Dedication to my wife', with the first stanzas identical, the second stanza having a first line that continues 'whose bodies smell of each other', and the third stanza being a variation on the verse above. Eliot made the dedication to his second wife, Valerie Fletcher, whom he had married the year before the first performance of this well-known play (at the Edinburgh Festival).

H.F. **Ellis,** *So This is Science!,* 1932

~ To Aristotle, whom I have always regarded with considerable contempt.

A burlesque on the phraseology and practice of popular works on science in the 1930s by a contemporary humorist and *Punch* contributor who describes himself for the purpose as 'Egregius Professor of all the Sciences at the Universities of Oxford and Cambridge'.

Buchi **Emecheta,** *Second-Class Citizen,* 1974

~ To my dear children, Florence, Sylvester, Jake, Christy and Alice, without whose sweet background noises this book would not have been written.

See below.

Buchi **Emecheta,** *Destination Biafra,* 1982

~ I dedicate this work to the memory of many relatives and friends who died in this war, especially my eight-year-old niece, Buchi Emecheta, who died of starvation, and her four-year-old sister Ndidi Emecheta, who died two days afterwards of the same Biafran disease at the CMS refugee centre in Ibuza; also my aunt Ozili Emecheta and my maternal uncle Okolie Okwuekwu, both of whom died of snake bites as they ran into the bush the night the federal forces bombed their way into Ibuza. I also dedicate *Destination Biafra* to the memory of those Ibuza women and their children who were roasted alive in the bush at Nkpotu Ukpe. May the spirit of Umejei, the Father founder of our town, guide you all in death, and may you sleep well.

Buchi Emecheta is a Nigerian novelist who moved to Britain in 1962 at the age of eighteen and overcame very difficult social conditions, as a black woman, to begin to write her novels, of which the second was *Second-Class Citizen* (above). Most of her more recent novels have been set in West Africa, and have shown her keen championship of women's rights and, frequently, her anger at racial injustice and warfare. The novel here is set in Nigeria in the 1960s, and described the events that led up to the bloody birth of Biafra.

George **Etherege**, *The Man of Mode*, 1676

~ To Her Royal Highness The Duchess. Madam, Poets, however they may be modest otherwise, have always too good an opinion of what they write. The world, when it sees this play dedicated to your Royal Highness, will conclude I have more than my share of that vanity. But I hope the honour I have of belonging to you will excuse my presumption. 'Tis the first thing I have produced in your service, and my duty obliges me to what my choice durst not else have aspired. [...] Authors, on these occasions, are never wanting to publish a particular of their patron's virtues and perfections; but your Royal Highness's are so eminently known, that, did I follow their examples, I should but paint those wonders here of which every one already has the idea in his mind. Besides, I do not think it proper to aim at that in prose which is so glorious a subject for verse; in which hereafter if I show more zeal than skill, it will not grieve me much, since I passionately desire to be esteemed a poet than to be thought, Madam, Your Royal Highness's most humble, most obedient, and most faithful servant, George Etherege.

The well-known Restoration comedy, which was the dramatist's last play, was dedicated by Etherege to the Duchess of York, Mary of Modena, second wife of the future King James II. The spelling is modernised here.

❧ F ❧

Frederick William **Faber**, *Hymns*, 1849

~ To the Earl of Arundel and Surrey, these hymns are affectionately inscribed, with the belief that to him it will be the truest token of gratitude for so many kindnesses thus to connect his honoured name with our dear St. Philip.

The final reference here is to the Oratory of St Philip Neri, which Faber had joined the previous year, having become a Roman Catholic three years before that. He later became the head of the London Oratory. Faber was the author of such well-known hymns as 'My God, how wonderful thou art!' and 'Hark! Hark! my soul, angelic songs are swelling'.

Michael **Fairless**, *The Roadmender*, 1901

~ To My Mother: and to Earth, my Mother, whom I love.

See below.

Michael **Fairless**, *The Gathering of Brother Hilarius*, 1901

~ To those dearworthy ones to whom I owe all; I give that which is theirs already.

'Michael Fairless' was the pseudonym of Margaret Fairless Barber, an enormously popular English 'inspirational' writer in the early twentieth century. Her most widely read book was *The Roadmender* (above), which is permeated with her love of nature and her deep religious spirit. The book can still be found by the score in secondhand bookshops, although it makes sentimental, even mawkish reading today. Both the books here were published posthumously, soon after her untimely death from a spinal illness when she was only thirty-two.

Gerald **Fairlie**, *With Prejudice*, 1952

~ This book is written entirely for my own pleasure, and is egotistical in the extreme. [...] I dedicate it to Joan, with my love; and also to those of my friends who, on hearing an attractively repeatable libel about me, would instinctively say: 'I don't believe it of him!' whether or not they did. [...]

The dedication, to the writer's wife, appears as part of the Preface to the book, which is autobiographical. Fairlie was the original of the fictional character Bulldog Drummond, and a friend of his creator, the army officer and novelist 'Sapper' (real name Herman McNeile).

J. Meade **Falkner**, *Moonfleet*, 1898
~ To all Mohunes of Fleet and Moonfleet in Agro Dorcestrensi, Living or Dead.

This is the dedication to the book that brought wide popularity to its author, a children's adventure story set in the eighteenth century and clearly based on, or at any rate inspired by, Stevenson's *Treasure Island*. Moonfleet is the name of a fictional Dorset village, near the sea, said to take its name from the Mohunes, 'a great family who were once lords of all these parts'. Hence the Latin phrase in the dedication meaning 'in the county of Dorchester'. The hero of the book is the boy John Trenchard, who lives in Moonfleet: he is witness to a smuggling, is kidnapped to Holland, and returns to Dorset with a price on his head.

Jeffery **Farnol**, *The Broad Highway*, 1910
~ To Shirley Byron Jevons, the friend of my boyhood ambitions, this work is dedicated as a mark of my gratitude, affection, and esteem.

Jeffery **Farnol**, *The Glad Summer*, 1951
~ Dedicated to my daughter, Charmian Jane, the devoted critic and Sternest Critic of her humble, highly respectful sire: Jeffery Farnol.

Two dedications from the first novel of the prolific novelist and from one of his last, published the year before his death. Most of his stories are of the romantic 'cloak-and-dagger' variety.

Howard **Fast**, *My Glorious Brothers*, 1950
~ To all men, Jew and Gentile, who have laid down their lives in that ancient and unfinished struggle for human freedom and dignity.

Howard **Fast**, *The Establishment*, 1979
~ To Molly. Welcome to this best of all possible worlds.

Many of the American writer's novels have both a historical and a 'class consciousness' theme, as does the first of the two here, set in ancient Israel.

Lt Col P.H. **Fawcett**, *Exploration Fawcett*, 1954
~ The lot of the one left behind is ever the harder. Because of that – because she as my partner in everything shared with me the burden of the work recorded in these pages – this book is dedicated to my wife, 'Cheeky'.

The book is actually a compilation by Brian Fawcett, the son of the explorer, archaeologist and ethnologist, from his father's manuscripts, letters, log-books and other records. Percy Harrison Fawcett disappeared in 1925 in the Matto Grosso, South America, after a series of explorations made in an endeavour to find a mysterious lost city referred to as 'Z'. He was then fifty-seven, and of his twenty-four years of married life, only ten had been spent with his wife.

Leslie **Fiedler,** *Freaks,* 1978

~ To my brother who has no brother, To all my brothers who have no brother.

The book is a factual study of cases of abnormal physical development among humans, that is, of 'freaks'.

Eugene **Field,** *A Little Book of Western Verse,* 1889
TO MARY FIELD FRENCH

1

A dying Mother gave to you
   Her child a many years ago;
How in your gracious love he grew,
   You know, dear, patient heart, you know.

2

The Mother's child you fostered then
   Salutes you now and bids you take
These little children of his pen
   And love them for the author's sake.

3

To you I dedicate this book,
   And, as you read it line by line,
Upon its faults as kindly look
   As you have ever looked on mine.

4

Tardy the offering is and weak, –
   Yet were I happy if I knew
These children had the power to speak
   My love and gratitude to you.

                        E.F.

Eugene Field was the American author of many poems with childhood days as their subject. He seems in some ways to have suffered from a sort of 'childhood regression', perhaps in an attempt to escape the realities of the adult world. His dedication below is self-revelatory in this respect.

Eugene **Field,** *Love Songs of Childhood,* 1894

~ To Mrs Bell Angier. Dearest Aunt: Many years ago you used to rock me to sleep cradling me in your arms and singing me pretty songs. Surely you have not forgotten that time, and I recall it with tenderness. You were very beautiful then. But you are more beautiful now, for in the years that have come and gone since then, the joys and sorrows of maternity have impressed their saintly grace upon the dear face I used to kiss and made your gentler heart gentler still. Beloved lady, in memory of many years to be recalled only in thought, and in token of my gratitude and affection, I bring you these little love songs and reverently I lay them at your feet.

One senses the mood here, a hundred years on, even if a little goes a very long way. See also the dedication above.

Nathan **Field**, *A Woman is a Weathercock*, 1609

~ To any Woman that hath beene no Weather-Cocke. I did determine, not to have Dedicated my Play to any Body, because forty shillings I care not for, and above, few or none will bestowe on these matter, especially falling from so famelesse a pen as mine is yet. And now I looke up, and finde to whom my Dedication is, I feare I am as good as my determination: notwithstanding, I leave a libertie to any Lady or woman, that dares say she hath beene no weather-Cocke, to assume the Title of Patronesse to this my Booke. If she have beene constant, and be so, all I will expect from her for my paynes, is that she will continue so, but till my next Play be printed, wherin she shall see what amendes I have made to her, and all the sex, and so I end my Epistle, without a Latine sentence.

A refreshingly direct dedication to an Elizabethan comedy, and one that reveals how much the usual dedicatory fee for a play was. The Preface to this bawdy comedy explains that the printer had insisted on some sort of dedication, and that he was essentially appealing to the public for sales. 'A woman is a weathercock' expresses the same sexist values as Virgil's 'Mutabile semper femina' and Verdi's 'La donna è mobile'.

Henry **Fielding**, *The History of Tom Jones*, 1749

~ To the Honourable George Lyttleton, Esq.; one of the Lords Commissioners of the Treasury. Sir, Notwithstanding your constant refusal, when I have asked leave to prefix your name to this dedication, I must still insist on my right to desire your protection of this work. To you, Sire, it is owing that this history was ever begun. It was by your desire that I first thought of such a composition. So many years have since past, that you may have, perhaps, forgotten this circumstance: but your desires are to me in the nature of commands; and the impression of them is never to be erased from my memory. Again, Sir, without your assistance this history had never been completed. [...] I mean no more than that I partly owe to you my existence during great part of the time which I have employed in composing it. [...] Lastly, It is owing to you that the history appears what it now is. If there be in this work, as some have been pleased to say, a stronger picture of a truly benevolent mind than is to be found in any other, who that knows you, and a particular acquaintance of yours, will doubt whence that benevolence hath been copied? [...] I will detain you, sir, no longer. Indeed I have run into a preface, while I professed to write a dedication. But how can it be otherwise? I dare not praise you; and the only means I know of to avoid it, when you are in my thoughts, are either to be entirely silent, or to turn my thoughts to some other subject. Pardon, therefore, what I have said in this epistle, not only without your consent, but absolutely against it; and give me at least leave, in this public manner, to declare that I am, with the highest respect and gratitude, Sir, Your most obliged, obedient, humble servant, Henry Fielding.

George Lyttleton, 1st Baron Lyttleton, professionally a prominent politician, was a minor poet but a major patron of his day, the friend not only of Fielding but of Pope, James Thomson and other literary contemporaries. The lengthy dedicatory epistle dwells on Lyttleton's apparent motives for not wanting a dedication to himself, and on the fact that the work is actually as worthy and virtuous as its patron. Fielding based the character of the kindly, generous Mr Allworthy, who first finds the baby Tom Jones, on his patron.

Jane **Findlater** and Mary **Findlater**, *Crossriggs*, 1908
~ To Kate Douglas Wiggin and Nora Archibald Smith, two sisters, from two sisters, Mary and Jane Findlater.

See KATE DOUGLAS WIGGIN's own dedications, below.

H.A.L. **Fisher**, *A History of Europe*, 1935
~ *Laetitiae Sacrum.*

The brief Latin dedication could be understood as 'Devoted to joy', but was actually intended to mean 'Dedicated to Lettice', this being the name of the famous historian's wife, née Ilbert, whom he had married in 1899.

John **Fiske**, *The American Revolution*, 1891
~ To Mrs. Mary Hemenway, in recognition of the rare foresight and public spirit which saved from destruction one of the noblest historic buildings in America, and made it a centre for the teaching of American history and the principles of good citizenship, I dedicate this book.

Mrs Hemenway had preserved the Old South Meeting-House, Boston, where in the late nineteenth century John Fiske had given a course of lectures in aid of the preservation fund. Fiske was Professor of American History at Washington University, St Louis, from 1884.

George Hamlin **Fitch**, *Comfort Found in Good Old Books*, 1911
~ To the memory of my son Harold, my best critic, my other self, whose death has taken the light out of my life.

Julia **Fitzgerald**, *The Jewelled Serpent*, 1984
~ *The Jewelled Serpent* is dedicated to Miss Rita Hayworth, in memory of her unforgettable beauty and grace in the film, *Salome.*

Sir Percy **Fitzgerald**, *Jock of the Bushveld*, 1907
~ It was the youngest of the High Authorities who gravely informed the inquiring Stranger that 'Jock belongs to the Likkle People'! That being so, it is clearly the duty, no less than the privilege, of the Mere Narrator to dedicate the Story of

Jock to Those Keenest and Kindest of Critics, Best of Friends, and Most Delightful of Comrades, 'The Likkle People'.

Sir Percy Fitzgerald, a South African politician and author, is now best remembered for this story of a dog and his master in the South African goldfields. The 'Likkle People' were Fitzgerald's children: three sons and a daughter. He died in 1931, all his sons having predeceased him.

Leonore **Fleischer**, *Dolly*, 1987

~ To the unsinkable Dolly, who has a big brain under that big yellow wig, and a big heart inside that big chest, this book is respectfully dedicated.

The combination of book title and personal description will prompt the reader to identify the dedicatee and biographee. She is of course none other than the great American country-and-western singer, Dolly Parton.

Ella Adelia **Fletcher**, *The Woman Beautiful*, 1900

~ To the lovely women, sixty years young, whose noble womanhood wins beauty from the passing years, this book is inscribed in loving esteem and admiration.

The book has the subtitle: 'A Practical Treatise on the Development and Preservation of Woman's Health and Beauty'.

Giles **Fletcher**, *Of the Russe Common Wealth*, 1591

~ To the Queenes most excellent Majestie. Most gracious Soveraigne, beeyng employed in your Majesties service to the Emperour of Russia, I observed the State, and manners of that Countrey. And having reduced the same into some order, by the way as I returned, I have presumed to offer it in this smal Booke to your most excellent Majestie. [...] The Almightie stil blesse your Highnese with a most long, and happy reigne in this life, and with Christ Jesus in the life to come. Your majesties most humble subject, and servant, G. Fletcher.

Giles Fletcher, English diplomat and writer, had just returned from a two-year appointment as Envoy to Russia, then under the rule of Tsar Feodor I, the son of Ivan the Terrible. His dedication to Queen Elizabeth was no doubt to Her Majesty's pleasing, unlike his actual report, which was in danger of offending the Russian court by its description of that country as 'a Tyrannical state ... without true knowledge of GOD', with a 'poore oppressed people'.

John **Florio**, *Essayes Written in French by Montaigne Done into English*, 1613

~ To the most Royal and Renowmed Majestie of the High-Borne Princesse Anna of Denmarke, By the Grace of God Queene of England, Scotland, France, and Ireland, &c. Imperiall and Incomparable Majestie. Seeing with me, all of me is in your Royall possession, and whatsoever pieces of mine have heretofore, under other starres passed the publike view, come now of right to be under the predomination of a Power, that both contains all their perfections, and hath influences of a more sublime nature. I could not but also take in this part (wherof time had worn-out the edition) which the world hath long since had of mine, and lay it at your Sacred feet, as a memoriall of my devoted dutie, and to shew that where I am, I must be all I am, and can not stand dispersed in my observance, being wholly (and therein happy), Your sacred Majesties most humble and loyall servant, John Florio.

To modern eyes, a convoluted dedication by a man who, nevertheless, was a gifted translator and lexicographer of the day. His translation of Montaigne was popularly received, and gave Shakespeare some of the background material for *The Tempest*. But Florio, the son of an Italian immigrant to England, is still best remembered for his great Italian–English dictionary entitled *A Worlde of Wordes* (1598). He subsequently revised and enlarged this as *Queen Anna's New World of Words*, thus paying tribute to his queen not merely in a dedication but in the very title itself.

Robert **Fludd**, *Utriusque Cosmi … metaphysica, physica, atque technica Historia*, 1617–24

~ To God, the most High, my incomprehensible Creator, may there be glory, praise, honour, blessing, and triumphant victory, world without end. Amen.

Translated from the Latin, and effectively a dedicatory prayer. The Latin title of Fludd's work means 'A metaphysical, physical and technical history of both man and the world'. There was a second dedication, to James I, which by an error in the author's Latin made it seem as if the king was a god. Fludd himself was a physician and prominent Rosicrucian.

Margot **Fonteyn**, *Autobiography*, 1975

~ To Love and Courage.

Perhaps the famous ballerina consciously based her dedication on the familiar 'love and marriage' coupling?

Samuel **Foote**, *The Englishman in Paris*, 1753

~ My Bookseller informs me, that the bulk of his Readers, regarding in a work of this kind the quantity more than the quality, will not be contented without an additional half sheet; and he apprehends that a short Dedication will answer the purpose. But as I have no obligations to any great man or woman in this country, and as I will take care that no production of mine shall want their patronage, I don't know any person whose good office I so much stood in need of as my Bookseller's. Therefore, Mr. Vaillant, I think myself obliged to you for the correctness of the Press, the beauty of the Type, and the goodness of the Paper with which you have decorated this work of, Your humble servant, Sam Foote.

Booksellers not merely sold books but printed, bound and published them down to the early nineteenth century. Today, an author would make an appreciative dedication of this type to his publisher. That few do is of course partly a matter of logistics: the dedication itself has to be printed, in one operation, before it can be published, in another, and pages cannot be added while the work is nearing completion, as they formerly could and as doubtless Foote did in his work.

Ford Madox **Ford**, *The Good Soldier*, 1915

~ My Dear Stella, I have always regarded this as my best book – at any rate as the best book of mine of a pre-war period; and between its writing and the appearance of my next novel nearly ten years must have elapsed, so that whatever I may have since written may be regarded as the work of a different man – as the work of *your* man. For it is certain that without the incentive to live that you offered me I should scarcely have survived the war-period and it is more certain still that without your spurring me again to write it I should never have written it again. And it happens that, by a queer chance, *The Good Soldier* is almost alone amongst my books in being dedicated to no one: Fate must have elected to let it wait the ten years that it waited – for this dedication. [...] And so I subscribe myself in all truth and in the hope that you will accept at once the particular dedication of this book and the general dedication of the edition. Your F.M.F.

The book, generally regarded as Ford's finest and most readable novel, was begun in 1913 on the author's fortieth birthday, and was published the following year. This dedicatory letter, however, was written as a special introduction to the novel in the collected edition of Ford's works published much later in the United States, and is dated 9 January 1927. It is addressed to Stella Bowen, the painter with whom Ford lived in the country after the war, and who later published an account of their relationship, *Drawn from Life* (1940).

John **Ford**, *The Broken Heart*, 1629

~ To the most worthy deserver of the noblest titles in honour, William, Lord Craven, Baron of Hampstead-Marshall. My lord, The glory of a great name, acquired by a greater glory of action, hath in all ages lived the truest chronicle to his own memory. In the practice of which argument, your growth to perfection, even in youth, hath appeared so sincere, so unflattering a penman, that posterity cannot with more delight, read the merit of noble endeavours, than noble endeavours merit thanks from posterity, to be read with delight. Many nations, many eyes have been witnesses of your deserts, and loved them; be pleased, then, with the freedom of your own name, to admit *one*, amongst all, particularly into the list of such as honour a fair example of nobility. [...] Your lordship strove to be known to the world when the world knew you least, by voluntary but excellent attempts; like allowance I plead of being known to your lordship (in this low presumption), by tendering, to a favourable entertainment, a devotion offered from a heart that can be as truly sensible of any least respect as ever profess the owner in my best, my readiest services, a lover of your natural love to virtue. John Ford.

An elegant, even over-ornate tribute by the famous Caroline dramatist to William Craven, Earl of Craven, as a noted patron of letters.

John **Ford**, *'Tis Pity She's a Whore*, 1631

~ To the truly noble John, Earl of Peterborough, Lord Mordaunt, Baron of Turvey. My lord, Where a merit of truth hath a general warrant, there love is but a debt, acknowledgment a justice. Greatness cannot often claim virtue by inheritance; yet, in this, yours appears most eminent, for that you are not more rightly heir to your fortunes than glory shall be to your memory. Sweetness of disposition ennobles a freedom of birth; in both, your lawful interest adds honour to your own name, and mercy to my presumption. Your noble allowance of these first fruits of my leisure, in the action, emboldens my confidence of your as noble construction in this presentment; especially since my service must ever owe particular duty to your favours, by a particular engagement. The gravity of the subject may easily excuse the lightness of the title, otherwise I had been a severe judge against mine own guilt. Princes have vouchsafed grace to trifles offered from a purity of devotion; your lordship may likewise please to admit into your good opinion, with these weak endeavours, the constancy of affection from the sincere lover of your deserts in honour. John Ford.

In among the flattering tributes to his patron, Ford tactfully points out that the seriousness of the subject of his drama (in fact incestuous love) is belied by its apparently flippant title.

E.M. Forster, *The Celestial Omnibus and other stories*, 1911
~ To the memory of the Independent Review.

That is, to the journal that published the author's first story in 1904 but that ceased publication shortly after.

E.M. Forster, *A Passage to India*, 1924
~ To Syed Ross Masood, and to the seventeen years of our friendship.

Masood was a striking and personable Muslim patriot to whom Forster was tutor from 1906 and for whom he developed an intense passion, travelling with him in India in 1912–13.

Frederick Forsyth, *The Odessa File*, 1972
~ To all Press reporters.

The famous thriller involves the hunt by a journalist for a war criminal and his incidental uncovering of a Nazi arms-smuggling ring.

Frederick Forsyth, *The Dogs of War*, 1974
~ For Giorgio, and Christian and Schlee, and Big Marc and Black Johnny, and the others in the unmarked graves. At least we tried.

Dian Fossey, *Gorillas in the Mist*, 1983
~ To the memories of Digit, Uncle Bert, Macho, and Kweli.

Understandably, the author dedicates her book to four of the animals to which it is devoted. Other gorillas featuring in the account are Flossie, Beethoven, Puck, Effie, Marchesa, Old Goat, Rafiki, Icarus and Pantsy.

Helen **Fowler**, *The Intruder*, 1952

~ To Mrs V. Bennett, whose gentle but persistent encouragement has urged more than one of her protégés to efforts they would not otherwise have made.

Frank **Fox**, *Australia*, 1911

~ To the fierce sun of Australia, which tempers man as fire tempers steel; to the gracious sun of Australia, which makes nature teem with bounty; to the glowing sun of Australia, which warms the heart, enkindles the eye, ruddies the cheeks, this is a tribute.

Pamela **Frankau**, *The Winged Horse*, 1953

~ For you, there can be no doubt whose book this is, nor how it came to be written. Nor, I think, need I remind you of the hot grey morning on the highway – with the boat waiting at Pier Ninety – when we first talked of these people. That was three years ago, Levitt was Levitt then, and Carey was Carey. But I was not the person who writes these words; nor were you the person who accepts them today. So I dedicate the finished endeavour to that you, and to this one, and to the alchemy for which I cannot find a name.

The novelist does not name her dedicatee, who was almost certainly not her husband, Marshall Dill, Jr. (Their marriage was later dissolved.) Levitt and Carey are two characters in the book, a story of loves and loyalties in an Anglo–American commercial setting. Frankau, who died in 1967, was the daughter of the novelist Gilbert Frankau and the granddaughter of the novelist Julia Davis, who wrote under the name of 'Frank Danby'.

Julian **Franklyn**, *A Dictionary of Rhyming Slang*, 1960

~ To Eric Partridge, with respect for his learning, admiration of his industriousness, and appreciation of his human qualities.

ERIC PARTRIDGE was a lexicographer who made slang and non-standard English his special study. See his own dedications, below.

George MacDonald **Fraser**, *Royal Flash*, 1970

~ For Kath, again, and for Ronald Colman, Douglas Fairbanks, jun., Errol Flynn, Basil Rathbone, Louis Hayward, Tyrone Power, and all the rest of them.

The writer, famous for his novels (like this one) based on the adult military exploits of Flashman, the bully in *Tom Brown's Schooldays*, dedicated this book, as others, to his wife Kathleen, and here additionally to a selection of film stars.

Michael **Freedland**, *Irving Berlin*, 1974

~ For my children, Fiona, Dani and Jonathan, who had the good sense to choose my wife as their mother.

Maybe not an original device, but a pleasant family tribute, all the same.

Brian **Freemantle**, *Goodbye to an Old Friend*, 1973
~ Only Maureen knows what I mean by 'friend'. So this is her book.

Georg Wilhelm **Freytag**, *Lexicon Arabico–Latinum*, 1830 –7
~ To Frederick William III, King and Most August and Powerful Master, Father of the Fatherland, Protector and Most Liberal Patron of Letters, Arts and all the sciences, This, the fruit of his studies, the height of which is equalled only by the grateful and submissive spirit of devotion, George Wilhelm Freytag, most devoted Worshipper of the Glory of your Kingdom, Gives Greeting (or Dedicates to you).

Translated from the German. The work, an Arabic–Latin dictionary, is dedicated to the King of Prussia.

David **Frost**, *'I Gave Them a Sword': Behind the Scenes of the Nixon Interviews*, 1978
~ To the memory of my father, the Reverend W.J. Paradine Frost, whose example I have tried to follow.

One of the many books by the prolific and hard-hitting reporter and television producer.

Rose **Fyleman**, *The Fairy Green*, 1919
~ To all teachers of little children in general and one in particular.

This was the second collection of children's poems by the English writer who gained immortality with the opening line of her very first published poem, contributed to *Punch* in 1917: 'There are fairies at the bottom of our garden!'.

❦ G ❦

Sandy **Gall**, *Gold Swop*, 1977

~ To Africa, in all her savagery and splendour, and to all my African friends who made this book possible.

A book by the veteran English television reporter and newsreader.

Paul **Gallico**, *The Poseidon Adventure*, 1969

~ For John Tucker Hayward, Yankee Bat-Boy; Admiral U.S.N.; Friend.

John **Galsworthy**, *The Forsyte Saga*, 1922

~ To my wife, I dedicate The Forsyte Saga in its entirety, believing it to be of all my work the least unworthy of one without whose encouragement, sympathy and criticism I could never have become even such a writer as I am.

A self-effacing tribute, in his best-known and finest work, to the author's wife. She was Ada, the former wife of John Galsworthy's first cousin, Arthur John Galsworthy, whom he married in 1905 and who regularly assisted and supported him in his writing. They had no children.

John **Galt**, *The Radical*, 1832

~ To the right honourable Baron Brougham and Vaux, late Lord High Chancellor of England. To you, my Lord, 'the head and front' of our party, I inscribe these sketches. No individual has, with equal vehemence, done so much to rescue first principles from prejudice, or to release property from that obsolete stability into which it has long been the object of society to constrain its natural freedom. To you belongs the singular glory of having had the courage to state even in the British Parliament, 'that there are things which cannot be holden in property'; thus asserting the supremacy of nature over law, and also the right of man to determine for himself the extent of his social privileges. What dogma of greater importance to liberty had been before promulgated? What opinion, more intrepidly declared, has so well deserved the applause and admiration of NATHAN BUTT?

Satirical dedications like this were still flourishing in the nineteenth century. John Galt was a Scots-born essayist and novelist who here published the political 'Autobiography' of one Nathan Butt. His dedicatory words now read strangely, addressed to the distinguished politician, reformer and educationist that Lord Brougham was.

Ernest K. Gann, *Twilight for the Gods*, 1956
~ To the young men of the California Maritime Academy, and their officers, who lead them down to the sea ...

The novel is a maritime adventure set in the 1920s.

Ernest K. Gann, *The Aviator*, 1981
~ For my friends and comrades who pioneered the world aloft. For those who survived ... fair winds. For the many who were lost ... fair winds.

Two books on his favourite subjects, aircraft and ships, by the American author who achieved international fame with his novel *The High and the Mighty* (1953), about the passengers of a disabled plane flying from Hawaii to San Francisco. Gann himself had long and varied experience as an air pilot.

Garcilaso de la Vega, *Tragedies*, 1587
~ To Philip Prince of the Spains: In presuming with audacious temerity to dedicate my unpolished verses to Your Highness, and to submit them to your indulgent patronage, I beseech Your Highness to overlook their defects, and to accept them, not as something deserving of criticism, but as something which will take advantage of your favour to render it safe from slanderers. Then indeed shall I feel myself amply and satisfactorily rewarded for my humble effort, and shall be encouraged to serve Your Highness with other greater efforts. May Our Lord grant Your Highness many long years of prosperity.

Translated from the Spanish. The dedicatee is Philip II of Spain.

Garcilaso de la Vega, *A General History of Peru*, 1617
~ To the Most Glorious Virgin Mary, daughter, mother, and virginal wife of her Creator, supreme princess of all creatures; by the Inca, Garcilaso de la Vega, thy unworthy servant, in adoration of thy worship. [...]

Translated from the Spanish; original title: *Storia General del Perù*. The first paragraph only of a long dedication to the Virgin Mary, by the Peruvian historian (related to the identically named writer above) known as 'El Inca' ('the Inca'), who served in Spain as an army captain fighting the Moors. The translation here is from an English edition of the work, published in two volumes (as was the original) in 1869–71.

Jane Gardam, *Bilgewater*, 1976
~ For WP + $V^A \times 47$, 1918–1965.

The English author Jane Gardam, short-listed for the 1978 Booker Prize with her *God on the Rocks* (1977), is best known as a children's writer. She made her reputation with three psychological novels describing the traumatic 'experience' undergone by their central character, in each case an adolescent girl. The novel here, with its private, even cryptic dedication, was the third to appear.

William **Gardiner**, *The Music of Nature*, 1832

~ To Thomas Moore, Esq. My dear Sir, In dedicating this work to you, I am well aware that the sanction of your name will confer upon it an honor much above its merits; but to whom could I address my performance with so much propriety, as to our greatest Lyric Poet, who has united the *Music of Nature* to his verse, with a success unattained by any other writer of the present age. I am, dear Sir, with great regard, Your obliged and faithful Servant, William Gardiner.

Gardiner was a musical composer (of sorts) who cobbled together extracts from classical composers and revamped them for use in church voluntaries and the like, unabashedly garbling the original melodies and tempi in the process. This book has a descriptive subtitle as follows: 'An Attempt to Prove that what is Passionate and Pleasing in the Art of Singing, Speaking, and Performing upon Musical Instruments, is Derived from the Sounds of the Animated World', in other words, that classical music derives from animal calls, birdsong and the like. The idea may seem absurd, but has been pursued by others since, such as the Cambridge musician David Hindley in the 1980s. The views of the author of *Lalla Rookh* on the subject remain uncertain, and it is not even clear whether Gardiner consulted the poet before dedicating his work to him. See also MOORE's own dedications, below.

Erle Stanley **Gardner**, *The D.A. Breaks an Egg*, 1957

~ I dedicate this mystery of fiction to that expert solver of mysteries in real life, my friend Dr. LeMoyne Snyder.

Snyder was a leading criminologist and personal friend of Gardner, who was working with him on the investigation of a real murder while dictating the final chapters of this book.

Jonathan **Gash**, *Spend Game*, 1980

~ To Wu Ch'ang, ancient Chinese god of wealth and good luck who hands out gold mountains to the humble and pious of heart, this book is humbly and piously dedicated. A story for John and Julie, Susan, Julia and the Port Sunlight Players, Pat and Reg, Elizabeth.

See below.

Jonathan **Gash**, *The Grail Tree*, 1981

~ To the Chinese god Kuan Ti, Guardian of antique dealers and pawnshops, this book is most sincerely and respectfully dedicated. He is also the god of war. Lovejoy. A story for friends in Tripoli, for Tom in dock, Susan, and the Berwick lifeboat men.

See below.

Jonathan **Gash**, *The Sleepers of Erin*, 1983

~ A story for Freda and Gers, for Susan, Glen, Babs, and Yvonne who wanted such a start. This book is dedicated as a humble offering to the memory of the ancient Chinese god T'ai Sui, who afflicts with poverty and pestilence all those who do not dedicate humble offerings to his memory. Lovejoy.

'Jonathan Gash' is the pseudonym of the English bacteriologist Dr John Grant in his successful role as a writer of detective fiction. The detective featuring in all his stories is an antiques dealer named Lovejoy who specialises in Oriental curios. Most of Gash's stories have a double dedication like this, one to the appropriate Chinese deity, and the other to his family, friends and acquaintances. Lovejoy sometimes puts in a comment, too.

Josephine S. **Gates**, *More About Live Dolls*, 1903
~ Dedicated to all the wee Madonnas wherever they may be, whose pure sweet mother love for their dolls is to me a sacred thing, and whose hunger for them to be alive is most pathetic.

Bob **Geldof**, *Is That It?*, 1986
~ To Paula and Fifi, more than words can say ...

The forthright bestselling autobiography of the famous Irish rock star, published in the year that he was awarded the KBE for his humanitarian fund-raising (through his Band Aid and Live Aid charities) and that he married his girlfriend, TV pop programme host Paula Yates. The dedication, which the book reproduces in handwritten facsimile, is thus to his wife and their young daughter Fifi Trixibelle.

Uri **Geller** and Guy Lyon Playfair, *The Geller Effect*, 1986
~ I dedicate this book to all those heads of corporations and individuals who believe in me and whose identity I have to protect.

A somewhat sinister dedication by the great fork-bender and master, or manipulator, of 'mind over matter'.

Eugene D. **Genovese**, *Roll, Jordan, Roll: The World the Slaves Made*, 1975
~ My wife, Elizabeth Fox-Genovese, to whom this book is dedicated, did not type the manuscript, do my research, darn my socks, or do those other wonderful things one reads about in acknowledgments to someone 'without whom this book could not have been written'. Nor did she work so hard on this book that she deserves to be listed as co-author; if she had, she would be listed as co-author. She did, however, take time from writing her doctoral dissertation to criticize each draft, review painstakingly the materials, help me rewrite awkward formulations, and offer countless suggestions, corrections, and revisions. And while under the pressure that anyone who has written a dissertation will readily appreciate, she made an immeasurable if intangible contribution to the writing of this book by living it with me.

An author who can clearly distinguish between what a dedication should be, and what it should not, yet so often is ...

Gerald of Wales, *The History and Topography of Ireland, c.* 1188
~ It pleased your Excellency, invincible king of the English, duke of Normandy, count of Anjou and Aquitaine to send me from your court, with your beloved

John, to Ireland. And there, when I had seen many things not found in other countries and entirely unknown, and at the same time worthy of some wonder because of their novelty, I began to examine everything carefully. [...] I have, therefore, collected everything, and have chosen out some of them. Those which I have thought worthy of being remembered I have, I hope usefully, put together and propose them for your attention – which scarcely any part of history escapes. I could, as others have done, have sent your Highness some small pieces of gold, falcons, or hawks with which the island abounds. But since I thought that a high-minded prince would place little value on things that easily come to be – and just as easily, perish – I decided to send to your Highness those things rather which cannot be lost. By them I shall, through you, instruct posterity. For no age can destroy them.

Translated from the Latin by John J. O'Meara; original title: *Topographia Hibernia*. Gerald of Wales (Giraldus Cambrensis) was a Welsh ecclesiastic and historian who had been sent to Ireland in 1185 by Henry II, to whom he was chaplain, in order to accompany Prince John's military expedition to that land. He compiled his firsthand account of the country and its people while there, and published it on his return.

André **Gide**, *The Counterfeiters*, 1925

~ I dedicate my first novel to Roger Martin du Gard, as a token of profound friendship. A.G.

Translated from the French by AR; original title: *Les Faux-Monnayeurs*. Roger Martin du Gard was a distinguished novelist and dramatist (and Nobel prizewinner) whose own novel, *The Thibaults*, which made his reputation, was being published in seven parts at the time when Gide's work appeared.

Val **Gielgud**, *A Fearful Thing*, 1975

~ My dear Rodney, I have felt for some time that I owed you a book – for two reasons. The first that had it not been for your kindness and generosity in the matter of *Wychwood* I should have had neither the leisure nor the background enabling me to spend a part of my declining years in the writing of fiction. Secondly I feel that your singular determination to spend so much of your time in travelling – to my mind both dangerously and uncomfortably in aeroplanes – demands, almost requires, that you should console yourself with the perusal of works of fiction. Here is one accordingly. And I shall be neither surprised nor affronted if you choose to pass it over to the nearest and most attractive air hostess, or alternatively to leave it at the most convenient airport. And it may amuse you to pick out what it must obviously remind you of: the prejudices and points of view which have so often led to agreeable squabbles in the environment of *Penance Pond*. Ever yours, V.G.

Val Gielgud, the elder brother of the actor John Gielgud, was the Head of Sound Drama at the BBC from 1929 to 1963 and the author of a number of plays and novels, such as the present one, published when he was seventy-five. It is dedicated to his friend Rodney

Millington, who appears from the wording here to have provided, wholly or partly, his home at 'Wychwood' in the village of Barcombe near Lewes, Sussex. (Presumably 'Penance Pond' was in turn the name of Millington's house.) Gielgud died in 1981. For a dedication to him in turn, see DOROTHY SAYERS' play *The Man Born To Be King*, below.

Denis **Gifford**, *The Golden Age of Radio*, 1985

~ For Big, Stinker, Mrs Bagwash, Ernie, Nausea, Lewis the Goat, Basil and Lucy, Mr Walker, and all at Top Flat, Broadcasting House.

A tribute to some of the comedians and characters heard on radio in the 'golden age' of broadcasting, with all the ones here featuring in *Band Wagon*, 1938–9. 'Big' is Arthur Askey ('Big-Hearted Arthur', who had his own comedy series, *Big's Broadcast*); 'Stinker' is Richard Murdoch; 'Mrs Bagwash' is the charlady in the programme, the mother of 'Nausea' and aunt of 'Ernie'; 'Lewis the Goat' is Murdoch's goat, which he kept, together with 'Basil' and 'Lucy', Askey's pigeons, in the 'Top Flat', otherwise on the roof of Broadcasting House. 'Mr Walker' is the cockney comedian Syd Walker. Gifford would have heard all this as a young boy of twelve or so.

Martin **Gilbert**, *The Holocaust*, 1986

~ Dedicated to those Jews who are refused permission to leave the Soviet Union today, whose parents, children, and other relations were murdered in Nazi Europe; and in particular to professor Alexander Lerner, refused an exit visa since 1971, two of whose daughters, aged five and three, were killed by the Nazis in 1941, in the hope that he, and his fellow Jews not allowed to leave, may soon be granted exit visas.

Alexander Lerner is a Russian Jew who provided much firsthand information for Gilbert's detailed and harrowing account of the murder of six million Jews by the Nazis in the Second World War. One of Lerner's daughters, born after the war, was allowed to leave the Soviet Union for Israel, but the professor and his wife (now no longer alive) were constantly refused permission to emigrate to their homeland. Of course, much has happened even since this book was published that could well have altered the situation.

Henry **Glapthorne**, *Poëms*, 1639

~ To the Right Honourable Jerome, Earle of Portland. My Lord, Dedications from some writers are mere customes; from others complements; but from mee neither, my muse being yet too young to be authorised by custome, to intrude upon a Patron, (this being the earliest flight of her ambition:) and my reason too old to suffer mee to be guilty of complement to one so furnished with all reality and worth as is your Lordship. [...]

Glapthorne was only twenty-nine when he wrote this work, dedicated to Jerome Weston, 2nd Earl of Portland. He regards his dedication as differing from the norm, if only because the work is his first.

Henry **Glapthorne**, *The Tragedy of Albertus Wallerstein*, 1640

~ To the great example of Vertue and True Mecenas of Liberall arts, Mr. William

Murrey, of his Majesties Bed-chamber. [...] Works of this nature have alwaies assumed this priviledge to aspire the noblest for their Protectors. Since then authorisd by custome, worthiest Sir, it cannot bee a diminution to your fame, nor repugnant to the gravity of your most serious imployments to have him by publike profession known your servant, who hath long since by particular devotion been the humblest of your honorers, Hen. Glapthorne.

William Murray, 1st Earl of Dysart, had been educated with the young Prince Charles (the future Charles I), and the two boys, who were almost exactly the same age, had become friends. Charles appointed him a Gentleman of the Bedchamber in 1626, and kept him in service from then on. Compare this dedication with the one above.

Oliver **Goldsmith** (attrib.), *The History of Little Goody Two-Shoes*, 1765
~ To all Young Gentlemen and Ladies Who are good, or intend to be good, This Book is inscribed by Their old Friend in St Pauls Church-yard.

It is not certain that Goldsmith was the author of this work, although the Introduction contains his known political sentiments and is one of the main reasons for ascribing it to him. On the other hand, the 'old friend in St Paul's Churchyard' was without any doubt the London bookseller and pioneer children's publisher John Newbery, whose first book specifically for children was *A Little Pretty Pocket Book* (1744). No doubt Goldsmith, if he was the author, was capitalising on Newbury's established reputation. The full title-page of the famous children's story reads nicely as follows: 'The History of Little Goody Two-Shoes; otherwise called, Mrs. Margery Two-Shoes. With the Means by which she Acquired her Learning and Wisdom, and in Consequence thereof her Estate; set forth at large for the Benefit of those, Who from a State of Rags and Care, And having Shoes but half a Pair; Their Fortune and their Fame would fix, And gallop in a Coach and Six. See the original Manuscript in the Vatican at Rome, and the Cuts by Michael Angelo. Illustrated with the Comments of our great modern Critics. London: Printed for J. Newbery, at the Bible and Sun in St. Paul's Church-yard, 1765. Price Six-Pence'.

Oliver **Goldsmith**, *She Stoops to Conquer*, 1773
~ To Samuel Johnson, LL.D. Dear Sir, By inscribing this slight performance to you, I do not mean so much to compliment you as myself. It may do me some honour to inform the public, that I have lived many years in intimacy with you. It may serve the interests of mankind also to inform them, that the greatest wit may be found in a character, without impairing the most unaffected piety. I have, particularly, reason to thank you for your partiality to this performance. The undertaking of a comedy, not merely sentimental, was very dangerous; and Mr. Colman, who saw the piece in its various stages, always thought it so. However, I venture to trust it to the public; and, though it was necessarily delayed till late in the season, I have every reason to be grateful. I am, dear Sir, your most sincere friend, and admirer, Oliver Goldsmith.

Colman, the theatre manager, had been slow to make arrangements for Goldsmith's famous play, and it was thus Dr Johnson who finally persuaded him, by 'a kind of force', to promise that it would be produced, even though he himself predicted that it would be a box office failure. It was enormously successful, although Goldsmith could not bring himself to enter the theatre on the opening night until the last act had started, when he was just in time to hear a solitary hiss.

Joe **Gores**, *Hammett*, 1975
~ For the Op, for the great H.M., *agent provocateur*, and for the ladies, bless 'em, Ev, Milli, Pearl, Dorth, flappers all.

Paula **Gosling**, *Loser's Blues*, 1980
~ To Elaine, Ilsa, Janet, Frances, Liz, Abbie and Emmy – for putting up with my talk, my nonsense ... and all that jazz.

The story centres on a jazz player and his group.

Edmund **Gosse**, *Firdausi in Exile, and Other Poems*, 1896
TO AUSTIN DOBSON
Neighbour of the near domain,
Stay awhile your passing wain!
Though to give is more your way,
Take a gift from me to-day! [...]

The first four of twenty-four lines of verse, saying how the two have for ten years been the 'best of neighbours', have shared critical praise and censure, and so on, and that their names have become linked both as friends and as poets in sympathy with each other. But Gosse was first and foremost a critic and essayist, rather than a poet. See AUSTIN DOBSON's quite different kind of dedication, above.

Stephen **Gosson**, *The School of Abuse*, 1579
~ To the right noble Gentleman, Master Philip Sidney Esquier, Stephene Gosson wisheth health of body, wealth of minde, rewarde of vertue, advauncement of honour, and good successe in godly affaires. [...]

This is merely the opening salutation in a dedicatory epistle that is in essence a justification for his work, which is an attack on poets and actors. The dedication was made to Sir Philip Sidney, the famous courtier and poet, without permission, either with satirical intent or genuinely. Either way, Sidney wrote his *Apology for Poetry* (1595) at least partly as a confutation of Gosson's attack. Compare the next dedication below.

Stephen **Gosson**, *The Ephemerides of Phialo*, 1586
~ [...] It was a custome right worshipfull, among the Heathens, when they had travayled the Seaes, and escaped the danger, to sacrifice some part of their treasure to that god, which they judged to bee their deliverer: and sith it hath beene my fortune to beare sayle in a storme, since my first publishing the *Schoole of Abuse*, and too bee tossed by such as fome without reason, and threaten me death without a cause, feeling not yet my finger ake, I can but acknowledge my safetie in your

worships patronage, and offer you Phialo my chiefest juell, as a manifest pledge of my thankefull heart. [...]

This dedication, like the one above, is to Sir Philip Sidney, and it seems likely that he did not particularly welcome either of them. As Gosson states in his extended maritime metaphor here, he had been attacked after his *School of Abuse*, and now offered this work, a romance, by way of a reply.

Elizabeth **Goudge**, *Towers in the Mist*, 1936

~ Dedicated to my father. 'Here now have you, most dear, and most worthy to be most dear Sir, this idle work of mine; which, I fear, like the spider's web, will be thought fitter to be swept away than worn to any other purpose. But you desired me to do it, and your desire to my heart is an absolute commandment'.

Elizabeth Goudge bases her quotation directly on the famous dedication to SIR PHILIP SIDNEY's *Arcadia*.

Clara E. **Grant**, *Farthing Bundles*, 1929

~ To my neighbours, known as my 'little mates', who have enriched my life and its relationships, I dedicate this book.

A personal account of charity and educational work among poor East End children in London.

Daniel **Green**, *Great Cobbett: The Noblest Agitator*, 1983

~ To E.D.J.G., who may grow up to enjoy Cobbett's company, and to my bankers, who although not in the book trade made this book possible.

A book about William Cobbett, the civil rights activist, and presumably dedicated to the author's son.

Daniel **Green**, *Bunter Sahib*, 1985

~ This work is dedicated *sans permission* but with all due apologies to William Wilberforce, Lord Byron, the Grand Old Duke of York, Charles Lamb, Omar Khayyam, Harriette Wilson, Mary Anne Clarke, Bishop Heber, and to the late Frank Richards.

The book is a fictional account of the life of the great-great-grandfather of Billy Bunter, the famous fat schoolboy in the stories about Greyfriars School by Frank Richards, set in India in the 1820s. The dedication is made to a selection of well-known literary and other nineteenth-century figures, who appear to lack any common link except for the fact that they are all contemporary to this period, if one allows Omar Khayyam to be represented by Edward Fitzgerald's popular free translation of him. Mary Anne Clarke was the mistress of Frederick Augustus, the 'Grand Old Duke of York' (George III's son). Harriette Wilson was a 'woman of fashion' and noted courtesan. All part of the world of Bunter's ancestor.

Roger Lancelyn Green and Walter Hooper, *C.S. Lewis: A Biography*, 1974
~ Fratribus unanimis Clive Staples et Warren Hamilton Lewis hunc librum dedicant scriptores amantissimi.

'The writers dedicate this book most affectionately to the two harmonious brothers Clive Staples and Warren Hamilton Lewis' (translated from the Latin by AR). Warren Hamilton Lewis was the elder brother of the scholar, Christian apologist and children's writer C. S. LEWIS, who died in 1963. See his own dedications, below.

Kate Greenaway, *Marigold Garden*, 1885
> You little girl,
> You little boy,
> With wondering eyes,
> That kindly look,
> In honour of
> Two noble names
> I send the offering
> Of this book.

This is generally regarded as being the best of the picture books by the well-known (and still influential) artist, verse-writer and illustrator of children's books. It would appear to have been dedicated to two particular children, although not Kate Greenaway's own, as she never married.

Graham Greene, *It's a Battlefield*, 1934
~ For David and Anne in London, and for Nils and Ingeborg in Oslo.

A dedication that was only in the first edition of this lesser-known book by Graham Greene, with later editions having no dedication.

Graham Greene, *Journey Without Maps*, 1936
~ To my wife: 'I carry you like a passport everywhere.' – William Plomer: 'Visiting the Caves'.

A later edition of this, published in 1978, had a different dedication: 'To my cousin Barbara Strachwitz'. The book describes Greene's travels in Liberia in the 1930s, when his cousin did in fact accompany him. For particulars of his wife, see *The Heart of the Matter*, below.

Graham Greene, *The Little Train*, 1946
~ To the guard of the twelve o'clock to Brighton.

This was Greene's first picture book for children, originally published anonymously by Eyre and Spottiswoode when he was a director of that London publishing house. Later editions omit the dedication.

Graham Greene, *The Heart of the Matter*, 1948
~ To V.G., L.C.G. and F.C.G.

A family dedication, with V.G. the author's wife Vivien, née Dayrell-Browning, whom he married in 1927, L.C.G. his daughter Lucy Caroline (to whom he also dedicated *Doctor Fischer of Geneva*, see below), and F.C.G. his son Francis.

Graham **Greene**, *The Comedians*, 1965

~ Dear Frere, When you were the head of an great publishing firm I was one of your most devoted authors, and when you ceased to be a publisher, I, like many others on your list, felt it was time to find another home. This is the first novel I have written since then, and I want to offer it to you in memory of more than thirty years of association – a cold word to represent all the advice (which you never expected me to take), all the encouragement (which you never realized I needed), all the affection and fun of the years we shared. [...]

Alexander Stuart Frere became managing director of William Heinemann Ltd in 1932 and the firm's chairman in 1945 (to 1961). Many authors become such firm friends with a publisher's chairman that when the chairman leaves or retires, they take their custom elsewhere, as Greene did. Heinemann published many of Greene's earlier books, but not this one.

Graham **Greene**, *A Sort of Life*, 1971

~ For the survivors, Raymond Greene, Hugh Greene, and Elisabeth Dennys.

Members of Greene's family who, like him, led long and full lives. Raymond Greene, a noted physician and writer on medical matters, was Graham Greene's elder brother. Sir Hugh Greene, who died in 1987, aged seventy-six, was Director General of the BBC and Graham Greene's younger brother. Elisabeth Dennys, née Greene, was Graham Greene's sister, and the wife of Rodney Onslow Dennys, Somerset Herald of Arms, whom she married in 1944, when both were working for the Foreign Office.

Graham **Greene**, *Doctor Fischer of Geneva, or the Bomb Party*, 1980

~ To my daughter, Caroline Bourget, at whose Christmas table at Jongny this story first came to me.

Greene's only daughter was also one of the three dedicatees of *The Heart of the Matter*, above.

Germaine **Greer**, *The Female Eunuch*, 1970

~ This book is dedicated to LILLIAN, who lives with nobody but a colony of New York roaches. [...] Lillian the beautiful who thinks she is ugly, Lillian the indefatigable who thinks she is always tired. It is dedicated to CAROLINE, who danced, but badly, painted, but badly. [...] Caroline who smarts at every attack, and doubts all praise, who has done great things with gentleness and humility, who assaults the authorities with valorous love and cannot be defeated. It is for my fairy godmother, JOY with the green eyes. [...] It is for KASOUNDRA, who makes magic out of skins and skeins and pens. [...] For MARCIA, whose mind contains everything and destroys nothing. [...]

A dedication to five close women friends by the famous feminist author, who gained instant acclaim (or notoriety) with the publication of this book, on the subordinate roles so often played by women.

Lady Augusta **Gregory**, *Seven Short Plays*, 1911

~ To you, W.B. Yeats, good praiser, wholesome dispraiser, heavy-handed judge, open-handed helper of us all, I offer a play of my plays for every night of the week, because you like them, and because you have taught me my trade.

Lady Gregory was an Irish landowner who entered the world of theatre only in her late forties, after her husband's death, with a hidden talent for writing comedies. But for Yeats, she might never have realised this. Both she and he were directors of the famous Abbey Theatre, Dublin, founded in 1904, and in 1911 she took the company on a triumphant visit to America.

Martin **Greif**, *The Gay Book of Days*, 1982

~ For Molly. Vale canis nobilis et fidelis. Sit tibi terra levis.

'Farewell noble and faithful dog. May the earth be light to you' (translated from the Latin by AR). The book itself is 'an evocatively illustrated who's who of who is, was, may have been, probably was, and almost certainly seems to have been gay during the past 5,000 years'. The dedication to the author's dog seems absolutely right in the circumstances.

William Elliot **Griffis**, *Sir William Johnson and the Six Nations*, 1891

~ Like my friend, the late Judge John Sanders, of Scotia, Schenectady County, N.Y., who took off his hat when meeting descendants of the heroes of Oriskany, the bloodiest, the most stubbornly contested, and perhaps the decisive battle in the War of the American Revolution, the writer makes his bow to the people of the Mohawk Valley, and to them, and to the memory of their brave ancestors, dedicates this sketch of one of the Makers of America.

Sir William Johnson was born in Ireland, but went to America in 1838 where he successfully traded with the Indians, especially those of the Six Nations, and was superintendent of Indian affairs from 1855 to 1874, being created a baron in the former year. Griffis was an American clergyman and writer of books on Japan.

Geoffrey **Grigson**, *A Dictionary of British Plant Names*, 1974

~ For *La grande cuisinière (sur une échelle)*.

The 'great cook (on a ladder)' was Grigson's wife Jane, an established writer on cookery. It is fitting that the tribute should be in French, the language of *haute cuisine* (itself perhaps punningly hinted at in the 'ladder' reference). Compare JANE GRIGSON's own dedication below.

Geoffrey **Grigson**, *The Goddess of Love*, 1978

~ Tais Philtatais.

'To the [female] dearest ones', a brief classical dedication by the author of the book, itself a study of Aphrodite, the Greek goddess of love.

Jane **Grigson**, *The Observer Guide to British Cookery*, 1984

~ For all the producers and sellers of good things, for all the chefs, for all the friends and colleagues who have helped so generously with this book.

Jane Grigson was the widow of GEOFFREY GRIGSON (see above), the poet and literary scholar who died in 1985. She herself died in 1990.

George **Grossmith** and Weedon **Grossmith**, *The Diary of a Nobody*, 1892

~ *The Diary of a Nobody* originally appeared in *Punch*, and is re-published by permission of the publishers, Messrs. Bradbury and Agnew. The Diary has been considerably added to. The excellent title was suggested by our mutual friend, F.C. Burnand, to whom we have the great pleasure of dedicating this volume.

SIR F.C. BURNAND was not only the editor of *Punch* (for twenty-six years from 1880) but the author of a number of good-humoured burlesques and theatrical adaptations, together with other popular books. See his own dedication (above) for *A New History of Sandford and Merton*.

Elizabeth **Grymestone**, *Miscelanea, Meditations, Memoratives*, 1604

~ To my loving sonne, Bernye Grymeston. My dearest sonne, there is nothing so strong as the force of love, there is no love so forcible as the love of an affectionate mother to her naturall childe; there is no mother can either more affectionately shew her nature, or more naturally manifest her affection, than in advising her child out of her owne experience, to eschew evill and encline them to do that which is good. [...] Wherefore, with as many good wishes to thee as good will can measure, I abruptly end, desiring God to blesse thee with sorrow for thy sinnes, thankefulnesse for his benefits, feare of his judgments, love of his mercies, mindfulnes of his presence, that living in his feare, thou mayst die in his favor, rest in his peace, rise in his power, remaine in his glory for ever and ever. Thine assured loving Mother, Elizabeth Grymeston.

Elizabeth Grymestone, or Grimston, née Bernye, was a poet and 'moral' writer, who here dedicates her work, mainly on religious topics, to her son Bernye, the only one to survive of her nine children. The book appeared posthumously, the year after her death. The dedication is in the form of a lengthy epistle, and only a brief extract is given here.

Neil M. **Gunn**, *The Green Isle of the Great Deep*, 1944

~ For Old Hector and others like him who were friendly to many a Highland boy, this phantasy.

The Scottish novelist Neil M. Gunn here dedicates his book to one of its central characters, Old Hector, who had appeared in an earlier story, *Young Art and Old Hector* (1942), a pastoral idyll about an old shepherd and a young boy, written as a warning on the dangers of fascism.

Q.F.C. **Guns** and Phyl Theeluker, *Middle Watch Musings*, 1911

~ To our many naval friends who can claim to come under the category of 'cheerful souls', this book is respectfully dedicated by the authors.

A whimsical naval account with equally whimsical pseudonyms for its authors. The first name can be interpreted as 'QF (i.e. quick-firing) sea guns'.

John **Gwynn**, *An Essay on Design*, 1749

~ To His Grace the Duke of Rutland. My Lord, Though this address, made without leave or Application, is perfectly unmixed with mercenary Views, yet Your Grace will give me leave to own that it is not altogether disinterested. I think myself interested in the Honour and Advantage of my country, and consequently in the Arts which I have endeavoured to recommend. I address Your Grace as a Lover and Judge of those Arts, and as a Nobleman whom Fame has long since pointed out for one of their most distinguished Patrons. What is usually said, I may be allowed to repeat. And in respect to that Delicacy, which is always attendant on good Sense, true Taste, generous Education, and the most polite Converse, I will not presume to say more. I am, may it please your Grace, Your Grace's most humble, and most obedient Servant, J. Gwynn.

Gwynn was an architect and one of the founders of the Royal Academy; his book centred on the lack of facilities that then existed for art training. The dedicatee was John Manners, 3rd Duke of Rutland, father of the Marquis of Granby.

❦ H ❦

John **Habberton**, *Helen's Babies*, 1876

~ Everyone knows that there are in the United States hundreds of thousands of fathers and mothers, each one of whom possesses the best children that ever lived. I am, therefore, moved by a sense of the eternal fitness of things to dedicate this little volume to the Parents of the Best Children in the World, with the reminder that it is considered the proper thing for each person to whom a book is dedicated to purchase and read a copy.

This popular children's novel, subtitled 'Some Accounts of their Ways, Innocent, Crafty, Angelic, Impish, Witching, and Repulsive', claimed to be a tale of a holiday in which a young uncle looked after his sister's children, but was actually based on the doings of Habberton's own young sons. By all accounts many of the dedicatees did purchase a copy, or at any rate many parents did, and although at first rejected by many publishers, the book became a bestseller and remained a firm favourite for many years.

H. Rider **Haggard**, *King Solomon's Mines*, 1885

~ This fruitful but unpretending record of a remarkable adventure is hereby respectfully dedicated by the narrator, Allan Quatermain, to all the big and little boys who read it.

Two years later, the hero would have a further series of adventures in a book titled with his name.

H. Rider **Haggard**, *Allan's Wife*, 1889

~ My Dear Macumazahn, It was your native name which I borrowed at the christening of that Allan who has become as well known to me as any other friend I have. It is therefore fitting that I should dedicate to you this, his last tale – the story of his wife, and the history of some further adventures which befell him. [...] Perhaps they will bring back to you some of the long past romance of days that are lost to us. [...] To you then, Macumazahn, in perpetual memory of those eventful years of youth which we passed together in the African towns and on the African veldt, I dedicate these pages, subscribing myself now as always, Your sincere friend, Indanda.

The dedicatee was Rider Haggard's friend Arthur Cochrane. In the story itself, the African name is used of Allan Quatermain, who explains: 'It was from this habit of watching at night that I first got my native name of Macumazahn, which may be roughly translated as "he who sleeps with one eye open".' The adoption of native names by both real and fictional Europeans was quite common, especially those who, like Haggard, were fascinated by Zulu culture. In *King Solomon's Mines* (see above), for example, Sir Henry Curtis is known as Incubu, and Commander John Good as Bongwan. See also the next dedication below.

H. Rider Haggard, *Nada the Lily*, 1892

~ Sompseu: For I will call you by the name that for fifty years has been honoured by every tribe between Zambesi and Cape Agulhas, – I greet you. Sompseu, my father, I have written a book that tells of men and matters of which you know the most of any who still look upon the light; therefore, I set your name within that book and, such as it is, I offer it to you.

The dedicatee here was Sir Theophilus Shepstone, the important South African statesman, who gained the recognition of Cetewayo as king of the Zulus and who annexed the Transvaal in 1877. He was known by the Africans as 'Father' or 'Sompseu' from his great prowess in hunting. The name itself is Zulu for 'mighty hunter'.

H. Rider Haggard, *Regeneration: Being an Account of the Social Work of the Salvation Army in Great Britain*, 1910

~ I dedicate these pages to the Officers and Soldiers of the Salvation Army, in token of my admiration of the self-sacrificing work by which it is their privilege to aid the poor and wretched throughout the world.

A leap to the pragmatic from the author of *She* (1887) and other romantic adventures. It sprang from his appointment in 1905 by the Colonial Office to enquire into the work of the Salvation Army in the United States, with a view to establishing similar settlements in South Africa.

Gordon S. Haight, *George Eliot: A Biography*, 1968

~ To Elinor Southwood Lewes Ouvry.

The dedicatee is the wife of Ernest Carrington Ouvry, born Elinor Lewes, and the granddaughter of George Henry Lewes, George Eliot's 'husband'.

Elizabeth Forsythe Hailey, *Joanna's Husband and David's Wife*, 1986

~ For my father and mother, who were there at the beginning, and for my husband, who had better be there at the end.

Alex Haley, *Roots*, 1976

~ It wasn't planned that *Roots'* researching and writing finally would take twelve years. Just by chance it is being published in the Bicentennial Year of the United States. So I dedicate *Roots* as a birthday offering to my country, within which most of *Roots* happened.

The award-winning family chronicle by the black American writer.

Joseph **Hall**, *Meditations and Vows*, 1605

~ The First Centurie is dedicated to the Right Worshipfull Sir Robert Drurie, Knight, my singular good Patron: All increase of true Honour and vertue. Sir, that I haue made these my homely Aphorismes publike, needs no other reason, but that though the world is furnished with other writings, euen to satietie and surfeit; yet of those which reduce Christianitie to practice, there is (at least) scarcitie enough: wherein (yet) I must needes confesse, I had some eye to my selfe. [...] Why I haue Dedicated them to your name, cannot be strange to any, that knowes you my Patron, and mee your Pastor. The regard of which bond, easily drew me on to consider, that whereas my bodie, which was euer weake, began of late to languish more; it would not be inexpedient (at the worst) to leaue behind me this little monument of that great respect, which I deseruedly beare you. [...] Your Worships humbly deuoted, Ios Hall.

This is the best-remembered work of Joseph Hall, later bishop successively of Exeter and Norwich. At the time of writing this, he was about to take up the post of headmaster of Blundell's School, Devon, but instead an offering of a living at Hawstead, near Bury St Edmunds, Suffolk, came from Lady Drury, and he decided to accept the benefice. However weak of body Hall may have felt himself to be, he lived on for another fifty years, to the age of eighty-two, and became well-known as a writer of classical-style verse satires, as well as an influential churchman.

Radclyffe **Hall**, *Adam's Breed*, 1926

~ Dedicated to our three selves.

Radclyffe **Hall**, *The Master of the House*, 1932

~ To our three selves.

All the writer's books, including *The Well of Loneliness* (1928), her once banned study of lesbian experience, have more or less identical dedications. The 'three selves' are the author herself and her two lovers, Veronica Batten and Lady Una Troubridge.

Charles **Hallock**, *The Fishing Tourist*, 1873

~ To Salmo, King of Game Fish, these few lines are respectfully dedicated by an old retainer.

The American author founded the sportsman's journal *Forest and Stream* in the year this was published, and later edited *Nature's Realm* and *Western Field and Stream*.

Charles **Hamilton**, *The Hedàya*, 1791

~ To Warren Hastings, Esq., late Governor-General of Bengal, etc. Sir, After the labour of several years, I am at last enabled to present you with a translation of the *Hedàya*. To you, Sir, I feel it incumbent upon me to inscribe a work originally projected by yourself, and for some time carried on under your immediate patronage. However humble the translator's abilities, and however imperfect the execution of these volumes may be, yet the design itself does honour to the wisdom and benevolence by which it was suggested. [...] I have the honour to be, with the utmost respect, and the most lively gratitude and esteem, Sir, your most obedient, and most humble Servant, Charles Hamilton.

Hamilton was an Irish orientalist who had been given the task of translating this work from the Persian by the Governor General (Warren Hastings) and Council of Bengal. It took him five years. The work itself, whose title translates as 'Guide', is a commentary on Muslim laws. Warren Hastings, the dedicatee, was the English colonial administrator who only three years before had been impeached for corruption and cruelty in his administration of India.

Olphar **Hamst**, *Handbook of Fictitious Names*, 1868
~ To the memory of Joseph-Marie Quérard I dedicate this humble attempt at emulating him.

Quérard was the author of a fascinating dictionary of apocryphal and pseudonymous writers entitled *Les Supercheries littéraires dévoilées* ('Literary frauds unmasked') (1845–56). Olphar Hamst (whose real name, anagrammatically, was Ralph Thomas) had written a life of Quérard, who had died in 1865, and followed this up with his own, similar work.

Helene **Hanff**, *Underfoot in Show Business*, 1980
~ The day I finished the book, I celebrated by phoning Maxine in Hollywood. 'Do you want to hear the dedication?' I asked her. 'Go ahead,' said Maxine. So I read it to her: To all the stagestruck kids who ever have, or ever will, set out to crash the theatre. 'What do you think of it?' I asked. 'It's MUCH too sentimental,' said Maxine. 'Why don't you just dedicate it to me?' So what the hell – This book is for Maxine.

Helene Hanff's name became well-known in Britain in 1981 with the production of her play *84 Charing Cross Road*, about the correspondence between an American author and the manager of a London bookshop, based on her own correspondence with bookseller Frank Doel. Her earlier work here is dedicated to her friend, the American actress Maxine Stuart.

Helene **Hanff**, *Q's Legacy*, 1985
~ In grateful memory of Sir Arthur Quiller-Couch, 'not to pay a debt but to acknowledge it'.

See some of QUILLER-COUCH's own dedications, below.

Patrick **Hannay**, *Sheretine and Mariana*, 1622
~ To the Trulie Honourable and Noble Lady Lucie Countess of Bedford. It is a continued custome (Right honourable) that what passeth the Presse, is Dedicated to some one of eminent quality: Worth of the personage to whom, or a private respect of the partie by whom it is offered, being chiefe causes thereof, the one for protection and honour, the other for a thankfull remembrance. Moved by both these, I present this small Poem (now exposed to publike censure) to your Honour: first knowing the foreplacing of your Name (for true worth so deservedly well

knowne to the world) will not only be a defence against malignant carpers, but also an addition of grace. Secondly, the obligation of gratitude (whereby I am bound to your Ladyships service) which cannot be cancelled, shall be hereby humbly acknowledged. If it please (that being the end of these endevours) I have my desire. Daine to accept thereof (Madam) with a favourable aspect, whereby I shall be incouraged, and more strictly tyed to remaine, Ever your Honour's, in all humble dutie, Patrick Hannay.

Hannay's heroic-style poem, based on Hungarian history, is almost unread today. But he dedicated it to a popular patron of literature, Lucy Russell, Countess of Bedford, the recipient of similar tributes from such well-known figures as BEN JONSON, JOHN DONNE, MICHAEL DRAYTON and GEORGE CHAPMAN.

George Simon **Harcourt**, 2nd Earl Harcourt, *Account of the Church and Remains of the Manor-house of Stanton Harcourt, in the County of Oxford*, 1808
~ To Richard Gough, Esq., George Simon, Earl Harcourt (although personally unknown to that distinguished antiquary) inscribes the following pages.

It is not so much the work itself here that is of interest, as it is simply a record of very local family history, but the fact that the dedication is made by a nobleman to a 'commoner', and not the other way round, as was more usual. Gough, a noted and now elderly antiquarian (he died the following year, aged seventy-three), was delighted at the tribute.

Julius **Hare**, *The Mission of the Comforter*, 1846
~ To the honoured memory of SAMUEL TAYLOR COLERIDGE, the Christian Philosopher, who through dark and winding paths of speculation was led to the Light, in order that others by his guidance might reach that light, without passing through the darkness, these sermons on the work of the Spirit are dedicated with deep thankfulness and reverence by one of his many pupils whom his writings have helpt to discern the sacred concord and unity of human and Divine truth.

A grave and stately dedication to the author of the *Rime of the Ancient Mariner*. In the original it was set out in fifteen lines of unequal length, forming a cross configuration with the word 'light' at the centre.

Marion **Harland**, *John Knox*, 1900
~ To my friend and pastor, Reverend George Alexander, D.D., whose Scottish ancestors, for three hundred years, bravely kept the Faith he holds and teaches, this Book, written with a willing hand and a full heart, in the Scotland secured to the Protestant Church by John Knox, is affectionately dedicated. Marion Harland.

'Marion Harland' was the pseudonym of Mrs Maria Virginia Terhune, née Hawes, wife of an American clergyman, Edward Payson Terhune, and mother of the American writer of dog stories, Albert Payson Terhune. She herself was a fairly prolific author, publishing her first novel in 1854 and following it with travel accounts, books on household management, and biographies, as here.

Thomas **Harman,** *Caveat or Warening for Commen Cursetors vulgarely called Vagabones,* 1567
~ To the ryght honorable and my singular good Lady, ELIZABETH COUNTES OF SHREWSBURY, Thomas Harman wisheth all joye and perfite felicitie, here and in the worlde to come. [...]

A lengthy dedicatory address to Elizabeth Talbot, Countess of Shrewsbury, follows, together with a similar epistle to the reader. The work itself is a detailed study of beggars and vagrants, subdivided by the author into twenty-four different types, and including a guide to their special cant or vocabulary ('pelting speche'). The Countess was Harman's near neighbour, and he appealed to her as patron for her generosity to such people, 'aboundantly powringe out dayely your ardent and bountifull charytie uppon all such as commeth for reliefe unto your luckly gates'. 'Cursetors' are tramps, people who wander about the country, or what we might today call 'travelling people' (the word is modern English 'cursitor', no longer used in this sense).

Ida Husted **Harper,** *The Life and Work of Susan B. Anthony,* 1899
~ To Women, for whose freedom Susan B. Anthony has given fifty years of noble endeavour, this book is dedicated.

The dedicatee was an American advocate of women's suffrage, and founder (in 1869) of the National Woman Suffrage Association. Susan B. Anthony died in 1906, aged eighty-six.

Joel Chandler **Harris,** ed., *Young Folks Library, Volume II, The Merry Maker: Funny Leaves for the Younger Branches,* 1902
~ Younger Branches: – He who creates laughter creates happiness; come then and laugh at my doings and appreciate me! For where one is found willing and capable to do so, thousands are found whose only pleasure is to make you cry! Laughter is your privilege! Come then and enjoy it, ring a chime of merry little laughs that shall be heard after afar off, and cheer the hearts of those that love you! I love you! I therefore dedicate my pen to you and in this my book draw upon you for thousands of laughs! And be sure you honor my draughts as you all have a great fund at your disposal. Yours affectionately, Krakemsides, castle of Burstenonde-lafen.

A little of this, by the American author of the famous Uncle Remus stories, goes rather a long way. But children will certainly have found much of it grist to their whimsical mill of mirth.

John **Harris,** Navigantium atque Itinerantium Bibliotheca, or a compleat Collection of Voyages and Travels, 1705
~ To the Queen's most excellent Majesty: Madam, Your gracious Acceptance of my late Book, which I had the honour to Dedicate to His Royal Highness, makes me presume to lay this at Your Majesty's Feet. The Discoveries that have been successively made of the Religions, Manners, Customs, Politicks, and Natural Products of all parts of the World, will here give Your Majesty an agreeable and

useful Entertainment: And, I'm sure, it will add to your satisfaction to see, that they have been chiefly made by those of Your Own Nation. [...]

Harris's work, a travel and exploration anthology 'Consisting of above Four Hundred of the Most Authentick Writers', is dedicated to Queen Anne. His earlier work, the first volume of a 'Lexicon Technicum; or an Universal English Dictionary of Arts and Sciences, explaining not only the terms of Art, but the Arts themselves', had been dedicated to her husband, George, Prince of Denmark.

Jane Ellen **Harrison**, *Themis: A Study of the Social Origins of Greek Religion*, 1912
~ TO GILBERT MURRAY, *kharistérion.*

The dedication appears in the second edition of the book, published in 1928, to which Gilbert Murray had contributed an additional 'Excursus on the Ritual Forms Preserved in Greek Tragedy'. Harrison and Murray were not only contemporaries at Cambridge, but classical scholars of considerable standing in their own right, as well as personal friends. The Greek word (in Greek letters in the original) translates as 'in token of thanksgiving'. It is tempting to see it as a private pun on Harrison's surname, but this may be simply a coincidence.

Michael **Harrison**, *The World of Sherlock Holmes*, 1973
~ To Agner Damgaard Henriksen, who, in 1959, was Titularly Invested, as a holder of the Irregular Shilling, in the Conanical *persona* of 'A Case of Identity' – Irregular Greetings! As Director-general of the Danish Baker Street Irregulars (*Sherlock Holmes Klubben i Danmark*), no less than as the dedicated and hardworking Editor for many years of their journal, *Sherlockiana*, Hr. Henriksen has done nobly indeed in 'the Cause of keeping green the Master's memory'. It was with 'The Delicate Case of the King of Scandinavia', as Watson so delicately puts it, that the then unknown Holmes was launched on his glittering, royally-patronized career. It was thus through Scandinavia that Holmes first became known to the world; Scandinavia is still the place where such dedicated Sherlockians as A.D. Henriksen ensure that his fame will endure. So – my heartfelt good wishes to a truly Great Sherlockian, and – in his own language – gid han og hans charmerende familie må nyde al den lykke, som hans ven, Michael Harrison, kunne ønske dem.

The book is a 'biography' of Sherlock Holmes, against a background of (real) contemporary London. The author, a prolific writer on many subjects, from novels to travel commentaries, was an authority on Holmes and his creator Conan Doyle, and like his Danish colleague mentioned here, was invested into the 'Baker Street Irregulars' (the detective police force employed by Holmes in the stories) under the 'Titular Investiture' (i.e., named after a particular story) of 'The Camberwell Poisoning Case', so was thus authorised to 'go everywhere, see everything, overhear everyone' like his fictional counterparts. The Danish greeting at the end translates: 'To him and his charming family, his friend, Michael Harrison, sends very best wishes for all possible happiness'.

Michael **Hartland**, *Seven Steps to Treason*, 1985

~ For my daughters, Ruth and Susanna, neither of whom bears the slightest resemblance to anyone in this book.

L.P. **Hartley**, *Facial Justice*, 1960

~ Dedicated with homage, acknowledgments and apologies to the memory of Nathaniel Hawthorne.

Hartley's story is a fable about life after World War Three, where no choice is left to the individual and where all humans are divided into categories, Alpha to Gamma. The heroine (Jael 97) has Alpha good looks, and thus is 'facially overprivileged', and the cause of discontent among other women. She is therefore obliged to submit to 'Facial Justice' and adopt a new, Beta face, given her by the 'Equalisations (Faces) Centre'. For much of the time she wears a veil to conceal her fresh mask, and this makes it likely that Hartley was inspired by Hawthorne's similar allegorical story, 'The Minister's Black Veil', in *Twice-Told Tales*. In this, a Puritan minister goes through life concealing his face, saying that his veil is a symbol of the curtain that hides every man's heart. Hence Hartley's tribute and acknowledgment to the American writer.

Arnold **Haskell**, *Ballet*, 1938

~ To Ninette de Valois, whose artistry, knowledge, inspiring leadership, consistency, and courage have made the ballet at Sadler's Wells into a national treasure, and who, by doing so, has added an exciting new chapter to the history of the art. And to her company, of the Vic-Wells Ballet, as she would wish. A.L.H.

Dame Ninette de Valois was one of Britain's greatest pioneering ballet dancers and directors, founding the Sadler's Wells Ballet (now the Royal Ballet) in 1931. The 'Vic-Wells Ballet' was a former name for the company, which gave its first performance that year at the Old Vic, then moved to the newly built Sadler's Wells Theatre. Haskell, who died in 1980, was a leading writer on ballet and a governor of both the Royal Ballet and the Royal Ballet School. His book here did much to popularise ballet, which until then had been regarded by many as an even more esoteric art than it is now.

Macdonald **Hastings**, *Mary Celeste: A Centenary Record*, 1972

~ To Susan Harriet Selina Hastings – no mystery she – with her father's love.

The *Mary Celeste* (popularly referred to as the *Marie Celeste*) was a brigantine found abandoned between the Azores and Portugal in 1872, with no trace of the crew. Macdonald Hastings, who died in 1982, was a copious writer on a wide range of subjects, from children's books to shooting and cookery, and was the father of Max Hastings, editor of the *Daily Telegraph*.

William **Hayley**, *A Philosophical, Historical and Moral Essay on Old Maids*, 1785

~ Dear Madam, – Permit me to pay my devotions to you, as the ancients did to their threefold Diana; and to reverence you in three distinct characters; as a Poet, as a Philosopher, and as an Old Maid. Although the latter name may, in vulgar estimation, be held inferior to the two preceding, allow me to say, it is the dignity with which you support the last of these titles, that has chiefly made me wish you to appear as the Protectress of the little volumes, which I have now the honour to lay before you. Your virtues and your talents induce me to consider you as the President of the chaste community, whose interest I have endeavoured to promote in the following performance. [...]

A rather unkind dedication to Mrs Elizabeth Carter, a contemporary poet and writer (and translator), who would have been sixty-eight years old at the time of publication. Not surprisingly, she took offence, and complained that the dedication made her look ridiculous. Despite being known as 'Mrs', she in fact never married, so to that extent could be said to have merited the epithet of 'Old Maid'.

Adrian **Hayter,** *Sheila in the Wind,* 1959

~ I dedicate this book to all those of varied colour, creed, social status and occupation – some of them I still write to, but I never even knew the names of most – who without thought of reward helped me on my way. 'It is nothing,' they said, but without that 'nothing' my own efforts would not have been enough.

The book tells the true story of a sailing venture undertaken on board the yawl *Sheila II*, when the author sailed single-handed from England to his native New Zealand in the 1950s, taking five years over the journey.

Marcella **Hazan,** *The Classic Italian Cookbook,* 1980

~ To Victor, my husband, *con tutto il mio amore e profonda tenerezza.* Without his confidence I would not have started this work, without his support I would soon have abandoned it, without his hand next to mine I would not have given it its final form and expression. His name really belongs on the title page.

The author, born in Italy in 1924, married in 1955, and she and her family now live in New York. The musical Italian tribute really translates itself.

Christopher **Headington,** *Illustrated Dictionary of Musical Terms,* 1980

~ For Peter Corlett, and those other friends for whom learning is a serious delight.

Peter Corlett, a personal friend of the author, was an Oxford schoolmaster and musician whose lifelong experience of music had begun as a boy chorister.

Edward **Heath,** *Travels: People and Places in my Life,* 1977

~ To all those who have made my travels possible, who have accompanied me on my way and who have welcomed me on arrival.

An account by Britain's bachelor prime minister of his peregrinations and general globe-trotting encounters.

Frédérique **Hébrard,** *A Husband's Husband,* 1976

~ To my husband, who I would love even if he were not my husband.

Translated from the French by AR; original title: *Un mari c'est un mari*. The film of this book was directed by the writer's husband, Louis Velle, who played in it, as did their children.

Mary F. **Henderson**, *Practical Cooking*, 1876
~ To my friend, Mrs. Ellen Ewing Sherman, a lady who studies the comforts of her household, these receipts are affectionately dedicated.

Homely homage from one American housewife to another, with 'receipts' our modern 'recipes'.

William Ernest **Henley**, *Poems*, 1898

TO MY WIFE

Take, dear, my little sheaf of songs,
   For, old or new,
All that is good in them belongs
   Only to you;

And, singing as when all was young
   They will recall
Those others, lived by left unsung, –
   The best of all.

Henley is now probably best remembered for the lines 'What have I done for you, England my England, / What is there I would not do, England, my own?' His wife, née Anna Boyle, was a Scottish engineer's daughter. They married in 1878.

A.P. **Herbert**, *Still More Misleading Cases*, 1933
~ To the Right Honourable Viscount Buckmaster, P.C. My Lord, The humble author still delights to have the blessing of a great man printed at the beginning of his book; but he no longer thanks publicly by advertising the great man's virtues. By this respectful epistle I hope to restore an old and gracious custom. You, my Lord, are a great lawyer, a great Liberal, public servant and reformer, a man of courage and chivalry, principle and wit. [...] I should be proud indeed if you would bless this little book with your name and a kind word; but I only dare to ask it because these frolics in jurisprudence are sometimes essays in reform as well, and are shyly intended not only to amuse but to amend. [...] To you, my Lord, with admiration and respect, I dedicate this work. A.P. Herbert.

Viscount Buckmaster, who wrote the Introduction to this book, had been Solicitor General before being appointed Lord Chancellor in 1915. He died the year after the book was published, aged seventy-three. A.P. Herbert's work was the fourth in a series of books on legal cases and anomalies in the law, the earlier ones being *Uncommon Law*, *Misleading Cases in the Common Law* and *More Misleading Cases*.

A.P. **Herbert**, *What a Word!*, 1935
~ To you, my gallant and innumerable Warriors, who have generously supported

me with encouragement and ammunition, my warm thanks, and for reward, this work.

A.P. Herbert's 'Warriors' were his many correspondents, who were encouraged by him to preserve the 'King's English'. The book has the subtitle: 'An Account of the Principles and Progress of "The Word War" conducted in "Punch", to the great Improvement and Delight of the People, and the lasting Benefit of the King's English, with many Ingenious Exercises and Horrible Examples'. The work was typical of 'APH', the popular novelist, legal reformer, and 'word worrier'.

George **Herbert**, *The Temple*, 1633

> Lord my first fruits present themselves to thee.
> Yet not mine neither: for from thee they came
> And must return. Accept of them and me,
> And make us strive who shall sing best thy name.
> > Turn their eyes hither who shall make a gain.
> > Theirs who shall hurt themselves or me, refrain.

Herbert is now best remembered for the hymns that have arisen from his poems, such as 'Teach me my God and King', 'King of Glory, King of Peace', and the popular 'The God of Love my Shepherd is' (with the second word now usually 'King'). This collection of his poems appeared posthumously in the year of his death, and had an address to the reader from the printers, beginning: 'The dedication of this work having been made by the authour to the Divine Majestie onely, how should we now presume to interest any mortall man in the patronage of it?' Despite such material considerations, however, they undertook to publish the poems as they were.

Oliver **Herford**, *The Bashful Earthquake*, 1898

~ To the Illustrator, in grateful acknowledgment of his amiable condescension in lending his exquisite and delicate art to the embellishment of these poor verses, from his sincerest admirer, The Author.

Herford was an English-born American humorist of the whimsical variety, who illustrated his own work. The dedication is thus to himself.

Robert **Herrick**, *Hesperides*, 1648

~ To the Most Illustrious, and Most Hopeful Prince, Charles, Prince of Wales.

> Well may my Book come forth like Publique Day,
> When such a Light as You are leads the way:
> Who are my Works Creator, and alone
> The Flame of it, and the Expansion,
> And look how all those heavenly Lamps acquire
> Light from the Sun, that inexhausted Fire:
> So all my Morne, and Evening Start, from You
> Have their Existence, and their Influence too.
> Full is my Book of Glories: but all These
> By You become Immortall Substances.

Prince Charles, the future Charles II, was eighteen at this time. The work itself is a major collection of poems, over 1,000 in number, with No. 213 describing the birth of the Prince in pastoral, even religious terms, so that shepherds bring the baby gifts like the Magi: 'But is't a trespass if we three / Should wend along his babyship to see?'.

James **Herriot**, *Vets Might Fly*, 1976
~ To my dogs, Hector and Dan, faithful companions of the daily round.

An appropriate dedication by the best-selling author of veterinary fiction, based on his professional experiences.

Maurice **Hewlett**, *Pan and the Young Shepherd*, 1899
~ This book in all love and honour to H.B.H.

A four-line stanza follows: 'What I have is yours; What I do is through you. Take the best of me / To hearten the rest of me.' The dedicatee is the author's wife, Hilda Beatrice Hewlett, née Herbert, whom he had married in 1888. The previous year he had had his initial success with the medieval romance *The Forest Lovers*. Other romances followed (see below for just one).

Maurice **Hewlett**, *The Queen's Quair or, The Six Years' Tragedy*, 1904
~ By his permission and with good reason this tragic essay is inscribed to Andrew Lang.

LANG was himself a prolific writer of historical and romantic novels, and was of Scottish origin. Hewlett's novel here has Mary, Queen of Scots as its central character.

Georgette **Heyer**, *Simon the Coldheart*, 1925
~ To the memory of my father – this, his favourite.

Georgette **Heyer**, *The Conqueror*, 1931
~ To Carola Lenanton, in friendship and in appreciation of her own incomparable work done in the historic manner dear to us both.

Many of Georgette Heyer's historical novels were set in Regency times, but this one has the Norman Conquest of Britain as its theme.

Thor **Heyerdahl**, *Early Man and the Ocean*, 1978
~ To the countless challengers whose opposition made me an admirer of early man and a friend of the living sea. To the erudite experts on whose pioneering work this book entirely depends and who nevertheless left loopholes that made me turn to early man for lessons in fields where there are no surviving authorities.

A more pragmatic work than the author's original book that had brought him worldwide fame forty years earlier, *The Kon-Tiki Expedition*.

Jack **Higgins**, *The Eagle Has Landed*, 1975

~ For my children, Sarah, Ruth, young Sean and little Hannah, who each in their separate ways have suffered and sweated through this one, but most of all for Amy, who has learned to live with that significant little click each time she lifts the telephone for more than two years now ...

'Jack Higgins' is the pseudonym of Harry Patterson, who dedicated this novel about an imaginary Britain under SS rule to his wife and children. (He has since remarried.)

Patricia **Highsmith**, *The Glass Cell*, 1965

~ To my dear cat Spider, born in Palisades, New York, now a resident of Positano, my cellmate for most of these pages.

Patricia **Highsmith**, *People Who Knock on the Door*, 1983

~ To the courage of the Palestinian people and their leaders in the struggle to regain a part of their homeland. This book has nothing to do with their problem.

Nor it has, as it deals with a family and society in crisis in the American Midwest.

John Buxton **Hilton**, *The Anathema Stone*, 1980

~ For Ryan and Miranda, whose hospitality, patience and patio enabled this book to be licked into shape.

Eric **Hiscock**, *The Bells of Hell Go Ting-a-Ling-a-Ling*, 1976

~ To R, who marched away, with love.

The autobiography of the writer noted for his books on boating, navigation and travel.

Katharine L. **Hoare**, *The Art of Tatting*, 1910

~ Dedicated by gracious permission to Her Majesty, the Queen of Roumania, whose love and knowledge of the arts of the thread have never failed to encourage fellow-needlewomen of all classes and in many countries.

That is, to Queen Elizabeth, wife of Carol I, who wrote novels under the pen name of 'Carmen Sylva' and who also provided an introduction to this book.

Jane Aiken **Hodge**, *Red Sky at Night*, 1978

~ For Brigid Brophy and Maureen Duffy and their campaign for Public Lending Right, that is payment for the use of our books in libraries.

A campaign that was successful, with 'PLR' introduced in 1984. But it benefits novelists such as the three ladies named here rather than writers of reference works, whose books in many cases cannot be borrowed from a public library, especially if they have 'Dictionary' in the title!

William **Hogarth**, *The No-Dedication, c.* 1753

~ The No-Dedication, not dedicated to any prince in Christendom, for fear it might be thought an idle piece of arrogance, not dedicated to any man of quality, for fear it might be thought too assuming, not dedicated to any learned body of men, as either of the Universities or the Royal Society, for fear it might be thought an uncommon piece of vanity; nor dedicated to any one particular friend, for fear of offending another; therefore dedicated to nobody; but if for once we may suppose nobody to be everybody, as everybody is often said to be nobody, then this work is dedicated to everybody. By their humble and devoted, William Hogarth.

Hogarth had intended to publish a supplement to his work on aesthetics, *The Analysis of Beauty* (1753), but never got round to it. He did, though, draft this droll dedication for it. It is in a sense a forerunner of 'alternative' publications and programmes of the twentieth century, especially ones that were pastiches of their staid opposite number, such as *Not The Times* and, on television, *Not The Nine O'Clock News*.

Timothy **Holme**, *The Neapolitan Streak*, 1980

~ To the two Johns who insisted that Peroni should live.

A reference to the novel's central character, police inspector Achille Peroni, of the Verona police force.

Oliver Wendell **Holmes**, *The Guardian Angel*, 1867

~ To James T. Fields, a token of kind regard from one of many writers who have found him a wise, faithful, and generous friend.

At the time of publication of this book, Fields was editor of the *Atlantic Monthly*, a distinguished American literary journal founded in 1857 and actually given its name by Holmes (for its Boston base), who became one of its leading contributors.

Winifred **Holtby**, *Anderby Wold*, 1923

~ To David and Alice is dedicated this imaginary story of imaginary events in an imaginary farm.

Winifred **Holtby**, *The Land of Green Ginger*, 1927

~ To a philosopher in Peshawar who said that he wanted something to read.

Winifred **Holtby**, *Mandoa! Mandoa!*, 1933

~ To Vera Brittain, V.S.V.P.L., irrelevantly.

The feminist writer and novelist, who died in 1935 at the age of only thirty-seven, was the subject of Vera Brittain's biographical study, *Testament of Friendship* (1940). The abbreviation, doubtless a privately shared one, may have begun with words such as 'Very Special'. Vera Brittain, also irrelevantly, was the mother of the politician and co-founder of the Social Democratic Party in Britain, Mrs Shirley Williams.

Kenneth **Hopkins**, *Body Blow*, 1962

~ To E.H. Visiak, as dedicated a scholar as Dr Blow, but luckier with his Domestics ...

The story concerns two 'unworldy academics', Dr Blow and Professor Manciple, who are able to solve crimes that baffle the police. E.H. Visiak, aged eighty-four when the novel was published, wrote on a range of academic and other subjects, but was first and foremost an authority on Milton.

William **Hornby**, *The Scourges of Drunkennes*, 1618

~ To all the impious and relentlesse-harted ruffians and roysters under Bacchus' regiment Cornu-apes wisheth remorse of conscience and more increase of grace.

The main dedicatory epistle to this work, whose title page had a woodcut of a wild man holding a whip in his right hand and a pipe in his left, was one in verse to the author's 'loving Kinsman and approved Friend, Mr. Henry Cholmely, Esquire'. This was followed by a metrical address headed as shown here. Hornby was a reformed drunkard, and his poem is a plea to others to follow his example. 'Cornu-apes' is a punning Latin version of his surname, from *cornu*, 'horn' and *apes*, 'bee' (i.e. 'Hornbee'). No doubt he intended his work to be enjoyable, despite its grimly sober subject.

Geoffrey **Household**, *Rogue Male*, 1939

~ To Ben, who knows what it feels like.

The novel, the author's second, which made him famous, is a thriller, in which an 'English man of rank' plans to assassinate a European dictator, presumably Hitler, and is himself hunted over England by an enemy agent.

A.E. **Housman**, *More Poems*, 1936

> They say my verse is sad: no wonder;
>   Its narrow measure spans
> Tears of eternity and sorrow,
>   Not mine, but man's,
>
> This is for all ill-treated fellows
>   Unborn and unbegot,
> For them to read when they're in trouble
>   And I am not.

This collection of Housman's poems appeared posthumously, in the year of his death.

Frankie **Howerd**, *On The Way I Lost It*, 1977

~ For my mother and family. For my friends. For those not so friendly, whose assessments of me are probably the most accurate. For the printers of this book for their seemingly inexhaustible supply of the first-person singular.

A typical mock self-deprecation by the popular comedian for the dedication of his autobiography.

John **Howlett**, *Orange*, 1985

~ To the people of Liverpool, with gratitude for their generosity and good humour; and in the hope that nothing of the sort is ever visited upon them. And for Julian Rouse whose dream suggested this story and whose insistence finally persuaded me to write it.

The novel has an imaginary civil war in Liverpool as its subject.

Geoffrey **Hughes**, *Words in Time: A Social History of the English Vocabulary*, 1988

~ To all workers at the alveary.

An alveary, as distinct from an aviary or even an apiary, is a beehive, and in a figurative sense a dictionary, or the compilers of one. The latter sense derived from a work by the sixteenth-century lexicographer John Baret. This was entitled simply *Alvearie* (1580) and was explained by its author in a note to the reader as being so named 'for the apt similitude betweene the good Scholers and diligent Bees in gathering their waxe and honie into their Hiue'. Hughes could therefore have had any group of dictionary compilers in mind when making his dedication, as his book is about the changing meanings of words over the centuries and the lexicographers who have recorded them. But perhaps he was particularly referring to the compilers of the famous *Oxford English Dictionary*, which he describes as 'the great storehouse of semantic change in English', especially since this was the work from which he extracted much of his material.

Robert M. **Hughes**, *General Johnston*, 1893

~ I take pride in dedicating to the Army of Tennessee, as a tribute to its constancy and valor, this sketch of the great captain who led it in its palmy days, and with whose renown it is inseparably associated.

General Joseph E. Johnston was a leading Confederate general who never experienced a direct defeat in the American Civil War and who commanded the Army of Tennessee in 1864 only to be outmanoeuvred that year by General Sherman and relieved of his post. Even so, he again led the Army the following year, but then surrendered to Sherman. He died in 1891.

Thomas **Hughes**, *Tom Brown's Schooldays*, 1857

~ To Mrs. Arnold of Fox Howe this book is (without her permission) dedicated by the author, who owes more than he can ever acknowledge or forget to her and hers.

The famous school story is set in Rugby School, where Hughes himself had been during the early years of the headmastership of Thomas Arnold. The dedication is thus to Arnold's wife, née Mary Penrose. Fox Howe was the Arnolds' Lake District home. Arnold himself died in 1842, one day short of his forty-eighth birthday.

Victor **Hugo**, *Cromwell*, 1827

~ To my father. Let the book be dedicated to him As the author is devoted to him. V.H.

Translation from the French by AR; original title as in English. The rhyming couplet appears to be Hugo's original.

Victor **Hugo**, *The Toilers of the Sea*, 1866

~ I dedicate this book to the rock of hospitality and of liberty, to that nook of ancient Norman soil where dwells the noble little nation of the sea: to the Isle of Guernsey, severe yet kind, my present asylum, my probable tomb.

Translated from the French; original title: *Les Travailleurs de la mer*. The novel is set in Guernsey, in the Channel Islands, where Hugo lived for fifteen years from 1855, banished from France by Napoleon III. In the event his tomb was none other than the Paris Pantheon.

Robert A. **Hume**, *An Interpretation of India's Religious History*, 1911

~ To my Indian brothers, Christian and non-Christian, with love and hope.

Hume was an American Congregational clergyman and missionary, in India from 1874 to 1926.

Major S. Leigh **Hunt** and Alexander S. Kenny, MRCSE, AKC, *Tropical Trials*, 1883

~ This book is dedicated by the authors to Anna Tatam, as a token of esteem and respect; and, also, as a tribute to the memory of her late husband, by whose bedside, during his last painful illness, contracted when on service in India, she maintained an almost ceaseless vigil extending over many months.

The book has the subtitle, 'A Hand-book for Women in the Tropics', with the credentials of Major Hunt given as 'Madras Army' and of Mr Kenny as 'Demonstrator of Anatomy at King's College, London. Author of "The Tissues and Their Structure," and joint author with Major S. Leigh Hunt of "On Duty under a Tropical Sun.".' Let us not mock: the two men undoubtedly had valuable practical and theoretical advice to impart, much of it gained from experience and their respective professional backgrounds.

Evan **Hunter**, *Love, Dad*, 1981

~ This is for all the sons and daughters, all the mothers and fathers.

The novel depicts the gradual dissolution of a family.

Laurence **Hutton**, *A Boy I Knew, Four Dogs, and Some More Dogs*, 1900

~ To Mark Twain, the creator of Tom Sawyer, one of the best boys I ever knew.

Hutton was primarily an American drama critic, but also wrote a number of chatty little books and collections of reminiscences, like this one. Mark Twain's *Tom Sawyer* had been published in 1876.

William De Witt **Hyde**, *The College Man and the College Woman*, 1906

~ To Theodore Roosevelt, who as legislator, commissioner, secretary, colonel, author, governor, vice-president, president and peacemaker, has wrought in the world what he was taught in college and shown the power for good a college man can be.

Hyde, an educationist and ordained Congregational minister, here summarises Roosevelt's key achievements in basically chronological order. He had become vice president of the United States in 1901, president in 1904, and in 1905 had been instrumental in ending the Russo–Japanese War on signing the Treaty of Portsmouth that year.

❦ I ❦

Brian **Innes**, *The Red Baron*, 1983
~ For Jeffrey, to whom, without this book ...

A rather patent variation on the traditional 'For X, without whom ...' formula.

Dorothy Hammond **Innes**, *What Lands Are These?*, 1981
~ To my Mother, who always used to hope I would write a book some day.

A novel by the wife of HAMMOND INNES.

Hammond **Innes**, *The Doomed Oasis*, 1960
~ To the Royal Air Force and the Officers of the Trucial Oman Scouts, with my admiration for the work they do in circumstances of difficulty, often of great hardship; and with my appreciation of their cooperation, without which this book could not have been written.

Hammond **Innes**, *The Big Footprints*, 1977
~ Dedicated to the memory of Billy, who was my publisher for over thirty years, a friend whose enthusiasm was a constant source of encouragement; that the last book of mine he was to read should have been this story of Africa is strangely appropriate and the best tribute I can offer him.

The author's tribute to Sir William Collins, head of the publishers of the same name, who died in 1976. Collins had supported Hammond Innes as a struggling young writer, providing him with a guaranteed income.

Hammond **Innes**, *Solomons Seal*, 1980
~ For Frances, who has twice helped to smooth our way in the southern hemisphere.

Hammond **Innes**, *The Black Tide*, 1982
~ To Marjory and Ian, in admiration, for reasons that will be apparent to all their many friends.

Wallace Irwin, *Chinatown Ballads*, 1906
~ To the City of Dreams that has passed again to the magic box of the Dreamer, this collection of rhymed memories is affectionately dedicated.

Wallace Irwin was an American journalist and humorist, with this book just one of many.

❧ J ❧

John P. Jackson, *The Passion Play at Ober-Ammergau*, 1880

~ To his most gracious majesty, Ludwig II, King of Bavaria, the illustrious representative of a noble dynasty, under whose fostering care Ober-Ammergau and its sacred tragedy have together grown and flourished for centuries: the genial and high-minded patron of music and the drama in Germany, this volume, which owes so much to his royal favor, is, with permission, most respectfully dedicated.

The dedicatee is now more popularly remembered as the 'mad king of Bavaria' who worshipped Wagner and who commited suicide by drowning. But he was all the same a noted patron of art and music, as witness this tribute.

Naomi Jacob, *Me: A Chronicle about Other People*, 1933

~ To all those people who have helped me, taught me, made me laugh, and shown me what a good place the world can be, and especially to Henrietta Carlotta Francesca Maria Simeone (Simmy) and, because I know that she won't mind his name following hers, a very gallant little Chinese gentleman, whose real name is Hi Ling Choo Foo, but who is always called Sam.

Naomi Jacob, who died in 1964, worked as a teacher, secretary and actress, and after her first novel was published in 1926, became a voluminous writer of fiction. This was her first attempt at autobiography, with a wealth of theatrical anecdotes.

James I, *A Declaration concerning the Proceedings with the States Generall, of the United Provinces of the Low Countreys, in the Cause of D. Conradus Vorstius*, 1642

~ To the Honour of our Lord and Saviour Jesus Christ, the Eternal Sonne of the Eternal Father, the onely THEANTHROPOS, Mediatour and Reconciler of Mankind, In signe of Thankefulnesse, His most humble and most obliged Servant, James, by the Grace of God, King of Great Britaine, France and Ireland, Defender of the Faith, Doeth dedicate, and consecrate this his Declaration.

If lesser mortals dedicate their books to kings and queens, to whom shall a king dedicate his writings? This is the logical, even the only, answer. James was here writing on the nature and attributes of God, in answer to Conrad Vorstius. The dedication, which appears in Latin and French, as well as English, is interesting in being one of the earliest in English to God. The Greek word in the text translates as 'god-man', one of the titles of Christ.

Storm Jameson, *The Hidden River,* 1955
~ For Carol and Carl Brandt, the true authors of this book, with love and respect.

David F. Jamison, *The Life and Times of Bertrand du Guesclin,* 1864
~ To W. Gilmore Simms, Esq., LL.D. My dear Sir: In looking abroad for one to whom I might inscribe this volume, I know of no one to whom I can more worthily dedicate it than to you – to you, my nearest neighbour and one of my oldest friends; to you, who first suggested the work as one suited to my capacity, my tastes, and to what little learning I possessed; who watched over its progress with scarcely less interest than if it had been your own; and who cheered me on, through the years of labour it has cost me, to its final completion now. [...]

A study of the famous fourteenth-century French soldier and Constable of France.

Fred T. Jane, *The British Battle Fleet,* 1912
~ To those who in all ages built the ships of the British Navy, and to the unknown men who have worked those ships and so made possible the fame of many admirals.

A dedication by the founder of such standard military annual publications as *Jane's Fighting Ships* and now *Jane's All the World's Aircraft, Jane's Weapon Systems,* and the like. The first two of these titles had already appeared by the time this book was published.

Francis Jeffrey, *Essays,* 1848
~ To the Reverend SYDNEY SMITH, the original projector of the Edinburgh review, long its brightest ornament, and always my true and indulgent friend, I now dedicate this republication from love of recollections, and in token of unchanged affection and esteem. F. JEFFREY.

Jeffrey and Sydney Smith had been joint founders of the *Edinburgh Review* in 1802, and Jeffrey was its editor until 1829. Sydney Smith, as an essayist and wit, has remained the greater literary luminary, however. The quarterly *Edinburgh Review,* one of the most influential critical journals of its day, was published regularly until 1929.

Herbert Jenkins, *Bindle,* 1916
~ To my mother, who as her son's best friend is probably his worst critic.

Jerome K. Jerome, *The Idle Thoughts of an Idle Fellow,* 1886
~ To the very dear and well beloved Friend of my prosperous and evil days. To the friend, who, though in the early stages of our acquaintanceship, he did ofttimes disagree with me, has since come to be my very warmest comrade. To the friend who, however often I may put him out, never (now) upsets me in revenge. To the friend who, treated with marked coldness by all the female members of my household, and regarded with suspicion by my very dog, nevertheless, seems day by day to be more drawn by me, and in return, to more and more impregnate me with the odour of his friendship. To the friend who never tells me of my faults,

never wants to borrow money, and never talks about himself. To the companion of my idle hours, the soother of my sorrows, the confidant of my joys and hopes, my oldest and strongest Pipe, this little volume is gratefully and affectionately dedicated.

A nice dedication, whose puns and gentle humour give extra value the second time round, once the identity of the 'dedicatee' is revealed.

Annie Fellows **Johnston**, *The Little Colonel's Holidays*, 1901
~ Dedicated to 'the Little Captain' and his sisters, whose proudest heritage is that they bear the name of a Nation's hero.

One of a series of children's stories about 'the Little Colonel', with which the American author made her name. The first such story was *The Little Colonel* (1895) itself, telling the tale of Lloyd Sherman, a little American girl living in the South after the Civil War. The 'Nation's hero' then was General Sherman, while 'the Little Colonel' is the girl's nickname, given her because she has a temper matching that of her grandfather, 'the Old Colonel', otherwise Colonel Lloyd, an ex-Confederate soldier. 'The Little Captain', the dedicatee here, is thus the girl's brother.

R.F. **Johnston**, *From Peking to Mandalay*, 1908
~ To David Playfair Heatley, whose presence in the east would bring happiness to exile, and whose absence in the west has caused his banished friend to turn many times with longing to the setting sun.

See below.

R.F. **Johnston**, *Lion and Dragon in Northern China*, 1910
~ To Sir James Haldane Stewart Lockhart, K.C.M.G., Commissioner of Weihaiwei, in memory of two moonlit nights at Lutao-K'ou, five frosty mornings at Pei-k'ou temple, and a hundred breezy gallops over the hills and sands of Weihaiwei.

Sir Reginald Fleming Johnston was a colonial administrator and scholar who had a lifelong link with China, holding various government posts there and making a series of intrepid journeys into the interior, either alone or with his bull terrier. In 1904 he was seconded to Weihaiwei as assistant to Sir James Lockhart, the commissioner, and dedicated his second book on China to him. He later became a virtual Buddhist, adopted a Chinese name (Lin Shao Yang), and became tutor to the young Chinese emperor, Hsuan Tung (P'u-i), then still in his teens. He died in 1938.

Graham **Jones**, *Own Goals*, 1985
~ This book is dedicated to goalkeepers and journalists everywhere (the risks are about the same). And to the players, staff and supporters of Halifax Town football club. If anyone needs cheering up, you do.

The book is a compilation of verbal and other gaffes, made by people who have 'opened their mouth and put their foot in it'. Jones is himself a journalist, and a self-confessed perpetrator of such errors, such as his pronouncement that 'Sheffield United are in the First Division to stay'. They promptly plummeted to the fourth division.

Tristan **Jones**, *A Star to Steer Her By*, 1985
~ To the meek, who shall inherit what's left of the earth, and to Ivan Buenza Gonzalez, of San Sebastian, Spain, for his intense loyalty in difficult times.

The book tells how a one-legged sailor crossed the Atlantic single-handed on board the 'Outward Leg'.

Erica **Jong**, *Fear of Flying*, 1973
~ For Grace Darling Griffin. And for my grandfather, Samuel Mirsky.

A novel that with its uninhibited and explicit sexual narrative would doubtless be an eye-opener to many grandfathers. But presumably not Samuel Mirsky. Or was this his granddaughter's way of opening his eyes after all?

Ben **Jonson**, *Volpone, or The Fox*, 1607
~ To the Most Noble and Most Equal Sisters, the Two Famous Universities, For Their Love and Acceptance Shown to His Poem in the Presentation; Ben Jonson, The Grateful Acknowledger Dedicates Both It and Himself. There follows an Epistle, if you dare venture on the length. [...]

Jonson tactfully addresses both Oxford and Cambridge Universities as 'equal', and his 'lengthy epistle' (which is spared readers here) states his aims in writing comedies. 'In the Presentation' means 'in performance'.

Ben **Jonson**, *The Alchemist*, 1610
~ To the Lady, Most Deserving her Name, and Blood: Mary, Lady Wroth. Madam, In the age of sacrifices, the truth of religion was not in the greatness, and fat of the offerings, but in the devotion, and zeal of the sacrificers: else, what could a handful of gums have done at the sight of a hecatomb? Or, how might I appear at this altar, except with those affections, that no less love the light and witness, than they have the conscience of your virtue? If what I offer bear an acceptable odour, and hold the first strength, it is your value of it, which remembers, where, when, and to whom it was kindled. Otherwise, as the times are, there comes rarely forth that thing, so full of authority, or example, but by assiduity and custom, grows less, and loses. This, yet, safe in your judgment (which is a Sidney's) is forbidden to speak more; lest it talk, or look like one of the ambitious faces of the time: who, the more they paint, are the less themselves. Your Ladyship's true honourer, Ben Jonson.

Lady Mary Wroth, whose name could also be spelt 'Worth' (hence 'most deserving her name'), was the eldest daughter of the 1st Earl of Leicester, and a niece of Sir Philip Sidney. She married Sir Robert Wroth in 1604. The somewhat baffling first sentence of the dedication is a direct reference to a passage in Seneca's *De Beneficiis* (I, vi, 2), a work that includes several examples of heroic self-sacrifice. Lady Mary is also included in the multiple dedication to GEORGE CHAPMAN's *Homer's Iliad*.

Ben **Jonson**, *The New Inn*, 1631

~ To the Reader. If thou be such, I make thee my patron, and dedicate the piece to thee: if not so much, would I had been after the charge of thy better literature. Howsoever, if thou canst but spell, and join my sense, there is more hope of thee, than of a hundred fastidious impertinents, who were there present the first day, yet never made piece of the prospect the right way. [...] So do I trust myself and my book, rather to thy rustic candour, than all the pomp of their pride, and solemn ignorance to boot. Fare thee well, and fall to. Read. Ben Jonson.

Jonson's comedy was poorly received on its first performance, and was not even heard out by many. Hence his direct appeal to the members of his audience. When first published, in 1629, it had the following subtitle: 'As It Was Never Acted, but Most negligently Played by Some; the King's Servants; and More Squeamishly Beheld and Censur'd by Others, the King's Subjects'. This later edition was subtitled: 'Now at Last Set at Liberty to the Readers, His Majesty's Servants and Subjects, to Be Judg'd of'.

Kate **Jordan**, *The Creeping Tides*, 1913

~ To John Masefield: An expression of appreciation, and because years ago, when shipwrecked in New York, he drifted to harbor among the old streets of Greenwich Village, where this story is laid. [...]

A quotation from Masefield's *The Tragedy of Man* follows. Kate Jordan was an Irish-American novelist and dramatist, who died in 1926.

Michael **Joseph**, *Charles: The Story of a Friendship*, 1943

~ To Eleanor Farjeon, who understands.

Charles was Michael Joseph's beloved Siamese cat Charles O'Malley, whom he acquired in 1930. The book was published in the year after Charles's death. Eleanor Farjeon, the fine children's writer, was equally a cat lover. Compare the next dedication below for more of the same.

Michael **Joseph**, *Cat's Company*, 1946

~ This book, originally dedicated (in 1930) to 'My little daughter Shirley who loves cats and "tikkens" as much as I do' is now dedicated to my daughter Shirley, who is no longer little, and no longer calls them 'tikkens', but still loves cats.

The daughter of the well-known publisher was born in 1928, so would have been two years old at the time of the book's original publication, and twenty-eight when the second edition appeared.

André **Jute**, *Reverse Negative*, 1980

~ For my Mother, who held faith, and for Roz, who held dinner, and for Stuart, who held forth.

❦ K ❦

Nikolai **Karamzin,** *A History of the Russian State,* 1816–17

~ To His Majesty Emperor Alexander Pavlovich, Autocrat of all the Russias. Most Gracious Majesty, I offer Your Imperial Majesty with veneration the fruit of my ardent labours of twelve years. I do not boast of zeal and constancy: encouraged by You, how could I not have these? In 1811, in the happiest and most memorable moments of my life, I read to You, Sire, certain chapters of this History – on the horrors of Batu's invasion, and the exploits of the hero, Dmitry Donskoi – at a time when a dense cloud of woes hung over Europe, equally threatening our dear fatherland. You listened to me with wondrous attention, and you compared the long-gone past with the present, and did not envy the glorious dangers of Dmitry, for you foresaw even more glorious dangers for yourself. The magnanimous presentiment was fulfilled: the cloud broke over Russia, but we were saved, we were glorified. The enemy was destroyed, Europe was liberated, and the head of Alexander shone in the resplendent wreath of immortality. Sire, if the happiness of Your virtuous heart equals Your glory, then You are the happiest of all mortals. A new age dawned. The future is known only to God, but we, to judge by the potential of our reasoning, await a secure peace, so desired for the people and the Crowned Heads, who wish to rule for the good of their people, and for the progress of morality, virtue, Science, Art, and welfare both public and private. Having by victory removed the obstacles in this truly Royal action, having bestowed a golden peace upon both us and Europe, what will You, Sire, not accomplish in the vigour of your manliness, in the course of the long life that is promised to You both by the laws of Nature and the fervent prayers of Your subjects! Be vigilant, beloved Monarch! The reader of the human heart reads the thoughts, History tells the deeds of magnanimous sovereigns and inspires her most remote posterity with love for their sacred memory. Grant your favourable acceptance to this book which serves as proof of this. The History of the people belongs to the Tsar. Most Gracious Majesty! Your Imperial Majesty's loyal subject, Nikolai Karamzin.

Translated from the Russian by AR; original title: *Istoriya gosudarstva Rossiyskogo.* A grandiose yet genuine personal tribute to Alexander I by one of Russia's most influential writers, prefacing his major historical work. Batu Khan, the grandson of Genghis Khan (Chingiz Khan), was the Mongol ruler who led the army that conquered Russia, Poland and Hungary in the thirteenth century; Dmitry Donskoi was the Russian prince who won a major victory over the Golden Horde at the Battle of Kulikovo a century later. Alexander I had joined the coalition against Napoleon and had helped destroy his retreating army.

Leonard **Katz**, *Uncle Frank: The Biography of Frank Costello*, 1974
~ The old man died on December 5, 1971. Except for his family the event could hardly be called a tragedy. Just an old man who died at the age of 79. The old man was my father, Joseph Katz, a New York City cab driver for most of his life. […] I miss him very much and lovingly dedicate this book to his memory. Leonard Katz.

George S. **Kaufman** and Moss Hart, *The Man Who Came to Dinner*, 1939
~ To Alexander Woollcot, for reasons that are nobody's business.

Alexander Woollcot, the acid-tongued American columnist and critic, was the inspiration for this play's central character, Sheridan Whiteside. The co-authors could not initially agree on the wording of the dedication, so eventually came up with this compromise. Many moviegoers will happily recall the excellent film version of the play, first screened in 1941. In this, Whiteside was played by Monty Woolley, who had made his name in the stage role.

James **Kavanagh**, *The Celibates*, 1985
~ To my brother Bob, who left the priesthood but lived and died a priest. To all the former priests and nuns who lovingly labored among the people and would labor still if law and history could submit to reality and love! To Gene Burk, John David Hamilton and Gerry.

A story in which priests are tempted to leave the ministry with its obligatory vows of celibacy.

Richard **Kearton**, *Wild Life at Home*, 1901
~ To a host of dear old comrades, toiling within sound of the beloved hum of Fleet Street.

John **Keats**, *Poems*, 1817

TO LEIGH HUNT, ESQ.

Glory and loveliness have passed away;
  For if we wander out in early morn,
  No wreathed incense do we see upborne
Into the east, to meet the smiling day:
No crowd of nymphs soft voic'd and young, and gay,
  In woven baskets bringing ears of corn,
  Roses, and pinks, and violets, to adorn
The shrine of Flora in her early May.
But there are left delights as high as these,

And I shall ever bless my destiny,
That in a time, when under pleasant trees
    Pan is no longer sought, I feel a free,
A leafy luxury, seeing I could please
    With these poor offerings, a man like thee.

A dedication to the well-known poet, critic and champion of Romanticism. Keats was obliged to move fast: 'On the evening when the last proof-sheet was brought from the printer, it was accompanied by the information that if a "dedication to the book was intended it must be sent forthwith". Whereupon he withdrew to a side-table, and in the buzz of a mixed conversation, ... he composed and brought to Charles Ollier, the publisher, the Dedication Sonnet to Leigh Hunt' (Charles and Mary Cowden Clarke, 'Recollections of Writers', in Buxton Forman's edition of Keats, vol. 4). Hunt essentially replied in kind in the first sonnet in his *Foliage* (1818):

TO JOHN KEATS

'Tis well you think me truly one of those,
Whose sense discerns the loveliness of things;
For surely as I feel the bird that sings
Behind the leaves, or dawn as up it grows,
Or the rich bee rejoicing as he goes,
Or the glad issue of emerging springs,
Or overhead the glide of a dove's wings,
Or turf, or trees, or midst of all repose;
And surely as I feel things lovelier still,
The human look, and the harmonious form
Containing woman, and the smile in ill,
And such a heart as Charles's, wise and warm, –
    As surely as all this, I see, ev'n now,
    Young Keats, a flowering laurel on your brow.

There is little doubt which is the better poet. Still, Hunt strongly supported Keats, as a Romantic, and in 1816 printed his early sonnet 'O Solitude' in *The Examiner*, as well as other poems subsequently. Charles here is the publisher mentioned, Charles Ollier, who already published Hunt, and who through him came to publish Keats. These *Poems* were not a success, however, which Keats attributed to Ollier's apathy, and he thereafter changed to another publisher. Compare the next dedication below.

John **Keats**, *Endymion: A Poetic Romance*, 1818
~ Inscribed to the Memory of Thomas Chatterton.

That is, to the 'Boy Poet', who had committed suicide in a lonely London garret at the age of only eighteen in 1770. But this was not the original dedication. That was: 'Inscribed, with every feeling of pride and regret and with "a bowed mind", to the memory of the most English of poets except Shakespeare, Thomas Chatterton'. Keats's original Preface referred to this earlier version: 'One word more – for we cannot help seeing our own affairs in every point of view – should anyone call my dedication to Chatterton affected I answer as followeth: "Were I dead, Sir, I should like a Book dedicated to me".' However, John

Hamilton Reynolds, a poet and close friend of Keats, together with other friends, advised that both the original dedication *and* the preface were unsuitable, so that Keats wrote back, in a letter of 9 April 1818, 'Since you all agree that the thing is bad, it must be so', and proposed the shorter dedication, as above.

Harriet L. **Keeler,** *Our Native Trees and How to Identify Them,* 1900
~ To the memory of Phyllis and Nicholas, my loving companions through field and wood, this volume is dedicated.

The identity of the dedicatees, which can perhaps be guessed anyway, is confirmed when one sees the picture of two dogs under the names.

Helen **Keller,** *The Story of My Life,* 1902
~ To Alexander Graham Bell, who has taught the deaf to speak and enabled the listening ear to hear speech from the Atlantic to the Rockies, I dedicate this story of my life.

A famous dedicator and dedicatee here. Through illness, Helen Keller became blind, deaf and dumb before she was even two years old. She grew up to lecture in America and abroad on behalf of the blind, and wrote many books while working for social reform. This book appeared when her 'life' was still only twenty-two years old. She died aged eighty-eight in 1968. Alexander Graham Bell, of course, was not only the inventor of the telephone but a pioneer in training teachers of the deaf.

Kitty **Kelley,** *Elizabeth Taylor: The Last Star,* 1981
~ Nino de su rubia osita – siempre.

A private Italian dedication for this biography of the famous film star. It translates: 'Little boy, from his little blonde bear – always'.

William **Kemp,** *Kemp's Nine Daies Wonder,* 1600
~ To the true Ennobled Lady, and his most bountifull Mistris, Mistris Anne Fitton, Mayde of honour to the most sacred Mayde Royall Queene Elizabeth. Honorable Mistris, In the waine of my little wit, I am forst to desire your protection, else every Ballad-singer will proclaime me bankrupt of honesty. [...] Three reasons moove mee to make publik this journey, one to reprove lying fooles I never knew: the other, to commend loving friends, which, by the way, I daily found: the third, to shew my duety to your honorable selfe, whose favours (among other bountiful friends) makes me (dispight of this sad world) judge my hart Corke, & my heeles feathers, so that, methinkes, I could flye to Rome (at least, hop to Rome, as the olde Proverb is) with a morter on my head. In which light conceite, I lowly begge pardon and leave, for my Tabrer strikes his hunts up, I must to Norwich. Imagine, Noble Mistris, I am now setting from my Lord Mayors, the houre, about seaven; the morning, gloomy; the company, many; my hart, merry. Your worthy Ladyships most unworthy servant, William Kemp.

William Kemp, a friend of Shakespeare, was a comedian and dancer who became popular through his jigs at the end of plays. In 1599 he undertook to dance a morris dance from London to Norwich. The work here is an account of that journey, which took him twenty-three days (of which only nineteen were spent actually dancing). Kemp seems to have confused the dedicatee, 'Mistris Anne Fitton', with her younger sister, Mary Fitton, who was (as he says) Maid of Honour to Queen Elizabeth and (as he does not say, but appropriately) famous for the dances she performed in court masques.

Henry Clarence **Kendall**, *Australasia*, 1880

TO A MOUNTAIN

To thee, O father of the stately peaks,
Above me in the loftier light – to thee,
Imperial brother of those awful hills,
Whose feet are set in splendid spheres of flame,
Whose heads are where the gods are, and whose sides
Of strength are belted round with all the zones –
Of all the world, I dedicate these songs. [...]

Kendall, who died in 1882, aged forty-one, was an Australian journalist and poet who wrote a number of evocative, if lightweight, descriptive poems on the Australian landscape, and in particular on the bush and (as here) mountain scenery. This is just the first of several stanzas dedicated to a mountain, no doubt a particular one, but unnamed here.

Edward **Kenealy**, *Poems*, 1864

~ To the Right Honourable Sir ALEXANDER EDMUND COCKBURN, Bart., Lord Chief Justice of England, etc., etc., etc., this volume is most respectfully inscribed by one, who shares in the fervent admiration, honour, and regard which the whole Bar feel, for the Judge, the Jurist, and the Scholar.

A dedication that reads strangely when considered against subsequent events. Kenealy, a barrister, was leading counsel for Arthur Orton, the 'Tichborne Claimant' (who professed to be the eldest son, actually lost at sea, of Sir James Tichborne, and so inherit his estate), but conducted the case so grotesquely and coarsely, while simultaneously making scurrilous statements about his colleagues, including his former friend Sir Alexander Cockburn, that he was professionally disbenched and disbarred. This was in 1874, only ten years after the polite and keenly appreciative tribute here.

Gerald **Kersh**, *They Die With Their Boots Clean*, 1942

~ From Guardsman Gerald Kersh, No. 2663141, Coldstream Guards, to Sergeant Bill (Spider) Kelly; Trained Soldier Phillips; Sergeant Ding-Dong Bell of the Musketry Class; [etc.] We had some good times in Caterham. [...] These are good fellows, They are the backbone of things. Therefore, to them, this book, unworthy as it is, is dedicated. Gerald Kersh.

A readable, firsthand description of life in the army ranks in the Second World War. The author lists around fifty of his army 'other ranks' cronies by name (and nickname) in this expansive dedication.

Gerald **Kersh**, *Brain and Ten Fingers*, 1943

~ TO CHARLES EVANS. [...] This book is for the people of Jugoslavia; good people in trouble. It was written for a people – or rather, for the indomitable spirit of a people. But I want to dedicate it to you, as a token of personal affection and old-established admiration. In publishing *Brain and Ten Fingers* you are helping me to express my goodwill to the people about whom it was written: I am grateful to you for this, as for certain other things. I think that you are a good man, and regard you as a good friend; and so I beg you not to allow your natural modesty to prevent your acceptance of this dedication.

Charles Evans was chairman of Kersh's publishers, William Heinemann. The book is a novel about the lives and deeds of Yugoslav guerrillas in the Second World War.

Ken **Kesey**, *One Flew Over the Cuckoo's Nest*, 1962

~ To Vik Lovell, who told me dragons did not exist, then led me to their lairs.

The American author's famous novel about the inmates of a psychiatric ward, later brilliantly filmed (1975) with Jack Nicholson in the main role as McMurphy.

Frances Parkinson **Keyes**, *Lady Blanche Farm*, 1940

~ To Catherine and Henry Deming, whose efficient, faithful and devoted service has lightened my labours as a housekeeper and facilitated my progress as an author, I dedicate this book with gratitude and affection.

Frances Parkinson **Keyes**, *Joy Street*, 1951

~ To Lebaron Barker, who kept insisting that this book must be written until I gave in and did it, and to the memory of Elizabeth Soule Sweetser, who long before Lebaron Barker was born, and also long before he or anyone else thought of me as an author, was confident that some day I would write books which would be a credit to the Boston of which she was the fine flower.

When this was published, Frances Parkinson Keyes, née Wheeler, was at the height of her long and productive life as a novelist. She died, aged eighty-five, in 1970.

Martha A. **Kidder**, *Æonian Echoes*, 1911

TO MY FATHER AND MOTHER

Father, who trained my youthful mind,
My sternest critic, just and kind,
My book I offer thee to-day,
The tribute of my love alway!

Mother, the dearest name on earth,
Whose care hath shielded me from birth,
No pen can write how much I owe!
No love so great my heart shall know.

Parental priority here, over any husband or lover – if there was one.

Charles **Kightly**, *The Customs and Ceremonies of Britain*, 1986
~ To Martha Rhoden's Tuppenny Dish, The Shropshire Bedlams, and The York Gentleman.

Three cute British curiosities, in which the book itself abounds.

Stephen **King**, *The Shining*, 1977
~ This is for Joe Hill King, who shines on.

The famous 'book of the film'.

Charles **Kingsley**, *Hypatia*, 1851
~ To My Father and My Mother. My dear Parents, When you shall have read this book, and considered the view of human relationship which is set forth in it, you will be at no loss to discover why I have dedicated it to you, as one paltry witness of an union and of a debt which, though they may seem to have begun at birth, and to have grown with your most loving education, yet cannot die with death: but are spiritual, indefeasible, eternal in the heavens with that God from whom every fatherhood in heaven and earth is named. C.K.

This was Kingsley's first historical novel, subtitled 'New Foes with an Old Face', and set in the fifth century in Alexandria. The eponymous central character was an Ancient Greek philosopher, renowned for her learning and beauty, who met a hideous death when torn to pieces by the Alexandrian monks, as the book describes in its final chapter.

Charles **Kingsley**, *Westward Ho!*, 1855
~ To the Rajah Sir James Brooke, K.C.B., and George Augustus Selwyn, D.D., bishop of New Zealand, this book is dedicated by one who (unknown to them) has no other method of expressing his admiration and reverence for their characters. That type of English virtue, at once manful and godly, practical and enthusiastic, prudent and self-sacrificing, which he has tried to depict in these pages, they have exhibited in a form ever purer and more heroic than that in which he has drest it, and than that in which it was exhibited by the worthies whom Elizabeth, without distinction of rank or age, gathered round her in the ever glorious wars of her great reign.

The famous novel is set in the Elizabethan era, with much bloodthirsty narrative and a romantic subtext. Sir James Brooke had set out in his private schooner in 1838 to bring civilisation to the Malay Archipelago and became governor ('Rajah') of Sarawak. George Selwyn was a missionary and the first bishop to New Zealand. He was later bishop of Lichfield, and gave the name of Selwyn College, Cambridge, founded in his honour. Kingsley clearly links their nineteenth-century pioneering endeavours with the heroic exploits of Elizabethan times, as portrayed in his book.

Charles **Kingsley**, *The Heroes*, 1856

~ To my children, Rose, Maurice and Mary, a little present of old Greek fairy tales.

The book, actually subtitled 'Greek Fairy Tales for my Children', was written by Kingsley as an 'improvement' on Nathaniel Hawthorne's retelling of the Greek myths in *A Wonder-Book for Boys and Girls* (1852) and *Tanglewood Tales* (1853), which he found 'distressingly vulgar'. At the time of publication, Rose was eleven, Maurice nine, and Mary, who later became Mrs Harrison and wrote novels as 'Lucas Malet', four. For a dedication to Mary alone, see MAJOR ARTHUR GLYN LEONARD's book, below.

Charles **Kingsley**, *The Water-Babies*, 1863

~ To my youngest son, Grenville Arthur, and to all other good little boys.

Kingsley's wife, Fanny Kingsley, recorded the following account of the inception of the famous children's book: 'Sitting at breakfast one spring morning this year [1862], the father was reminded of an old promise, "Rose, Maurice, and Mary have got their book [see above], and baby must have his." He made no answer, but got up at once and went into his study, locking the door. In half an hour he returned with the story of little Tom. This was the first chapter of "The Waterbabies", written off without correction.' 'Baby' was seven years old when the book was published the following year. He later went to work in Australia.

Charles **Kingsley**, *The Roman and the Teuton*, 1864

~ Dedicated to the gentlemen of the University who did me the honour to attend these lectures.

The work has the subtitle: 'A Series of Lectures Delivered before the University of Cambridge'. The dedication is probably genuine, rather than ironic, as it might have been from another writer.

Charles **Kingsley**, *Hereward the Wake*, 1866

~ To Thomas Wright, Esq., F.S.A., etc. My dear Wright: Thus does Hereward, the hero of your youth, reappear at last in a guise fitted for a modern drawing-room. To you is due whatever new renown he may win for himself in that new field. You first disinterred him, long ago, when scarcely a hand or foot of him was left standing out from beneath the dust of ages. You taught me, since then, how to furbish his rusty harness, botch his bursten saddle, and send him forth once more, upon the ghost of his gallant mare. Truly he should feel obliged to you; and though we cannot believe that the last infirmity of noble minds endures beyond the grave, or that any touch of his old vanity still stains the spirit of the mighty Wake; yet we will please ourselves – why should we not? – with the fancy that he is as grateful to you as I am this day. Yours faithfully, C. Kingsley.

Thomas Wright was an antiquarian and historian whose special interest centred on individuals influential in medieval times, and who helped to found the Camden, Percy and Shakespeare societies. That anyone has heard of Hereward the Wake today is entirely due to Kingsley's book. He was actually an eleventh-century Lincolnshire outlaw who led a revolt of the British, aided by a Danish fleet, against William the Conqueror. He is said to have been pardoned by William and to have died at Maine, killed by the Normans. Kingsley tells a legendary version of his exploits, together with those of his wife Torfrida and his mare Swallow. 'Wake' means 'watchful'. He is commercially commemorated in Peterborough, with its modern Hereward Shopping Centre. This despite the fact that he plundered the town with the help of the Danes. But who cares – his historic name and the literary link are good for business!

Henry **Kingsley**, *The Recollections of Geoffry Hamlyn*, 1859

~ To my father and mother, this book, the fruit of so many weary years of separation, is dedicated, with the deepest love and reverence.

This was the first book by the younger brother of CHARLES KINGSLEY, and is partly autobiographical, with the author represented by the main character, Geoffry Hamlyn. Like his hero, Kingsley had gone to Australia to seek his fortune in the gold rush of the early 1850s. He failed to find gold, but instead gathered much narrative material over the five years he was away, and used it for this book. See also below.

Henry **Kingsley**, *Ravenshoe*, 1862

~ To my brother Charles Kingsley I dedicate this tale in token of a love which only grows stronger as we both get older.

Henry Kingsley was thirty-two when he wrote this, the best-known of his twenty-one novels. (Charles was now fifty-three.) Later, Henry's relations with Charles would be soured by his frequent requests for loans of money. He died in mid-career as a novelist, still only forty-six, in 1876.

Reverend T.H. **Kinnane**, *Mary Immaculate, Mother of God*, 1878

~ To the immaculate, ever sinless, ever Virgin Mary, holy Mother of God: To the purest, the most holy, the most exalted soul ever created by the Almighty: To thee, 'the Glory of Jerusalem', 'the Joy of Israel', 'the honour of our people': To thee, 'fair as the moon', 'bright as the sun', 'beautiful', 'sweet and comely as Jerusalem': To thee, 'garden enclosed', 'fountain sealed', 'work of the Most High', 'the only one', 'perfect one', 'full of grace' and 'blessed among women': To thee, 'the delight of the Blessed Trinity', 'the tabernacle of the Holy Ghost', 'the Virgin Mother of the Redeemer' [...] In petition for thy all powerful help at every moment of life, but more specially in temptation and at the awful moment of death, this little book is most affectionately and most reverentially dedicated.

The Irish Roman Catholic author has pulled out all the epithets he can think of here to describe the subject of his book. Strange, though, that amidst all this adulation the word 'love' is lacking.

Rudyard **Kipling**, *Plain Tales from the Hills*, 1888

~ To the wittiest woman in India I dedicate this book.

It is still not certain who the 'wittiest woman' was. It may have been Kipling's mother, or his sister Alice, or some young woman whom he had met in India. It could not have been his wife, as he married only in 1892. The most likely seems to have been his sister, who had contributed one story to the collection when it originally appeared.

Rudyard **Kipling**, *Stalky & Co*, 1899
~ To Cormell Price, Headmaster, United Services College, Westward Ho!, Bideford, Devon, 1874–1894.

Kipling had himself been at this school for four years from 1878, and the novel is based on his time and experiences there. Cormell Price, an unconventional man, was a personal friend of William Morris, Swinburne and Rossetti.

Joshua **Kirby**, *Dr Brook Taylor's Method of Perspective made easy, both in Theory and Practice*, 1755
~ [...] I shall not follow the common method of dedicators, by attempting a panegyrick upon your amiable qualifications, which might appear like flattery, and offend your modesty; I shall only beg leave to say, that your own inimitable performances are greater instances of your genius in the arts of design, your knowledge of the Human passions, and your contempt of vice and Folly, than it is in my power to express. [...]

Kirby's work, based on Taylor's two treatises on linear perspective, was dedicated to William Hogarth, and had a rather unusual frontispiece by this artist. Kirby knew Hogarth personally, as well as other famous painters such as Gainsborough and Reynolds. His work here was originally published in two parts, in 1715 and 1719 respectively.

H.H. **Kirst**, *A Time for Scandal*, 1973
~ The book that follows is dedicated to my first dog, Anton the Newfoundland, and to Muckel the poodle, fellow-creatures to whom I am indebted for moments of unadulterated joy.

Translated from the German; original title: *Verdammt zum Erfolg*. Hans Hellmut Kirst made his reputation as a writer after the Second World War, and achieved world fame with his fictional trilogy *08-15*, comprising *The Revolt of Lance-Corporal Asch* (1954), *The Strange War of Warrant Officer Asch* (1954), *The Final Victory of Lieutenant Asch* (1955), later filmed.

Mary **Kistler**, *The Jarrah Tree*, 1977
~ To my 'quiet' husband, who can't pass up an adventure. I thank him for a wonderful life in strange, exciting places. And I offer him a special toast to the Spanish years.

Arthur **Koestler**, *The Thirteenth Tribe: The Khazar Empire and its Heritage*, 1976
~ To Harold Harris, the editor with whom I have never quarrelled, and who suggested the title for this book.

Harris was Koestler's editor at Hutchinson, who published the book.

Jerzy **Kosinski**, *Being There*, 1971

~ For Katherina v. F., who taught me that love is more than the longing to be together.

The dedicatee is Katherina von Fraunhofer, now (since 1987) the author's second wife, his first wife having died in 1968 after only six years of marriage. Kosinski, a Polish-born American writer, has made a reputation as the author of picaresque or 'oddball' novels, of which this is an example. (A gentle, illiterate gardener comes by chance to be catapulted to international prominence in the United States.) The novel was an award-winning film of 1978, with Peter Sellers in the main role, his last major part.

Judith **Krantz**, *Mistral's Daughter*, 1982

~ For Ginette Spanier, who opened the doors of Paris for me, with much love and the memory of many years of friendship. For Steve, who has all my love. This book could never have been written without him.

Thomas **Kyd**, *Cornelia*, 1594

~ To the vertuously Noble, and rightly honoured Lady, the Countesse of Sussex. Having no leysure (most noble Lady) but such as evermore is traveld with the afflictions of the minde, then which the world affoords no greater misery, it may bee wondred at by some how I durst undertake a matter of this moment, which both requireth cunning, rest and oportunity; but chiefely, that I would attempt the dedication of so rough, unpollished a worke to the survey of your so worthy selfe. But beeing well instructed in your noble and heroick dispositions, and perfectly assur'd of your honourable favours past (though neyther making needles glozes of the one, nor spoyling paper with the other Pharisaical embroderie), I have presum'd upon your true conceit and entertainement of these small endevours, that thus I purposed to make known my memory of you and them to be immortall. A fitter present for a Patronesse so well accomplished I could not finde then this faire president of honour, magnanimitie, and love. Wherein, what grace that excellent *Garnier* hath lost by my defaulte, I shall beseeche your Honour to repaire with the regarde of those so bitter times and privie broken passions that I endured in the writing of it. And so vouchsafing but the passing of a Winters weeke with desolate *Cornelia*, I will assure your Ladiship my next Sommers better travell with the Tragedy of *Portia*. And ever spend one howre of the day in some kind service to your Honour, and another of the night in wishing you all happines. Perpetually thus devoting my poore selfe, Your Honors in all humblenes. T.K.

Little is known about the life of Thomas Kyd, except that he served an unknown lord for some years, was arrested for heresy in 1593 because of his association with Christopher Marlowe, was very likely tortured, and died soon after his release from prison in 1594, the year of publication of this play, aged only thirty-six. The play was his version of the Senecan tragedy of the same name by the French dramatist Robert Garnier, as he mentions in his dedication. His promised play, *Portia*, thus never materialised. His dedicatee was Frances Radcliffe, née Sidney, wife of Thomas Radcliffe, 3rd Earl of Sussex. She died in 1588, leaving a bequest for the foundation named after her as Sidney Sussex College, Cambridge.

The wording of the dedication may need the odd gloss: *traveld* means 'laboured' (and thus *travell*, near the end, 'labour'); *cunning* is 'skill'; *heroick* is 'virtuous'; *needles glozes* is 'unnecessary flattery' (literally 'needless glosses'); *conceit* is 'opinion'; *entertainement* is 'reception'; *president* is 'precedent' (in the special sense 'sign', 'token').

❧ L ❧

John Lacy, *The Dumb Lady*, 1669

~ To the high-born and most hopeful Prince Charles, Lord Limrick and Earl of Southampton. [...] When I began to write this dedication my hand shook, a fear possessed me, and I trembled; my pen fell from me, and my whole frame grew disordered as if blasted with some sudden upstart comet. Such awe and reverence waits on dignity, that I now find it fit for me to wish I had been refused the honour of my dedication, rather than undertake a task much too great for me. [...]

The young hopeful here was the seven-year-old Charles Fitzroy, the eldest of Charles II's illegitimate sons by Barbara, Duchess of Cleveland, one of his many mistresses. Three years later, Lacy dedicated his play *Old Troop* to the same Duchess's third son, Prince George, later Duke of Northumberland. Lacy, both actor and dramatist, was a great favourite with Charles II, who would doubtless have enjoyed the dedication quoted here.

Charles Lamb, *Poems*, 1797

~ The few following poems, creatures of the fancy and the feeling in life's more vacant hours, produced, for the most part, by love in idleness, are, with all a brother's fondness, inscribed to Mary Anne Lamb, the author's best friend and sister.

Lamb was twenty-two this year, and his sister thirty-three. The previous year, in tragic circumstances, she had killed their mother, when the latter intervened in a row between Mary and an apprentice girl. Brother and sister lived together for the rest of their lives, neither marrying.

Charles Lamb, *Works*, 1818

TO MARTIN CHARLES BURNEY, ESQ.
Forgive me, Burney, if to thee these late
And hasty products of a critic pen,
Thyself no common judge of books and men,
In feeling of thy worth I dedicate.
My *verse* was offered to an older friend;
The humbler *prose* has fallen to thy share:
Nor could I miss the occasion to declare,

What spoken in thy presence must offend –
That, set aside some few caprices wild,
Those humorous clouds that flit o'er brightest days,
In all my threadings of this worldly maze,
(And I have watched thee almost from a child)
Free from self-seeking, envy, low design,
I have not found a whiter soul than thine.

The volume contained miscellaneous writings in verse and prose, with the poetry dedicated to Coleridge, the 'older friend', who had published four sonnets by Lamb in a volume in 1796. In 1818, when this collection was published, Coleridge was forty-six, and Burney, a barrister, thirty, while Lamb was forty-three.

Charles **Lamb**, *Essays of Elia*, 1823

~ To the Friendly and Judicious Reader, who will take these papers as they were meant; not understanding every thing perversely in the absolute and literal sense, but giving fair construction as to an after-dinner conversation, allowing for the rashness and necessary incompleteness of first thoughts; and not remembering, for the purpose of an after taunt, words spoken peradventure after the fourth glass. The author wishes (what he would will for himself) plenty of good friends to stand by him, good books to solace him, prosperous events to all his honest undertakings, and a candid interpretation to his most hasty words and actions. The other sort (and he hopes many of them will purchase his book too) he greets with the curt invitation of Timon, 'Uncover, dogs, and lap,' or he dismisses them with the confident security of the philosopher, 'You beat but in the case of ELIA'.

Lamb sent this to his publisher with the following letter: 'To J. Taylor, Esq. Dear Sir, – I should like the enclosed dedication to be printed unless you dislike it. I like it. It is in the olden style. But if you object to it put forth the book as it is, only pray don't let the printer mistake the word *curt* for *curst*.'

George **Lamming**, *Season of Adventure*, 1960

~ Especially for Neville Dawes, whose secret is clean in this adventure, joining his wishes to my deep gratitude for the State of Ghana during my stay with Sophia, Mary Manful, Vick Merz and Suhame, Sonny, Freda and the African families at Technology, Claud Ennin, Katsina and Ado Kufour, Abdul Atta and Alex Boyo, Four Fingers Bertie Opoku, Good Ol' Jo Reindorph and the C.P.P. youth on Kingsway weekends in Kumasi.

The Barbadian author's novel is set in San Cristobal, in the Caribbean. The tributes seem both convivial and cordial.

Rom **Landau**, *Search for Tomorrow*, 1938

~ To my friends in the Near East, Arab and non-Arab, hoping that my affection for them, no less than my desire for truth, may be reflected in these pages.

A book on the problems of the Middle East.

Walter Savage **Landor**, *The Hellenics*, 1847

~ To Pope Pius IX. Never till now, most holy father! did I hope or desire to offer my homage to any potentate on earth; and I now offer it only to the highest of them all. There was a time when the cultivators of literature were permitted and expected to bring the fruit of their labour to the Vatican. Not only was incense welcome there, but ever the humblest produce of the poorest soil. 'Verbenam, pueri, ponite thuraque'. If those better days are returning, without what was bad or exceptionable in them, the glory is due entirely to your Holiness. You have restored to Italy hope and happiness; to the rest of the world hope only. But a single word from your prophetic lips, a single motion of your earth-embracing arm, will overturn the firmest of seats of iniquity and oppression. [...]

And more in the same vein. Pope Pius IX had been elected only the previous year, and his initial reforms had not yet given way to his reactionary policies, which doubtless made Landor regret his generous dedication. The work itself was a retelling of various Greek myths. The Latin quotation translates as 'Place sacred boughs, boys, and incense'.

Andrew **Lang**, *Letters on Literature*, 1892

~ Dear Mr. Way, After so many letters to people who never existed, may I venture a short one, to a person very real to me, though I have never seen him, and only know him by his many kindnesses? Perhaps you will add another to these by accepting the Dedication of a little work, of a sort experimental in English, and in prose, though Horace – in Latin and in verse – was successful with it long ago? Very sincerely yours, A. Lang. To W.J. Way, Esq., Topeka, Kansas.

Lang was a voluminous writer of books, plays, poetry, stories, and essays of all kinds, as well as a contributor to the *Encyclopaedia Britannica* of articles on such diverse topics as 'Apparitions', 'Fairy', 'Molière' and 'Scotland'. Here he refers to his earlier *Letters to Dead Authors*, which inspired the present collection of letters on literary topics, but this time to imaginary people.

Charles **Larson**, *Muir's Blood*, 1976

~ For Pearl and Frank, my sister and brother in everything but the minor matter of blood.

John **Latham**, *A General History of Birds*, 1821–8

~ Sir, – The work which I submit to the public under your Majesty's most gracious patronage has been the labour and amusement of many years. Having through the kindness of many friends had an opportunity of examining most of the specimens mentioned therein, I trust that the descriptions will be found faithful. That your Majesty may long reign over a loyal people, the Patron and encourager of Science and Art in their branches, is the sincere wish of Your Majesty's Devoted and grateful subject and servant, John Latham.

A somewhat stilted dedication to George IV. The elderly author, a retired doctor, began his *magnum opus* at the age of eighty-one, completing it seven years later. He lived on to be ninety-six, at which advanced age he was visited by Lord Palmerston, who found him unable to read through poor eyesight, but otherwise 'well, hearty, and cheerful, eating a good dinner at five'.

Henry **Lawes**, *Second Book of Ayres and Dialogues*, 1655

~ To the Honourable the Lady Dering, wife to Sir Edward Dering, of Surenden Dering, Bart. Madam, I have consider'd, but could not finde it lay in my power to offer this booke to any but your Ladiship. Not only in regard of that honour and esteem you have for musick, but because those Songs which fill this Book have receiv'd much lustre by your excellent performance of them; and (which I confesse I rejoice to speake of) some, which I esteem the best of these ayres, were of your own composition, after your noble husband was pleased to give the words. For (although your Ladiship resolv'd to keep it private), I beg leave to declare, for my own honour, that you are not only excellent for the time you spent in the practice of what I set, but are your self so good a composer, that few of any sex have arriv'd to such perfection. So as this Book (at least a part of it) is not dedicated, but only brought home to your Ladiship. [...] I wish all prosperity to your Ladiship and to him who (like yourself) is made up of all harmony; to say nothing of the rest of his accomplishments of wisdome and learning. May you both live long, happy in each other, when I am become ashes; who while I am in this world, shall be ever found, madame, Your Ladiship's humble admirer and faithful servant, Henry Lawes.

A musical compliment to a musical lady and her poetic husband. Sir Edward Dering, whose country seat of Surrenden Dering was at Pluckley, west of Ashford, Kent, was an antiquarian and politician aged fifty-seven at the time of this dedication, and married to his third wife, née Unton Gibbs (his 'ever dear Numps' as he called her in his letters to her). She took singing lessons from Lawes, as he mentions, and as her husband's *Household Book* duly records: '1649, June 1. Paid Mr. Lawes, a month's teaching on my wife, 1*l*. 10*s*.'.

Frederick **Lawrence** and Emmeline Pethick Lawrence, eds., *Votes for Women*, 1913

~ To the brave women who to-day are fighting for freedom: to the noble women who all down the ages kept the flag flying and looked forward to this day without seeing it: to all women all over the world, of whatever race, or creed, or calling, whether they be with us or against us in this fight, we dedicate this paper.

'This paper' was the official organ of the Women's Social and Political Union of Great Britain, which advocated militant suffragist action without violence, much in the spirit expressed here. Women did not get the vote in Britain until 1918, and even then had to be aged thirty or more. Votes for women at twenty-one came only in 1928.

T.E. **Lawrence**, *The Seven Pillars of Wisdom*, 1926

TO S.A.

I loved you, so I drew these tides of men into my hands
and wrote my will across the sky in stars

To earn you Freedom, the seven pillared worthy house,
                    that your eyes might be shining for me
                              When we came.

Death seemed my servant on the road, till we were near
                    and saw you waiting:
When you smiled, and in sorrowful envy he outran me
                    and took you apart:
                              Into his quietness.

Love, the way-weary, groped to your body, our brief wage
                    ours for the moment
Before earth's soft hand explored your shape, and the blind
                    worms grew fat upon
                              Your substance.

Men prayed me that I set our work, the inviolate house,
                    as a memory of you.
But for fit monument I shattered it, unfinished: and now
The little things creep out to patch themselves hovels
                    in the marred shadow
                              Of your gift.

Much literary detective work has been engaged to determine the identity of 'S.A.'. The poem was partly the work of Robert Graves, who changed many of Lawrence's original words and phrases. In response to his queries, Lawrence had told Graves that 'S.A.' was 'a certain Sheikh Achmed', with whom he had a sort of 'blood-brotherhood' before the war, but he later said that 'S.A.' was 'rather an idea than a person', then that (splitting the two initials) 'one is a person and one is a place'. In *T.E. Lawrence* (1979), Desmond Stewart tackles the problem and comes to the conclusion that 'S.A.' could well have been one of two young men loved by Lawrence: either Dahoum, whose real name was said to be Saleem Ahmed, or Sharif Ali ibn al-Hussein, the young Arab warrior who succeeded him, and that of the two, the latter is the more probable, especially in view of certain references in the poem itself.

Edward **Lear**, *The Complete Nonsense Book*, 1912

~ To the great-grandchildren, grand-nephews, and grand-nieces of Edward, 13th Earl of Derby, this book of drawings and verse (the greater part of which were originally made and composed for their parents) is dedicated by their author, Edward Lear.

For four years from 1832, Lear was engaged by the Earl of Derby at his home, Knowsley Hall, near Liverpool, to draw the creatures in the private menagerie there. While so employed, Lear began to amuse the Earl's grandchildren with rhymes and drawings, and this led to his *Book of Nonsense* (1846). The book went into twenty-one subsequent editions, of which this was one.

James **Leasor**, *The Chinese Widow*, 1975
~ For Dr Louis Moss, who pioneered acupuncture in Britain.

F.R. **Leavis** and Q.D. Leavis, *Dickens the Novelist*, 1970
~ We dedicate this book to each other as proof, along with *Scrutiny* (of which for twenty-one years we sustained the main burden and the responsibility), of forty years and more of daily collaboration in living, university teaching, discussion of literature and the social and cultural context from which literature is born, and above all, devotion to the fostering of that true respect for creative writing, creative minds and, English literature being in question, the English tradition, without which literary criticism can have no validity and no life.

The influential Cambridge literary critic and educationist Frank Raymond Leavis, who died in 1978, had married another English scholar, his former pupil Queenie Dorothy Roth (died 1981) in 1929, and three years later he and his wife helped to launch the literary and critical quarterly *Scrutiny*. Leavis's subsequent books were almost all created out of essays originally written for this journal, while it was the journal itself, which they kept going for twenty-one years, that eventually made their reputation. Their mutual dedication is sometimes quoted as summarising their life's work.

John **Le Carré**, *The Honourable Schoolboy*, 1977
~ For Jane, who bore the brunt, put up with my presence and absence alike and made it all possible.

Presumably for Le Carré's second wife, née Valerie Jane Eustace, whom he married in 1972.

Brian **Lecomber**, *Talk Down*, 1978
~ This book is dedicated to the following: [...], in memory of thousands of hours instructing in many different cockpits and many different skies.

The listing runs to 399 individual names, making it a fair bidder for the record multiple dedication.

Gerald Stanley **Lee**, *Crowds ...*, 1913
~ Gratefully inscribed to a little Mountain, a great Meadow, and a Woman. To the Mountain, for the sense of time; to the Meadow, for the sense of space; and to the Woman for the sense of everything.

Lee was an American Congregational clergyman and writer, lecturing (from 1898) on literature and the arts.

Harper **Lee**, *To Kill a Mockingbird*, 1960
~ For Mr. Lee and Slice, in consideration of Love & Affection.

The American author's first and award-winning novel, presumably dedicated to her husband and child, the latter called by a nickname.

Vernon Lee, *Belcaro*, 1883
~ To A. Mary F. Robinson.

'Vernon Lee' was the pseudonym of Violet Paget, the English novelist, essayist and art critic who lived in Italy from 1871, when she was fifteen. The book is subtitled 'Essays on sundry Æsthetical Questions' and is virtually an entire dedication in itself. The author intended that it should be so, and in the opening chapter, headed 'The Book and its Title. To one of my Readers, the First and Earliest', justifies her concept, and gives her view on conventional dedications, as follows: 'A little while ago I told you that I wished this collection of studies to be more especially yours. So now I send it you, a bundle of proofs and of MS., to know whether you will have it. I wish I could give you what I have written in the same complete way that a painter would give you one of his sketches; that a singer, singing to you alone, might give you his voice and his art; for a dedication is but a drop of ink on a large white sheet, and conveys but a sorry notion of property. Now, this book is intended to be really yours; yours in the sense that, were it impossible for more than one copy of it to exist, that one copy I should certainly give to you.' The chapter also describes how the book came by its name, from a joint visit made to Belcaro Castle, Siena, by both women. The final sentence of the book again evokes the mutual associations of 'that early winter afternoon on the ilex-girded battlements of Belcaro'. Violet Paget died in Italy in 1935, aged seventy-nine.

Richard **Le Gallienne**, *The Maker of Rainbows*, 1912
~ That this volume shall be entirely in keeping with its fairy tale contents, I dedicate it to my good friends its publishers, Harper and Brothers, in remembrance of kindly relations between them and its writer seldom found out in a fairy tale.

Harper and Brothers were the forerunners of the American publishers now known as Harper & Row. Le Gallienne had gone from Britain to settle in America in 1901.

Major Arthur Glyn **Leonard**, *The Lower Niger and its Tribes*, 1906
~ To the Natives of Southern Nigeria in particular, and of West Africa in general, this Work is dedicated, in all true sincerity and sympathy, not only as a small memento of ten years' personal touch, but in the best and truest interests of themselves, and of Humanity, by one who has always endeavoured to labour on their behalf with the strenuous and untiring energy of a sincere and heartfelt sympathy. Further, as one who voluntarily and unselfishly devoted some of the best years of her life in the same good cause, it is in all esteem and respect dedicated to the memory of Miss MARY KINGSLEY, and to the African Society that emanated therefrom, the object and motive of which is to advance the glorious cause of civilisation and progress.

Mary Kingsley was the daughter of CHARLES KINGSLEY, and she travelled extensively in West Africa as an ethnologist. She died in South Africa of typhoid fever contracted while nursing British soldiers wounded in the Boer War. She was thirty-seven.

Rhoda **Lerman**, *Eleanor*, 1980

~ To Curtis Roosevelt, whose grace and wisdom led me, painfully, to know his grandmother.

A fictional work based on the young years of Eleanor Roosevelt, with factual help from the family.

Desmond **Leslie** and George Adamski, *Flying Saucers Have Landed*, 1953

~ I would like to dedicate Book One to Shaun and to Christopher-Mark, who will know much more about these things than their father by the time they are grown up. Desmond Leslie. Book Two of this work is dedicated to people, everywhere and in every world. George Adamski.

Book One, with twenty chapters, is by Leslie; Book Two, of just three chapters, is by Adamski. The Foreword to the book, regarded as a sensation when originally published, states that 'this book is neither intended for, nor humbly dedicated to, the statistician, nor anyone else who mistakes figures from facts'. It concludes: 'It is to this sort of fool; to the lonely heretic who likes to walk alone down strange untrodden paths; to him who believes that all things are possible, particularly those things held by other men to be impossible; to him who leaves no stone unturned, and to him who gives a second chance to "the stone rejected by the builders", that this book is dedicated'. By the time they had grown up, no doubt Shaun and Christopher-Mark had indeed discovered, along with many other people, that the whole thing was a hoax, and that no flying saucers had landed in California or anywhere else, as Adamski had claimed. The book's photographs went along with the dupe, and while claiming to show a 'Venusian flying saucer or "Scout Ship"' ('photographed at 9.10 a.m. 13 December 1952 at Palomar Gardens, California, by George Adamski through his six-inch telescope') were actually of a mock-up consisting of table tennis balls mounted into a tobacco jar, a hospital operating theatre light, and a vacuum cleaner. The dedication in the Foreword, however, does hint at the hoax that the authors knew would one day be unmasked. Adamski, a Polish immigrant to the USA, where he originally worked as a chef in a roadside café on the highway that led to the famous Mount Palomar Observatory, died in 1965.

C.S. **Lewis**, *The Allegory of Love*, 1936

~ To Owen Barfield, wisest and best of my unofficial teachers.

The first and still the best-known work of the Oxford critic and theologian who had been converted back to Christianity some five or six years earlier. Owen Barfield was the Oxford English don, the same age as Lewis, who became his 'solicitor and philosopher-critic' (as the *DNB* put it).

C.S. **Lewis**, *Out of the Silent Planet*, 1938

~ To my brother, W.H.L., a lifelong critic of the space-and-time story.

See also ROGER LANCELYN GREEN's dedication (above).

George **Leycester**, *The Civil Wars of England*, 1649

~ To the honour and glory of the infinite, immense, and incomprehensible majesty of Jehovah, the fountaine of all excellencies, the Lord of Hosts, the Giver of all Victories, and the God of Peace.

Philip **Lindsay**, *The Devil and King John*, 1943

~ Dedication for Neville Thomson. My dear Neville, here, at last, is the book of which we have talked so often, here it lies for you to open, and I hope, it will not disappoint you after all my boasting. [...] Take it now that it is completed – if a book ever can be completed, which no novelist would believe, for there is always so much more to be written, so much that should be rewritten – take it, with my love, knowing I shall be waiting – fearfully, I confess – to hear your verdict. Philip Lindsay.

Lindsay usually prefaced his historical novels with lengthy dedicatory epistles like this. Here only the opening and closing lines are quoted. The book itself is based on the life of King John. Both dedicator and dedicatee had been close friends from childhood.

Judge Ben B. **Lindsey** and H.J. **O'Higgins**, *The Beast*, 1910

~ To those who have helped: the hundreds whose names I have not had room to mention; the thousands whose names I do not even know. B.B.L.

Benjamin (known as Ben) Barr Lindsey, who died in 1943, was an American jurist and authority on juvenile court laws and juvenile delinquency. He wrote the book in collaboration with Harvey Jerrold O'Higgins, a Canadian-born journalist and novelist.

Eric **Linklater**, *Position at Noon*, 1958

~ To my dear Mu who demanded a dedication I offer this with love.

One of the many novels by the author of the bestseller *Private Angelo* (1946). He was writing continuously almost right up the final months before he died in 1974, aged seventy-five. The dedicatee is presumably his wife Marjorie, whom he had married in 1933.

Robert **Littell**, *The Amateur*, 1981

~ this booK IS dedicAted to tHE GrAndpaReNts LeoN anD syD littElL anD their GranDchilDreN jonATHaN october And jeSSE AUGUsT littelL.

A spy story involving the CIA and a cryptologist. Presumably the latter could crack this apparently wayward dedication, with its combination of upper and lower case letters.

David **Livingstone**, *Missionary Travels and Researches in South Africa*, 1857

~ To Sir Roderick Impey Murchison, President of the Royal Geographical Society, this work is affectionately offered as a token of gratitude for the kind interest he has always taken in the Author's pursuits and welfare; and to express admiration of his eminent scientific attainments, nowhere more strongly evidenced than by the striking hypothesis respecting the physical conformation of the African continent, promulgated in his Presidential address to the Royal Geographical Society in 1852, and verified three years afterward by the Author of these travels.

Murchison was not merely President of the RGS but a noted geologist. Livingstone published this account of his travels two years after his discovery (and naming) of the Victoria Falls on the Zambezi, followed by his rapturous welcome on return to Britain. Murchison's name remains on the map in many parts of the world today, including Australia, New Zealand and various African countries.

Richard **Llewellyn**, *A Few Flowers for Shiner*, 1950
~ Dedicated to all workmen.

Thomas **Lodge**, *A Margarite of America*, 1596
~ To the noble, learned and vertuous Ladie, the Ladie Russell, T.L. wisheth affluence on earth, and felicitie in heaven. Madam, your deep and considerate judgement, your admired honor, & happy readings have drawne me to present this labor of mine to your gracious hands and favorable patronage: wherein, though you shall find nothing to admire, yet doubt I not but you may meet many things that deserve cherishing. [...] So hope I (Madame) on the wing of your sacred name to be borne to the temple of Eternitie, where though envie barke at me, the Muses shall cherish, love, and happie me. Thus hoping your Ladiship will supply my boldnesse with your bountie and affabilitie, I humbly kisse your most delicate handes, shutting up my English duety under an Italian copie of humanitie and curtesie. From my house this 4. of Maie 1596. Your Honors in all zeale, T. Lodge.

Lodge, now remembered as a writer of prose romances, here retells a story that he claimed to have found in the Jesuit library at Santos, Brazil, during his South American voyage made five years previously.

William **Loe**, *A Months Minde*, 1620
~ To his much respected good frend Mr. Thomas Barker one of the assistants of the worthy companie of the Marchants Adventurers, residing at Hamborough. The blessing of both worlds in Christ Jesus. Welbeloved. There is nothing more comfortable to a spirituall minded man then to muse & meditate of his departure hence into the blessed sight of Christ in the other life. Yet to a worldling that would build up a rest for his body here, & sing a requiem to his soule in this vale of teares, nothing is more fearefull & hiddeous then for him to heare death spoken of. We must therefore examine our selves, whether we can sing a song of Sion in this exile and banishment, whether we can solace our selves, in hymnes & songs, of our ends and departure hence. [...] O then let us meditate & muse to our selves, and sing, & say to our soules that our end & the last things are not the least but the best things that we can consider of to mortifie us, & make us meete for the saving mercies of god in Christ; to which I recommend you in my dearest love, & rest. Yours in life, & death. W. Loe.

Loe's work, forming part of the collection of religious verse known as *The Songs of Sion*, had death as its theme, and consisted of a series of 'thoughts' prefaced by a biblical verse and followed by a song or hymn of consolation. Loe, who was chaplain in ordinary to James I, had accepted the pastorate of the English church in Hamburg ('Hamborough'), and dedicated his writings to different English merchants there. Thomas Barker was one such merchant.

Norah **Lofts**, *Here Was A Man*, 1936

~ For Geoffrey, and my heart with it.

An early novel by the prolific popular British novelist, dedicated to the writer's first husband, whom she married in 1931. Compare the next dedication below.

Norah **Lofts**, *The Lost Ones*, 1968

~ For Eleanor Willy, who brought this subject to my notice and died before the story was told, Robert, my husband, and Pearl, my sister, who made complete concentration possible, Margery Weiner, who did the research. Their Book.

A historical romance centring on Princess Caroline, sister of George II, and so set in the 1760s. After the death of her first husband (see above), Norah Lofts remarried (in 1948), so that her husband here was Dr Robert Lorisch. She herself died in 1983 at the age of seventy-nine, the author of over fifty novels, most of them historical tales like this one.

John Luther **Long**, *Felice*, 1908

~ To the gentle strangers in our gates – who speak in other words and understand in other ways than ours – that both words and ways may be more and more one.

Long was an American novelist and playwright, whose short story *Madame Butterfly* (1898) was adapted for the stage and used as the basis for Puccini's famous opera. The 'strangers' here are Italians.

William Joseph **Long**, *Ways of Wood Folk*, 1899

~ To Plato, the owl, who looks over my shoulder as I write, and who knows all about the woods.

The American author was a Congregational clergyman and writer on nature and animal life. Aged thirty-three when this was published, he died in 1952, at the age of eighty-eight.

J. Alden **Lording**, *Young Folks' Nature Field Book*, 1906

~ This book is dedicated to my first wild pet, who was the most interesting and intelligent creature I have tamed. He chased the children into their houses by pinching their legs; he awoke the dog by pulling his tail; and he pecked the horses' feet, then jumped back and crouched low to avoid being kicked. Because of his thieving instinct, he kept me at war with the neighbors. His last mischievous act was to pull the corks from the red and the black ink bottles, tip them over, fly to the bed, and cover the counterpane with his tracks. I found him dead in the workroom the following morning, his black beak red, and his red mouth, black.

Now guess what sort of a pet he was …

Konrad Z. **Lorenz**, *King Solomon's Ring*, 1952

~ To Mr and Mrs J.B. Priestley, without whose timely help jackdaws would not – in all probability – be flying round Altenberg any more.

Translated from the German; original title: *Er redete mit dem Vieh, den Vögeln und den Fischen*, 1949. The book, subtitled (in English) 'New Light on Animal Ways', is about animals and animal nature, from Alsatian dogs to worms, but especially is about jackdaws, which the author reared in his native Austria. The German title is of biblical origin: 'He spoke with the beasts, the birds and the fishes', as King Solomon did (I Kings 4:33). A slight misreading of this gave rise to the legend that Solomon could speak *to* the animals with the aid of a magic ring. Hence the English title of the book.

Benson J. **Lossing**, *Mary and Martha, the Mother and the Wife of George Washington*, 1886

~ To my young countrywomen this brief sketch of the lives of two of the most illustrious exemplars of true womanhood is dedicated by the Author.

Washington's mother was Mary Ball, whom Augustine Washington married in 1731, the year before George's birth. His wife was Martha Dandridge, the widow of one Daniel Parke Custis. She was a good housewife and hostess, as befits her name. Lossing was an American engraver, journalist and historian who wrote several popular biographies and histories.

Pierre **Loti**, *The Marriage of Loti*, 1892

~ To Mademoiselle Sarah Bernhardt. Madame, To you who shine on high, the very obscure author of *Aziyadé* humbly dedicates this native tale. It seems to him that your name will cast a little of its great poetic charm on the book. The author was very young when he wrote this book, and he sets it at your feet, Madame, craving your very greatest indulgence.

Translated from the French by AR; original title: *Le Mariage de Loti*. The book was Loti's second, originally written at the age of thirty. Sarah Bernhardt was of course the famous French actress, 'the Divine Sarah', now at the height of her career. Loti's career as a naval officer sent him to distant and exotic places, many of which, as here, he used as settings for his novels. This one was located in Tahiti, and was illustrated by the author.

Herbert R. **Lottman**, *Albert Camus*, 1979

~ To all those who helped me for truth's sake, and to those who helped me for love of their friend Camus.

A biography of the famous French Existentialist writer.

James Russell **Lowell**, *Among My Books*, 1870

TO F.D.L.

Love comes and goes with music in his feet,
And tunes young pulses to his roundelays;
Love brings thee this: will it persuade thee, sweet,
That he turns proser when he comes and stays?

Dedicated by the well-known American poet and essayist to his second wife, Frances Dunlap, whom he had married in 1857.

Cyprian **Lucar**, *Lucarsolace*, 1590

~ To the Right Worshipfull his brother-in-law Maister William Rose Esquier and Alderman of the honorable Citie of London. [...] I would here earnestly desire you to be patron of my Lucarsolace, but I think it not necessarie; for as spurres unto those which cannot be stopped with bridles are needlesse, so intreaties to you who are thereunto perswaded, and have already granted my desire therein, will be superfluous. [...]

The full title of this book was: 'A Treatise named Lucar Solace, devided into fower Bookes, which in part are collected out of diverse Authors in diverse Languages, and in part devised by Cyprian Lucar, Gentleman'. It is basically a mathematical and engineering manual, with Book 4, for example, dealing with such matters as sinking wells, building chimneys, and the like, with several geometrical figures and folding plates illustrating new mechanical devices. 'Solace' here has its obsolete sense of 'entertainment', 'recreation', rather than 'comfort'. Hence such delights as a new type of fire engine, 'a kinde of squirt made to holde an hoggeshed of water'. No doubt his brother-in-law enjoyed the book.

Jeremy **Lucas**, *Whale*, 1981

~ The chapter called Spraylash is for Katie, for she, without knowing how, made it the way it is. The rest is for my mother.

Robert **Ludlum**, *The Chancellor Manuscript*, 1977

~ For Mary. The reasons increase each day. Above all, there is Mary.

Martin **Luther**, *On the Liberty of a Christian Man*, 1520

~ Of your person, excellent Leo, I have heard only what is honourable and good. [...] But of the Roman See, as you and all men must know, it is more scandalous and shameful than any Sodom or Babylon, and, as far as I can see, its wickedness is beyond all counsel and help, having become desperate and abysmal. It made me sick at heart to see that under your name and that of the Roman Church, the poor people in all the world are cheated and injured, against which thing I have set myself and will set myself as long as I have life. [...] Finally, that I come not before your Holiness without a gift, I offer you this little treatise, dedicated to you as an augury of peace and good hope; by this book you may see how fruitfully I might employ my time, as I should prefer to, if only those impious flatterers of yours would let me. It is a little book as respects size, but if I mistake not, the whole sum of a Christian life is set down therein, in respect to contents. I am poor and have nothing else to send you, nor do you stand in need of any but my spiritual gifts.

Translated from the German by Preserved Smith; original title: *Von der Freiheit eines Christenmenschen*. This extract from the dedication to Pope Leo X comes in the book by its translator, *The Life and Letters of Martin Luther* (1911). The work was one of Luther's campaigning pamphlets, written in either Latin or (as here) German. Preserved Smith, with his suitably Puritanical name, was an American historian who died in 1941.

Nan **Lyons** and Ivan **Lyons**, *Champagne Blues*, 1979
~ To Nat and Diane – for the shirts off their backs.

❦ M ❦

Hamilton Wright **Mabie**, *The Life of the Spirit*, 1898
~ To George A. Gordon: The race must become partner in the moral enterprise, fellow-worker with the universe at its ethical task, if its heart of rhythm and soul of fire are to stand fully revealed.

A not very specific spiritual statement addressed by the author, the American editor of the *Christian Union* magazine, to his friend, then a Congregationalist pastor in Boston.

Anne **McCaffrey**, *The White Dragon*, 1978
~ This book is irreverently dedicated to my brothers Hugh and Kevin for sibling rivalries, and the mature affections and loyalties that develop from early brawling!

Presumably the American science fiction writer did actually mean 'irreverently', not 'irrelevantly'?

Anne **McCaffrey**, *Dragondrums*, 1979
~ This book is dedicated (and about time) to Frederick H. Robinson, for many, many, many reasons, not the least of which is the fact that he is the Master Harper.

The SF novel, one of those on the 'dragonriders of Pern', has Masterharper Robinson as its central character.

James **McConnell**, *The Benedictine Commando*, 1981
~ For precious friends hid in death's dateless night.

A fictional account of the fate of a monastery caught up in battle in the Second World War. The dedication suggests a quotation.

W.G. **MacCullum**, *A Text-Book of Pathology*, 1916
~ To G.A. MacCullum, M.D. My Father And My Best Friend.

The author was Professor of Pathology and Bacteriology at the Johns Hopkins University, Baltimore.

Betty **Macdonald**, *The Plague and I*, 1948
~ For Dr. Robert M. Smith, Dr. Clyde R. Jensen, and Dr. Bernard P. Mullen,

without whose generous hearts and helping hands I would probably be just another name on a tombstone.

The popular American author gives an account of her life in a sanatorium as a tuberculosis patient, all described with a vivid and humorous touch.

Eva McDonald, *John Ruskin's Wife*, 1979
~ In fond remembrance of Mother, because it was *her* interest, so many years ago, in Effie Gray, which prompted me to write this book.

Effie (Euphemia) Gray was Ruskin's wife, whom he married in 1848. He found the concept of marriage distasteful, however, and it was annulled six years later, whereupon Effie married the painter John Millais (who painted her portrait, now in the Tate Gallery, London).

Frederika MacDonald, *Puck and Pearl*, 1887
English children, English born,
  Happy children, strong and rosy,
Who have never yet been torn
  From your homes so safe and cosy.
Who, when evening comes, delight
  In the dismal wintry weather
Round the fire, red and bright,
  Close to sit and talk together,
With the fire-glow on your faces,
  Talking of adventures bold,
All, how men of other races
  Saw strange sights in days of old:

Take these tales of your own times,
  Brought to show you how afar
Live in distant Eastern climes,
  Just such children as you are. [...]

The first of three such stanzas, concluding 'Signed by Puck, Pearl, and their Mamma'. The children's story has the subtitle 'The Wanderings and Wonderings of Two English Children in India'. Although a contemporary of GEORGE MACDONALD, and a writer in the same vein, Frederika MacDonald appears not to be related to her namesake's family.

George MacDonald, *Within and Without*, 1855
TO L.P.M.D.
Receive thine own; for I and it are thine
Thou know'st its story; how for forty days –
Weary with sickness and with social haze,
(After thy hands and lips with love divine
Had somewhat soothed me, made the glory shine,
Though with a watery lustre,) more delays

Of blessedness forbid – I took my ways
Into a solitude, Invention's mine;
There thought and wrote afar, and yet with thee.
Those days gone past, I came, and brought a book
My child, developed since in limb and look.
It came in shining vapours from the sea,
And in thy stead sung low sweet songs to me,
When the red life-blood labour would not brook.

G.M.D.

The famous Scottish children's author and writer of fairy tales dedicated this, his first book, to his wife of four years, Louisa Powell MacDonald. (In both his initials and hers 'M.D.' represented the single surname MacDonald.)

George **MacDonald**, *The Portent*, 1864

~ My dear Sir, Allow me, with the honour due to my father's friend, to inscribe this little volume with your name. The name of one friend is better than those of all the Muses. [...]

The dedicatory letter, which goes on to say more about the story ('It is a Romance'), was addressed to MacDonald's friend Duncan McColl. The novel itself is subtitled 'A Story of the Inner Vision of the Highlanders, commonly called *The Second Sight*'.

George **MacDonald**, *Unspoken Sermons*, 1867

~ These Ears of Corn, gathered and rubbed in my hands upon broken Sabbaths, I offer first to my Wife, and then to my other Friends.

See his first dedication above.

George **MacDonald**, *Dealings with the Fairies*, 1867

~ My children, You know I do not tell you stories as some papas do. Therefore, I give you a book of stories. You have read them all except the last. But you have not seen Mr. Hughes's drawings before. If plenty of children like this volume, you shall have another soon. Your Papa.

The collection of tales was illustrated by Arthur Hughes, who would soon become a close family friend. He was also the illustrator of the 1869 edition of *Tom Brown's Schooldays*, by his namesake (although no relation) Thomas Hughes, as well as stories by GREVILLE MACDONALD.

George **MacDonald**, *A Book of Strife in the form of the Diary of an Old Soul*, 1880

Sweet friend, receive my offering. You will find
Against each worded page a white page set: –
This is the mirror of each friendly mind,
Reflecting that, in this book we are met.

Make it, dear heart, of worth to you indeed: –
Let your white page be ground, my print be seed,
Growing to golden ears, that faith and hope shall feed.
Your old soul.

The book was a poem, highly rated by many at the time, with a stanza for each day of the year. It was largely inspired by the death from tuberculosis of two of the MacDonald children, Mary and Maurice. The dedication names no individual, but the author may have had one in mind.

George **MacDonald**, *Castle Warlock: A Homely Romance*, 1882

TO MRS. RUSSELL GURNEY

A broken tale of endless things,
    Take, lady: thou art not of those
Who in what vale a fountain springs
    Would have its journey close.

Countless beginnings, fair first parts,
    Leap to the light, and shining flow;
All broken things, or toys or hearts,
    Are mended where they go.

Then down thy stream, with hope-filled sail,
    Float faithful, fearless on, loved friend;
'Tis God that has begun the tale,
    And does not mean to end.

G.M.D.

MacDonald dedicated his story to Emelia Gurney, née Batten, the widow of Russell Gurney, lawyer, Member of Parliament and Recorder of London, who had died four years previously.

Greville **MacDonald**, *The Magic Crook*, 1911

To Miss Katharine King, aged 14

I wrote this tale, sweet Maid, for your delight –
    A fairy tale, wherein a child might see
    How joy and pain are roses on one tree,
Though one be sweet, the other cramped with blight.
It tells of fairy play and goblin spite,
    How greed spoils everything, how love sets free
    The joy of lamb and bird and honey-bee,
And tunes the music of their hearts aright.

Your Mother's truthful eyes give light to bear
    The grief and havoc wrought by things unkind;
    Your Father's purposeful and steadfast mind
Braves dragons that make weaker knights despair:
    Kitty! these God-sent gifts they gave to you:

Be happy, gentle, strong; be fearless, true!

Dr Greville MacDonald, professionally a nose and throat consultant at King's College Hospital, London, was the son of GEORGE MACDONALD, and a writer of children's stories in his own right, as well as his father's biographer (*George MacDonald and His Wife*, 1924). The story here, subtitled 'The Stolen Baby, A Fairy Story', actually had two dedications, the first as above, and the second 'To Curdie, the Old-English Sheep-dog, an important Person in the Story, and belonging to Miss Katharine King'. This is likewise in verse, with four stanzas. The dog appears to have been named after Curdie Peterson, the miner's son who is a central character in two of George MacDonald's children's stories, *The Princess and the Goblin* (1870) and *The Princess and Curdie* (1882). *The Magic Crook* was illustrated by Arthur Hughes, who also provided the pictures for some of George MacDonald's books (see above) as well as those by his son. But surely a young lady of this age would have outgrown such things, even then, when childhood lasted longer and innocence was still a valid virtue? Likewise the similar dedicatee below?

Greville **MacDonald**, *Trystie's Quest*, 1912

To Miss Mollie Gamble

A little baby-maid but four years old
  Came to my heart just begging that my hand
  Should cure her trouble, brought from some far land
Where mischief-making Fairies, all too bold,
Mix tears with joy – if all be true that's told.
  Then, quick, the Fairy Queen, with loving wand,
  Bound that small heart to mine with silken strand,
And numbered us within her magic fold.
Though I, each time I came, in healing must
  Bring to that child so many a sob and tear,
    She daily welcomed me with smiling glee.
For fourteen years, you, Child, in joyful trust
  Have cherished all I gave as very dear: –
    I think, whoe'er loves you, you'll still love me!

G. MᶜD.

A dedication to be compared to the one above. By this time, Greville MacDonald was well embarked on his secondary career (see above) as a writer of children's stories, which he maintained until his death in 1944. The book has the subtitle: 'Kit, King of the Pigwidgeons: A Fairy Story', and like the earlier tale was illustrated by Arthur Hughes.

John **MacDonald**, *One More Sunday*, 1984

~ To the memory of quiet Sunday mornings in South Congregational Church on Genesee Street in Utica, New York, with my grandfather, Edward Odell Dann, my great-aunt, Emily Grace Williams, my mother Margarite Dann MacDonald, my father, Eugene Andrew MacDonald, and my sister, Doris Jean MacDonald – now all at rest in Plot 63, Lot 814 and contiguous Lot 6325, in Forest Hill Cemetery in Utica.

A concise family dedication and documentation, although without any ages or dates to go with the names.

Philip **Macdonald**, *The Rasp*, 1924
~ To the Guv'nor.

This was the first detective novel of the author, who was the grandson of GEORGE MACDONALD. The novelist also wrote under the pen names Oliver Fleming, Anthony Lawless, and Martin Porlock.

Kevin **MacDonnell**, *Eadweard Muybridge, The Man who Invented the Moving Picture*, 1972
~ This book is dedicated to the pioneers of photography, whose wonder at the way in which light can create a picture never ceased, and whose greatest happiness lay in discovering some new application of the miracle.

Roger **McGough**, *In the Glassroom*, 1976
~ Dedicated to those who gaze out of windows when they should be paying attention.

A collection of poems by the Liverpool poet about, and for, schoolchildren.

Thomas **McGuane**, *Ninety-two in the Shade*, 1974
~ for Beck for Beck for Beck

Niccolò **Machiavelli**, *The Prince*, 1517
~ To Lorenzo the Magnificent. Those who desire to gain the favour of some Prince are accustomed to present themselves to him with those of their possessions that they prize the most or in which they see that he takes the greatest pleasure. From which it often happens that they come to be presented with horses, arms, cloth of gold, precious stones, and similar ornaments worthy of their greatness. Desiring thus to offer myself to Your Magnificence with some testimony of my servitude, I have found nothing among my possessions that I value so much as the knowledge of the deeds of great persons, which I have acquired through long experience of modern affairs and continuous reading of the ancients. On which I have thought and reflected at length and with great care, in order to reduce it now into a small volume which I send to Your Magnificence. And although I judge this work unworthy to be presented to You, Your humanity is nevertheless an assurance that You will accept it in good part, knowing that from Your hands can come no greater gift than that of giving You the means to comprehend in a short time what I have understood over so many years, with great labour and danger to my person. And I have not embellished this book or filled it with long sentences, or with resonant and inflated words, or with any other outer allurement or embellishment that many use to adorn their works. For my intention is either that nothing should bring it honour, or that purely the novelty of the material

and its gravity should make it worthy of recommendation. Nor should I further wish to be accused of presuming, from my small and low estate, to dare to discourse on the government of Princes and to set forth their rules. For as those who draw landscapes stay down in the plain in order to consider the appearance of the mountains and high places, and then climb these to gain a better prospect of the low places, it is advisable to be a Prince to know the nature of the people well, and for the nature of Princes to be popular. Accept, then, Your Magnificence, this little gift with the same heart with which I send it to You. In reading and carefully considering it, You will perceive the keen desire that I have for You to attain the greatness that good fortune and Your other qualities promise You. And if Your Magnificence, from the peak of Your prominence, should sometimes turn Your eyes toward those humble places where I live and breathe, You will learn how unworthily I bear a great and continuous malignity of fortune.

Translated from the Italian by AR; original title: *Il Principe*. The famous Italian political philosopher's greatest work, outlining his theory of government and containing several maxims relating to statecraft. Lorenzo the Magnificent (il Magnifico), a member of the powerful Medici family, was the son of Piero and the grandson of the original Lorenzo the Magnificent, who died in 1492. He ruled Florence from 1513 until he died six years later, aged twenty-seven, murdered by a remote relative. 'They' in the second sentence refers to the princes mentioned in the previous sentence. The translation aims to reflect the original Italian style, with its quick leaps from one thought to another, and its frequent use of the anacoluthon (starting a sentence one way and finishing it in another).

Helen MacInnes, *The Hidden Target*, 1980
~ To Sir William Stephenson – a man well-named Intrepid – with admiration and affection.

Sir William, a Canadian born in 1896, served in British intelligence in the Second World War under the code name 'Intrepid', with his exploits described in his biography by H.M. Hyde, *The Quiet Canadian* (1962) (called *Room 3603* in the USA), and in two books by his near-namesake, William Stevenson: *A Man Called Intrepid* (1977) and *Intrepid's Last Case* (1984).

Compton Mackenzie, *Guy and Pauline*, 1915
~ To General Sir Ian Hamilton, G.C.B., D.S.O., and the General Staff of the Mediterranean Expeditionary Force.

A quite irrelevant dedication for a pastoral love story. Mackenzie had just been posted to Sir Ian's staff at a time when the Mediterranean Expeditionary Force were involved in the Gallipoli campaign of the First World War. His tribute was thus essentially an ego-boosting exercise. In volume 5 of his ten-volume autobiography *My Life and Times* (1963–71) he comments: 'Two or three reviewers were to find that dedication a bit of showing off on my part. Well, well ...'

Compton Mackenzie, *Poor Relations*, 1919
~ This theme in C major with variations is inscribed to the romantic and

mysterious Captain C by one who was privileged to serve under him during more than two years of war.

Compare the dedication above.

Compton **Mackenzie**, *Extraordinary Women*, 1928

~ My dear NORMAN DOUGLAS: Your delightful commentary on the birds and beasts of the Greek Anthology took no account of the peculiar Æolian fauna whose life I have ventured to observe in this book. Nor can I recall that you, the most erudite of living Sirenians, have ever turned your naturalist's eye to study the migration of these Ægean creatures into Tyrrhenian waters. So I offer you this little treatise on what can hardly without a smile be called natural history as a kind of footnote to your own enchanting volumes; for it was you who sent me to Sirene by the magic of your conversation so dearly enjoyed among the fogs of London fifteen years ago. Why we are not both there now I cannot think; but under a vine-wreathed bower conjured by fancy I drink to our long friendship in the wine of the country. Yours ever, Compton Mackenzie.

NORMAN DOUGLAS began his career as a writer with books on zoology, but went on to travel books and fiction, making his reputation with the novel *South Wind* (1917). 'Sirene' is a reference to his earlier travel book *Siren Land* (1911), for the dedication to which see above.

Compton **Mackenzie**, *The South Wind of Love*, 1937

~ TO NEWMAN FLOWER. My dear Newman, It was to you in your room at La Belle Sauvage that I first put into words my conception of The Four Winds of Love, which alone would make your name at the head of this dedicatory letter appropriate. That the long process of elaboration ultimately resulted in my being unable to fit it into your list makes me more anxious than ever to inscribe to you this volume so that I can have a chance to thank you for an association of seventeen years without a single disagreement. You thought (and you may yet be right) that four volumes would be a mistake. I could not squeeze my tale into two. You could have compelled me to do so, but you generously allowed our contract to be broken in order that I might write the tale in my own way. [...] Well, with all its faults, my dear Newman, I offer you The South Wind of Love and with it my gratitude for more than can be expressed with a book however long. Yours ever, Compton Mackenzie.

Newman Flower, who died in 1964, was head of Cassell & Co., Compton Mackenzie's publishers. In the end the author got his way with a full quota of volumes: he began his six-volume novel with *The East Wind* in 1937, went on, as described here, with *The South Wind* published that same year, then continued in *The West Wind* (1940), *West to North* (1940), and *The North Wind* (1944, 1945, two volumes).

Compton **Mackenzie**, *The Monarch of the Glen*, 1941

~ To Pilot Officer Robert Boothby, M.P., R.A.F. My dear Bob, I do not propose to involve myself with any institution or individual by saying why I particularly choose this moment to dedicate to you a farce; but I want to commemorate a friendship of twenty years, and this dedication gives me a chance to say how precious that friendship has been, is and always will be to Yours ever, Compton Mackenzie.

Robert Boothby, who died in 1986, the same age as the century, was Parliamentary Private Secretary to the Chancellor of the Exchequer (Winston Churchill) for four years in the 1920s and Parliamentary Secretary to the Ministry of Food for two years in the Second World War, after which he occupied several political and honorary posts, becoming Baron Boothby in 1958. In 1941 both he and Mackenzie had been in legal trouble, so had a common bond, commemorated in this dedication.

Compton **Mackenzie**, *Keep the Home Guard Turning*, 1943
~ To Lt.-Col. F.W. Sloper, O.B.E., and the original Second Inverness-shire (West) Battalion of the Home Guard, with a special greeting to the Commanders of C, D and E Companies and to the Subalterns, N.C.O.'s, and Volunteers of my own F Company. My dear Colonel, The process of keeping the Home Guard turning has had the effect of making this dedication retrospective because the Battalion as you commanded it no longer exists. It might imperil the whole future strategy of the war if I were to reveal what has taken its place, and so I shall say no more than a word of gratitude to you for your unfailing appreciation of Home Guard problems in the Islands, so many of which have been solved by laughter. I fear you will not recognize in these pages anybody who served under you, and I may add that I have seldom gone to so much trouble in a book to avoid living models for what really are imaginary portraits. Slàinte mhath! Yours ever, Compton Mackenzie.

'The Islands' were the Outer Hebrides, where Mackenzie wrote the book (on the island of Barra), and where he would set his enjoyable novel *Whisky Galore* four years later. The two Gaelic words that end his letter are a toast: 'Good health!'

Faith **Mackenzie**, *As Much As I Dare*, 1938
~ To M.C.M. When I asked you for your opinion of my portrait of you in this book, you said the impression was that of an amiable lunatic, a sort of Mr. Dick. 'Perhaps that's what I am. Anyway don't alter it. I like it.' If I have not stressed your earthquake tendency, it is partly because the foundations of this book would not stand the strain, and partly because I think the tendency is more familiar to the world in general than what you are pleased to call the 'amiable lunatic' side of your personality which it has been my fortune to enjoy for so many years.

The autobiography of Faith Compton Mackenzie, wife of COMPTON MACKENZIE, whom she married in 1905, and dedicated to him. (He remarried after her death in 1960.) Mr Dick is the amiable lunatic in Dickens's *David Copperfield*.

Charles **Macklin**, *Love à la Mode*, 1759 and *The Man of the World*, 1781
~ My Lord, – The permission, with which your Lordship has been pleased to

honour me, calls forth warmest acknowledgements of respect and gratitude. The polite condescension, with which, before that time, I had been admitted to your Lordship's presence, was always considered by me as the happiest incident of my life. I knew from what a height your Lordship beheld me in my humble station. You looked, I may say, from Shakespeare's Cliff, and saw, more than half way down, a man gathering Samphire. Repeated obligations taught me to flatter myself that in the evening of my days, I had obtained a patron; and what at first was vanity, soon turned to gratitude. [...] The honour of being distinguished by Lord Camden, has put me on better terms with myself; and, though I feel the symptoms natural to a long life, I can boast with pride, that I know the value of the obligation, and to whom I am indebted. [...] That the memory of Lord Camden, and the obligations which he has bestowed upon me, may be the last to fade from my mind, is a consummation devoutly to be wished for. I have the honour to remain, my Lord, your Lordship's most grateful and most devoted humble Servant, Charles Macklin.

This dedication was the one to the reprinted edition, in 1793, of the two earlier plays named above. Macklin was now extremely old, and also very poor. His friends clubbed together to try and extricate him from this state, and by issuing this reprint as a subscription edition managed to collect the princely some (for those days) of £1,582 11s. This provided Macklin, now ninety-four, with an annuity of £200 and one for his wife of £75 in case she survived him. He eventually lived to be ninety-eight, dying in 1797. It is likely that he himself at least drafted the dedication, which was to Charles Pratt, 1st Earl Camden. Macklin's second wife did survive him, but all his children, perhaps unsurprisingly, predeceased him.

Roderick MacLeish, *Prince Ombra*, 1983
~ For Brad Morse, who has come to the sensible conclusion that the world can be saved and goes on trying, with love and admiration these thirty years later ...

A novel combining the supernatural with the criminal.

Fiona Macleod, *The Sin-eater and Other Tales*, 1895
~ To George Meredith, in gratitude and homage, and because he is Prince of Celtdom.

The author was the first famous Fiona! 'Fiona Macleod' was the pseudonym of the Scottish writer William Sharp, who became popular with his mystic Celtic tales and stories of peasant life. The novelist and poet George Meredith, despite his Welsh surname, was born in Portsmouth and lived all his life in the south of England. He thus lacked any hereditary Celtic spirit, and hardly merited Sharp's particular epithet.

Larry McMurtry, *The Desert Rose*, 1983
~ For Leslie, for the use of her goat.

John J. McNamara, *The Billion Dollar Catch*, 1987
~ With love for Lisa, Emily, Sarah and Joan, and admiration for those who work to defeat chemical addiction.

Thomas **Macquoid** and Katharine Macquoid, *Pictures and Legends from Normandy and Brittany*, 1878

~ To Elizabeth Clarke. Dear Elizabeth, You suggested the idea of 'Pictures and Legends from Normandy and Brittany'; and we lovingly dedicate the book to you, in memory of your true and life-long friendship for us and for our children. Affectionately yours, Thomas & Katharine Macquoid.

Griffith J. **McRee**, *Life and Correspondence of James Iredell*, 1857

~ In memory of the Honorable James Iredell, late Governor of the State of North Carolina, senator of the United States, etc., etc., this record of a father, whose genius he inherited, and whose virtues he emulated; in memory of him to whose parental care I am indebted for the greatest of all blessings – an admirable wife, this volume is affectionately inscribed by Griffith J. McRee.

James Iredell, who had died four years previously, was the son of an identically named jurist father who had gone to America and become Comptroller of Customs at Edenton, North Carolina, in 1768. As the dedication implies, McRee had married Iredell's daughter.

Maurice **Maeterlinck**, *Wisdom and Destiny*, 1898

~ To Mme Georgette Leblanc: I dedicate to you this book, which is, as it were, your work. There is a collaboration loftier and more real than that of the pen; it is the collaboration of thought and example. And thus I have not been compelled laboriously to imagine the thoughts and actions of an ideal sage, or to frame in my heart the moral of a beautiful but shadowy dream. I had only to listen to your words, and to let my eyes follow you attentively in life; for then they were following the words, the movements, the habits, of wisdom itself.

Translated from the French by Alfred Sutro; original title: *La Sagesse et la destiné*. Georgette Leblanc was the well-known actress and singer who was the sister of the French novelist Maurice Leblanc, author of the stories about the gentleman crook (and detective) Arsène Lupin. Maeterlinck dedicated many of his plays to her.

Norman **Mailer**, *The Presidential Papers*, 1963

~ This book is dedicated to some ladies who have aided and impeded the author in his composition. They are Beverly Rentz Sugarfoot Bentley, Jeanne Louise Slugger Campbell; my daughters Susan, Dandy, Betsy, Kate; my adopted daughter Jeanne H.W. The Invaluable Johnson; my secretary Anne Morse Towel-Boy Barry; my sister Barbara Jane Alson; and Sadie and Hetty Diggs and Every-Mae.

The book itself is an almost equally diverse collection of essays considering President John F. Kennedy from all angles, including that of 'Hero'.

Manohar **Malgonkar**, *The Devil's Wind*, 1972

~ To Sunita, in memory of the day we brought the dog back and other shared adventures.

Sir Thomas **Malory**, *Le Morte Darthur*, 1485

~ [...] Thenne to procede forth in thys sayd book, whyche I dyrecte unto alle noble prynces, lordes and ladyes, gentylmen or gentylwymen that desyre to rede or here redde of the noble and joyous hystorye of the grete conquerour and excellent kyng Kyng Arthur, somtyme kyng of thys noble royalme, thenne callyd Brytaygne, I wyllyam Caxton symple persone present thys book followyng, whyche I have enprysed tenprynte and treateth of the noble actes, feates of armes, of chivalrye, prowesse, hardynesse, humanyte love, curtosye, and veray gentylnesse, wyth many wonderfull hystoryes and adventures. [...]

Malory completed his great medieval prose romance in 1470, but William Caxton printed it in 1485, supplying a Prologue, part of which formed the dedication quoted here. 'I have enprysed tenprynte' means 'I have undertaken to print'.

Ethel **Mannin**, *Late Have I Loved Thee*, 1948

~ To Isabel Foyle, in devoted friendship, and deep gratitude for introducing me to Fr. McGrath's *Life of Father John Sullivan, S.J.*, without which I should not have discovered that most human of saints, Augustine of Hippo, or been moved to write this novel – which, if it does no more than induce non-Catholics like myself to read Fr. McGrath's book, and the beautiful impassioned writing of St. Augustine, will have been worth doing.

Ethel Mannin, born at the turn of the century, was a prolific writer, active into her late seventies, of novels, stories, travel books, children's books and works on education.

Gideon **Mantell**, *Geology of the South-East of England*, 1833

~ To his most excellent Majesty, William the Fourth, this work on the geology of the South-East of England is, with his Majesty's gracious permission, most humbly inscribed, by his Majesty's faithful and devoted subject, and servant, The Author.

Gervase **Markham**, *The English Husbandman*, 1613

~ To the Right Honourable and his singular good Lord, the Lord Clifton, Baron of Layton: It was a custome (right honourable and most singular good Lord), both amongst the auntient Romans, and also amongst the wise Lacedemonians, that every idle person should give an account of the expence of his howers. Now I that am most idel, and least imployed in your familie, present here unto your Lordship's hands an account of the expence of my idle time, which how well or ill, it is, your noble wisedome must both judge and correct. [...]

Markham may have been something of a hack, but he was hardly idle by modern standards in the 'expence of his howers' (spending of his hours). He wrote many works on country pursuits and on the art of war, and several plays and poems.

Jeannette **Marks** and Julia **Moody**, *A Holiday with the Birds*, 1910

~ This book on birds is inscribed to one of them – Captain Speckles of the Gull Marines, a brave voyageur on the Atlantic Ocean.

George **Markstein**, *The Goering Testament*, 1978
~ To the girl who drove a staff car and knew the route.

A thriller based on fact.

Christopher **Marlowe**, *The Jew of Malta, c.* 1590
~ To my worthy friend, Mr. Thomas Hammon, of Grays Inn, &c. This play, composed by so worthy an author as Mr. Marlowe, and the part of the Jew presented by so unimitable an actor as Mr. Alleyn, being in this later age commended to the stage; as I ushered it unto the Court, and presented it to the Cock-pit, with these Prologues and Epilogues here inserted, so now being newly brought to the press, I was loath it should be published without the ornament of an Epistle; making choice of you to whom to devote it; than whom (of all those gentlemen and acquaintance within the compass of my long knowledge) there is none more able to tax ignorance, or attribute right to merit. Sir, you have been pleased to grace some of mine own works with your courteous patronage: I hope this will not be the worse accepted, because commended by me; over whom none can claim more power of privilege than yourself. I had no better a New Year's gift to present you with; receive it therefore as a continuance of the inviolable obligement, by which he rests still engaged; who, as he ever hath, shall always remain, *Tuissimus*, Tho. Heywood.

Although Marlowe's tragedy was first performed in about 1590, it was not published until 1633, when this 'Epistle Dedicatory' was prefaced to it by the playwright Thomas Heywood. 'Mr. Alleyn' was Edward Alleyn, the actor and founder of Dulwich College, London (and thus also of Alleyn's School, named after him, as part of the same foundation of 1619). The dedication is here given in modern English, with the Latin farewell equating to 'all yours'.

Christopher **Marlowe** and George **Chapman**, *Hero and Leander*, 1598
~ To the Right Worshipfull, Sir Thomas Walsingham, Knight. Sir, we thinke not our selves discharged of the duty we owe to our friend when we have brought the breathles bodie to the earth. [...] By these meditations (as by an intellectual will) I suppose my self executor to the unhappily deceased author of this Poem; upon whom knowing that in his life time you bestowed many kinde favours, entertaining the parts of reckoning and worth which you found in him with good countenance and liberall affection, I cannot but see so far into the will of him dead, that whatsoever issue of his braine should chance to come abroad, that the first breath it should take might be the gentle aire of your liking. [...] At this time seeing that this unfinished Tragedy happens under my hands to be imprinted; of a double duty, the one to your selfe, the other to the deceased, I present the same to your most favourable allowance, offering my utmost selfe now and ever to be readie, at your Worships disposing: E.B.

Marlowe, who had died an early and violent death at the hands of a secret agent in a Deptford tavern in 1593, when still in his twenties, had left this narrative poem unfinished. It was completed by his friend GEORGE CHAPMAN. Sir Thomas Walsingham, the dedicatee, was the brother of Sir Francis Walsingham, Secretary of State to Elizabeth I, for whom Marlowe had acted as espionage agent on the government's behalf.

Don **Marquis**, *archy and mehitabel*, 1927
~ Dedicated to Babs with Babs knows what and Babs knows why.

One of the best-known wry works by the American writer, featuring Archy the cockroach and Mehitabel the cat. The text appears in small letters throughout, as it is ostensibly typed by Archy, who was unable to reach the shift key. But Marquis could, of course, to type this dedication to his wife!

Ngaio **Marsh**, *Last Ditch*, 1977
~ For the family at Walnut Tree Farm.

This was not the home of the New Zealand author, who lived in Christchurch for many years until her death in 1982.

Alan **Marshall**, *I Can Jump Puddles*, 1955
~ To my daughters Hephzibah and Jennifer, who can jump puddles too.

The book is the autobiography of an Australian disabled by polio who struggled to walk again.

John Westland **Marston**, *Our Recent Actors: Recollections of Recent Distinguished Performers of Both Sexes*, 1888
~ To Joseph Knight, Esq., of Lincoln's-Inn, Barrister-at-law. My dear friend: It may probably have occurred to you, as it has done to myself, to glance in leisure moments at the dedications which were published a century or two ago. I confess to having read them with considerable amusement, and, perhaps, with a slight feeling of contempt; for the poet's praise of his patron was usually in such superlatives that he often evinced more imagination in his dedication than in his poem. Were the patron a warrior, he was at least an Achilles; were he a poet, one would think that Homer and Shakespeare ought to hold up his train; were he a legislator, Solon or Lycurgus would be eclipsed; while in the event of the book being inscribed to a lady, the three Goddesses who contended for the Golden Apple were at once superseded in their respective attributes by the modern divinity. One naturally reproaches such clients, to use the old phrase, with insincerity and servility. And yet I have at length learned, from experience, some toleration for them, for you have taught me that seeming hyperbole may well consist with truth. [...] Accept from me these Recollections, touching an art in which we are both deeply interested, and believe, dear Knight, in the profound and grateful affection of yours always, Westland Marston.

A dedication that is interesting for its reflections on earlier dedications, notably the famous

Elizabethan ones. Both dedicator and dedicatee were noted theatre critics of the day, and Knight had met leading authors and playwrights at Marston's London home. Marston died in 1890, and Knight in 1907.

Karl **Marx**, *Capital*, 1887

~ Dedicated to my unforgettable friend, Wilhelm Wolff, intrepid, faithful, noble protagonist of the proletariat. Born in Tarnau on June 21, 1809; Died in exile in Manchester on May 9, 1864.

Translated from the German; original title: *Das Kapital* (1867). Wolff was a German revolutionary and a friend of both Marx and Engels. After the defeat of the Revolution of 1848–9 in Germany, he emigrated first to Switzerland, then in 1851 to London, living in Manchester from 1854.

A.E.W. **Mason**, *The Four Feathers*, 1902

~ This book is dedicated to Miss Elspeth Angela Campbell.

This is the best-known of the writer's historical novels and tales of adventure, even if the identity of the dedicatee is not immediately obvious.

Robert Alexander **Mason**, *Friar Tuck*, 1912

~ Many there are who respond to the commonplace, monotonous call of Duty, and year after year uncomplainingly spend their lives on the treadmill of Routine: but who still feel in their hearts the call of the open road, the music of the stars, the wine of the western wind, and the thrilling abandon of a mad gallop out beyond speed limits and grass signs to where life has ceased to be a series of cogs and – a man is still a man. To the members of this fraternity, whose emblem, hidden behind deep and steadfast eyes, is often missed by man, but always recognized by dogs and horses: I dedicate this book, in the hope that for an hour or two it may lift the pressure a little.

A true 'escapist' dedication and book.

Philip **Massinger**, *The Bondman*, 1624

~ Right Honourable, – However I could never arrive at the happiness to be made known to your lordship, yet a desire, born within me, to make a tender of all duties and service to the noble family of the Herberts, descended to me as an inheritance from my dead father, Arthur Massinger. Many years he happily spent in the service of your honourable house, and died a servant to it. [...]

The playwright's father had been a confidential servant, or house steward, at Wilton House, to Henry Herbert, 2nd Earl of Pembroke, and had retained this post under the latter's son, William, 3rd Earl, Shakespeare's patron and friend.

Philip **Massinger**, *A New Way to Pay Old Debts*, 1633

~ [...] I was born a devoted servant to the thrice noble family of your incomparable lady, and am most ambitious, but with a becoming distance, to be known to your lordship. [...]

A brief extract from a much longer dedicatory epistle to Robert Dormer, 1st Earl of Carnarvon, Master Falconer of England, who ten years on would be killed at Newbury fighting in the Civil War as a Royalist. His 'incomparable lady' was his wife Anna Sophia, daughter of Philip Herbert (the son of Henry Herbert in the dedication above), Earl of Montgomery and 4th Earl of Pembroke. Massinger constantly referred to his connection with the Herbert family in his dedications, and desperately sought their patronage. He was born in Salisbury, where his father had a post with the Herberts at nearby Wilton House (see above), and it is possible that he was named after SIR PHILIP SIDNEY, brother of the wife, Mary Herbert, née Sidney, of Henry Herbert, 2nd Earl of Pembroke.

John **Masters**, *Bhowani Junction*, 1954

~ This book might have been dedicated to the Anglo-Indian communities of India and Pakistan. But so many thousands of Anglo-Indians, over so many years, have dedicated their lives to the service of the railway that I am happy to follow their example. This book, therefore, is inscribed with respect and admiration to Number 1 Down mail, which was to many a prideful train, to them an obstinate ideal of service.

One of the early books that made the author's name, this one devoted to the post-war conflict in British India that was waged just before the Independence of India in 1947. Masters had been an army officer in India, and turned to writing after retiring from the army in 1948.

John **Masters**, *Pilgrim Son*, 1971

~ To the bone of England, which bred us, and the star of America, which led us.

The novelist's autobiography, telling how he went to live and work in the USA.

John **Masters**, *The Field-Marshal's Memoirs*, 1975

~ For Tom Hamill, Artist, Big Chief Tamale; companion of long trails, the high hard days; friend.

Masters was writing almost right up to his death in 1983 at the age of sixty-nine.

Berkely **Mather**, *The Pagoda Tree*, 1979

~ To Juliet O'Hea, who has guided, encouraged and launched more authors than Helen has ships – from one of the former, in affection and gratitude.

Presumably a tribute to the author's agent or to his editor at his publishers, William Collins, Sons & Co.

Thomas **Maurice**, *The History of Hindustan*, 1820

~ To His Royal Highness Prince Augustus Frederick. Duke of Sussex, K.G., D.C.L., Earl of Inverness, baron of Arklow, &c., &c., &c., and what far transcends all titles, the Patron and Genius of Toiling Science, these pages are respectfully and gratefully inscribed, by His Highness's most humble, obliged, and devoted servant, Thomas Maurice.

The royal dedicatee, a noted patron of the arts and sciences, was the sixth son of George III and Queen Charlotte. This was the second edition of the book, whose full title continued: 'its Arts, and its Sciences, as Connected with the History of the Other Great Empires of Asia, during the Most Recent Periods of the World'. Maurice himself was an oriental scholar and historian and a prodigious but hardly inspiring writer. (His works were described by Byron in *Richmond Hill* as 'the petrifactions of a plodding brain'.) He also wrote several poems, mainly on the deaths of noted contemporaries.

Sir Herbert **Maxwell**, *The Life of Wellington*, 1900
~ To the British Army in profound admiration for its past and equal confidence for its future, this memoir of the Great Example is dedicated by the Author.

The 'Great Example', of course, being the subject of the book.

William **Mayne**, *Sand*, 1964
~ Dedicated to PHYSETER CATODON, ESQ. for much kind help.

The children's novel tells how a group of schoolboys discover the remains of a sperm whale buried beneath the sand on the coast of a seaside town in north-east England. *Physeter catodon*, otherwise the dedicatee and 'hero' of the story, is the scientific name of the particular species found.

William **Mayne**, *The Incline*, 1972
> Put her away, this doll of seasons
>   Elapsed and succeeded,
> Named and forgotten, played and done,
>
> Elapsed and succeeded.
>   Let her story rest that
> On her wax face was recorded.
>
> Put her away, this doll of seasons,
>   Empty now of reminiscence;
> After such life and voice
>
> No more to speak of things
>   Named and forgotten, played and done.
> Time no more to recall how
>
> Once those cheeks received
>   Wonders now turned mortal,
> Named and forgotten, played and done –
>
> Softly impressed is softly lost.
>   Elapsed and succeeded,
> Named and forgotten, played and done –

Dumb is the wax, its voices gone.

A touching farewell to a child's doll by the well-known children's author. And presumably a farewell, too, to the dedicatee, whose name will be found by reading down the initial letters of each line. This acrostic device was also used by LEWIS CARROLL in his dedications to *The Hunting of the Snark* and *Sylvie and Bruno* and for the end poem in *Through the Looking-Glass*. Mayne's poem is clever enough to repeat an identical line meaningfully for four of the five Ns that occur in the name.

Mark **Medoff**, *Children of a Lesser God*, 1980
~ For Phyllis French and Bob Steinberg, who gave everything to it.

The play is about the endeavours of James Leeds, a speech therapist, to break through to his deaf pupil, Sarah Norman, with whom he falls in love. In the London première the pupil was played by a deaf actress, Elizabeth Quinn, while the play itself is based on the experiences of the American deaf actress, Phyllis French, who married the stage scenic and lighting designer who had fallen in love with her, Bob Steinberg. The play was thus written for these two and naturally dedicated to them.

Herman **Melville**, *Billy Budd*, 1924
~ Dedicated to Jack Chase, Englishman. Wherever that great heart may now be, Here on earth or harbored in Paradise, Captain of the maintop in the year 1843 in the U.S. Frigate *United States*.

Melville had begun this famous short novel in 1886 but had left it only half-finished at the time of his death in 1891. It was eventually published in 1924. The story itself is set on board HMS *Bellipotent* in the year 1797.

Antony **Melville-Ross**, *Shadow*, 1984
~ Bad form it may be, but I dedicate this book to my friend and editor, Richard Ollard.

Surely most editors would be only too appreciative of such a tribute, bad form or not?

Yehudi **Menuhin**, *Unfinished Journey*, 1976
~ To Diana, my heavenly host on this earthly way, and to those unique and irreplaceable predecessors and successors, parents and children, without whose dedicated upbringing there would be no pages to fill, this book is offered.

The world-famous violinist's autobiography, dedicated to his wife, whom he married in 1947. Presumably the 'heavenly host' reference is a deliberate pun.

Eunice A. **Messer**, *Children, Psychology and the Teacher*, 1967
~ For NEIL GAVIN who arrived when the manuscript was half-completed and caused the author to reconsider some cherished theories.

A textbook by a Scottish educational psychologist, and evidently one receptive to new ideas and theories.

Thomas **Middleton**, *The Wisdom of Solomon Paraphrased*, 1597

~ To the right Honourable and my very good Lord, Robert Devoreux, Erle of Essex and Ewe, Vicount of Hereford, Lorde Ferrers of Chartley, Bourcher, and Louayne, Maister of her Majesties Horse and Ordonance, Knight of the honourable order of the Garter, and one of her Majesties most honorable privie Counsell. The Summers Harvest (right Honourable) is long since reapt, & now it is sowing time againe. Behold, I have scattred a few seedes upon the yong ground of unskilfulnesse. If it beare fruit, my labour is well bestowed; but if it be barren, I shall have lesse joy to set more. The husbandman observes the courses of the Moone, I, the forces of your favor: he desireth sun-shine, I, cheerefull countenance: which once obtayned, my harvest of joy will soone bee ripened. My seedes, as yet, lodge in the bosome of the earth, like Infantes upon the lappe of a Favourite, wanting the budding spring-time of their growth, not knowing the Est of their glorie, the west of their quietnesse, the South of their summer, the North of their winter; but if the beames of your aspectes lighten the small moytie of a smaller implanting, I shall have an every-day-harvest, a fruition of content, a braunch of felicitie. Your Honours addicted in all observance, Thomas Midleton.

A poetic and quite charming dedication for the future dramatist's earliest pamphlet. Sir Robert Devereux, 2nd Earl of Essex, had been the leading favourite of Queen Elizabeth, but offended her on secretly marrying the widow of Sir Philip Sidney. In the year when this pamphlet was published, he was appointed Earl Marshal of England. Four years later, however, he was executed for treason, aged only thirty-five, his death warrant signed by Elizabeth. Compare MIDDLETON's dedication below.

Thomas **Middleton**, *The Witch*, 1613

~ To the Truely-Worthie and Generously-Affected THOMAS HOLMES, Esquire. Noble Sir, As a true testemonie of my readie inclination to your service, I have (meerely uppon a tast of your desire) recovered into my hands (though not without much difficultie) this (ignorantly-ill-fated) labour of mine. Witches are (*ipso facto*) by the law condemn'd, & that onely (I thinck) hath made her lie so long in an imprisond obscuritie. For your sake alone She hath thus far conjur'd herself abroad; and beares noe other charmes about her, but what may tend to your recreation, nor no other spell but to possess you with a belief, that as She, so He that first taught her to enchant, will alwaies be Your devoted THO. MIDDLETON.

This dedication implies that friends of the author, and his patron, could well ask for a manuscript copy of a play, and that the author might have some problem recovering his manuscript, presumably from the company that had performed the work, if the play had failed, as Middleton's evidently had ('ignorantly-ill-fated').

Lina **Mikdadi**, *Surviving the Siege of Beirut*, 1983

~ This book is dedicated to my city and its heroic inhabitants, those who stayed; to my daughters Leyla and Rashe, who survived the siege; and to my nephews and nieces Marwan, Catherine, Ridha, Hania, Richard, Husni and Alana Les

Moyler who never saw the siege. May they all grow and live by principles and ideals, whatever these may be.

George Mikes, *How to be Decadent*, 1977

~ To my old friend Emeric Pressburger – the only man I know who is not decadent. But – I hope – he can learn.

Pressburger, the well-known journalist and film scriptwriter, was an emigrant from Hungary to Britain, as the shrewd humorist Mikes himself was.

John Stuart Mill, *On Liberty*, 1859

~ To the beloved and deplored memory of her who was the inspirer, and in part the author, of all that is best in my writings – the friend and wife whose exalted sense of truth and right was my strongest incitement, and whose approbation was my chief reward – I dedicate this volume. [...] Were I but capable of interpreting to the world one-half of the great thoughts and noble feelings which are buried in her grave, I should be the medium of a greater benefit to it, than is ever likely to arise from anything that I can write unprompted and unassisted by her all but unrivaled wisdom.

This moving tribute to the philosopher's late wife surprised those friends who knew him as a calm and outwardly undemonstrative person. Mill had married Mrs Taylor, a widow, in 1851, having been her close friend for some twenty years previously. She died in the year this work was published, two years his junior at fifty-one. Mill later revealed in his *Autobiography* (1873) that a similar tribute to his wife-to-be had been prefixed to some of the presentation copies of his *Principles of Political Economy* (1848) when it was first published, but that her dislike of publicity had prevented him from including this in later editions.

Jeff Millar, *Private Sector*, 1979

~ For everybody who said *yes* when it would have been just as easy to say *no*.

John Miller, *Former Soldier Seeks Employment*, 1989

~ This book is dedicated to: Queen and Country, serving them gave me some great material; [...] Levi Strauss for my genes; [...] anybody with a 38DD, please call; [...] Andy Dunlop, the only man I know who can sit up while lying down; [...] Lou Reed. I never said your wife was fat but I know who did; [...] the provisional IRA. Come out and fight like men, you bastards; [...] the estate agent who sold me my house. You knew the roof leaked, didn't you?; [...] my wife Sarah, who has been more than I could have hoped for in every department as a wife, a mistress and a mother and for giving me two beautiful children, Kate and James.

Just eight, fairly representative, of the total fifty-nine dedications to individuals, organisations, restaurants, clubs and the like that occupy two whole pages of the unpleasantly lurid but unputdownably readable autobiography of an ex-Scots Guardsman-turned-mercenary and 'soldier of fortune'.

Russell **Miller**, *The House of Getty*, 1985
~ To my family, with heartfelt thanks that our name is not Getty.

An account of the life and family of Paul Getty, the American oil magnate and billionaire who died in 1976.

Spike **Milligan**, *Mussolini: His Part in My Downfall*, 1978
~ This book is dedicated to Erin Pizzey in her lonely fight to stop brutal physical and physiological violence on women and children.

A typically 'caring' yet completely irrelevant dedication by the British humorist and campaigner for worthy causes. Erin Pizzey opened a refuge for battered women in London in 1971 and attracted much publicity by her frequent prosecutions (for overcrowding) and by her clashes of will with other campaigners and feminists. Milligan's book is one of a series of autobiographical recollections dealing with his army life and experiences in the Second World War, the first of which was *Adolf Hitler: My Part in his Downfall* (1971).

John **Mills**, *Up in the Clouds, Gentlemen Please*, 1980
~ For Mary, without whose understanding of the author's sometimes childish tantrums, and his deplorable lack of control in adjusting his life to masquerading as a writer, these recollections of the past would never have been completed.

An autobiography of the famous film actor, dedicated to his wife, the playwright Mary Hayley Bell, whom he married in 1941.

A.A. **Milne**, *Once a Week*, 1914
~ [To] my collaborator who buys the ink and paper, laughs, and in fact does all the really difficult part of the business.

That is, to Dorothy (Daphne) Milne, née de Selincourt, wife of the popular children's writer, novelist and playwright, whom he had married the previous year and who gave him strong moral support and 'collaboration' without actually doing any of the writing.

A.A. **Milne**, *When We Were Very Young*, 1924
~ To Christopher Robin Milne or, as he prefers to call himself, Billy Moon, this book which owes so much to him is now humbly offered.

Otherwise to Milne's son, the famous Christopher Robin of the 'Pooh' books, aged four when this collection of verse for young children appeared. 'Billy' was Christopher Robin's name for himself, and 'Moon' his babyish attempt at saying 'Milne'.

A.A. **Milne**, *Winnie the Pooh*, 1926
~ To Her. Hand in hand we come, Christopher Robin and I, to lay this book in

your lap. Say you're surprised? Say you like it? Say it's just what you wanted? Because it's yours – because we love you.

When this, the best-known and most popular of Milne's children's books appeared, Christopher Robin was five years old. The main dedication, of course, is to Milne's wife (see above).

A.A. **Milne,** *Now We Are Six,* 1927
~ To Anne Darlington now she is seven and because she is so speshal.

The book, a further collection of verse for young children, has a title that relates to the age at the time of Milne's son, Christopher Robin. Anne Darlington was one of the little boy's close childhood friends. She was eight months older, and lived half a mile from the Milne home in London. Like him, she was an only child, and his parents were as fond of her almost as much as they were of their own son. Perhaps she represented the daughter the Milnes wanted (and planned to name Rosemary) but never had. All of this made Anne 'speshal'. There were hopes that the two children would grow up to marry, but although their friendship lasted to about the age of twenty-five, their lives then went different ways and this never happened. Christopher Milne married his cousin, Lesley de Selincourt, in 1948.

A.A. **Milne,** *The House at Pooh Corner,* 1928
You gave me Christopher Robin, and then
  You breathed new life in Pooh.
Whatever of each has left my pen
  Goes back homing to you.
My book is ready, and comes to greet
  The mother it longs to see –
It would be my present to you, my sweet,
  If it weren't your gift to me.

Dedicated, as were earlier books (see above), to Milne's wife.

Christopher **Milne,** *The Enchanted Places,* 1974
~ For Olive Brockwell, 'Alice' to others but 'Nou' to me. To remind you of those enchanted places where the past will always be the present.

An autobiography by the son of A.A. MILNE, dedicated to his childhood nurse, who features in his father's verses as 'Alice' ('They're changing the guard at Buckingham Palace, / Christopher Robin went down with Alice'). No doubt 'Nou' was a pet form of 'Nanny'.

William **Milns,** *The Well-Bred Scholar,* 1797
~ To the Superintendents of Schools. Gentlemen, in dedicating to you the following essays on polite literature, I am influenced by a stronger motive than the mere propriety of such an address. Aware of the prejudices usually conceived by the ignorant, the envious, and the illiberal, against every new attempt to render the way to learning either shorter, or smoother, I wish to submit the sketches of

my plan to the judgment of those only who are best qualified to decide on its reasonableness, without considering whether it has long use for its authority or not. [...] My design, however, is not to write strictures on the established modes of private or public instruction, but simply to explain those which I have found most successful in real practice. Should they prove serviceable to other teachers in the discharge of some of the most important duties of society, I shall think my humble labours very amply rewarded. I remain, gentlemen, with sincere respect, your most obedient servant, William Milns.

A treatise on education in the days when education was education, published in New York and subtitled: 'Practical Essays on the Best Methods of Improving the Taste, and Assisting the Exertions of Youth in their Literary Pursuits'.

John Milton, *Comus*, 1637

~ To the Right Honourable John, Lord Viscount Brackley, son and heir-apparent to the Earl of Bridgewater, etc. My Lord, – This Poem, which received its first occasion of birth from yourself and others of your noble family, and much honour from your own person in the performance, now returns again to make a final dedication of itself to you. Although not openly acknowledged by the Author, yet it is a legitimate offspring, so lovely and so much desired that the often copying of it hath tired my pen to give my several friends satisfaction, and brought me to a necessity of producing it to the public view, and now to offer it up in all rightful devotion, to those fair hopes and rare endowments of your much-promising youth, which give a full assurance to all that know you of a future excellence. Live, sweet Lord, to be the honour of your name; and receive this as your own from the hands of him who hath by many favours been long obliged to your most honoured Parents, and, as in this representation your attendant *Thyrsis*, so now in all real expression, Your faithful and most humble Servant, H. Lawes.

This is thus not Milton's own dedication to the work, but that of Henry Lawes, who published it himself anonymously. Lawes was the young musician who set to music the songs of many well-known contemporary writers such as Carew, Lovelace and Herrick, and it was at his request that Milton composed the masque of *Comus*, to celebrate the inauguration of John Egerton, 1st Earl of Bridgewater, into his duties as Lord President of Wales. When the masque was performed at Ludlow Castle in 1634, the Earl's fifteen-year-old daughter Alice and her two young brothers John (the dedicatee) and Thomas, aged eleven and nine, who were under the instruction of Lawes, took the leading parts, with Lawes himself playing the Attendant Spirit. The descriptive subtitle of the work was thus: 'A Maske presented at Ludlow Castle, 1634: on Michaelmasse night, before the Right Honorable John Earl of Bridgewater, Lord President of Wales'. The younger John Egerton succeeded his father as Earl of Bridgewater in 1649.

R.J. Minney, *Carve Her Name With Pride*, 1956

~ For TANIA who is old enough now to read this story of her brave and wonderful mother.

The book tells the story of the Second World War secret agent Violette Szabo, the young widow of a French officer, born Violette Reine Elizabeth Bushell in Paris in 1921 as the daughter of an English father and French mother. Her daughter Tania was born in occupied France in 1941 at a time when her mother was working aginst the Gestapo. Violette was executed at Ravensbruck by a German firing squad three years later. The heroic and tragic story was made into a successful movie of the same name in 1958, with Virginia McKenna in the leading role.

Mary Russell **Mitford** (Miss Mitford), *Country Stories*, 1837
~ To the Rev. William Harness, whose old hereditary friendship has been the pride and pleasure of her happiest hours, her consolation in the sorrows and her support in the difficulties of life, this little volume is most respectfully and affectionately inscribed by The Author.

Harness had formed a lifelong friendship with Mary Mitford, and his father had acted *in loco parentis* to her mother at her marriage and had given her away. BYRON had wanted to dedicate *Childe Harold* to Harness, his school friend at Harrow, but had been persuaded not to for fear of damaging his reputation.

Nancy **Mitford**, *Pigeon Pie*, 1940
~ To Phyllis Blake, Margaret Candler, and, of course, to the wonderful Old Songster of Kew Green himself, I dedicate this book.

Molière, *A School for Husbands*, 1661
~ To the Duke of Orleans, only brother of the King. Your Grace, I herewith present France with things that are hardly well proportioned. There is nothing so great and so superb as the name that I put at the head of this book, and nothing baser than what it contains. Everyone will find this combination strange, and some will doubtless say, referring to the imbalance, that it is like placing a crown of pearls and diamonds on a clay statue, or showing someone into a mean hut through magnificent portals and grand triumphal arches. But, Your Grace, what must serve as an excuse is that in this enterprise I had no other choice, and that the honour I have in being a subject of Your Royal Highness has imposed on me the absolute necessity of dedicating to you the first work of mine that I myself am publishing. It is not a gift that I make to Your Royal Highness, but a duty that I discharge. And acts of homage are never regarded by the things they bear. I have thus been bold enough, Your Grace, to dedicate a trifle to Your Royal Highness, because I could not do otherwise. And if I excuse myself here from expatiating on the fine and glorious truths that could be told of Your Royal Highness, it is through the understandable fear that these great ideas should even further reveal the unworthiness of my offering. I have vowed to remain silent until I can find a more suitable place to say such fine things, and all that I have claimed in this Epistle is to justify my action to the whole of France and to be proud enough to tell you yourself, Your Grace, that I am, with all possible deference, Your Royal Highness's most humble, obedient and faithful servant, I.B.P. Molière.

Translated from the French by AR; original title: *L'Ecole des Maris*. Philippe I, son of

Louis XIII and brother of Louis XIV, became Duke of Orleans in 1660 and was Molière's patron and protector. The initials before Molière's name (the pseudonym he adopted) represent his real name of Jean-Baptiste Poquelin.

Molière, *The Bores*, 1661

~ To the King. Sire, I add a scene to the comedy, and it is a kind of tiresome thing, as tedious as a man who dedicates a book. Your Majesty knows about him more than anyone in his kingdom, and nowadays Your Majesty does not regard himself as exposed to the fury of dedicatory epistles. But although I am following the example of others and number myself among those whom I have played, I yet dare say to Your Majesty that what I have done is not so much to offer You a book as to have good grounds for thanking You for the success of this comedy. I owe it, Sire, this success, which has exceeded all expectations, not only to the glorious approval with which Your Majesty originally honoured the play, and which resulted so splendidly in that of everyone else, but to the command You gave me to add another boring character, about which You had the goodness to reveal to me your own ideas, and which has everywhere been found to be the finest part of the work. It must be admitted, Sire, that I have never done anything with such ease, nor so rapidly, than this part on which Your Majesty commanded me to work. I had a joy in obeying You which was worth more to me than Apollo and all the Muses. And I conceive, by that, what I would be capable of executing for an entire comedy, if I had been inspired by such commands. Those who are born of high rank can envisage the honour of serving Your Majesty in the greatest employment, but as for me, the greatest glory to which I can aspire is to delight You. I limit there the ambition of my desires, and I think that in some way it is not without benefit to France to contribute something towards the entertainment of the king. If I fail to do so, it will not be through lack of zeal or application, but only through ill fortune, which often follows the best intentions, and which certainly would noticeably trouble, Sire, Your Majesty's most humble, obedient and faithful servant and subject, I.B.P. Molière.

Translated from the French by AR; original title: *Les Fâcheux*. A typical tongue-in-cheek tribute to Louis XIV by the shrewd and witty playwright, who sailed dangerously close to the wind on more than one occasion.

Molière, *The School for Wives*, 1662

~ To Madame. Madame, I am the most diffident man in the world when I have to dedicate a book, and am so unfamiliar with the style of the dedicatory epistle that I hardly know where to begin. Another author in my place would have first found a hundred fine things to say to Your Royal Highness on the title of THE SCHOOL FOR WIVES and the offering that he made you. But I, Madame, admit my inadequacy to you. I know nothing of the art of finding common links between things so disproportionate, and whatever fine words of wisdom my fellow authors give me daily on such subjects, I fail completely to see what Your Royal Highness could have in common with the comedy that I present to you. There is no difficulty, indeed, in knowing how you should be praised. The thing, Madame, is all too obvious, and from whatever point one considers you, one finds glory on glory and qualities on qualities. You have these, Madame, by way of rank and birth, which make you respected throughout the world. You have them by way of grace of both mind and body, which make you admired by all those persons who see you. You have them by way of the soul, which, if one may be so bold to say so, make you loved by all those who have the honour of approaching you – I mean that sweetness full of charms with which you deign to temper the pride of the grand titles that you bear, that all-favouring goodness, and generous affability that you show to everyone. And it is particularly these last that I mean, and about which I truly feel that I shall never one day fall silent. But once again, Madame, I lack the means of treating here such patent truths, and these are things, in my view, of both too wide a scope and too lofty a merit to be encompassed in an epistle and mingled with trifles. All things considered, Madame, I see nothing left for me but simply to dedicate my comedy, and to assure you that, with all possible respect, I am, Madame, Your Royal Highness's most humble, obedient and obliged servant, I.B.P. Molière.

Translated from the French by AR; original title: *L'Ecole des Femmes*. 'Madame' was Henrietta Anne, Duchess of Orleans and the fifth daughter of Charles I of England. She had been taken to France at the age of two and brought up a Catholic, but returned to England at the Restoration in 1660. The following year she married Philippe, Duke of Orleans (see the first dedication above), known as 'Monsieur'. She was still only eighteen when Molière wrote his flattering tribute to her, and was all the things he implies: well-bred, beautiful and intelligent. Two years after the publication of Molière's play here she was the godmother of his first child. She died tragically young at twenty-six, believed poisoned by agents of her husband. See also RACINE's dedication to her for *Andromache*.

Molière, *The Criticism of the School for Wives*, 1663

~ To the Queen Mother. Madame, I well know that Your Majesty has no need of all our dedications, and that these alleged duties, which are elegantly said to be discharged to You, are acts of homage which, to tell the truth, Your Majesty could well do without. But nevertheless I do have the audacity to dedicate the CRITICISM OF THE SCHOOL FOR WIVES to You, and I could not miss the small opportunity of expressing my joy to Your Majesty on Your happy recovery, which restores to our wishes the best and greatest princess in the world, and which promises us long years of vigorous health for You. As everyone regards these things from the point of view that concerns him, I rejoice, in this general gladness, at being able to have the further honour of entertaining Your Majesty. You prove so well, Madame, that true devotion is not at all contrary to honest entertainment. You descend so humanly from Your lofty thoughts and important occupations to the pleasure of our plays, and do not disdain to laugh with the same mouth as that with which you make your prayers to God. I say my mind is flattered in the hope of this glory, and I await the moment with the greatest impatience in the world. And when I shall enjoy that happiness, it will be the greatest joy that could be received, Madame, by Your Majesty's most humble, obedient and faihtful servant, I.B.P. Molière.

Translated from the French by AR; original title: *La Critique de l'Ecole des Femmes. The School for Wives* (see above) had caused considerable concern regarding its alleged indecency and irreverence, and Molière now ridiculed his objectors in this one-act prose comedy. His main defence, sensibly enough, was that the play was a good one because it had given pleasure. If it had offended, there must be something wrong with the accepted rules of moral conduct. His dedicatee was the mother of Louis XIV, Anne of Austria.

Molière, *Amphitryon*, 1668

~ To His Most Serene Highness, His Grace the Prince. Your Grace, with all deference to our wits, I see nothing more tedious than dedicatory epistles, and Your Most Serene Highness will find it fitting, if he chooses, that I should not follow the style of those gentlemen, and that I should refuse to utilise two or three miserable ideas which have been fashioned and refashioned so many times that they are in every way quite exhausted. The name of the Great Condé is too glorious a name to be treated as other names are, and it should only be applied, this illustrious name, to uses that are worthy of it, so that to say fine things of it I would wish to put it at the head of an army rather than at the head of a book, and I regard it as much more capable of opposing the enemy forces of this state than opposing the criticism of the enemies of a comedy. It is not, Your Grace, that the glorious approbation of Your Most Serene Highness has not been a powerful protection for all these kinds of works, and that one is not convinced of the wise words of Your mind as much as the intrepidity of Your heart and the greatness of Your soul. The whole world knows that the lustre of Your excellence is not confined within the limits of that indomitable value accorded it by even those worshippers that it overwhelms, and that it extends, this excellence, to the most demanding and refined kind of knowledge, and that the decisions of your judgment on all works of the mind do not fail to be agreed by the most delicate of sentiments. But it is also known, Your Grace, that all these glorious approbations which we vaunt to the public cost us nothing to have printed, and that they are things that we can dispose as we will. It is known, indeed, that a dedicatory epistle says anything one wishes, and that an author is empowered to enlist the most august persons, and to adorn with their great names the first mere pages of his book, and that he has the liberty to assume, as much as he wishes, the honour of their greatness, and to make of his protectors that which they never dreamed of being. Your Grace, I will debase neither Your name nor Your goodness in combatting the censors of *Amphitryon*, and in attributing to myself a glory that I may well not have deserved, and I take the liberty of offering You my comedy only in order to be able to tell You that I have an unceasing regard, with profound veneration, for the great qualities that You add to the august blood that You possess, and that I am, Your Grace, with all possible respect and all imaginable zeal, Your Most Serene Highness's most humble, obedient and obliged servant, Molière.

Translated from the French by AR; original title as in English. Molière's august dedicatee here was Louis II, Prince of Condé, leader of the last of the great French aristocratic rebellions known as the 'Fronde', and one of the most outstanding generals in Louis XIV's army. Hence his popular title of 'The Great Condé'. Attacks on Molière's plays were nothing knew, simply because almost all of them alluded directly or indirectly to the affectations and indiscretions of royalty and the aristocracy. *Amphitryon* contained many references to the amatory ventures of the king, Louis XIV, and was staged at a time when he was embroiled with an aristocratic married lady, Madame de Montespan, an involvement that was widely known outside royal circles and that had begun the previous year. It lasted thirteen years and resulted in six children, all subsequently legitimated.

Michel de **Montaigne**, *Essays*, 1635

~ To Monseigneur, the Most Excellent Cardinal, duc de Richelieu. Monseigneur, I cannot give the essays to you, because they are not mine, but cognizant, nevertheless, that all that is illustrious in our age passes through your hands or owes you homage, I have thought that the name of your Eminence ought to adorn the frontispiece of this book. It is true, Monseigneur, that the homage rendered here to you, by my agency, is very irregular; though it is not in my power to bestow these essays upon you, I dare to give them to you as a legacy: that is to say, that, as soon as I shall be entombed within the sepulchre, I consign to you this orphan which was committed to me in order that it may please you henceforth to hold the place of guardian and protector. [...]

Translated from the French; original title: *Essais.* The dedication to Cardinal Richelieu was made by Marie de Gournay, Montaigne's *fille d'alliance* or adopted daughter, whom he had first met in 1588 when he was fifty-five and she twenty-two. She was not only a great enthusiast of his works but an accomplished woman of letters, and it was soon agreed that she should be his literary executor, a timely arrangement as he died four years later. Montaigne had begun his *Essays* in 1572, and the first and second books were published in 1580. An enlarged edition of these then appeared in 1588 together with a third book. Marie de Gournay's edition of 1635 was not only dedicated to Richelieu but had been prepared with his assistance. She in turn was 'entombed within the sepulchre' in 1645, aged seventy-nine.

Maria **Montessori**, *The Montessori Method*, 1912

~ I place at the beginning of this volume, now appearing in the United States, her fatherland, the dear name of Alice Hallgarten of New York, who by her marriage to Baron Leopold Franchetti became by choice our compatriot. Ever a firm believer in the principles underlying Case dei Bambini, she, with her husband, forwarded the publication of this book in Italy, and, throughout the last year of her short life, greatly desired the English translation which should introduce to the land of her birth the work so near her heart. To her memory I dedicate this book, whose pages, like an ever-living flower, perpetuate the recollection of her beneficence.

Translated from the Italian by Anne E. George; original title: *Metodo della pedagogia scientifica applicata all'educazione infantile* (1909). Maria Montessori was the internationally famous physician and educator who initiated the scientifically based 'Montessori method' or system of education for young children that is still widely followed today. Her first Casa dei Bambini ('Children's House', or school for young children) was opened in a slum district of Rome in 1907. Baron Leopoldo Franchetti was an Italian politician who died in Rome in 1917 at the age of seventy.

Guiy de **Montfort**, *All the Queen's Men*, 1980

~ This book is respectfully dedicated to the Memory of Lord Mountbatten, the Rt Hon. Airey Neave, MP and all those who have died for the love and honour of their country ... And for the children of Cambodia, in whose suffering innocence is reflected the cracked mirror of our time. This is for you, that you might forgive us ... For my lady, with love and gratitude. For my father, who never understood it all.

The story tells of a fictitious terrorist plot in 1978 to capture the Royal Yacht *Britannia* with Queen Elizabeth's husband, the Duke of Edinburgh, on board. The four-part dedication appears on two pages: the first two, to public figures, on one side of the page, and the second two, privately, on the other. Both Lord Mountbatten, the great-grandson of Queen Victoria, and Airey Neave, Conservative politician and former intelligence officer, were murdered by the IRA in 1979.

Carlotta **Monti** with Cy **Rice**, *W.C. Fields and Me*, 1971

~ I dedicate this book to myself, for the many years of loving service and kindness I willingly gave him.

Carlotta Monti was film star W.C. Fields's mistress from 1932, when she was twenty-four (and he fifty-three), to his death in 1946.

George Washington **Moon**, *The Bishop's English*, 1903

~ Dedicated to the memory of my ancestor Thomas Aldam, of Warmsworth, in the County of York, one of the earliest members of 'The Society of Friends'. A good man, who died in peace with all men, and loving trust in God, A.D. 1660.

The subtitle of this small book explains its aim: 'A series of criticisms on the Right Rev. Bishop Thornton's Laudation of the Revised Version of the Scriptures; and also on the English of the Revisers, showing that the version put forth by them contains errors against religion and morals so unpardonable as totally to unfit it for circulation'. In short, the Reverend is inveighing against the Revised Standard Version of the Bible, which had been published in 1881 (New Testament) and 1885 (Old Testament), with the former not well received by many, who objected to the annoying and apparently inaccurate alteration of many familiar words and passages. But some of this critic's objections hardly hold water. For example, he maintains that the rendering of I John 4:21 as 'And this commandment have we from him, that he who loveth God love his brother also' implies that we should love God's brother! The author was returning to the fray, having several years previously taken up the gauntlet against Dean Alford in *The Dean's English*. Even so, he writes in the present book, 'I am an old man now, being in my eightieth year, and consequently not so "keen of fence" as I was then, but I may still be able to do something which, if not redoubtable, may haply be deemed of public service in an attempted overthrow of disgraceful error.' So never give up, and never say die!

Chas **Moore**, *CB Language*, 1981

~ Dedicated to: Chris Cohen, my loyal typist, Irv, the Chicken Choker, The L.A. Shifter, The Hungry Eye, Mother Trucker, The Cricket, The Tulsa Flash.

The code names of fellow CBers. Moore himself was Mr Blue Sky.

Doris Langley **Moore**, *Ada, Countess of Lovelace*, 1977

~ To Mary Clapinson, Most Notable for Detection of Manuscripts and Deciphering of Handwritings.

Presumably a tribute to the author's editor.

George **Moore**, *Confessions of a Young Man*, 1888

~ To Jacques Blanche. The soul of the Ancient Egyptian awoke in me when my youth died, and I had the idea of preserving my past, its spirit and shape, in art. So dipping my paintbrush into my memory, I painted his cheeks so that they should take on an exact resemblance of life, and I wrapped death in the finest of winding-sheets. Rameses II could not have received more pious care! Let this book be as lasting as his pyramid! I wanted to inscribe your name here, dear friend, as an epitaph, for you are my youngest and dearest friend; and in you is all that is gracious and discerning in these dismal years that drain away into the mud of the twentieth century.

Translated by AR. The dedication is in French, but the book itself, an autobiography of the Irish novelist, is in English. Moore, who died in 1933, was still only thirty-six and obviously suffering from severe symptoms of *fin de siècle*. Jacques Blanche, then twenty-seven, was a gifted French portrait painter. Hence the appositeness of the artistic references: even double appositeness, for Moore had himself had ambitions to be a painter when young and had studied art in Paris.

John Trotwood **Moore**, *Gift of the Grass: being the Autobiography of a Famous Racing Horse*, 1911

~ Great horses are like great men: they achieve greatness because greatness is born in them. [...] And so I dedicate this book to four of them that I knew and loved – all of a family, and all unbeaten champions of their day. They were gentlemen without knowing it, friends without pay, generals unbooked, and heroes without feathers or trappings: Little Brown Jug, 2:11¼; Hal Pointer, 2:04½; Brown Hal, 2:12½, and Star Pointer, 1:59¼, – immortal quartet of the unbeaten Hals.

The American author and journalist wrote a good deal of 'local colour' literature about Tennessee, and was the father of the poet Merrill Moore.

Thomas **Moore**, *Odes of Anacreon Translated into English Verse*, 1801

~ To his Royal Highness the Prince of Wales. Sir, In allowing me to dedicate this Work to Your Royal Highness, you have conferred upon me an honour which

I feel very sensibly: and I have only to regret, that the pages which you have thus distinguished are not more deserving of such illustrious patronage. Believe me, Sir, With every sentiment of respect, Your Royal Highness's very grateful and devoted Servant, Thomas Moore.

This was the poet's first work, dedicated to the future George IV.

Thomas **Moore**, *Epistles, Odes and Other Poems*, 1806

~ To Francis, Earl of Moira, General in His Majesty's Forces, Master-general of the Ordnance, Constable of the Tower, etc. My Lord, It is impossible to think of addressing a Dedication to your Lordship without calling to mind the well-known reply of the Spartan to a rhetorician, who proposed to pronounce an eulogium on Hercules. 'On Hercules!' said the honest Spartan, 'who ever thought of blaming Hercules?' In a similar manner the concurrence of public opinion has left to the panegyrist of your Lordship a very superfluous task. I shall, therefore, be silent on the subject, and merely entreat your indulgence to the very humble tribute of gratitude which I have here the honour to present. I am, my Lord, with every feeling of attachment and respect, Your Lordship's very devoted Servant, Thomas Moore.

Francis Rawdon-Hastings, 1st Marquis of Hastings and (in the Irish peerage) 2nd Earl of Moira was a colonial administrator and army officer who had fought the Americans in the Civil War. Moore had made his acquaintance socially early in his career as a poet, and frequently stayed with him in England at his country seat near Castle Donington, Leicestershire.

Thomas **Moore**, *Irish Melodies*, 1808–34

~ To the Marchioness Dowager of Donegal. It is now many years since, in a Letter prefixed to the Third Number of the Irish melodies, I had the pleasure of inscribing the Poems of that work to your Ladyship, as to one whose character reflected honour on the country to which they relate, and whose friendship had long been the pride and happiness of their Author. With the same feelings of affection and respect, confirmed if not increased by the experience of every succeeding year, I now place those Poems in their present new form under your protection, and am, with perfect sincerity, Your Ladyship's ever attached friend, Thomas Moore.

The ten parts of this work were published irregularly between the dates mentioned. Hence the reference to the 'Third Number' and the original dedication.

Thomas **Moore**, *Intercepted Letters: or The Twopenny Postbag*, 1813

~ To Stephen Woolriche, Esq. My dear Woolriche, It is now about seven years since I promised (and I grieve to think that it is almost as long since we met) to dedicate to you the very first Book, of whatever size or kind, I should publish. Who could have thought that so many years would elapse, without my giving the least signs of life upon the subject of this important promise? Who could have imagined that a volume of doggerel, after all, would be the first offering that Gratitude would lay upon the shrine of Friendship? If you continue, however, to be as much interested about me and my pursuits as formerly, you will be happy to hear that doggerel is not my *only* occupation. [...] In the mean time, my dear Woolriche, like an orthodox Lutheran, you must judge of me rather by my *faith* than by my *works*; and however trifling the tribute which I here offer, never doubt the fidelity with which I am, and always shall be, Your sincere and attached Friend, The Author.

Thomas **Moore**, *Sacred Songs*, 1816
~ To Edward Tuite Dalton, Esq., this first number of sacred songs is inscribed, by his sincere and affectionate friend, Thomas Moore.

Thomas **Moore**, *Lalla Rookh*, 1817
~ To Samuel Rogers, Esq., this Eastern Romance is inscribed by his very grateful and affectionate friend, Thomas Moore.

Samuel Rogers was a fellow poet, but English, not Irish like Moore, and a friend of many famous literary names of the day, such as Byron, Scott and Wordsworth.

Thomas **Moore**, *Fables for the Holy Alliance*, 1823
~ To Lord Byron. Dear Lord Byron, Though this Volume should possess no other merit in your eyes, than that of reminding you of the short time we passed together at Venice, when some of the trifles which it contained were written, you will, I am sure, approve the dedication of it with pleasure, and believe that I am, My dear Lord, Ever faithfully yours, T.B.

Moore had been a friend of BYRON since the latter had come back to England from the eastern Mediterranean in 1831. On his death, Byron left his 'Memoirs' to Moore who, although destroying the original, used material from it to compile his *Letters and Journals of Lord Byron* (1830).

Thomas **Moore**, *The Summer Fête*, 1831
~ To the Honourable Mrs. Norton. For the groundwork of the following Poem I am indebted to a memorable Fête, given some years since, at Boyle Farm, the seat of the late Lord Henry Fitzgerald. In commemoration of that evening – of which the lady to whom these pages are inscribed was, I well recollect, one of the most distinguished ornaments – I was induced at the time to write some verses, which were afterwards, however, thrown aside unfinished, on my discovering that the same task had been undertaken by a noble poet, whose playful and happy *jeu d'esprit* on the subject has since been published. It was but lately, that, on finding the fragments of my own sketch among my papers, I thought of founding on them such a description of an imaginary Fête as might furnish me with situations for the introduction of music. Such is the origin and object of the following Poem,

and to Mrs. Norton it is, with every feeling of admiration and regard, inscribed by her father's warmly attached friend. Thomas Moore.

The 'noble poet' mentioned by Moore was FRANCIS EGERTON, whose own dedications see above.

Hannah More, *Hints towards Forming the Character of A Young Princess*, 1805

~ To the Right Reverend The Lord Bishop of Exeter (Dr. John Fisher). My Lord, Could it have been foreseen by the Author of the following pages, that, in the case of the illustrious Person who is the subject of them, the standard of Education would have been set so high; and especially, that this Education would be committed to such able and distinguished hands, the work might surely have been spared. But as the Second Volume was gone to the press before that appointment was announced, which must give general satisfaction, it becomes important to request, that if the advice suggested in any part of the Work should appear presumptuous, Your Lordship, and still more the Public, who might be more forward than Your Lordship in charging the Author with presumption, will have the candour to recollect, that it was offered, not to the learned Bishop of Exeter, but to an unknown, and even an imaginary Preceptor. Under these circumstances, Your Lordship will perhaps have the goodness to accept the Dedication of these slight Volumes, not as arrogantly pointing out duties to the discharge of which you are so competent, but as a mark of the respect and esteem with which I have the honour to be, My Lord, Your Lordship's most obedient and most faithful servant, The Author.

This work, with its pedantic dedication, was intended to be a recommendatory guide to the correct education and upbringing that should be given to the nine-year-old Princess Charlotte, daughter of the future George IV. In a Preface to this same treatise, Hannah More wrote: 'Had the Royal Pupil been a Prince, these Hints would never have been obtruded on the world, as it would then have been naturally assumed, that the established plan usually adopted in such cases would have been pursued'. In other words, princes got a 'proper' education, but princesses did not! Sadly, whatever education Princess Charlotte did or did not eventually receive, she died in childbirth in 1817 at the age of only twenty-one. Hannah More began life as a dramatist, but went on to become a religious and didactic writer, as here (and as below).

Hannah More, *Christian Morals*, 1813

~ As a slight memorial of sincere esteem and cordial friendship, this little sketch of Christian Morals is, with strict propriety, inscribed to the Rev. Thomas Gisborne, of Yoxall Lodge; in his writings and in his life, a consistent Christian moralist.

Gisborne knew most of the intellectual evangelicals of his day, and himself wrote several moralist and Christian philosophical works, as well as poems in the style of Cowper. Hannah More was now nearly seventy. She lived to be eighty-eight, and died in 1833.

Speer **Morgan**, *Belle Starr*, 1979

~ For Virginia Lee Morgan and Ralph Speer, Sr., who never told me any of this.

Christopher **Morley**, *Pipefuls*, 1920

~ This book is dedicated to three men, Hulbert Footner, Eugene Saxton and William Rose Benét. Because if I mentioned only one of them, I would have to write books to inscribe the other two.

Of the three American dedicatees, the best known is the last, who was not only a poet and novelist but editor of *The Reader's Encyclopedia* (1948). Morley was himself equally if not more prolific, and edited the eleventh edition of the famous *Bartlett's Quotations* (1937).

Robert **Morley**, *Robert Morley's Book of Worries*, 1979

~ To scrambled eggs on toast this book is affectionately dedicated.

A whimsical dedication to a whimsical book by the well-known British film actor, as a sequel to the equally diverting *Robert Morley's Book of Bricks*, published the previous year.

Sheridan **Morley**, *Marlene Dietrich*, 1976

~ For Margaret who's never cared for her and for the rest of us who always have.

A biography of the famous film star by the son of the film star above. The dedication is to his wife (on the one hand) and son and two daughters (on the other).

Desmond **Morris**, *The Book of Ages*, 1983

~ To my mother, who at 85 finally admits to being 'over 29'.

Reverend Robert **Morrison**, *Dictionary of the Chinese Language*, 1815

~ To the honorable the Court of Directors of the United East India Company, at whose sole expense the following work is printed, it is most respectfully dedicated by their much obliged and very obedient humble servant, The Author.

Morrison was a missionary in China and translator to the East India Company. His Chinese dictionary was long regarded as one of the best in any language.

Jedediah **Morse**, *Geography Made Easy: Being an Abridgement of the American Geography*, 1784

~ To the Young Masters and Misses throughout the United States, the following Easy Introduction to the useful and entertaining Science of Geography compiled particularly for their Use is dedicated, with his warmest wishes for the early Improvement in every thing that shall make them truly happy, by their sincere Friend, Jedediah Morse.

Morse was known as the 'Father of American Geography' and by vocation was a Congregational clergyman. His book was the first geography published in the United States. Samuel Morse, inventor of the Morse code, was his son.

Stella **Morton**, *Garden of Paradise*, 1942
~ To the children who still play in paradise.

Peter **Morwood**, *The Horse Lord*, 1983
~ For my father, who had to leave early.

Fynes **Moryson**, *An Itinerary*, 1617
~ To the Right Honourable, William, Earle of Pembroke, Lord Chamberlaine of
his Majesties Household, one of his Majesties most Honourable Privie Counsell,
and Knight of the most noble order of the Garter, &c. Right Honourable, Since
I had the happinesse imputed to Salomons Servants by the Queene of Sheba to
stand sometimes before You, an eye and eare witnes of your Noble conversation
with the worthy Earle of Devonshire, (my deceased Lord and Master) I ever
admired your vertues and much honoured your Person. And because it is a thing
no lesse commendable, gladly to receive favours from men of eminent worth, then
with like choice to tender respect and service to them, I being now led by powerfull
custome to seeke a Patron for this my Worke, and knowing that the weakest frames
need strongest supporters, have taken the boldnes most humbly to commend it
to your Honours protection: which vouchsafed, it shall triumph under the safegard
of that massy shield; and my selfe shall not only acknowledge this high favour
with humblest thankefulnesse, but with joy imbrace this occasion to avow my selfe
now by publike profession, (as I have long been in private affection,) Your Honours
most humble and faithfull servant, Fynes Moryson.

The dedicatee was the famous Earl of Pembroke who gave his name to Pembroke College,
Oxford, and who, as William Herbert, was thought by some to be the object of
SHAKESPEARE's well-known dedication to 'Mr W.H.' (which see below). Moryson had the
equivalent of a 'travelling fellowship' from Cambridge to make his way across Europe and
record everything he saw and heard in detail. He originally wrote his *Itinerary* in Latin,
but then translated it.

Maisie **Mosco**, *The Waiting Game*, 1987
~ This novel is dedicated to my friends Masha and Vladimir Slepak, with the
hope that Mr Gorbachev's *glasnost* will include ending their long and harrowing
wait to leave the Soviet Union.

A novel on the oppression of Soviet Jews.

Maria J. **Moss**, *A Poetical Cook Book*, 1864
~ When I wrote the following pages, some years back at Oak Lodge, as a pastime,
I did not think it would be of service to my fellow-creatures, for our suffering
soldiers, the sick, wounded, and needy, who have so nobly fought our Country's
cause, to maintain the flag of our great Republic, and to prove among Nations
that a Free Republic is not a Myth. With these few words, I dedicate this book
to the Sanitary Fair to be held in Philadelphia, June, 1864.

This, of course, was the time of the American Civil War, which would continue for another full year.

Peter **Motteux**, *Beauty in Distress*, 1698

~ To the Honourable HENRY HEVENINGHAM, Esq. Sir, – As Beauty in Distress has always found Protection from the Generous and the Brave, to throw herself into honorable hands and hospitable walls, she seeks a Patron here; fearless even of greater dangers than those she has happily escap'd, when your condescending goodness emboldens her to aspire to favours which her humble thoughts wou'd scarce permit her to expect. But while my fair Unfortunate rests secure under so auspicious a roof, my unhappier hero will inevitably be lost there. He'll find that sweetness of temper, that gracefulness, that tenderness of soul, and every qualification so much above him, that where he enters with Pride, he will sit down with envy. He will find you dividing your equally grateful conversation betwixt the gravity of the wise, the gayety of the witty, and the easy sprightliness of the fair, and entertaining the solid, the ingenious, and the beauteous, so as to improve the first, cheer the second, and charm the last. [...] For my part, I hope never to seem so impudent as to debase with flattery the real worth which I wou'd extol. But I ought to finish this address, lest I usurp some of those moments which are due to your more entertaining diversions; and as the business of this epistle is not more to secure to this tragedy the honour of your patronage than to assure you of the deep respect of the author, I cannot conclude better than with a solemn protestation of being eternally, with the utmost veneration, Your most humble and most obedient Servant, PETER MOTTEUX.

This unctuous dedication, in the original some four times as long as the extract quoted here, became notorious when it was discovered that it had actually been written by the patron himself, who is alleged to have offered to pay Motteux five guineas for the use of his name. (According to the eighteenth-century historian John Oldmixon, 'One Mr. Heveningham bought a dedication of Motteux, haggled with him about the price, and bargained for the number of lines and the superlatives of eulogy: not contented with this, he wrote the dedication himself, and made the miserable author put his name to it.') Motteux, a gifted Huguenot dramatist who had fled to England in 1685 after the revocation of the Edict of Nantes, had the singular misfortune to die in a London brothel on his fifty-eighth birthday.

Louise Chandler **Moulton**, *At the Wind's Will*, 1899

TO HOPE

Undying Hope, Memory's immortal heir,
    To thee I consecrate this sheaf of song, –
In darkest gloom, of thee I am aware;
    Thy magic is to make the weak soul strong.

The poems of the American poet, who married William U. Moulton in 1855, when she was twenty, were published in a collected edition in 1909.

Richard **Mulcaster,** *Positions,* 1581

~ To the most vertuous ladie, his most deare, and soveraine princesse, Elizabeth by the grace of God Queene of England, Fraunce, and Ireland, defendresse of the faith &c. My booke by the argument, most excellent princesse, pretendeth a common good, bycause it concerneth the generall traine and bringing up of youth, both to enrich their minds with learning, and to enable their bodies with health; and it craves the favour of some speciall countenaunce farre above the common, or else it can not possiblie procure free passage. [...] I am therefore driven upon these so violent considerations to presume so farre as to present it, being my first travell that ever durst venture upon the print, into your majesties most sacred handes. For in neede of countenaunce, where best abilitie is most assurance, and knowne vertue the fairest warrant, who is more sufficient then your excellencie is, either for cunning to commend, or for credit to commaunde? And what reason is there more likely to procure the favour of your majesties most gracious countenance, either to commende the worke, or to commaunde it waie, then the honest pretence of a generall good wherein you cannot be deceived? [...] I know your Majesties pacience to be exceeding great in verie petie arguments, if not, I should have bene afraid to have troubled you with so many wordes, and yet least tediousnesse do soure even a sweete and sound matter, I will be no bolder. God blesse your Majestie, and send you a long, & an healthfull life, to his greatest glorie, and your Majesties most lasting honour. Your Majesties most humble and obedient subject, Richard Mulcaster.

The complete dedication, a third as long again as these opening and closing passages addressed to Queen Elizabeth, apologises for the length of the book, explains its title (as meaning 'groundes' for the advancement of learning) and refers to the interest in education taken by the Queen's father, Henry VIII. The book itself is a surprisingly modern educational treatise, advocating among other things physical training, music in schools, direct contact between teachers and parents, and recognised qualifications and commensurate salaries for teachers. Education for women was also an essential part of the programme. Mulcaster himself graduated from Oxford as a Hebrew scholar and became the first headmaster of Merchant Taylor's School, London, and it was while he held this post that he wrote this work. In 1596 he then moved to become High Master of St Paul's School. A few words may need glossing in the excerpted text here: *travell* is 'labour', *countenaunce* is 'favour', *sufficient* is 'suitable', *cunning* is 'ability', *least* is 'lest'. In Mulcaster's third rhetorical question, *to commaunde it waie* is 'to approve its passage', i.e., to give the work the royal thumbs-up.

Charles **Murchison,** comp. and ed., *Palaeontological Memoirs and Notes of the Late H.F.,* 1868

~ To Colonel Sir Proby T. Cautley, K.C.B., Member of the Council of India, this volume, embracing the results of those studies of his departed friends and colleagues on the fossil fauna of the Sewalik Hills, which obtained for them worldwide reputation in science, is dedicated by The Author.

'H.F.' was Hugh Falconer, a Scottish palaeontologist and botanist, who had found fossilised mammals and reptiles in the Sewalik Hills, India, in 1832. Murchison, his friend, was the cousin of the famous geologist, Sir Roderick Murchison, and was himself a doctor but also an amateur geologist. Colonel Cautley, who designed the Ganges Canal, was likewise a 'fossil-hunter' and presented his Indian collection to the British Museum.

Frances **Murray**, *Payment for the Piper*, 1983

~ This novel is dedicated to my friends in the Staff Room of the Ladies' College, Guernsey, and in particular to Margaret Surridge, Elaine Berry and Anne Forsyth who were so helpful in providing me with material about old New Zealand. Teaching has its frustrations but they are compensated by the friends one makes.

Dr James **Murray** *et al.*, eds., *A New English Dictionary on Historical Principles*, 1888–1928

~ To the Queen's Most Excellent Majesty this Historical Dictionary of the English Language is by her gracious permission dutifully dedicated by the University of Oxford. A.D. MDCCCXCVII.

This was the first dedication to what is now the *Oxford English Dictionary*, originally published in parts, letter by letter of the alphabet. Its main editor, Dr Murray, had suggested that the whole work, then still being compiled, should be dedicated to Queen Victoria. In August 1897 she accepted, and the third volume (letters D and E) included a flyleaf with this dedication. No doubt it was felt that to have placed the dedication in the first volume would have been presumptuous. (A subsequent volume also had what amounted to a dedication: 'This sixth volume is a memorial of the munificence of the Worshipful Company of Goldsmiths who have generously contributed five thousand pounds towards its production'.) Finally, the tenth volume, published in 1928, had the following new dedication (and effective rededication): 'This Dictionary of the English Language which was dedicated in 1897 to Her Majesty Queen Victoria is now on its completion presented by His Majesty's gracious permission to King George the Fifth by the Chancellor, Master and Scholars of the University of Oxford'. Compare the dedications to the *Supplement* (under BURCHFIELD) and to the second edition of the *OED* (under SIMPSON).

A.W. **Mykel**, *The Windchime Legacy*, 1981

~ To three lives which, in ending, started it all.

A spy story.

❦ N ❦

Sir William Napier, *History of the War in the Peninsula,* 1828–40
~ To Field-Marshal the DUKE OF WELLINGTON. This history I dedicate to your Grace because I have served long enough under your command to feel why the soldiers of the Tenth Legion were attached to Caesar.

Napier had taken a prominent part in the Peninsular War in which he had been seriously wounded, reaching the rank of brevet lieutenant-colonel. After the war he decided to write its history, gathering material from various sources and acquaintances, including Wellington himself, who passed on to him the whole of the correspondence of Napoleon's son, Joseph Bonaparte, which had been taken at the battle of Vittoria in 1813. This was carefully deciphered by Napier's wife Caroline, whom he had married in 1812. The first volume of his *magnum opus* duly appeared in 1828, but its publishers, John Murray, lost money on it and declined to proceed with the remaining volumes. Napier therefore published these himself, at his own expense. The sixth and final volume appeared in 1840. The work long remained a classic account of its subject and is still regarded as a prime authority today.

R.K. Narayan, *A Tiger for Malgudi,* 1983
~ To Charles Pick, who, to my great joy, brought me to the windmill again.

Ogden Nash, *Hard Lines,* 1931
~ To Mrs. Parker, Mr. Hoffenstein, and Mr. Roget, without a handy set of whose works this book could not have been written so quickly.

i.e., Dorothy Parker, Samuel G. Hoffenstein, and Mark Roget. The first two were witty and original American poets; the third was the compiler of the famous *Thesaurus*, still in its subsequent versions and editions a basic resource of many writers. But Nash's own wit and humour is individual, and not quite as derivative as his dedication implies. *Hard Lines* was his first collection of verse.

Ogden Nash, *There's Always Another Windmill,* 1969
~ Once more for Frances. Who else is there?

As one might guess, Nash's wife, whom he married in 1931, the year of his first published collection of verse (see above).

George Jean Nathan, *Beware of Parents,* 1943
~ To George Jean Nathan, Jr.

Who did not exist: the book was a bachelor author's advice to parents.

Nikolay **Nekrasov**, *Frost the Red-Nosed*, 1863

To My Sister

Once again now you take me to task
For ignoring the call of my muse,
For not writing more as you ask,
But just doing each day as I choose.
I don't bar my muse from my head
Just to deal with each day to its end,
Is the gift that she gave me now dead,
That formerly made me her friend? [...]
My muse that has quietened of late
I am hesitant now to caress,
And her last song I sadly await
Is for you, dear, no more and no less. [...]

Translated from the Russian by AR; original title: *Moroz, krasnyy nos*. The powerful poem, describing a brave and attractive peasant woman and her hard life in the vast, frozen Russian forest, was not in fact Nekrasov's last inspiration by 'his muse', and in 1879, albeit posthumously and unfinished, appeared the long satirical folk-poem by which he is chiefly remembered, *Who Can Be Happy in Russia?*

Walter **Nelson**, *The Minstrel Code*, 1979

~ This book is dedicated to those whose job it is to make sure it can't happen.

A fictional account of a plan by a terrorist organisation to take the Queen hostage in a suicide mission.

E. **Nesbit**, *The Railway Children*, 1906

~ To my dear son, Paul Bland, behind whose knowledge of railways my ignorance confidently shelters.

Paul Bland was the eldest son of the children's writer Edith Nesbit, who had married Hubert Bland in 1880. The book itself remains a classic today. Its author deliberately used a single initial for her books in order to disguise her sex.

John Henry **Newman**, *Loss and Gain*, 1874

~ To the Very Rev. Charles W. Russell, D.D., President of St Patrick's College, Maynooth, &c. &c. My dear Dr Russell, – Now that at length I take the step of printing my name in the Title-page of this Volume, I trust I shall not be encroaching on the kindness you have so long shown to me, if I venture to follow it up by placing yours in the page which comes next, thus associating myself with you, and recommending myself to my readers by the association. Not that I am dreaming of bringing down upon you, in whole or part, the criticisms, just or unjust, which lie against a literary attempt which has in some quarters been thought out of keeping with my antecedents and my position; but the warm and sympathetic interest which you took in Oxford matters thirty years ago, and the benefits which I derived personally from that interest, are reasons why I am desirous of prefixing your name to a Tale, which, whatever its faults, at least is a more intelligible and exact representation of the thoughts, sentiments, and aspirations, then and there prevailing, than was to be found in the anti-catholic pamphlets, charges, sermons, reviews, and storybooks of the day. These reasons, too, must be my apology, should I seem to be asking your acceptance of a Volume, which, over and above its intrinsic defects, is, in its very subject and style, hardly commensurate with the theological reputation and the ecclesiastical station of the person to whom it is presented. I am, my dear Dr Russell, Your affectionate friend, John H. Newman.

The great English theologian, Anglican turned Roman Catholic, originally published this novel, the first of two, anonymously in 1848. Russell, head of Maynooth College, near Dublin, still today one of Europe's leading Roman Catholic seminaries, was a close personal friend of Newman and did much to bring about his conversion. Newman's novel, religious in content and turgid in style, like his dedicatory epistle here, is now virtually unread, as is his other, *Callista* (see below).

John Henry **Newman**, *Callista*, 1856
~ To Henry William Wilberforce. To you alone, who have known me so long, and who love me so well, could I venture to offer a trifle like this. But you will recognize the author in his work, and take pleasure in the recognition.

Wilberforce was a Roman Catholic journalist and author and the youngest son of William Wilberforce, the famous philanthropist. He studied classics at Oxford in the vacations with Newman, and it was the latter who had suggested that Wilberforce should abandon his academic specialty, law, and take holy orders. In 1850 Wilberforce and his wife, until then Anglicans, converted to Catholicism as Newman had done five years earlier. Newman's second of two novels was about the persecution and martyrdom of the third-century Christian convert, the sculptor Callista.

Beverley **Nichols**, *Are They The Same At Home?*, 1927
~ Dedicated with appropriate sentiments to my dear enemy the Baroness Clifton, in the knowledge that one of us should know better and that one of us does.

The book is a 'series of bouquets diffidently distributed' to famous contemporaries of Nichols, such as the conductor Thomas Beecham and the writer Aldous Huxley. In the 'bouquet' to himself Nichols tells how 'I have been seriously informed, by Baroness Clifton, writing with girlish ardour in the *Sunday Express*, that I deserve to be (*a*) eaten by lions; (*b*) raked into the gutter; (*c*) hacked with a pike until my blood spattered the pavement'. Not much love lost there. Nichols, a gifted writer, expended much of his literary talents on sentimental autobiographical accounts and journalistic social sniping. He died in 1983, aged eighty-four.

Beverley **Nichols**, *Down the Garden Path*, 1932
~ To Marie Rose Antoinette Catherine de Robert d'Aqueria de Rochegude d'Erlanger, whose charms are as gay and numerous as her names.

The book, a wistful but entirely self-centred account of the writer's country cottage and garden, was very popular for many years, and in its way epitomised the *dolce far niente* indulged in by those who had the means and the leisure (and the taste for it) in the early 1930s.

Meredith **Nicholson**, *The Little Brown Jug at Kildare*, 1908
~ To you at the Gate.

The American novelist is said to have seen an unknown girl standing by a gate but to have passed by without speaking to her. The missed opportunity was something he recalled, and regretted, for the rest of his life.

Florence **Nightingale**, *Introductory Notes on Lying-In Institutions*, 1871
~ To the Midwife Phaenarete: If I may dedicate, without 'permission', these small *Notes* to the shade of Socrates' mother, may I likewise, without presumption, call to my help the questioning shade of her son, that I who write may have the spirit of questioning aright, and that those who read may learn, not of me, but of themselves? And further has he not said, 'The midwives are respectable women and have a character to lose'?

The famous 'Lady with the Lamp' had founded an institution for the training of nurses in 1860, when she herself was forty. Socrates' mother, Phaenarete, was a midwife. A 'lying-in institution' is of course what we would now call a maternity home (or something similar).

Larry **Niven**, *The Integral Trees*, 1983
~ This book is dedicated to Robert Forward, for the stories he's sparked in me, for his help in working out the parameters of the Smoke Ring, and for his big, roomy mind.

In this science fiction story the 'Smoke Ring' is the doughnut-shaped gaseous envelope round a neutron star which had evolved a variety of life-forms.

Kathleen **Norris**, *The Rich Mrs Burgoyne*, 1912
> To Kathleen Mary Thompson
> Lover of good books, who never fails to find
> Some good in every book, your namesake sends
> This book to you, knowing you always kind
> To small things, timid, and in need of friends.

Kathleen Norris, née Thompson (hence 'namesake'), was the wife of Charles G. Norris, brother of Frank Norris, himself the best-known, and most substantial, of the three novelists, despite being the shortest lived (died 1902, aged only thirty-two). All were prolific enough, however.

Sir Thomas **North**, *The Lives of the Noble Grecians and Romanes*, 1603
~ To the most high and mighty princesse Elizabeth, by the grace of God, of England, Fraunce, and Ireland Queene, defender of the faith: &c. Under hope of

your highnes gratious and accustomed favor, I have presumed to present here
unto your Majestie, Plutarkes lyves translated, as a booke fit to be protected by
your highnes, and meete to be set forth in Englishe. For who is fitter to give
countenance to so many great states than such an highe and mightie Princesse?
Who is fitter to revive the dead memorie of their fame than she that beareth the
lively image of their vertues? Who is fitter to authorize a worke of so great learning
and wisedome than she whome all do honor as the Muse of the world? Therefore
I humbly beseech your Majestie, to suffer the simplenes of my translation to be
covered under the amplenes of your highnes protection. For, most gracious
Sovereigne, though this booke be no booke for your Majesties selfe, who are meeter
to be the chiefe storie, than a student therein, and can better understand it in
Greeke, than any man can make it Englishe: yet I hope the common sorte of your
subjects, shall not onely profit them selves hereby, but also be animated to the
better service of your Majestie. [...] And therefore that your hignes may give grace
to the booke, and the booke may doe his service to your Majestie: I have translated
it out of French, and doe here most humbly present the same unto your highnes,
beseeching your Majestie with all humilitie, not to reject the good meaning, but
to pardon the errours of your most humble and obedient subject and servaunt,
who prayeth God long to multiplye all graces and blessings upon your Majestie.
Written the sixteene day of January. 1579. Your Majesties most humble and
obedient servaunt, Thomas North.

This was North's most significant translation, of Plutarch's *Lives*. His version was not from
the original Greek, however, but from the French, as he makes clear here in the dedication
to Queen Elizabeth and as the work's full title meticulously details: 'The Lives of the Noble
Grecians and Romanes, compared together by that graue learned Philosopher and
Historiographer, Plutarke of Chæronea: Translated out of Greeke into French by James
Amyot, Abbot of Bellozane, Bishop of Auxerre, one of the King's Priuy Counsel, and Great
Amner of Fraunce; and out of French into Englishe by Thomas North.' ('Amner' is
'almoner'; the title of the senior chaplain to the French court was *Grand aumônier de France*.)
The work is important not only for the stylishness of North's translation, but for the fact
that it was the source for all Shakespeare's Roman plays, such as *Julius Caesar* and *Antony
and Cleopatra*, while others of his plays, such as *A Midsummer Night's Dream*, are also
indebted to it. *Antony and Cleopatra* in many places follows North's text almost word for
word. No copyright problems then!

❦ O ❦

Joyce Carol **Oates**, *Angel of Light*, 1981
~ This novel is for Robert Fagler, in honor of his service in the House of Atreus; and for our lost generations.

In classical mythology the House of Atreus was the family of Atreus, father of Agamemnon and Menelaus, who shocked the gods by feeding Thyestes, his brother, with his own child. The tragic story has been an inspiration for both Greek dramatists and subsequent writers, from Milton and Shakespeare to Sartre. Oates's story is about corruption in Washington.

Colonel H.A. **Oatts**, *Loch Trout*, 1958
~ To A.M.O. Who has fished with me for nigh on forty years and unravelled many of life's tangles.

Presumably to the piscatorial author's wife.

Edna **O'Brien**, *Casualties of Peace*, 1966
~ For Rita Tushingham whose coat it is.

The film actress dedicatee had by now leapt to fame with her performances in *A Taste of Honey* (1961), *The Knack* (1965) and other movies.

Flann **O'Brien**, *The Hard Life*, 1961
~ I honourably present to Graham Greene, whose own forms of gloom I admire, this misterpiece.

A droll compliment by the Irish writer to the great English novelist, whose own dedications see above.

Flann **O'Brien**, *The Dalkey Archive*, 1964
~ I dedicate these pages to my Guardian Angel, impressing upon him that I'm only fooling and warning him to see to it that there is no misunderstanding when I go home.

The Irish novelist would in fact 'go home' two years after this was published, at the age of fifty-five.

Sean O'Casey, *The Plough and the Stars*, 1926
~ To the gay laugh of my mother at the gate of the grave.

The Irish dramatist's mother, now elderly, was born Susanna Casey, and in turn bore him in 1880. He was the youngest of her surviving children.

John Odmark, *An Understanding of Jane Austen's Novels*, 1981
~ This book is dedicated to my grandfather Luther Owen, who has always thought I should have become a lawyer, and to my wife Helga, who suspects I would have had more time if I had.

The dedication comes as the last two sentences in the Preface to the book, whose author died just before its publication, aged thirty-eight.

John Ogilby, *Atlas Japaniensis*, 1670
~ To the Supream, most high and Mighty Prince Charles II. By the Grace of God, of Great Britain, France, and Ireland King, Defender of the Faith, &c. These Strange and Novel Relations concerning Both the Ancient and Present Estate of the So Populous and Wealthy Empire of Japan, being a Book of Wonders, Dedicated with all Humility, Lies Prostrate at the Sacred Feet of Your Most Serene Majesty: by the Humblest of Your Servants, and Most Loyal Subject, John Ogilby.

Ogilby was a Scottish translator and printer, whose works included translations of several classical authors and of Aesop's *Fables*. The work here, whose full title was 'Atlas Japaniensis: being remarkable Addresses, by way of embassy, from the East India Company of the United Provinces to the Emperor of Japan', was a compilation based on the writings of the classical poet Montanus.

Alfred Ollivant, *The Taming of John Blunt*, 1911
~ To the Future.

Ollivant never repeated the success of his famous dog story, *Owd Bob* (1898). He had taken up writing when his career as an artillery officer had been brought to an abrupt end by a spinal injury. He died in 1927, aged fifty-three.

Baroness Orczy, *The Scarlet Pimpernel*, 1905
~ To Julia Neilson and Fred Terry, whose genius created the rôles of Sir Percy and Lady Blakeney on the stage, this book is affectionately dedicated.

The famous novel followed its success as a stage version two years earlier, in which Fred Terry played Sir Percy Blakeney, the 'Scarlet Pimpernel', while his wife, Julia Neilson, took the part of Marguerite, Lady Blakeney. BARONESS ORCZY had written the play in collaboration with her husband, Montague Barstow.

Baroness Orczy, *Eldorado*, 1906
~ To my life-long friend, David Murray, R.A. To you, my dear David, I inscribe

and dedicate this book, not only because you liked it so, but in token of my admiration for your genius, and for your devotion to a sister art. Emmuska Orczy.

Murray, who died in 1933 at the age of eighty-four, was a Scottish landscape painter. The novel was the author's fourth about the famous Scarlet Pimpernel, who had made his bow to his reading public the previous year (see above). 'Emmuska' was the pet form of the first name of Emma Magdalena Rosalia Marie Josefa Barbara Orczy, the Hungarian-born author better known as Baroness Orczy, who had arrived in England at the age of fifteen in 1880.

Baroness **Orczy**, *Petticoat Government*, 1909
~ To Theodore Watts-Dunton, the kind friend whose appreciation has cheered me, the idealist whose work has guided me, the brilliant intellect whose praise has encouraged me, this book is dedicated in token of admiration, regard and friendship. Emmuska Orczy.

Watts-Dunton had made his name as novelist with *Aylwin* (1898), a thinly disguised portrait of Dante Gabriel Rossetti. He encouraged many writers, and even took Swinburne into his own house for several years to look after him when the poet was at a low ebb. See SWINBURNE's own dedication to him, below.

Baroness **Orczy**, *Mam'zelle Guillotine*, 1940
~ To all those who are fighting in the air, on the water and on land for our country and our homes, I dedicate this romance because it is to them that we shall owe a happy issue out of all our troubles and a lasting peace. Emmuska Orczy.

The ninth and last of the adventures of the Scarlet Pimpernel (see above) who gallantly rescued victims from the guillotine in the French Revolution. Baroness Orczy's dedication was both patriotic and prophetic for her adopted homeland.

James **Orton**, *The Proverbialist and the Poet*, 1852
~ To the lovers of Sense-Shortness, and Salt, this work is respectfully inscribed.

The reference appears to be to some proverb or quotation.

Thomas **Otway**, *Venice Preserv'd*, 1682
~ To Her Grace the Duchess of Portsmouth. Madam, – Were it possible for me to let the world know how entirely your Grace's goodness has devoted a poor man to your service; were there words enough in speech to express the mighty sense I have of your great bounty towards me; surely I should write and talk of it for ever: but your Grace has given me so large a theme and laid so very vast a foundation, that imagination wants stock to build upon it. I am as one dumb when I would speak of it, and when I strive to write, I want a scale of thought sufficient to comprehend the height of it. Forgive me, then, Madam, if (as a poor peasant once made present of an apple to an emperor) I bring this small tribute, the humble growth of my little garden, and lay it at your feet. Believe it is paid you with the utmost gratitude, believe that so long as I have thought to remember how very

much I owe your generous nature, I will ever have a heart that shall be grateful for it too. [...] May your Grace, who are so good a mistress, and so noble a patroness, never meet with a less grateful servant than, Madam, your Grace's entirely devoted creature, Thomas Otway.

An embarrassingly servile address to Charles II's mistress, Louise-Renée de Kéroualle, Duchess of Portsmouth (from 1673), the recipient of other dedications from famous writers, such as JOHN CROWNE. It is rather sad to see a fine and sensitive tragedian like Otway demeaning himself like this.

Ouida, *Bimbi*, 1882

~ A S.A.R. Vittorio Emanuele Principe di Napoli speranza dell'Italia queste novelle dettate per lui consacra riverente Ouida.

The Italian dedication translates: 'To His Royal Highness Victor Emmanuel, Prince of Naples, hope of Italy, these stories written for him are reverently dedicated by Ouida'. This was Victor Emmanuel III, then aged twelve, who became king of Italy in 1900 (until 1946). 'Ouida' was the pseudonym (from a childish pronunciation of her first name) of Louise de la Ramée, an English-born writer of romantic novels and short stories, the latter including those for children, as here.

❦ P ❦

Samuel **Page**, *Alcilia, or Philoparthen's Loving Folly*, 1619
~ To my approved and much respected friend, Iz. Wa.: –

> To thee, thou more than thrice beloved friend
> I too unworthy of so great a blisse:
> These harsh-tun'd lines I here to thee commend,
> Thou being cause it is now as it is:
> For hadst thou held thy tongue, by silence might
> These have been buried in oblivion's night.

> If they were pleasing, I would call them thine,
> And disavow my title to the verse:
> But being bad, I needs must call them mine,
> No ill thing can be cloathed in thy verse.
> Accept them then, and where I have offended,
> Rase thou it out, and let it be amended. S.P.

The dedicatee was the young Izaak Walton, aged twenty-six, who only when he was sixty gained fame with his treatise on fishing, *The Compleat Angler* (1653). (See his own dedication below.) This was the second edition of Page's poetic work. The first had appeared in 1613, 'by S.P.', which led some to assume that it was by the historian and travel-writer Samuel Purchas, his contemporary. When the third edition was published in 1628, these two dedicatory stanzas were replaced by six lines by 'the author to his book'.

A.B. **Paine**, *The Arkansaw Bear, a Tale of Fanciful Adventure*, 1898
~ Dedicated to Master Frank Ver Beck, for whose bedtime entertainment the Arkansaw Bear first performed.

The dedicatee was the young son of the book's illustrator. Albert Bigelow Paine was an American author best known for his biography of Mark Twain, which appeared in 1912, but who also wrote a number of children's books, like this one (and the one below). One of his plays, *The Great White Way* (1901), gave the familiar name of the New York theatre district.

A.B. **Paine**, *The Hollow Tree Snowed-in Book*, 1910
~ To all dwellers in the big deep woods of dream.

Thomas **Paine**, *The Rights of Man*, 1791–2

~ To George Washington, President of the United States of America. Sir, I present you a small Treatise in defence of those Principles of Freedom which your exemplary Virtue hath so eminently contributed to establish. That the Rights of Man may become as universal as your Benevolence can wish, and that you may enjoy the Happiness of seeing the New World regenerate in the Old, is the Prayer of, Sir, Your much obliged, and Obedient Humble Servant, Thomas Paine.

This was one of the great English political writer's most famous (and most notorious) works, attacking hereditary succession. It was branded as seditious, and Paine was obliged to flee to France where he was convicted of treason in his absence. Earlier, he had been sent to America by Benjamin Franklin, where he had served in Washington's army while pursuing his political writing.

Bernard **Pares**, *Russian Fables of Ivan Krylov*, 1942
   To Birds and Bears, wherever they be,
   Especially R., J., S. and C. –
   Or else, as you might possibly guess,
   To P., A., and R., with an E. and an S.

The book is a verse translation of Krylov's *Fables* with Russian and English texts on facing pages. The first edition, a hardback, was published in 1926 and was dedicated by its author, the Russian historian Sir Bernard Pares, to his eldest son Richard, then a Fellow of All Souls College, Oxford. The second edition, an abridged version in a Penguin paperback, had the new dedication quoted here, in order to include a wider range of members of the Pares family. The second line thus contains the initials of Richard's family: Richard himself, his wife Janet, and his two daughters Susan and Catherine. (Two more daughters, Elisabeth and Jenny, were born later.) The fourth line contains the initials, which happen to spell out the family surname, of Sir Bernard's own children: Peter (the second youngest son), Andrew (the youngest), Richard (again), Elisabeth (the second oldest) and Susan (the third child). Susan (Sue) had actually been christened Ursula, hence the reference to 'Bears' (as her name means 'little bear'). But Sir Bernard used nicknames based on 'Birds and Bears' for his children in any case, and, for instance, was writing letters to Andrew as 'Beloved Bearikin' right up to his death in 1949 at the age of eighty-two. Richard Pares, born in 1902, and in later life Professor of History at Edinburgh University, died in 1958, aged fifty-five.

John Ayrton **Paris**, *Philosophy in Sport Made Science in Earnest*, 1827

~ To Miss Maria Edgeworth. Madam, To whom can a work, which professes to blend amusement with instruction, be dedicated with so much propriety, as to one, whose numerous writings have satisfactorily demonstrated the practicability and value of such a union; – to one who has stripped Romance of her meretricious trappings, and converted her theatre into a temple worthy of Minerva? Justly has it been observed, that to the magic pens of Madame d'Arblay, and yourself, we are indebted for having the Novel restored to its consequence, and, therefore, to its usefulness; and I may be allowed to add, that your Harry and Lucy have shown how profitably and agreeably, the machinery of fiction may be worked for the dissemination of truth. That a life which has been so honourable to yourself, and so serviceable to the Commonwealth, may be long extended, and deservedly enjoyed, is the fervent wish of the author.

Paris was a doctor who wrote mainly on medicine but also a biography of Humphrey Davy. This present book is a popular treatise on physical science, with sketches by Cruikshank. Maria Edgeworth, now aged sixty, had been widely feted by her literary contemporaries. Her works were either novels on Irish life or English society, or books for children. Harry and Lucy were a brother and sister in one of her didactic books for children in the series *Early Lessons*, begun in 1801.

John **Parkinson**, *Paradisi in Sole Paradisus Terrestris*, 1629

~ To the Queens most excellent Maiestie. Madame: Knowing your maiestie so much delighted with all the faire flowers of a garden, and furnished with them as farre beyond others, as you are eminent before them, this my work of a Garden, long before this intended to be published, but now only finished, seemed as it were destined to be first offered into your Highnesse hands as of ryght challenging the propriety of Patronage from all others. Accept I beseech your Majestie this speaking Garden that may inform you in all the particulars of your store as well as wants, when you cannot see any of them fresh upon the ground: and I shall further encourage him to accomplish the remainder, who in praying that your Highnesse may enjoy the heavenly Paradise, after the many years fruition of this earthly, submitteth to be Your Majesties in all humble devotion, John Parkinson.

This was the first work of the apothecary and herbalist, with its full title continuing (in English): 'A garden of all sorts of pleasant flowers, which our English ayre will permitt to be nursed up; with a kitchen garden […] and an orchard' (etc). The work gives a description of all the plants and shrubs and bulbs of Parkinson's day, with a classification for each, under their varieties, and ending with a division into 'The Place', 'The Time', 'The Names' and 'The Vertues' of every plant. (The main Latin title translates as 'An Earthly Paradise of a Paradise in the Sun', with the latter phrase also intended as a pleasant pun on the author's name, as a 'Park in the sun'.) Parkinson dedicated his work to Queen Henrietta Maria, herself now blossoming out as the twenty-year-old wife of Charles I. As a result of its publication, Charles awarded Parkinson the title of 'Botanicus Regius Primarius', or the equivalent of royal head botanist.

Edward Abbott **Parry**, *Katawampus: Its Treatment and Cure*, 1895

~ To those virtuous and well-behaved children, Helen, Dorothy, Joan and Humffreys, this volume is respectfully dedicated by their affectionate Pater.

The book is a children's story about children who throw a tantrum ('Katawampus') when they don't get what they want, so that the dedication is ironic. Parry, an English judge, was father of the four children named. In the book they are respectively represented by nine-year-old Olga ('thought herself very wise and clever'), seven-year-old Molly ('a great chatterbox'), her younger sister Kate ('like the little girl you have all heard of, who had a curl hanging down from the middle of her forehead') and three-year-old Tomakin ('ready to sing and romp until six in the evening').

James **Parton,** *Life of Andrew Jackson,* 1860
~ To North Carolina and Tennessee, mother and daughter. One gave Jackson birth, the other opportunity.

Andrew Jackson, seventh President of the United States, was actually born in South Carolina. However, he was admitted to the North Carolina bar in 1787 and opened a law office in Tennessee the following year, becoming judge of the Tennessee Supreme Court in 1798 and major-general of the Tennessee Militia in 1802.

Eric **Partridge,** *Slang Today and Yesterday,* 1933
~ For my old and loyal friend Alan Steele.

Eric **Partridge,** *Words, Words, Words!,* 1933
~ For Mary and Frances Long, who, in their many kindnesses, waste no words and yet achieve eloquence.

Eric **Partridge,** *A Dictionary of Slang and Unconventional English,* 1937
~ To the memory of the late Alfred Sutro (of San Francisco), lover of lovely things in art and literature, devotee to knowledge, and true friend.

Eric **Partridge,** *A Dictionary of Clichés,* 1940
~ To the memory of the late A.W. Stewart, Professor of Chemistry, writer of thrillers, lover of good English, gratefully from the author whom he considerably helped in that excellent blood sport: cliché-hunting.

Eric **Partridge,** *A Dictionary of Abbreviations,* 1942
~ For my friend Hugh Kimber, who does not need it.

Eric **Partridge,** *Usage and Abusage,* 1942
~ In memoriam Dr C.T. Onions, C.B.E., from whose lucid lexicography, severely impeccable etymologies and humanely corrective English syntax I have learnt more than I can fittingly express in this respectful dedication.

Eric **Partridge,** *Shakespeare's Bawdy,* 1947
~ For F. Chesney Horwood, scholar and friend.

Eric **Partridge,** *Words at War: Words at Peace,* 1948
~ For Neil Bell.

Eric **Partridge,** *A Dictionary of the Underworld,* 1949
~ For M. Gustave Rudler, Maréchal Foch Professor of French in the University of Oxford, *hommage d'auteur, voeux et souhaits d'ami.*

Eric Partridge, *Here, There and Everywhere*, 1950
~ For H.L. Menken, who has made the American language his own and *The American Language* the world's.

Eric Partridge and **John W Clark**, *British and American English since 1900*, 1951
~ For Gregory Mitchell (of Onehunga, New Zealand), gratefully, for much friendly assistance in Maori and for many kind, thoughtful and generous actions over a period of many years. Eric Partridge.

Eric Partridge, *From Sanskrit to Brazil*, 1952
~ For John W. Clark, of the University of Minnesota, in memory of a delightful collaboration and in gratitude for many kindnesses.

Eric Partridge, *Chamber of Horrors*, 1952
~ To Ivor Brown, gracious guardian of English, appreciatively, 'Vigilans'.

Eric Partridge, *You Have a Point There*, 1953
~ For Hamish Hamilton, who doesn't need it.

Eric Partridge, *The Concise Usage and Abusage*, 1954
~ For the Headmaster and Masters of Cotton College: where I have spent so many happy and profitable days: this affectionate dedication.

Eric Partridge, *What's the Meaning?*, 1956
~ For Essie and Diana Browning, with affection.

Eric Partridge, *Origins: A Short Etymological Dictionary of Modern English*, 1958
~ *Piam in memoriam* Cecil Arthur Franklin, a kindly and generous man and a remarkable publisher.

Eric Partridge, *Name This Child*, 1959
~ To Carlile Norris, with deep respect and, if anything, deeper affection.

Eric Partridge, *Comic Alphabets*, 1961
~ Gratefully, to the Librarians of the British Museum (and their staffs), without whose constant and courteous assistance, and archangelic patience, this and most of my other books could not have been written.

Eric **Partridge**, *Smaller Slang Dictionary*, 1961
~ For Simeon Potter, a humanist among the philologers; a great philologist, with a generous sense of the humanities.

Eric **Partridge**, *Adventuring Among Words*, 1961
~ For Richard Middleton Wilson, Professor of English Language in the University of Sheffield: with the author's profound gratitude.

Eric **Partridge**, *A Dictionary of Catch Phrases*, 1977
~ For Norman Franklin, worthy son of a worthy father and, in his own right, a brilliant and generous publisher.

Eric **Partridge**, *A Dictionary of Catch Phrases* (ed. by Paul Beale), 2nd edn., 1985
~ While fully acknowledging the help and encouragement given to me by my publishers, I dedicate this second edition of *A Dictionary of Catch Phrases*, with profound gratitude, to the entire staff of St Luke's Ward and its associated clinics: cleaners; auxiliaries; nurses; doctors; consultants; surgeons; and others in the background – all who were on duty at the Leicester Royal Infirmary, 1–13 April and 30 October–3 November 1982, and in the clinics ever since. Without their skills and care I would have been denied the privilege and delight of editing this book. P.B.

A selection of dedications from the considerable output of the New Zealand-born philologist and lexicographer, whose particular area of interest in the English language was somewhat off-centre, and focused more on the unconventional, slang and improper. The dedications range from the private to the public, and include a number of eminent colleagues, British and American, working in the same field, as well as other professionals such as publishers and lecturers. F. Chesney Horwood, Dean of St Catherine's College, Oxford, had Partridge as one of his pupils. 'Vigilans' was the pseudonym used by Partridge for *Chamber of Horrors*, on errors and lapses in English. Most of Partridge's dictionaries (named as such) were published by Routledge & Kegan Paul, including both editions of the final work here, where the second dedication is of course that of its previously indisposed editor, Paul Beale, not of Partridge, who had died in 1979, aged eighty-five. Norman Franklin, dedicatee of the first edition, and Routledge's chairman until his retirement in 1988, was the son of Cecil Franklin (*Origins*), who had died in 1961.

Coventry **Patmore**, *The Angel in the House*, 1854–63
~ This Poem is inscribed to the memory of Her by whom and for whom I became a poet.

Patmore's first wife, Emily, née Andrews, whom he married in 1847 when she was twenty-three, was the inspiration of this long and popular sequence of poems in praise of married love. She died in 1862, leaving him with six children. The two had come by then to be regarded as an ideal Victorian couple, while the *Dictionary of National Biography* described Emily as 'a lady possessed of mental and personal charms far beyond the common'. Patmore went on to marry twice more, and died in 1896, aged seventy-three.

John **Paxton**, ed., *Everyman's Dictionary of Abbreviations*, 1974
~ To Nchls and Jnthy.

Presumably the latter name is an abbreviated 'Jonthy', itself short for Jonathan.

Laurence **Payne**, *Malice in Camera*, 1983
~ For Randolph Beard, Surgeon. A poor return for a life.

A tribute that is laconic in the extreme.

William **Payne**, *An Introduction to Geometry*, 1767
~ Sir, They who are permitted to prefix the names of princes to the treatises of science generally enjoy the protection of a patron, without fearing the censure of a judge. The honour of approaching your royal highness has given me many opportunities of knowing that the work which I now presume to offer will not partake of the usual security. For as the knowledge which your royal highness has already acquired of Geometry extends beyond the limits of an introduction, I expect not to inform you; I shall be happy if I merit your approbation. [...] Geometry is secure of your regard, and your opinion of its usefulness and value has sufficiently appeared by the condescension in which you have been pleased to honour one who has so little pretension to the notice of Princes as, Sir, your royal highnesses most obliged, most obedient and most humble servant, William Payne.

This dedication to Edward, Duke of York, may well have been the work of Dr Johnson.

Geoffrey **Payton**, *Payton's Proper Names*, 1969
~ To Mary, without whose constant encouragement and advice this book would have been finished in half the time.

Francis Greenwood **Peabody**, *Mornings in the College Chapel*, 1899
~ To my beloved and revered colleagues, the preachers to the university, and to the sacred memory of Phillips Brooks, of the first staff of preachers, who being dead yet speaketh among us, in grateful recollection of happy association in the service of Christ and the Church.

Peabody was an American Unitarian theologian, at this time Professor of Christian Morals at Harvard. Phillips Brooks was the American Episcopalian bishop (died 1893, aged fifty-eight) who gave the world the popular carol 'O Little Town of Bethlehem', written when he was thirty-three.

Josephine Preston **Peabody**, *Fortune and Men's Eyes*, 1900
~ To my Mother's presence and my Father's memory.

Brooklyn-born Josephine Peabody had just, aged twenty-six, turned from light lyric poetry to poetic drama when she wrote this, a one-act play about Shakespeare.

Henry **Peacham,** *Minerva Britanna,* 1612

~ To the Right High and Mightie HENRIE eldest sonne of our Soveraigne Lord
the King, PRINCE OF WALES, Duke of Cornwall and Rothsay, and Knight of the
most noble order of the Garter. Most excellent Prince, Having by more then
ordinarie signes, tasted heeretofore of your gratious favour; and evidently knowen
your Princely and generous inclination to all good Learning and excellencie, I am
emboldened once againe to offer up at the altar of your gratious acceptance these
mine Emblemes; a weake (I confesse,) and a worthlesse sacrifice, though an assured
pledge of that zeale and duetie I shall ever most religiouslie owe unto your Highnes:
shewing herein rather a will to desire, then worth to deserve, so peerlesse a
patronage. [...] What I have done, I most humbly offer up the same unto your
gratious view and protection: desiring of God to beautifie and enrich your most
hopeful & heroique minde with the divinest giftes of his grace and knowledge,
heartily wishing there were any thing in me worthy of the least favour and respect
of so excellent a Prince. To your Highnes, the most sincerely and affectionately
devoted in all dutie and service, HENRY PEACHAM.

The descriptive subtitle of Peacham's work gives a clue to its content and to the kind of
books he wrote and compiled: 'A Garden of Heroical Devises, furnished and adorned with
emblemes and impresa's of sundry natures, newly devised, moralized, and published by
Henry Peacham, M^r of Artes'. That is, a collection of mottoes, verses and the like with
accompanying drawings by himself. Peacham was a versatile author and illustrator, turning
his hand to a whole range of subjects, from language and manners to art and heraldry.

Hesketh **Pearson,** *Conan Doyle: His Life and Art,* 1943

~ To James Galbraith Mitchell. My dear James, You and I have disagreed about
most things under the sun, and as you come from somewhere in North Britain I
have been compelled to argue with you about everything under the sun. But on
one point at any rate we have always agreed: the immense superiority of the
Sherlock Holmes saga over all other detective fiction. And although you are quite
capable of disputing it, I think you agree with me that the Brigadier Gerard stories
are the best short adventure-yarns ever written. It is because from boyhood I have
never enjoyed any tales so much as those of Holmes and Gerard that I have written
this book, which is (partly) a tribute of gratitude to their creator for more happy
hours than I should care to count. Yours ever, the Author.

A dedication that is more implicit than explicit, and that is even more a compliment to the
creator of Holmes than the recipient of the letter. Pearson, the writer of many lively and
readable biographies, lived in the south of England, in Sussex. Hence the 'North-South
divide' that he refers to.

Joseph **Pennell** and Elizabeth **Pennell,** *Our Sentimental Journey through France and Italy,* 1888

~ To Lawrence Sterne, Esq. Dear Sir, We never should have ventured to address
you, had we not noticed of late that Mr. Andrew Lang has been writing to Dead

Authors, not one of whom – to our knowledge – has taken offence at this liberty. Encouraged by his example, we beg leave to dedicate to you this history of our journey, laying it with the most respectful humility before your sentimental shade, and regretting it is without that charm of style which alone can make it worthy. And as, in our modesty, we would indeed be unwilling to trouble you a second time, we must take advantage of this unhoped-for opportunity to add a few words of explanation about our journey in your honor. It is because of the conscientious fidelity with which we rode over the route made ever famous by you, that we have included ourselves in the class of Sentimental Travellers, of which you must ever be the incomparable head. [...] We have the honor to be, dear Sir, your most obedient and most devoted and most humble servants, Joseph Pennell, Elizabeth Robins Pennell.

The Pennells, husband and wife, were Americans who came to live in England in 1884, the year of their marriage, staying there until 1918. While there, they became acquainted with many literary figures, such as Aubrey Beardsley and Bernard Shaw. The journey they describe in the book here was one they made in their early thirties, following as closely as possible Sterne's route in *A Sentimental Journey Through France and Italy* (1768), in which the narrator travels from Calais to Rouen and Paris (but never actually reaches Italy). Sterne's narrator made the journey by post-chaise, but the Pennells made their excursion by tricycle, 'the only vehicle by which we could follow your wheel-tracks along the old post-roads'. For the reference to Andrew Lang, see his own dedication above.

Sholto **Percy** and Reuben **Percy**, *The Percy Anecdotes*, 1821–3
~ To Mrs Elizabeth Fry, the female Howard of her times, these anecdotes of beneficence are respectfully inscribed by her most devoted and obedient humble servants, Sholto Percy, Reuben Percy.

This is the dedication to the *Anecdotes of Beneficence* in volume I of the collection. Elizabeth Fry, who was the subject of one of the anecdotes, was the famous English Quaker philanthropist and prison reformer, and so in the latter capacity a 'female Howard', like the eighteenth-century prison reformer John Howard. 'Sholto Percy' and 'Reuben Percy' were the respective pseudonyms of Joseph Clinton Robertson and Thomas Byerley, both journalists, who claimed to be 'Brothers of the Benedictine monastery of Mount Benger', taking their pen name from the Percy coffee-house in Rathbone Place, London, where they used to meet regularly. Their *Anecdotes* appeared monthly in forty-four parts.

Thomas **Percy**, *Reliques of Ancient English Poetry*, 1765
~ To the Right Honourable Elizabeth, Countess of Northumberland, in her own right, Baroness Percy, Lucy, Poynings, Fitz-Payne, Bryan, and Latimer. Madam, those writers, who solicit the protection of the noble and great, are often exposed to censure by the impropriety of their addresses: a remark that will perhaps be too readily applied to him, who having nothing better to offer than the rude songs of ancient minstrels, aspires to the patronage of the Countess of Northumberland, and hopes that the barbarous productions of unpolished ages can obtain the approbation or notice of her, who adorns courts by her presence, and diffuses

elegance by her example. But this impropriety, it is presumed, will disappear, when it is declared that these poems are presented to your Ladyship, not as labours of art, but as effusions of nature, showing the first efforts of ancient genius, and exhibiting the customs and opinions of remote ages. [...] I am, Madam, your Ladyship's most humble and most devoted servant, Thomas Percy.

Percy's *Reliques* was a collection of medieval and later songs, ballads and other verse pieces, some of which were crude in style or subject matter. Their compiler was thus understandably anxious not to offend or alarm his titled patroness, the daughter of Charles Seymour, 6th Duke of Somerset. This was the first edition of the work, and the same dedication appeared in the second edition (1767) and the third (1775). The dedication itself, however, was composed by Dr Johnson, so was not Percy's own. The Duchess died in 1776, so when the fourth edition was published in 1794, it had an amended dedication: 'To Elizabeth, late Duchess, and Countess of Northumberland, in her own right Baroness Percy, etc., etc., etc., [...] this little work was originally dedicated; and as it sometimes afforded her amusement, and was highly distinguished by her indulgent approbation, it is now, with the utmost regard, respect and gratitude, consecrated to her beloved and honoured memory'. Percy, who later became Bishop of Dromore, in Ireland, was anxious to connect his name and family with that of the Northumberland Percys, and in particular wished to trace his ancestry back to Sir Ralph Percy, son of the 2nd Earl of Northumberland.

Louis **Perrier**, *Osteophytic Arthrosis*, 1862

~ To my father, to my mother: I will never forget the sacrifices that you made for me. To the memory of my grandfather, to my brothers and my sister. To Uncle Jacques Roux and his family. To all my relations, all my friends. To M. Ollier. To my masters.

Translated from the French by AR; original title: *L'Arthrose ostéophytique*. This all-embracing 'family and friends' dedication appeared in the thesis for the Bachelor of Science degree worked by the famous Dr Perrier, whose name is now universally associated with his particular brand of sparkling mineral water. His new qualification entitled him to practise as a specialist at Montpellier, France, where he had made a detailed study of arthritic patients and their treatment. Monsieur Ollier was the senior surgeon of the rheumatic establishment at Lyon where Perrier had undergone his medical training.

Fred **Perry**, *An Autobiography*, 1984

~ This book is dedicated to players and spectators alike, and to the game of tennis, which has done so much for me.

The life story of the famous British tennis player, published when he was seventy-five.

Walter Copland **Perry**, *Greek and Roman Sculpture*, 1882

~ To H.I.H. the Crown Princess of Germany and Prussia, Princess Royal of Great Britain and Ireland, whose skill as an artist has made her a discriminating patroness of art, this work is dedicated with profound respect by her loyal and obedient servant the author.

The dedicatee was Queen Victoria's daughter, Princess Victoria, who had married Prince (later Emperor) Frederick William of Prussia in 1858.

Laurence J. **Peter** and Raymond Hall, *The Peter Principle*, 1969

~ This book is dedicated to all those who, working, playing, loving, living and dying at their Level of Incompetence, provided the data for the founding and development of the salutary science of Hierarchiology.

As the Canadian-born American educationist explained it in this book: 'My analysis of hundreds of cases of occupational incompetence led me on to formulate *The Peter Principle*: In a Hierarchy Every Employee Tends to Rise to His Level of Incompetence'. See also the next dedication below.

Laurence J. **Peter**, *Why Things Go Wrong, or the Peter Principle Revisited*, 1985

~ To Stephen Pile, who believes that success is overrated, and whose glorification of failure everywhere should be a consolation to each of us as we confront our own areas of incompetence.

For STEPHEN PILE's own two dedications, see below.

Harry Mark **Petrakis**, *A Dream of Kings*, 1967

~ For my wife, Diana, who has endured me for twenty years.

A. **Phelps**, ed., *Lord Dunchester, or The End of Dr. Therne*, 1901

~ Dedicated to the sincerity, born of ignorance, of the members of all societies which mind other people's business.

Elizabeth Stuart **Phelps**, *The Gates Ajar*, 1868

~ To My Father, whose life, like a perfume from beyond the Gates, penetrates every life which approaches it, the readers of this little book will owe whatever pleasant thing they may find within its pages. E.S.P.

See below.

Elizabeth Stuart **Phelps**, *Beyond the Gates*, 1883

~ To My Brother Stuart, Who passed Beyond. August 29, 1883.

Massachusetts-born Elizabeth Stuart Phelps made her name with *The Gates Ajar* (above), a passionately emotional religious novel (or series of religious conversations), subtitled 'Our Loved Ones in Heaven' and published when she was twenty-four. The book was enormously popular, especially among the grieving and lonely, and the author continued the theme of 'the future life' in *Beyond the Gates* (here), which recounts the dream of a woman who believes she has died and gone to heaven. Further books continued similarly, such as *The Gates Between* (1887) and *Within the Gates* (1901), although the latter novel was really just a reworking of the former. Phelps's writing was undoubtedly at least partly inspired by deaths in her own family, as the dedications imply. In 1888 she married Herbert Dickinson

Ward, and collaborated with him on various biblical romances while continuing her own books. She died in 1911.

Robert **Phillips**, ed., *Aspects of Alice*, 1971

~ This book is for Master Graham van Buren Phillips, who can still look forward to his first fall down the rabbit-hole.

No doubt he has now tumbled? The book itself, as its name implies, and the dedication confirms, is a consideration of the Alice tales by LEWIS CARROLL.

Mary Orne **Pickering**, *Life of John Pickering*, 1887

~ To the eldest grand-daughter of my father and mother, whose childhood was blessed with their loving care; to the memory of her departed sister, and to the younger grand-children, who never had the happiness of knowing their grand-parents and sharing their affection, this imperfect memorial of my father and mother is tenderly shared by their aunt. Mary Orne Pickering.

Marge **Piercy**, *Small Changes*, 1972

~ For me. For you. For us. Even for them.

For the American feminist author, the 'them' here means 'men'. Compare the next dedication below.

Marge **Piercy**, *Vida*, 1980

~ For the street and alley soldiers.

That is, for the writer's militant fellow feminists.

Albert **Pierrepoint**, *Executioner: Pierrepoint*, 1974

~ To Anne my wife, who in forty years never asked a question, I dedicate this book with grateful thanks for her loyalty and discretion.

The autobiography of Britain's last hangman.

Nicolas **Pike**, *A New and Complete System of Arithmetic*, 1786

~ To His Excellency, James Bowdoin, Esquire, Governor and Commander in Chief of the Commonwealth of Massachusetts and President of the American Academy of Arts and Sciences. May it please your Excellency, the author of this System, anxious to procure for it a favorable Reception from his Fellow-citizens, takes the liberty of soliciting the Honour of your Excellency's Patronage. As this Work is the first of the kind composed in America, he feels he is entitled to the candid indulgence of the Learned in general – and from your Excellency's zeal for the advancement of the Sciences, and attachment to the Republic of Letters, he rests assured that the Public will pardon him the ambition of inscribing your Name to this Literary Attempt. That your Excellency may long continue the Ornament of your Country and the Delight of your Friends, is the ardent wish of, May it please your Excellency, Your Excellency's much obliged, Most Obedient, and very Humble Servant, Nicolas Pike.

Pike had originally offered to dedicate his work to George Washington, but the President declined on the grounds that 'there are several Characters in your part of the country who deservedly hold a high rank in the literary world, and whose names would add dignity to such a performance', so that therefore 'it would be more proper [...] to dedicate your Book to them' (letter of 20 June 1786). The dedication was thus made to the Governor of Massachusetts and founder of the American Academy of Arts and Sciences, as credited above.

Stephen **Pile**, *The Book of Heroic Failures*, 1979

~ To all those who have written terrible books on how to be a success, I dedicate this terrible book on how it's perfectly all right to be incompetent for hours on end, because I am and so is everyone I know.

Pile's droll collection of misadventures and disasters was itself anything but a failure. It was published by Routledge & Kegan Paul and was that somewhat staid firm's first bestseller since their publication of *Uncle Tom's Cabin* in 1852. Compare Pile's follow-up, below.

Stephen **Pile**, *The Return of Heroic Failures*, 1988

~ To Quin Xiang-Yi, who in 1846 was given the title 'distinguished failure' in recognition of his 20 years spent failing the Chinese Civil Service entrance exams. Buoyed up by this honour, he went on to fail several times more.

See above for the genesis of this book. Compare also LAURENCE PETER'S titles above, and his second dedication.

Chapman **Pincher**, *The Private World of St John Terrapin*, 1982

~ To Lord Forte, who preserved the fabric and the spirit.

The fifth novel of the distinguished British journalist and former defence correspondent, dedicated to Sir Charles Forte, chairman of the hotel and catering company Trusthouse Forte, who was raised to the peerage as Baron Forte in the year Pincher's book was published.

George **Pinckard**, *Notes on the West Indies*, 1806

DEDICATION TO FRIENDSHIP

Looking round, as it is said authors are wont, for a great personage to whose name I might dedicate my work, I have not found it possible to fix upon anyone to whom I could with so much propriety consign it, as to ... its Parent! Accept, then, Benign Power! thine offspring; cherish it even as Thou hast begotten it; and cause thy warmest influence ever to animate the heart of thy faithful and devoted servant, The Author.

An unusual dedication by the writer, an army doctor who had sailed with Sir Ralph Abercromby's expedition of 1895 to the West Indies. Originally composed in the form of letters to friends, the book describes his experiences there and his reaction to social and living conditions, especially for slaves.

L.G. **Pine**, *A Dictionary of Nicknames*, 1984

~ Do, dico, et dedico hunc librum nepti meae Emily Ruth Alice Pine.

A rather pretentious Latin address to a young child by the author declaring that he 'gives, shows and dedicates this book to my granddaughter'. But given the subject of the book, why not use the nickname that, like all children, she surely must have had?

D. Brian **Plummer**, *Off the Beaten Track*, nd (*c.* 1980)

~ I dedicate this book to Barry Cockroft of Yorkshire Television with whom I spent considerable time and also to Fiona Richmond with whom I spent no time at all – more's the pity.

A 'country lore' book about the handling and training of lurcher dogs, sparrowhawks and the like. 'Fiona Richmond' was the name assumed by a stage and porno movie actress prominent in the 1970s, here rather dubiously invoked to exorcise one of the author's hang-ups.

Su **Pollard**, *Hearts and Showers*, 1988

~ To all the men who have made it possible for me to write this and to all the people who have encouraged and bullied me in the process. Not forgetting the chemist who recommended hand ointment when me fingers started sticking to the pen.

A typically chatty tribute by the popular British TV actress and comedienne. The title of the book is a punning variation on the phrase 'hearts and flowers', used to denote something over-sentimental or cloyingly sweet. Su Pollard's life has not been roses all the way, as her autobiography reveals.

Ted **Pollock**, *The Rainbow Man*, 1981

~ For Barbara and Jill, who listened ... and listened ... and listened ...

Peter **Pook**, *Gigolo Pook*, 1975

~ To those readers who kindly wrote to tell me how our hero had cured them of their ills, from chronic depressions and nervous breakdown to insomnia.

One of a series of popular autobiographical (non-fictional) books, usually incorporating the author's name in the title, such as the earlier *Pook in Business* (1963) and *Bwana Pook* (1965).

Alexander **Pope**, *The Rape of the Lock*, 1714

~ Dedication to Miss Arabella Fermor. Madam, It will be in vain to deny that I have some regard for this piece, since I dedicate it to you. Yet you may bear me witness, it was intended only to divert a few young ladies, who have good sense and humour enough to laugh not only at the sex's little unguarded follies, but at their own. But as it was communicated with the air of a secret, it soon found its way into the world. An imperfect copy having been offered to a bookseller, you had the good-nature for my sake to consent to the publication of one more correct: this I was forced to before I had executed half my design, for the machinery was entirely wanting to complete it. [...] As to the following Cantos, all the passages of them are as fabulous as the vision at the beginning, or the transformation at the end (except the loss of your hair, which I always mention with reverence). The human persons are as fictitious as the airy ones; and the character of Belinda, as it is now managed, resembles you in nothing but in beauty. If this Poem had as many graces as there are in your person, or in your mind, yet I could never hope it should pass through the world half so uncensured as you have done. But let its fortune be what it will, mine is happy enough, to have given me this occasion of assuring you that I am, with the truest esteem, Madam, your most obedient, humble Servant, A. Pope.

The famous mock heroic poem was inspired by a real-life incident in which the twenty-year-old Sir Robert Petre, three years earlier, had mischievously cut a lock of hair from the head of the young and beautiful Lady Arabella Fermor, causing a feud between their two families. Pope's aim in writing the poem was to bring about a reconciliation between them by means of a good humoured treatment of the event, using his piece at the same time as a vehicle for satirising the superficial concerns of the society of the day. In the poem, 'Belinda' is thus Lady Arabella (retaining the appropriate 'bel' element to denote her beauty). Pope had originally planned a verse dedication, but Arabella Fermor rejected this in favour of a letter, part of which is quoted here.

Dennis **Potter**, *Pennies from Heaven*, 1981
~ To Nora Kaye, for seeing – and believing ...

Henry Codman **Potter**, *The East of To-day and To-morrow*, 1902
~ To John Pierpont Morgan, financier, philanthropist, friend: to whose munificence these opportunities for observation in the East were owing, and whose constructive genius, which upbuilds and never pulls down, has indicated the tasks which await Western civilization in Eastern fields.

The dedicatee was the famous American banker and entrepreneur who had consolidated the United States Steel Corporation the previous year.

Tyrone **Power**, *Impressions of America during the Years 1833, 1834, and 1835*, 1836
~ Dedication to the British public: Most persons have a patron, from whose power and influence they have derived support, and of whose favour they feel proud. I cannot claim to be of the few who are above this adventitious sort of aid, self-raised, and self-sustained; on the contrary, I have a patron, the only one I ever sought, but whose favour has well repaid my pains of solicitation. The patron I allude to is yourself, my Public, much courted, much abused, and commonly accused of

being either coldly neglectful or capriciously forgetful of all sorts of merit. [...] As an actor, when managers have appeared indifferent, or critics unkind, and my hopes have sunk within me, I have turned to your cheering plaudits, and found in them support from the present and encouragement for the future. [...]

Tyrone Power, the famous Irish actor, was first on stage in 1815, and a firm favourite in the United States. He was returning from his third visit to that country in 1841 on board the SS *President* when the ship sank and he was tragically drowned, aged still only forty-four. He was the grandfather of the film star and Broadway matinee idol of the same name, who died in 1931, and great-grandfather of the likewise identically named stage and screen actor who died in 1958.

John Cowper Powys, *A Glastonbury Romance*, 1933
~ To my youngest sister and oldest god-daughter, Lucy Amelia Penny.

One of the best-known lengthy esoteric novels by the English writer. He was the eldest of a family of eleven children, with two of his brothers, Theodore Francis and Llewellyn, also writers. A third brother, Albert Reginald, was a distinguished architect, and of his sisters, Gertrude Mary was a portrait painter and Marian an authority on old lace. Which leaves, among others, Lucy Amelia Penny, as complimented here.

J.B. Priestley, *Angel Pavement*, 1930
~ To C.S. Evans, because he is not only a good friend and a fine publisher, but also because he is a London man and will know what I am getting at in this London novel.

Charles Seddon Evans, who died in 1944, was Chairman of Priestley's publishers, William Heinemann, from 1932. Compare GERALD KERSH's second dedication above.

J.B. Priestley, *The Linden Tree*, 1947
~ To J.P. Mitchelhill. My dear Mitch, I hope you will accept, with my affectionate regards, the dedication of this play. You were enthusiastic about it from the first, and it took us back to the Duchess Theatre again, in the happiest circumstances, after an interval of nearly ten years, during which it looked as if we should never work together in the Theatre again. To have you on the management once more, together with my friends of the Westminster venture – and Dame Sybil and Sir Lewis Casson playing so beautifully – this has been happiness when I had almost ceased to dream of finding it in the Theatre. [...] So please accept the piece as a tribute to our friendship and your love of the Theatre. Yours ever, J.B.P.

Mitchelhill, who died in 1966, had been manager of the Duchess Theatre, London, in the 1930s, and had produced several of Priestley's plays there, beginning with *Dangerous Corner* (1932). Their collaboration resulted in a close and lasting friendship, as the dedication states. Dame Sybil is Dame Sybil Thorndike, the leading Shakespearean actress, who died in 1976.

J.B. **Priestley**, *Lost Empires*, 1965

~ To A.D. Peters, from an Old Client, an Old Friend, after forty years.

Peters, who died in 1973, was a well-known literary agent with many distinguished writers among his clients, including not only Priestley but such as Edmund Blunden, Rebecca West, Terence Rattigan, Evelyn Waugh and Norman Collins. It was Peters who was responsible for Priestley's plays at the Duchess Theatre in the 1930s (see above).

J.B. **Priestley**, *The Carfitt Crisis, The Pavilion of Masks*, 1975

~ Dedicatory Letter to Charles Pick, Chairman and Managing Director of Wm Heinemann Ltd. Dear Charles, I hope you will accept this dedication as at least some small token of my warm regard for you as an enthusaistic publisher and as a friend. If any reader chooses to see these two novellas as an old writer's toys, I shan't take offence, even though the ideas that can be discovered in them are serious ideas important to us in the present age. [...] I trust you will enjoy these novellas, a form quite new to me, and even if you don't, I shan't regret this dedication. Yours ever, J.B. Priestley.

Compare the first dedication above. Priestley was now eighty, and his long and active life would continue until his death in 1984 a month short of his ninetieth birthday.

William C. **Prime**, *Tent Life in the Holy Land*, 1858

~ To the memory of Nathaniel S. Prime, our revered and beloved father, who while we were climbing the mountains of Lebanon, on the morning of the twenty-seventh day of March, in the year eighteen hundred and fifty-six, did ascend into the Sublime and Solemn Company of the Patriarchs and Prophets of all Time, I dedicate this volume.

William Cowper Prime, who died in 1905, was an American journalist and writer on art who became editor of the *New York Journal of Commerce* from 1861 and who was later Professor of the History of Art at Princeton.

John **Proctor**, *The Historie of Wyates Rebellion, with the Order and Maner of Resisting the Same* (etc.), 1554

~ To the most Excellent and virtuous Lady, our most gracious Sovereign, Mary, by the grace of God, Queen of England, France, Naples, Hierusalem, and Ireland; Defender of the Faith; Princess of Spain, and Sicily; Archduchess of Austria; Duchess of Milan, Burgundy, and Brabant; Countess of Hapsburg, Flanders, and Tyrol; your Majesty's most faithful, loving, and obedient subject, John Proctor, wisheth all grace, long peace, quiet reign, from God the Father, the Son, and the Holy Ghost. [...]

A dedication that is remarkable for its enumeration of Mary Tudor's titles, which are usually abbreviated to '&c., &c., &c.' or the like. Wyatt's Rebellion, of the same year as the publication, was a revolt of about 3,000 men of Kent, led by Sir Thomas Wyatt, against Mary's proposed marriage to Philip II of Spain. The rebellion failed, and Wyatt was executed, together with hundreds of his followers. Proctor's work, as the title makes plain, was concerned with ways of crushing the rebellion, so was pro-Mary. She married Philip that same year, but lived only four more years, dying when she was still only forty-two. She is popularly remembered in the history books as 'Bloody Mary' for her persecution of Protestants in England.

Marcel **Proust**, *Swann's Way*, 1913

~ To Monsieur Gaston Calmette, in token of profound and affectionate gratitude. Marcel Proust.

Translated from the French by AR; original title: *Du Côté de chez Swann*. Calmette was the editor of the French newspaper *Figaro*, who the following year launched a campaign against the French premier and recent Minister of Finance, Joseph Caillaux, accusing him of financial irregularities and threatening to publish letters between Madame Caillaux, his former mistress, and himself. On learning of the campaign, Madame Caillaux came to Calmette's office and shot him dead.

Marcel **Proust**, *The Guermantes Way*, 1920

~ To Léon Daudet, author of *Shakespeare's Journey*, *The Child's Portion*, *The Black Star*, *Ghosts and the Living* and so many masterpieces. To my matchless friend in witness of gratitude and admiration. M.P.

Translated from the French by AR; original title: *Le Côté de Guermantes*. Léon Daudet was the journalist and writer son of the better-known novelist and short story writer Alphonse Daudet.

Alexander **Pushkin**, *Poltava*, 1829

> To you – but will the dark muse ever
> Her singing to your ear impart?
> Perhaps your modest soul will never
> Discern the strivings of my heart?
> Or will a poet's dedication
> As, once, the love he gave to you,
> Lack any answering indication,
> And simply not be known anew?
>
> At least accept the sounds I'm sending,
> The sounds so dear to you of late,
> And think: in days no longer blending,
> In days of my perfidious fate,
> Your lonely life and weary sadness,
> Your final words, the last of all,
> A single treasure are, a gladness,
> A single love left in my soul.

Translated from the Russian by AR; original title as in English. Pushkin's poem is a retelling of the romantic story in which the Cossack hetman Mazeppa falls in love with his godchild, set against the historical background of the struggle between Peter the Great of Russia and

Charles XII of Sweden, which culminated in crushing defeat for the latter at the Battle of Poltava in 1709. Pushkin had shortly before fallen passionately in love with the dazzlingly beautiful sixteen-year-old Natalya Goncharova (he himself was now thirty), but had been rejected by her when he proposed marriage. Stunned and hurt by this rebuke, he had left for the Caucasus, where a war was going on with Turkey, and had been rebuked for doing so without permission. But many fairy tales have a happy ending, and the following year, on his return, he once again proposed to Natalya and was accepted. It was, however, the discovery of a subsequent love affair between Natalya and the French baron Georges D'Anthès that resulted in Pushkin's death in a duel in 1837. He was thirty-eight.

George Haven **Putnam**, *Books and their Makers During the Middle Ages*, 1896

~ To the memory of my wife, who served me for years both as eyesight and as writing-arm and by whose hand the following pages were in large part transcribed, this work is dedicated.

George Haven Putnam, who died in 1930, was the son of the founder of the American publishers G.P. Putnam & Son, of which he was the president from 1872 until his death.

Howard **Pyle**, *The Garden Behind the Moon*, 1895

~ To the little boy in the Moon Garden, this book is dedicated by his Father.

Pyle was a popular American author and Art Nouveau illustrator who wrote many stories for children but chiefly fairy tales and retellings of folk tales. This book, a novel-length fantasy, was inspired by the death of his young son, and is an allegory on the meaning of life and mortality. Pyle himself died, aged fifty-eight, in 1911.

❧ Q ❧

Francisco de **Quevedo** y Villegas, *Toys of Childhood*, 1641

~ To no person at all whom God created on earth. I have considered that all writers dedicate their books with two purposes, which are seldom separated: one that such person should aid the publication with his blessed almsgiving; the other, that he should shield the work from critics. I consider (having been a critic myself for many years) that this serves to restrain only two of those who criticise: the fool who is persuaded that the critics have some reason to swear; and the presumptuous one who pays his money for this flattery. I have determined to write helter-skelter and to dedicate my book to fools and idiots, and let happen what may. […] Let everybody do as they please about my book, since I have said what I wished about everybody. Good-bye, Mæcenas, I take leave of dedications.

Translated from the Spanish; original title: *Juguetes de infancia*. Quevedo was an extremely prolific and wide-ranging Spanish satirist, moralist and poet, and this is just one of his numerous dedications.

Sir Arthur **Quiller-Couch**, *The Astonishing History of Troy Town*, 1888

~ To Charles Cannan. My dear Cannan, It is told of a distinguished pedagogue that one day a heated stranger burst into his study, and, wringing him by the hand, cried, 'Heaven bless and reward you, sir! Heaven preserve you long to educate old England's boyhood! I have walked many a weary, weary mile to see your face again,' he continued, flourishing a scrap of paper, 'and assure you that but for your discipline, obeyed by me as a boy and remembered as a man, I should never – no, never – have won the Ticket-of-leave which you behold!' In something of the same spirit I bring you this small volume. The child of encouragement is given to staggering its parent; and I make no doubt that as you turn the following pages, you will more than once exclaim, with the old lady in the ballad: 'O, deary me! this is none of I.' Nevertheless, it would be strange indeed if this story bore no marks of you: for a hundred kindly instances have taught me to come with sure reliance for your reproof and praise. Few, I imagine, have the good fortune of a critic so friendly and inexorable; and if the critic has been unsparing, he has been used unsparingly. Q.

Charles Cannan, scholar and university publisher, had become classical fellow and Dean of Trinity College, Oxford, four years previously, and Quiller-Couch, an undergraduate at the same college, had studied classics under him. The two men, with only a five-year age difference between them, had become firm friends. Hence this dedication by 'Q' for his second novel. Quiller-Couch also had a tribute to Cannan in the *Oxford Book of English Verse* which he would compile later (see below).

Sir Arthur **Quiller-Couch**, *The Splendid Spur*, 1889

~ To Edward Gwynne Eardley-Wilmot. My dear Eddie, Whatever view a story-teller may take of his business, 'tis happy when he can think, 'This book of mine will please such and such a friend,' and may set that friend's name after the title-page. For even if to please (as some are beginning to hold) should be no part of his aim, at least 'twill always be a reward: and (in unworthier moods) next to a Writer I would choose to be a Lamplighter, as the only other that gets so cordial a 'God bless him!' in the long winter evenings. To win such a welcome at such a time from a new friend or two would be the happiest fortune for my tale. But to you I could wish it to speak particularly, seeing that under the coat of JACK MARVEL beats the heart of your friend. Q.

One of the author's earliest novels, a historical romance set in 1642 at the time of the Civil War, with Jack Marvel as the hero. The dedicatee was a member of the family of the barrister Sir John Eardley Eardley-Wilmot, who had six sons and two daughters.

Sir Arthur **Quiller-Couch**, *Ship of Stars*, 1899

~ To Leonard Henry Courtney.

> Lord make men as towers –
> All towers carry a light.

Although for you heaven has seen fit to darken the light, believe me, it shines outwards over the waters, and is a help to men; a leading light tended by brave hands. We pray, Sir – we who sailed in little boats – for long life towers and the unfaltering lamp.

The dedicatee, Baron Courtney of Penwith, was a statesman and journalist who in middle age partially lost his sight.

Sir Arthur **Quiller-Couch**, ed., *The Oxford Book of English Verse*, 1900

~ To the president, fellows and scholars of Trinity College, Oxford, a house of learning, ancient, liberal, humane, and my most kindly nurse.

'Q' had studied classics at Trinity (see above) and stayed on for a fifth year as a lecturer in classics before leaving Oxford to take up journalism in London in 1887. It was as a result of his contribution to journalism and literature, and not least as compiler and editor of this anthology, that he was knighted in 1910. Compare his next dedication below.

Sir Arthur **Quiller-Couch**, ed., *The Oxford Book of English Prose*, 1925

~ To two houses of learning and hospitality, Trinity College, Oxford and Jesus College, Cambridge, *oikothen oikade*, and to Friendship.

'Q' was not only a former student of Trinity College, Oxford (see above) but in 1912 was appointed Professor of English Literature at Cambridge, where he became a fellow of Jesus College. His Greek tribute is the equivalent of 'home from home'.

Sir Arthur **Quiller-Couch,** *Castle Dor*, 1961

~ It was my father's intention to dedicate this book to Mr and Mrs Santo of Lantyan. F.F. Q.-C.

The dedicator is not, of course, the author, who had died in 1944, but his daughter, Foy Felicia Quiller-Couch (herself named after Fowey, in Cornwall, where 'Q' and his family had long lived, and which was the 'Troy Town' of the first title above). The story here was found lying in a drawer after the author's death. It was completed by Daphne du Maurier, another famous Cornish novelist, and duly published in the year stated.

A.J. **Quinnell,** *The Mahdi*, 1981

~ For all believers of Islam, that the simplicity and totality of their faith not blind them to the dangers.

A thriller by the American suspense novelist (whose real name is a closely kept secret).

❦ R ❦

Jean Racine, *Andromache*, 1667

~ TO MADAME. MADAME, It is not without reason that I place your illustrious name at the head of this work. And with what other name could I dazzle the eyes of my readers, if not that which has already so happily dazzled my audience? It was common knowledge that YOUR ROYAL HIGHNESS had deigned to attend to the direction of my comedy. It was known that you had loaned me some of your insights to add new ornaments to it. And finally it was known that you had honoured it with a few tears at the first reading I made of it to you. Forgive me, MADAME, if I dare to vaunt this happy beginning to its fortune. It consoles me superbly for the harshness of those who would have nothing further to do with it. I permit them to condemn *Andromache* as much as they will, so long as I am permitted to appeal with all the subtleties of their wit to the heart of YOUR ROYAL HIGHNESS. But, MADAME, it is not only with the heart that you judge the value of a work, it is with the intellect that no false light could mislead. Can we put on the stage a history that you did not know as well as ourselves? Can we act out an intrigue if you cannot penetrate all its motives? And can we conceive of sentiments so noble and delicate that they are infinitely below the nobleness and delicacy of your own thoughts? It is known, MADAME, and YOUR ROYAL HIGHNESS hides it in vain, that in the great degree of glory to which nature and fortune have been pleased to raise you, you do not disdain that humble glory that men of letters have reserved for themselves. And it seems that you have wished to have as much advantage over our sex in the wisdom and resolve of your mind as that in which you excel in yours by all the graces that surround you. The court regards you as judge of all that would be agreeable. And we, who work to please the public, no longer have to ask the learned if we are working according to the rules. The sovereign rule is to please YOUR ROYAL HIGHNESS. That is probably the least of your excellent qualities. But, MADAME, it is the only one of which I have been able to speak with any knowledge: the others are too elevated for me. I cannot speak of them without debasing them by the feebleness of my thoughts, and without abandoning the deep veneration with which I am, MADAME, YOUR ROYAL HIGHNESS's Most humble, obedient and faithful servant, Racine.

Translated from the French by AR; original title: *Andromaque*. On 17 November 1667, the actors of the Hôtel de Bourgogne had presented the play in the royal apartment of the Queen, Marie-Thérèse, wife of Louis XIV. The following day, the same troupe performed it publicly at the Hôtel itself. (The famous actor Montfleury, now aged sixty-seven, took the part of Orestes. He had such a large stomach that he tried to contain it with an iron band, but through bawling his lines, ruptured it and died.) For a similar dedication to this same 'Madame', Henrietta Anne, wife of Philip of Orleans, see MOLIÈRE's *School for Wives* above. Racine's dedication to the Princess is perfectly pitched, flattering but not fulsome, and acknowledging her active participation in the staging of the play. When he talks of appealing to Henrietta Anne's 'heart' he really means her intuition. And the mention of 'humble glory' is a typical Racinian combination of two opposed words, of which other examples occur in the play itself.

Betty **Radice**, *Who's Who in the Ancient World*, 1971
~ In memoriam Catherine Lucy Radice, 1947–1968, *sunt apud infernos tot milia formosarum.*

The Latin translates as 'In the underworld there are so many thousands of beautiful ones', the latter word being feminine. This must have been a tribute to the daughter of the author, a noted translator of, and writer on, Greek and Latin classical authors.

Allan **Ramsay**, *The Tea-Table Miscellany: A Collection of Choice Songs, Scots and English*, 1724
> To ilka lovely British lass
>   Frae Ladies Charlotte, Anne, and Jean,
> Down to ilk bonny singing Bess,
>   Wha dances barefoot on the green.
>
> Dear Ladies, Your most humble slave,
>   Who ne'er to serve you shall decline,
> Kneeling, wad your acceptance crave,
>   When he presents this small propine.
>
> Then take it kindly to your care,
>   Revive it with your tunefu' notes:
> Its beauties will look sweet and fair,
>   Arising saftly through your throats. [...]

Ramsay was a Scottish poet and anthologist who did much to revive Scots vernacular poetry. This was a collection of songs and ballads, and no doubt the four women mentioned in the verse dedication (which had four further stanzas) were real enough. The use of the vernacular may require a guiding glossary: *ilk* (*ilka*) is 'each', *frae* is 'from', *wha* is 'who', *wad* is 'would', *saftly* is 'softly'. A 'propine' is a gift. Note the use of 'British' to refer to both the Scottish and English songs in the book. And compare the next dedication below.

Allan **Ramsay**, *A Collection of Scotch Proverbs*, 1736
~ Dedicated to the Tenantry of Scotland, farmers of the Dales, and Storemasters of the Hills. Worthy Friends, The following hoard o' *Wise Sayings*, an' observations o' our forefathers, which hae been gathering through mony bygane ages, I hae collected wi' great care, an' restored to their proper sense, which had been

frequently tint by publishers that didna understand our landwart language, particularly a late large book o' them, fu' o' errors, in a stile neither *Scots* nor *English*. Having set them to rights, I couldna think them better bestowed than to dedicate them to you wha best ken their meaning, moral use, pith an' beauty. Some amang the gentle vulgar, that are *mair nice than wise*, may startle at the broadness, or (as they name it) coarse expressions. But that is nae worth our tenting: a brave man can be as meritorious in hodden-gray as in velvet. [...] Since dedicators scantily deserve that name, when they dinna gar the praises o' their patrons flow freely through their propine, I should be reckoned ane o' little havins to be jum in that article, when I hae sic guid ground to work upon, an' leal verity to keep me frae being thought a fleetcher.. [...] I am, Men an' Brethren, Your affectionate friend an' humble servant, Allan Ramsay.

The reader should imagine this being spoken with a broad Scots accent. But even then a little assistance may be needed with the vernacular. Here are some guidelines: *tint* is 'lost', *tenting* is 'heeding', *hodden-gray* is 'black and white coarse woollen clothes', *gar* is 'cause', *propine* is 'gift', *ane o' little havins* is 'one of poor manners', *jum in that article* is 'reserved in that respect', *leal verity* is 'true faithfulness', *fleetcher* is 'flatterer'.

Jay **Ramsay**, *Claw*, 1983
~ For Jack and Robin (who know my secret) and for Jack Martin (who is one) – friends for life.

The bird names are doubtless significant here.

Arthur **Ransome**, *Swallows and Amazons*, 1930
~ To the six for whom it was written in exchange for a pair of slippers.

The six dedicatees are the four children and two parents of the Altounyan family, on whom Ransome based the characters of his famous children's book. Three of the children keep their original Christian names in the book, but change their surname, becoming Susan, Titty and Roger Walker. Taqui Altounyan, the eldest girl, is metamorphosed into John Walker in the story. The slippers ('real Turks, bright scarlet, shaped like barges') had been given to Ransome by the family as a birthday present. See also the next dedication below.

Arthur **Ransome**, *The Picts and the Martyrs*, 1942
~ To Aunt Helen, C.F.C.A., Plus 100, A1. (These letters mean Certificated First Class Aunt. There are Aunts of all kinds, and all the good ones should be given certificates by their nephews and nieces to distinguish them from Uncertificated Aunts, like Nancy's and Peggy's G.A.)

Nancy and Peggy Blackett are the sisters who crewed the 'Amazon' in *Swallows and Amazons* (see above), and who feature in subsequent books by Ransome. The 'G.A.' was their Great Aunt, against whom the Amazons and 'the 2 D's' (Dick and Dorothea Callum) campaigned.

Terence **Rattigan**, *The Winslow Boy*, 1946
~ To Paul Channon, in the hope that he will live to see a world in which this play will point no moral.

The play is about a boy who is falsely accused of a petty theft, and the struggle to prove his innocence. The dedicatee, who was himself an eleven-year-old boy at the time of the play's first performance, grew up to become a leading Conservative politician and member of Mrs Thatcher's cabinet.

Ernest **Raymond**, *Tell England*, 1922

~ To the Memory of Reginald Vincent Campbell Corbet, who fell, while a boy, in the East, and George Frederick Francis Corbet, who passed, while a boy, in the West, is affectionately dedicated what little is best in this book, nothing else in it being worthy of them.

This, Raymond's first novel, follows a group of public schoolboy friends, Rupert Ray, Archibald Pennybet, and Edgar Gray Doe, from their school days through to the First World War. They see action at Gallipoli, but Doe is killed. The sentiment seems mawkish now, but was perfectly in tune with its time.

Ernest **Raymond**, *In the Steps of St Francis*, 1938

~ This book is offered to the Poverello himself, with humility but without fear, because he loved all things little and poor.

That is, to St Francis, the 'little poor one', as the Italian epithet describes him.

Ernest **Raymond**, *The Tree of Heaven*, 1965

~ To the good memory of Newman Flower, my publisher, counsellor and friend of forty years.

Newman Flower, who had died the previous year, was Chairman of the publishers Cassell & Co. Compare COMPTON MACKENZIE's dedication to him for *The South Wind of Love*.

Claire **Rayner**, *Long Acre*, 1978

~ For Joan Chapman, with gratitude for her ever-patient rusty shoulder.

Claire **Rayner**, *Woman*, 1986

~ For Amanda, the most important woman in my life.

Just two of the many books by one of Britain's leading 'agony aunts'. Amanda ('worthy to be loved') is her daughter, aged twenty-six when the second book appeared.

Desmond **Rayner**, *The Dawlish Season*, 1984

~ For my pseudonymous wives: Ada – Ann – Helen – Ida – Johnny – Ruth – Sheila, but quintessentially their joint and understanding begetter, Claire.

A novel by the husband of CLAIRE RAYNER (see above), with the names referring to her pseudonyms, whether as 'agony aunt' or novelist, for example 'Ann Lynton', 'Ruth Martin', 'Sheila Brandon', to give just three.

Al **Read**, *It's All in the Book*, 1985

~ To my 'ghost', Robin Cross – I had to tell somebody the story of my life, and he was the only fellow who would listen.

The autobiography, 'ghosted', as he says, of the popular British comedian.

Charles **Reade**, *Peg Woffington*, 1853

~ To T. Taylor, Esq., my friend and coadjutor in the comedy of 'Masks and Faces', to whom the reader owes much of the best matter in this tale; and to the memory of Margaret Woffington, falsely 'summed up' until to-day, this 'dramatic story' is inscribed by Charles Reade.

Reade began his long career as a theatre manager and dramatist in 1852, the year before this novel appeared, and that same year successfully produced the comedy *Masks and Faces*, on which the book is based. He had written the play jointly with his dedicatee, Tom Taylor, dramatist and editor of *Punch*, with the comedy itself based on an episode in the life of the eighteenth-century actress Peg Woffington, famous for her vigorous acting of 'breeches' parts, for her raucous voice, and for being the mistress of Garrick.

Walter **Redfern**, *Puns*, 1984

~ This book is devoted to my wife Angela. Living with me, while on and off it may have been a laugh a minute, must at times have been no joke. She enriches the life that feeds the works.

The book is an academic study of puns and word-play in English and French, by the Professor of French at the University of Reading.

Sidney A. **Reeve**, *The Thermodynamics of Heat-Engines*, 1903

~ To my wife, to whose devotion and aid (although she doesn't know entropy from carbonic acid) the existence of this book is due, it is dedicated.

John **Reeves**, *Murder Before Matins*, 1984

~ For Father Basil Foote, O.S.B., servant of the Church, editor of Gregorian chant, lover of books.

Forrest **Reid**, *The Garden God: A Tale of Two Boys*, 1905

~ To Henry James, this slight token of respect and admiration.

The well-known American writer and the lesser-known Irish one had been on friendly terms, until Reid's dedication brought their relationship to an end. Reid's view of childhood, and specifically boyhood, was not shared by James, and he had no desire to be associated with it. Compare the next dedication below.

Forrest **Reid**, *Peter Waring*, 1937

~ To E.M. Forster, now as then.

Unlike Reid and Henry James (see above), Reid and Forster, though so different as men and writers, had much in common, and formed a lifelong friendship. Reid had dedicated one of his best early novels, *Following Darkness* (1930), to Forster soon after they first met. Forster then half-jokingly suggested that the next novel should also be dedicated to him, but Reid did not oblige.

Forrest **Reid**, *Private Road*, 1940

> When you are old your eyes by chance may light
> Upon this book, in the quiet night
> Beside the drowsy fire memory may weave its spell.
> Then shall the writer enter like a ghost
> To stand beside his all unconscious host,
> Summoned from dim far fields his tale to tell.

One of Reid's later nostalgic autobiographies, with its preliminary verse not perhaps an actual dedication as such, but nevertheless an invitation to the reader to accept the book. Possibly the author had a particular person in mind, even if he does not name anyone. Reid was now sixty-five. He died seven years later.

Frederic **Remington**, *Pony Tracks*, 1895

~ This book is dedicated to the fellows who rode the ponies that made the tracks, by the Author.

Remington was an American painter, illustrator and sculptor who had travelled in the western United States and worked as a cowboy.

Ernest **Renan**, *Life of Jesus*, 1869

~ To the Pure Soul of my sister Henriette, who died at Byblus, on September 24th, 1861. Dost thou recall, from the bosom of God where thou reposest, those long days at Ghazir, in which, alone with thee, I wrote these pages, inspired by the places we had visited together? Silent at my side, thou didst read and copy each sheet as soon as I had written it, whilst the sea, the villages, the ravines, and the mountains were spread at our feet. When the overwhelming light had given place to the innumerable army of stars, thy shrewd and subtle questions, thy discreet doubts, led me back to the sublime Object of our common thoughts. One day thou didst tell me that thou wouldst love this book – first, because it had been composed with thee, and also because it pleased thee. Though at times thou didst fear for it the narrow judgments of the frivolous, yet wert thou ever persuaded that all truly religious souls would ultimately take pleasure in it. In the midst of these sweet meditations, the Angel of Death struck us both with his wing: the sleep of fever seized us at the same time – I awoke alone! [...] Thou sleepest now in the land of Adonis, near the holy Byblus and the sacred stream where the women of the ancient mysteries came to mingle their tears. Reveal to me, O good genius, to me whom thou lovedst, those truths which conquer death, deprive it of terror, and make it almost beloved!

Translated from the French; original title: *Vie de Jésus*. The father of the great French philosopher and historian had been drowned at sea when the little boy was only five. Renan's beloved sister, twelve years his senior, was thus the bread-winner of the family, and his second mother. In adulthood, she was his closest companion and counsellor. The two had travelled to the Middle East on a commissioned archaeological expedition, originally accompanied by Renan's wife, who had had to return home prematurely. Renan was particularly glad of the work, as he wished to visit the Holy Land in connection with material (and inspiration) that he required for a planned life of Jesus. In July 1861, after completing the survey, the two paid a visit to the Upper Lebanon, with Renan now writing his draft of the *Life* and Henriette copying it out page by page. When investigating ruins at Jubail (the ancient Byblus), however, in what is now Saudi Arabia, they both contracted malaria. Renan himself was dangerously ill for a time, but Henriette did not recover. She was buried there, aged just forty, in the 'land of Adonis'. The 'thees' and 'thous' of the translated dedication, rendering the French second person singular, are perhaps appropriate in this instance.

D.F. **Rennie**, *Peking and the Pekingese During the First Year of the British Embassy at Peking*, 1865

~ To the Hon. Sir F.W.A. Bruce, G.C.B., Late her Majesty's Envoy Extraordinary and Minister Plenipotentiary at the Court of Peking; and now H.M. Minister at Washington, the following volumes are dedicated, as a tribute of respect for the enlightened and conciliatory policy, based on the principle of recognizing right rather than might, which has characterized his administration at Peking; a policy auguring so favourably for the future of China, and which, having been mainly conducive to the extinction of the Taeping Rebellion, has already been attended with results of the highest importance to the cause of humanity; also, in grateful recollection of much personal kindness received by The Author.

Most of Sir Frederick Bruce's credentials and achievements are indicated here. A bachelor Scot, he died in Boston, USA, two years after this book appeared, aged only fifty-three.

Agnes **Repplier**, *The Fireside Sphinx*, 1901

~ In memory of Agrippina.

The American author's cat, whom she mentions in more detail in the Foreword to the book ('Dear little ghost, whose memory has never faded from my heart, accept this book, dedicated to thee, and to all thy cherished race'). Agnes Repplier was the author of scholarly and sensitive essays on 'all sorts and conditions of men', from *Books and Men* (1888) to *Americans and Others* (1912) and similar titles. She died in 1950, aged ninety-five.

Alice Hegan **Rice**, *Mrs Wiggs of the Cabbage Patch*, 1901

~ To my mother, who for years has been the good angel of the Cabbage Patch.

A children's novel by the American writer Alice Caldwell Hegan who the following year married the poet Cale Young Rice. The book itself was her most popular, about a widow, Mrs Wiggs, who lives in a tumbledown house called 'The Cabbage Patch' by the railroad tracks in a seedy city district.

Barnaby **Rich**, *The Honestie of This Age*, 1614
~ To the Right Honorable Syr Thomas Middleton, Knight, L. Maior of the Honorable Cittie of London. Most Honorable Lord, to avoid idlenes, I have with Domitian, endevoured to catch Flies; I have taken in hand a text that will rather induce hatred, then winne love. [...] Remayning then in some doubtfulnes of mind to whom I might bequeath it, that would eyther grace or give countenance unto it, I was prompted by Report of your Lordships worthinesse, that now in the course of your governement in this Honorable Cittie of London, you have set up those lights for the suppressing of severall sorts of sinnes, that as they have already advanced your applause amongst those that bee of the best approved honesty, so they will remaine for ever in record to your perpetuall prayse. Let not, therefore, my boldnes seems presumptuous that being altogether unknowne to your Lordship, have yet presumed to shelter my lines under your Honorable name, and thus in affiance of your Honorable acceptance, I rest to doe your Lordshippe any other kinde of service. Your Lordships to commaund, Barnabe Rich.

Rich, professionally an army captain, wrote a number of romances on the one hand and denunciatory pamphlets, such as this one, on the other. Here he inveighs against each of the deadly sins in turn, choosing his patron because of the latter's reputation as a moral reformer. Thomas Middleton should not be confused with the well-known dramatist of identical name, although oddly enough the previous year the playwright had written a pageant in celebration of his namesake's mayoralty. There appears to have been no family relationship between the men, nor did either claim it. The mayor's surname is still frequently spelled 'Myddelton' to differentiate between the two.

Jacob A. **Riis**, *Theodore Roosevelt the Citizen*, 1904
~ To the young men of America.

Riis was a Danish-born journalist and writer who campaigned for the improvement of social and recreational conditions among deprived children, especially in the slum tenements of lower New York. He was a close friend and admirer of Roosevelt, who was elected to the presidency in the year this was published, and cooperated with him in various projects.

Sally **Rinard**, *Pretensions*, 1985
~ In memory of my father, Richard I. Rinard, who started a love affair with the written word, watered it, and made it grow long enough to last a lifetime.

A not altogether satisfactory mixed metaphor – how do you water a love affair? – although one can see what the author means.

Roger **Riordan** and Tozo Takayanagi, *Sunrise Stories: A Glance at the Literature of Japan*, 1896
~ Dedicated to his excellency S. Kurino, His Imperial Majesty's Envoy Extraordinary and Minister Plenipotentiary to the United States of America, by the authors.

Viscount Shinichiro Kurino was minister to the USA for only two years, but later was minister at Rome, Paris and St Petersburg. He died in 1937.

Brian **Rix**, *My Farce from my Elbow*, 1975

~ I dedicate this book, written in my own indecipherable longhand, to the members of my audience – those who love me and those who loathe me – and to my wife Elspet, the members of my family plus my friends – who've been a bit ambivalent in their time, too. To all, my gratitude for their support.

The first autobiography of the well-known British actor and actor-manager, famous for his farces (as the punning title of his book indicates).

Field Marshal Lord **Roberts** of Kandahar, *Forty-One Years in India from Subaltern to Commander-in-Chief*, 1898

~ To the country to which I am so proud of belonging, to the army to which I am so deeply indebted, and to my wife, without whose loving help my 'Forty-One Years in India' could not be the happy retrospect it is, – I dedicate this book.

In that order! This was 1st Earl Roberts of Kandahar, Pretoria and Waterford, 'Bobs Bahadur' to his soldiers, and leading figure in the Indian Mutiny, Siege of Delhi, Relief of Lucknow, Battle of Cawnpore, and other famous Anglo-Indian engagements of the day. He would go on to hold supreme command in South Africa, relieve Kimberley there, capture Johannesburg, annexe the Transvaal and achieve similar military successes. He retired in 1904, aged seventy-two, to create a citizen army, dying ten years later. A truly 'imperial' life. His wife was Nora Henrietta Bews, whom he had married in 1859.

Frank **Robertson**, *Triangle of Death: The Inside Story of the Triads – the Chinese Mafia*, 1977

~ To Ruth, for everything (and a proprietary kowtow to the Chinese divinity, Wei T'o, Protector of Books).

Charles Mulford **Robinson**, *The Call of the City*, 1908

~ Affectionately dedicated to the Humdrum Club, Rochester, New York.

Robinson was an American journalist and authority on city planning.

Margaret Blake **Robinson**, *Souls in Pawn*, 1900

~ To my friends, my readers, my critics, – those present and to come, as well as to those who will taste my doctrine and label it as no good thing shall be labelled, – to these four I dedicate *Souls in Pawn* as a mark of my affection and esteem, and as a proof of my impartiality.

W. Heath **Robinson** and K.R.G. Browne, *How to be a Perfect Husband*, 1937

~ Dedicated (a) With Respectful Sympathy To: The Newly-Married, the About-To-Be-Married, the Long-Married, the Ex-Married, the Frequently-

Married, and even – such is our combined love for our fellow-creatures – People Who Would Not Marry If They Were Paid To Do So. (b) With Sympathetic Respect To: The President, Vice-President, Chucker-Out, and Other Officials of the Probate, Divorce, and Admiralty Division. W. Heath Robinson, K.R.G. Browne.

The book gives light-hearted practical guidance to husbands, with chapters headed, for example, 'Selection of a Mate', 'Courtship and Proposal', 'The Wedding', 'Early Married Life', 'The Young Idea', and so on, all in the fashionable 'men and marriage' spirit of the thirties. Heath Robinson is better remembered for his cranky mechanical contraptions than his role as a marriage consultant.

Gwen **Robyns,** *Barbara Cartland,* 1984
~ To Barbar with love – for sharing her memories with me, and those hours awash with laughter.

One of many biographies of the phenomenal romantic novelist and quasi-Everyone's-Favourite-Granny.

Will **Rogers,** *Letters of a Self-Made Diplomat to His President,* 1927
~ To Mrs. Calvin Coolidge, because she appreciates jokes even on her own husband.

One of the wry books by the famous American actor and humorist. Calvin Coolidge was US President at the time.

C.H. **Rolph,** *Further Particulars,* 1987
~ To my much-loved children and the equally cherished people they married, all of whom have been spared any mention in this book. They should be relieved about this. In case any of them is not, this seems the best place in which to offer public atonement, at the same time congratulating them all on their escape.

One of several volumes of autobiography by the former police inspector and campaigner for criminal reform, published when he was eighty-five.

Jules **Romains,** *The Chums,* 1921
~ I dedicate this new edition of *The Chums* to those Companies and Assemblies of young people who, in various parts of the world, have done this book the honour of taking it as a Counsellor of Joy and a Breviary of Facetious Wisdom; and in particular to 'Unanimist of B.L.D.' and the 'Litterateurs of Lausanne'. J.R.

Translated from the French by AR; original title: *Les Copains.* The original edition of this comic adventure was published in 1913. It describes the practical jokes played by a band of seven friends on members of the local community, and is designed to illustrate the author's theory of 'unanimism', a kind of universal brotherhood, in which the spirit of the individual merges with that of the group to which he belongs. 'B.L.D.' is presumably the town of Bar-le-Duc, east of Paris.

James **Ronald**, *This Way Out*, 1940

~ To My Creditors, whose increasing impatience has made this book necessary.

A rather desperate but certainly practical dedication.

Theodore **Roosevelt**, *The Rough Riders*, 1899

~ On behalf of the Rough Riders I dedicate this book to the officers and men of the five regular regiments which, together with mine, made up the cavalry division at Santiago. Theodore Roosevelt.

The Rough Riders, formerly the 1st Volunteer Cavalry, were the regiment of United States cavalry who had been recruited by Roosevelt for deployment in the Spanish-American War and who were composed mainly of cowboys, miners, college athletes and the like. The future US President was their second-in-command, and had led them in Cuba at the Battle of San Juan Hill the previous year.

Henry **Root**, *The Henry Root Letters*, 1980

~ To Mrs Root and Mrs Thatcher: two ordinary mothers.

The book contained the results of an epistolary leg-pull, in which spoof but apparently genuine letters were sent by one 'Henry Root' (real name William Donaldson) to various celebrities and officials. The purported writer of the letters was an impossibly patriotic retired wet-fish merchant, whose family consisted of his wife, 'Mrs Root', nineteen-year-old daughter 'Doreen', and fifteen-year-old son 'Henry Jr'. Letters to Mrs Thatcher ('Dear Leader!') from 'Henry Root' are reproduced in the book together with a reply from her private secretary and a signed photograph. Only a very small number of recipients suspected the hoax that the whole thing really was. A subsequent similar collection, entitled *The Further Letters of Henry Root*, was published later the same year and had the dedication: 'For the future Mrs Root, Doreen and Henry Jr.'. A third collection, *The Soap Letters* (1988), with Root in new personae ('Daniel Ziskie', 'Jeremy Cox', 'Angela Picano', 'Selina Sidey' et al), as well as his pseudonymous self, unfortunately has no dedication.

Honor **Rorvik**, *A Touch of Ginger*, 1987

~ I might never have started writing this book had it not been for my friend and teacher Fay Goldie. And I might never have finished writing it had it not been for my son Rolf, who, *after his death*, urged me to complete it.

H.J. **Rose**, *A Handbook of Greek Mythology*, 1928

~ Viro doctissimo deqve his studiis optime merito L.R. Farnell, D. Litt., Collegii Exoniensis apvd Oxonienses rectori, amicitiae ergo.

A classical dedication for a classical book by a classical scholar to another classical scholar! Lewis Richard Farnell, who died in 1934, was a noted Oxford classicist and college head. The Latin text translates: 'To the most learned man, and most worthy of these studies, L.R. Farnell, rector of Exeter College, Oxford, therefore in friendship'. Professor Herbert Rose died in 1961.

Lord **Rosebery**, *Pitt*, 1891

~ This little book has been written under many disadvantages, but with a sincere desire to ascertain the truth. My chief happiness in completing it would have been to give it to my wife; it can now only be inscribed to her memory.

A study of the famous English statesman by the 5th Earl of Rosebery, Archibald Philip Primrose, himself a leading politician and soon to be prime minister. He had married Hannah de Rothschild when he was thirty-one at a time when she had just succeeded to the considerable family fortune (notably the Rothschild family seat, Mentmore, in Buckinghamshire, with all its art treasures). She had died, however, in 1890, the year before this book was published, and her loss was such a grievous blow to Rosebery that he never fully recovered.

Christina **Rossetti**, *Sing-Song, a Nursery Rhyme Book*, 1872

~ Rhymes dedicated without permission to the Baby who suggested them.

But not one of the author's own, as she never married.

Edmond **Rostand**, *Cyrano de Bergerac*, 1897

~ I had wanted to dedicate this poem to the soul of CYRANO. But since this has passed into you, COQUELIN, it is to you that I dedicate it. E.R.

Translated from the French by AR; original title as in English. Constant-Benoît Coquelin was a famous actor of the Comédie Française who had played the name part in Rostand's play, which is why the soul had 'passed into him'. The play itself is a poetic 'cape and sword' drama set in seventeenth-century Paris, with Cyrano de Bergerac a chivalrous Gascon knight.

A.L. **Rowse**, *The Expansion of Elizabethan England*, 1955

~ To T.S. Eliot, who gave me my first introduction to the world of letters.

A compliment from one scholar to another.

Kenneth **Royce**, *The XYY Man*, 1970

~ For Andy, hoping that you are still out.

A novel on a criminal newly released from prison.

Berta **Ruck**, *The Youngest Venus*, 1928

~ Dedicated to any girl who imagines herself to be hopelessly unattractive!

One of many romantic novels by the prolific author who lived to be one hundred, dying in 1978.

Ruth Janette **Ruck**, *Place of Stones*, 1961

~ Y mae y llyfr hwn yn gyflwynedig i'm cyfeillion a'm cymdogion Cymreig, yn arbennig felly i bobl Nantmor, am eu caredigrwydd yn ein cynorthwyo i amaethu yn eu cwmwd godidog.

'This book is dedicated to my Welsh friends and neighbours, and specially so to the people of Nantmor, for their kindness in helping on the farm in their splendid commot'. Translated from the Welsh by AR. The book tells of the Welsh farm, Carneddi, that the author had bought in the Second World War. Its name translates as 'place of stones', the title of the book. A 'commot' is a Welsh administrative division in a 'cantred' ('hundred').

John **Ruskin**, *Modern Painters*, 1843

~ To the landscape artists of England this work is respectfully dedicated by their sincere admirer the author.

It was the first volume of this work, aiming to prove the superiority of modern landscape painters, such as Turner, over the 'old masters', that brought Ruskin to the notice of the public as an art critic.

John **Ruskin**, *The Ethics of the Dust*, 1866

~ To the real little Housewives, whose gentle listening and thoughtful questioning enabled the writer to write this book, it is dedicated with his love.

The famous art critic's book, subtitled 'Ten Lectures to Little Housewives on the Elements of Crystallization', consists of a collection of lectures on geology that the author had originally given at a girls' school, which, he explains in the Preface, 'in the course of various experiments on the possibility of introducing some better practise of drawing into the modern scheme of female education, I visited frequently enough to enable the children to regard me as a friend'. The first lecture is preceded by a list of 'personae' headed by 'Old Lecturer (of incalculable age)' (in fact forty-seven when the book was published) and giving the names and ages of the 'Little Housewives': Florrie ('on astronomical evidence presumed to be aged' nine), Isabel (11), May (11), Lily (12), Kathleen (14), Lucilla (15), Violet (16), Dora ('who has the keys and is the housekeeper') (17), Egypt ('so called from her dark eyes') (17), Sibyl ('so called because she knows Latin') (18), and Mary ('of whom everybody, including the Old Lecturer, is in great awe') (20). Presumably these were the girls' real names. Ruskin merely tells us that the school was 'far in the country', but it was actually Winnington Hall, just outside Northwich, in Cheshire. Such was its geology class of '66!

George **Willian** Erskine **Russell**, *Matthew Arnold*, 1904

~ Offered to Matthew Arnold's children with affectionate remembrance 'of that unreturning day'.

Among the children of the poet and educationist were Eleanor Arnold, who had published the *Matthew Arnold Birthday Book* in 1883, and the Hon. Mrs Armine Woodhouse, who brought out selections from her father's *Notebooks* in 1902. Arnold himself had died in 1888.

❦ S ❦

Paul **Sabatier,** *Life of St Francis of Assisi*, 1894

~ To the Citizens of Strasbourg. Friends! Here at last is the book that I told you about so long ago now. The result is very small by comparison with the effort; I can see that, alas, better than anyone. The widow of the Gospel put only one mite into the alms-box of the temple, but that mite, they say, won paradise for her. Accept this mite that I offer you today, as God accepted the mite of that poor woman, considering not her offering, but her love. *Feci quod potui, omnia dedi.* Do not reprove me too much for these long delays, for in a way you are the cause of them. Several times a day in Florence, Assisi and Rome, I have forgotten the document I was studying and have sensed something in me fly off to flutter at your windows. Sometimes, they opened to me ... One evening, two years ago, I was lost in thought at San Damiano, long after sunset. An old monk came to warn me that the sanctuary was closed. '*Per Bacco!*', he murmured softly as he led me out, all ready to receive my confidences, '*sognava d'amore o di tristezza?* Well, yes, I *was* dreaming of love and sadness, since I was dreaming of Strasbourg.

Translated from the French by AR, original title: *Vie de S. François d'Assise.* A brief but affecting dedication by the French historian and Protestant clergyman (not to be confused with Paul Sabatier the chemist, his better-known contemporary). Sabatier's life of St Francis presents the saint as a man frustrated by the extreme caution of his superiors at Rome. The Latin quotation translates as 'I have done what I could, I have given everything'. Apart from his exclamation ('By Bacchus!'), the rest of the Italian monk's question is repeated in Sabatier's reply in the final sentence.

Vita **Sackville-West,** *Challenge*, 1924

~ Acaba embeo sin tiro, men chuajañí; lirenas, berjaras tiri ochi busñe, changeri, ta armensalle.

This was the author's second book about her lover Violet Trefusis (née Keppel). The dedication, in its mysterious language, was a private one, understood by Violet alone. It was not deciphered until 1973, when a *Sunday Times* reader, a Mrs Ridler, discovered that the words were in Romany, and were taken from George Borrow's *The Zincali; An Account of the Gypsies of Spain* (1841). It appears to translate as follows: 'This book is yours, my witch; if you read it, you will find your sweet soul changed, and free'.

Carl **Sagan**, *Cosmos*, 1981

~ For Ann Druyan. In the vastness of space and the immensity of time, it is my joy to share a planet and an epoch with Annie.

See below.

Carl **Sagan**, *Contact*, 1985

~ For Alexandra, who comes of age with the Millennium. May we leave your generation a world better than the one we were given.

Ann Druyan (above) is Sagan's second wife, whom he married in 1981. Alexandra, his daughter by her, was born in 1982 (as can be deduced from the second dedication here). The famous American author and astronomer has three sons by his first marriage.

Giles **St Aubyn**, *Edward VII: Prince and King*, 1979

~ This book is dedicated to Eton College, whose sons figure so prominently in its pages, and to Members of my House, who for eighteen years prevented me from writing it. 1959–1976.

St Aubyn, the author of a number of royal and Victorian biographies, taught history at Eton and was Housemaster there during the years stated. He himself went to Wellington College.

Antoine de **Saint-Exupéry**, *Wind, Sand and Stars*, 1939

~ Henri Guillaumet, my comrade, I dedicate this book to you.

Translated from the French by AR; original title: *Terre des hommes*.

Antoine de **Saint-Exupéry**, *The Little Prince*, 1943

~ TO LÉON WERTH. I ask children to forgive me for dedicating this book to a grown-up. I have a good excuse: this grown-up is the best friend I have. I have another excuse: this grown-up can understand everything, even books for children. I have a third excuse: this grown-up lives in France where he is cold and hungry. He has real need of being comforted. If all these excuses are not enough, then I want to dedicate this book to the child that this grown-up once was. All grown-ups were children once. (But few of them remember it.) So I correct my dedication: TO LÉON WERTH WHEN HE WAS A LITTLE BOY.

Translated from the French by AR; original title: *Le Petit Prince*. A dedication in the simple but attractive style of the well-known children's (and grown-ups') book itself. Léon Werth, twenty-three years older than 'Saint-Ex', was an Israeli art critic and writer (and pacifist) who had sought refuge from the Gestapo in France during the Second World War. It was Werth who prompted Saint-Exupéry to write his famous *Letter to a Hostage* (1943), in which he called for unity among Frenchmen in the cause of peace.

Henry **St John**, 1st Viscount Bolingbroke, *A Dissertation upon Parties*, 1735

~ Sir, As soon as the demand of the Publick made it necessary to collect the following Papers together, and to prepare a second edition of them, I took the resolution of addressing them to you. The style of my dedication will be very different from that which is commonly employed to persons in your station. But if you find nothing agreeable in the style, you may perhaps find something useful, something that will deserve your serious reflection in the matter of it. I shall compare you neither to Burleigh, nor Godolphin. Let me not prophane the tomb of the Dead to raise altars to the Living. [...]

The start of a long and bitter dedicatory letter by Lord Bolingbroke to Sir Robert Walpole, his great opponent, then First Lord of the Treasury (the equivalent of Prime Minister) and Chancellor of the Exchequer. In 1712 Walpole, a Whig, had been ruined as effective opposition leader by leading Tories, including Bolingbroke, who had sent him to the Tower of London on a charge of corruption as Secretary for War. Two years later he had his revenge, when he brought about the impeachment of Bolingbroke for treason, so that the latter had to flee to France. A state of keen animosity existed between the two men from then on. (Once, they had been at Eton together, however.) Bolingbroke spent much of the last ten years of his life attacking his opponent in print. This particular piece had been originally published anonymously two years previously.

Nicholas **Salaman**, *The Frights*, 1981
~ For my Mother, who kept the frights at bay.

J.D. **Salinger**, *Franny and Zooey*, 1961
~ As nearly as possible in the spirit of Matthew Salinger, age one, urging a luncheon companion to accept a cool lima bean, I urge my editor, mentor, and (heaven help him) closest friend, William Shawn, *genius domus* of the *New Yorker*, lover of the long shot, protector of the unprolific, defender of the hopelessly flamboyant, most unreasonably modest of born great artist-editors, to accept this pretty skimpy-looking book.

See below.

J.D. **Salinger**, *Raise High the Roof Beam, Carpenters* and *Seymour: An Introduction*, 1963
~ If there is an amateur reader still left in the world – or anybody who just reads and runs – I ask him or her, with untellable affection and gratitude, to split the dedication of this book four ways with my wife and children.

This book, comprising two stories which had previously appeared in the New Yorker, was the last the popular American novelist and short story writer would publish. Salinger was still only forty-four, and apart from one final story in the *New Yorker* two years later, he now completely retired from the literary scene, thus depriving his public of much rewarding reading, and us here of further agreeable dedications like these two.

Thomas **Salmon**, *A New Geographical and Historical Grammar*, 1766
~ To His Majesty King George the Third, And to the British Princes and

Princesses, His Royal Brothers and Sisters, this new Geographical and Historical Grammar is Humbly Dedicated by the Author, Thomas Salmon.

George III was now twenty-eight. His brothers and sisters were (with ages) as follows: Edward Augustus, Duke of York (27, died the following year), William Henry, Duke of Gloucester (23), Henry Frederick, Duke of Cumberland (21), Princess Augusta (29), wife of Charles William Frederick, Prince of Brunswick-Wolfenbüttel, Princess Caroline Matilda (15), wife (marrying this year) of Christian VII, King of Denmark. It is not clear to what extent this book contributed to the education of any of these youthful royals. It was a work, as its subtitle explains, 'wherein the Geographical Part is Truly Modern; and the present state of the several Kingdoms of the World is so Interspersed as to render the Study of Geography both Entertaining and Instructive'. As indeed it should be, of course.

George **Sandys**, *A Relation of a Journey Begun An. Dom. 1610*, 1615

~ TO THE PRINCE. Sir, The Eminence of the degree wherein God and Nature have placed you doth allure the eyes, and the hopefulnesse of your Vertues win the love of all men. For Vertue, being in a private person an exemplary ornament, advanceth it selfe in a Prince to a publike blessing. And as the Sunne to the world, so bringeth it both light and life to a kingdome: a light of derection, by glorious example; and a life of joy, through a gracious government. For the just and serious consideration whereof, there springeth in minds not brutish, a thankfull correspondence of affection and duty; still pressing to expresse themselves in endevours of service. Which hath also caused me, (most noble Prince) not furnished of better means, to offer in humble zeale to your princely view these my doubled travels; once with some toyle and danger performed, and now recorded with sincerity and diligence. [...] Accept great Prince these weake endevours of a strong desire: which shall be alwaies devoted to do your Highnesse all acceptable service; and ever rejoyce in your prosperity and happinesse. George Sandys.

Sandys had been travelling extensively in the Middle East, and his journeyings took him to countries as varied as Turkey, Italy, Egypt and the Holy Land. He faithfully recorded all that he could with regard to the government, customs and especially religious customs of these lands, and on his return, five years after setting out, wrote up his account and presented it, as dedicated here, to the future Charles I, then aged fifteen. Compare his next dedication below.

George **Sandys**, *Ovid's Metamorphosis*, 1621–6

~ To the most High and Mightie Prince CHARLES, King of Great Britaine, France, and Ireland. Sir, Your Gracious acceptance of the first fruites of my Travels, when You were our Hope, as now our Happinesse; hath actuated both Will and Power to the finishing of this Peece: being limn'd by that unperfect light which was snatcht from the howers of night and repose. For the day was not mine, but dedicated to the service of your Great Father, and your Selfe: which, had it proved as fortunate as faithfull, in me, and others more worthy; we had hoped, ere many yeares had turned about, to have presented You with a rich and wel-peopled Kingdome; from whence now, with my selfe, I onely bring this Composure. [...]

But how ever unperfect, Your favour is able to supply; and to make it worthy of life, if you judge it not unworthy of your Royall Patronage. Long may you live to be, as you are, the Delight and Glorie of your People: and slowly, yet surely, exchange your mortal Diadem for an immortall. So wishes Your Majesties most humble Servant, George Sandys.

Sandys, the son of the Bishop of York, translated Ovid's *Metamorphoses* to while away the tediousness of his time in Virginia, where he was acting as secretary to the Governor. (This was at a time when the *Mayflower* had made her historic landing just months before.) No doubt Charles I enjoyed the tactful manner in which Sandys justifies his 'moonlighting'. Alas, he would 'exchange his mortal Diadem for an immortall' all too abruptly twenty-three years later, when executed as a tyrant and traitor, aged forty-nine.

William **Sandys** and Simon Andrew Forster, *The History of the Violin and Other Instruments Played on with the Bow*, 1864
~ Dedicated (with permission) to Lord Gerald Fitzgerald, and the nobility and gentry of the society of wandering minstrels.

Dorothy L. **Sayers**, *Busman's Honeymoon*, 1937
~ To Muriel St Clare Byrne, Helen Simpson, and Marjorie Barber. Dear Muriel, Helen, and Bar, With what extreme of womanly patience you listened to this tale of *Busman's Honeymoon* while it was being written, the Lord He Knoweth. I do not like to think how many times I tired the sun with talking – and if at any time they had told me you were dead, I should easily have believed that I had talked you into your graves. But you have strangely survived to receive these thanks. You, Muriel, were in some sort a predestined victim, since you wrote with me the play to which this novel is but the limbs and outward flourishes; my debt and your long-suffering are all the greater. You, Helen and Bar, were wantonly sacrificed on the altar of that friendship of which the female sex is said to be incapable; let the lie stick i' the wall! To all three I humbly bring, I dedicate with tears, this sentimental comedy. [...] Yours in all gratitude, Dorothy L. Sayers.

The novel is subtitled 'A Love Story with Detective Interruptions', and is the last story featuring the detective Lord Peter Wimsey, who finally married Harriet Vane in the book. The previous year, as she mentions, Sayers had written the play version in collaboration with Muriel St Clare Byrne, when it was staged at the Comedy Theatre, London. From now on, Sayers switched from detective fiction to religious works, such as the famous play below. Notice her part quotation from TENNYSON's famous dedication to *Idylls of the King*.

Dorothy L. **Sayers**, *The Man Born To Be King*, 1943
~ These plays are for Val Gielgud, who has made them his already.

This dramatic work for radio, subtitled 'A Play-Cycle on the Life of our Lord and Saviour Jesus Christ', was written by Dorothy Sayers at the request of J.W. Welch, then Director of Religious Broadcasting at the BBC. The work itself comprised twelve separate plays, which were broadcast over the period December 1941 to October 1942. They were produced by Val Gielgud, brother of the actor Sir John Gielgud, and caused some controversy with the Mrs Whitehouses of the day for their direct representation of Christ, who was heard to speak modern, often colloquial English (sample: 'Well, young man. What can I do for you?'), and who was shown to have a sense of humour. The production would hardly raise any hackles today, except among fundamentalists, perhaps.

Olive **Schreiner**, *The Story of an African Farm*, 1883
~ To my friend Mrs John Brown of Burnley, this little firstling of my pen is lovingly inscribed. Ralph Iron.

This latter name was the pseudonym under which the South African writer published her famous, protofeminist novel, with its symbolic 'anti-colonial' farm, and which first brought her to public notice. Compare her next dedication below.

Olive **Schreiner**, *Woman and Labour*, 1911
DEDICATED TO CONSTANCE LYTTON
'Glory of warrior, glory of orator, glory of song
Paid with a voice flying by to be lost on an endless sea –
Glory of virtue, to fight, to struggle, to right the wrong –
May, but she aimed not at glory, no lover of glory she;
Give her the glory of going on and on and still to be.'

Tennyson.

In the Introduction to this polemic work, Schreiner explained: 'I have inscribed it to my friend, Lady Constance Lytton; not because I think it worthy of her, nor yet because of the splendid part she has played in the struggle of the women fighting to-day in England for certain forms of freedom for all women. It is, if I may be allowed without violating the sanctity of a close personal friendship so to say, because she, with one or two other men and women I have known, have embodied for me the highest ideal of human nature, in which intellectual power and strength of will are combined with an infinite tenderness and a wide human sympathy.' Lady Constance was the sister of Victor Alexander George Robert Bulwer-Lytton, 2nd Earl of Lytton, who was as keen as she was on promoting the cause of women's suffrage and whose name was one of the few male ones to be included in the suffragettes' equivalent to *Who's Who*.

Sir Peter **Scott**, *Travel Diaries of a Naturalist*, 1985
~ To all those who have worked to protect the beauty and wonder of nature, and to those who have made it possible for me to travel and to enjoy that beauty and wonder in so many different parts of the world.

Peter Scott, who died in 1989 only a few days short of his eightieth birthday, became internationally known for his tireless lifelong promotion of wildlife preservation and for his ceaseless writing, painting, lecturing and travelling in pursuit of this cause.

Sir Walter **Scott**, *The Lay of the Last Minstrel*, 1805
~ To the Right Honourable Charles, Earl of Dalkeith, this Poem is inscribed by the Author.

Sir Walter Scott, *Marmion*, 1808

~ To the Right Honourable Henry Lord Montague, etc., etc., etc., this Romance is inscribed by the Author.

The different cantos of this work are individually dedicated to various friends of Scott, with a 'poetic epistle' for each. The actual dedicatees (with canto number) are: I 'to William Stewart Rose, Esq.'; II 'to the Rev. John Marriott, A.M.'; III 'to William Erskine, Esq.'; IV 'to James Skene, Esq.'; V 'to George Ellis, Esq.'; VI 'to Richard Heber, Esq.'.

Sir Walter Scott, *The Lady of the Lake*, 1810

~ To the Most Noble John James, Marquis of Abercorn, etc., etc., etc., this Poem is inscribed by the Author.

Sir Walter Scott, *The Vision of Don Roderick*, 1811

~ To John Whitmore, Esq., and to the Committee of Subscribers for Relief of the Portuguese Sufferers, in which he presides, this poem, The Vision of Don Roderick, composed for the Benefit of the Fund under their Management, is respectfully inscribed by Walter Scott.

In other words, aid for Portugal, which was now in the throes of the Peninsular War.

Sir Walter Scott, *Rokeby*, 1813

~ To John S.B. Morritt, Esq., this Poem, the scene of which is laid in his beautiful demesne of Rokeby, is inscribed in token of sincere friendship, by Walter Scott.

Morritt was a clerical scholar and traveller, who lived at Rokeby Park, Yorkshire. Scott stayed a fortnight there in 1809 and much admired it, telling Morritt that he wanted to set a poem there. He even went so far as to confide to Morritt that he was the author of *Waverley*, which had already begun to circulate anonymously, causing much speculation regarding its authorship (see below).

Sir Walter Scott, *Waverley*, 1814

~ [...] As I have inverted the usual arrangement, placing these remarks at the end of the work to which they refer, I will venture on a second violation of form, by closing the whole with a dedication: These volumes being respectfully inscribed to our Scottish Addison, Henry Mackenzie, by an unknown admirer of his genius.

This dedication, unusually, came at the end of the work to which it belonged, not the beginning. Scott had published *Waverley* anonymously in the year stated, and dedicated it to Henry Mackenzie, then Comptroller of Taxes for Scotland but also, more significantly, the author of the influential novel (also published anonymously) *The Man of Feeling* (1771). He was nicknamed 'the Addison of the North' as his book was similar to Addison's essays on Sir Roger de Coverley. The 1869 edition of Scott's novel, published by Adam and Charles Black of Edinburgh to mark the forthcoming centenary (in 1871) of the writer's birth, had the following dedication: 'To Mary Monica Hope Scott of Abbotsford, this edition of the novels of her great-grandfather, Walter Scott, is dedicated by the publishers'. The dedicatee, apart from being Scott's great-granddaughter, was the second daughter of

James Robert Hope-Scott, who himself had married Scott's granddaughter, Charlotte Harriet Jane Lockhart, and the wife-to-be (in 1874) of the Hon Joseph Constable Maxwell, third son of Lord Herries, who assumed the extra name of Scott (hers, that is) on marriage. Scott had himself dedicated *Tales of a Grandfather* (1828) to his grandson, the son of his daughter and J. Gibson Lockhart, in a letter beginning: 'Much respected sir, Although I have not arrived at the reverend period of life which may put me on a level with yours […].'

Comtesse de **Ségur**, *Good Children*, 1879

~ TO MY GRANDCHILDREN, Pierre, Henri, Marie-Thérèse de Ségur; Valentine, Louis de Ségur; Camille, Madeleine, Louis, Gaston de Malaret; Elisabeth, Henriette, Armand Fresneau; Jacques, Jeanne, Marguerite, Paul de Pitray. My dear little children, I wanted each one of you to have his name at the head of my works, but your number, always increasing and rapidly so, exceeded my courage, and I unite you all in a single dedication, which will not, I hope, be the last, although every year I lose a year of life, as good Monsieur de la Palisse would say. A little time more, and I will keep silent, to hide the infirmities of my spirit from the public. You will be my only little confidants. Your grandmother, Comtesse de Ségur, née Rostopchine.

Translated from the French by AR, original title: *Les Bons Enfants*. The popular French children's author became best known for *The Misfortunes of Sophie* (1859), and followed this with several more volumes for the children's book series *Bibliothèque Rose* ('Pink Library', referring to the colour of their binding). She was the daughter of a Russian count, Fyodor Vasilyevich Rostopchin, aide-de-camp to Paul I, and married another count, but this time a French one, Comte Eugène de Ségur. She was an invalid from about 1835, and while lying on her couch made up the stories about naughty or unfortunate children to entertain her eight children or, later, her grandchildren, as here. Compare the dedication below.

Comtesse de **Ségur**, *Bribouille's Sister*, 1880

~ To my granddaughter, Valentine de Ségur-Lamoignon. Dear child, I offer to you, charming, loved, and protected, the story of a poor half-imbecile boy, unloved, and deprived of everything. Compare his life to yours, and thank God for the difference.

Translated from the French by AR; original title: *La Sœur de Bribouille*. This grandchild is also included in the dedication above, but here has her married name added.

Hugh de **Selincourt**, *The Cricket Match*, 1924

~ To Frank W. Carter, in memory of many good games watched and played together, you in your small corner, I in mine.

De Selincourt, who died in 1951, aged seventy-two, was professionally literary critic of the *Observer* but made his name with his popular chronicles of village cricket, as here.

Maurice **Sellar**, *The Allies*, 1979

~ To Lorna, who sustained me with her blood, sweat, tears and tea.

Robert **Service**, *Songs of a Sun-Lover*, 1949

DEDICATION TO PROVENCE

I loved to toy with tuneful rhyme,
My fancies into verse to weave;
For as I walked my words would chime
So bell-like I could scarce believe;
My rhythms rippled like a brook,
My stanzas bloomed like blossoms gay:
And that is why I deem this book
    A verseman's holiday.

The palm-blades brindle in the blaze
Of sunsets splendouring the sea;
The gloaming is a lilac haze
That impish stars stab eagerly ...
O Land of Song! O golden clime!
O happy me, whose work is play!
Please take this tribute of my rhyme:
    A verseman's holiday.

The dedication to one of the many collections of light verse by the Canadian writer who died in 1958 at the age of eighty-four.

Ernest Thompson **Seton**, *The Biography of a Grizzly*, 1900

~ This book is dedicated to the memory of the days spent at the Palette Ranch on the Graybull, where from hunter, miner, personal experience and the host himself, I gathered many chapters of the history of Wahb.

One of the books on wildlife (and the need to protect it) by the English-born Canadian (much later, American) naturalist and writer, who founded the Woodcraft League, a Boy Scout-type organisation, in 1902 and who played a large part in founding the Boy Scouts of America themselves in 1910. In this story, Wahb is the name of the grizzly bear. See further dedications of his below.

Ernest Thompson **Seton**, *Lives of the Hunted*, 1901

~ To the preservation of our Wild Creatures, I dedicate this book.

Ernest Thompson **Seton**, *Two Little Savages*, 1903

~ To Woodcraft, by one who owes it many lasting pleasures.

This story was written to teach woodcraft to boys (see above), and tells how the 'two little savages', Yan and Sam, are taught its art by Caleb Clark, an old trapper.

Ernest Thompson **Seton**, *The Natural History of the Ten Commandments*, 1907

~ Dedicated to the Beasts of the Field by a Hunter.

Alfred J. Sewell, *The Dog's Medical Dictionary*, 1906

~ The reviser dedicates this book to P.E.B., who like himself wishes it to be a real help to our friend the dog in his hour of need, and hopes it may prove a worthy successor to the general work of his late partner.

This is the dedication to the new edition of the book, published in 1932, which was revised by F.W. Cousens. The grammar of the text makes it uncertain whether the reviser or P.E.B. hopes that the edition will be a worthy successor to the original, but common sense suggests that Sewell was Cousens' late partner, not P.E.B.'s.

Anna Sewell, *Black Beauty*, 1877

~ To my dear and honoured mother, whose life, no less than her pen, has been devoted to the welfare of others, this little book is affectionately dedicated.

Anna Sewell's mother, Mary Sewell, had begun to write moral verses and stories when she was nearly sixty, with her ballad *Mother's Last Words* (1860) selling over a million copies. But it was her only daughter's fame that would last, with her much loved and still popular 'autobiography' of a black mare. Anna, who never married, was a permanent cripple from her mid-30s, and died in 1878 aged fifty-eight, only a few months after her book was published, too soon for her to see it as the bestseller it became. Her mother died in 1884, aged eighty-seven.

Arabella Seymour, *Dangerous Deceptions*, 1988

~ To Orlando Hatten and Nick La Fourche, with love and kisses and special thanks for a great time in New York, Sept. '86 XXXX. And for Dave Diehl, Jeff & Lynne Halik, with love and friendship.

Sir Ernest Shackleton, *South*, 1919

~ To my comrades who fell in the white warfare of the south and on the red fields of France and Flanders.

The book is an account of the famous explorer's expedition to Antarctica in the ship *Endurance* over the two years from 1914, in the First World War. Hence the reference to 'warfare' symbolised by the two different colours.

William Shakespeare, *Venus and Adonis*, 1593

~ To the Right Honourable Henrie Wriothesley, Earle of Southampton and Baron of Tichfield. Right Honourable, I know not how I shall offend in dedicating my unpolisht lines to your Lordship, nor how the worlde will censure mee for choosing so strong a proppe to support so weake a burthen, onelye if your Honour seeme but pleased, I account my selfe highly praised, and vowe to take advantage of all idle houres, till I have honoured you with some graver labour. But if the first heire of my invention prove deformed, I shall be sorie it had so noble a god-father: and never after eare so barren a land, for feare it yeeld me still so bad a harvest, I leave it to your Honourable survey, and your Honor to your hearts content, which I wish may alwaies answere your owne wish and the worlds hopefull expectation. Your Honors in all dutie, William Shakespeare.

Shakespeare seems to have written only two dedicatory letters, both to the same patron, Henry Wriothesley, 3rd Earl of Southampton, some nine years younger than himself. This is the first, in which Shakespeare tactfully and modestly makes his offering. His promise of 'some graver labour' was probably fulfilled in *The Rape of Lucrece* (see below).

William **Shakespeare**, *The Rape of Lucrece*, 1594

~ To the Right Honourable Henry Wriothesly, Earle of Southampton, and Baron of Tichfield. The love I dedicate to your Lordship is without end: wherof this Pamphlet without beginning is but a superfluous Moiety. The warrant I have of your Honourable disposition, not the worth of my untutord Lines makes it assured of acceptance. What I have done is yours, what I have to doe is yours, being part in all I have, devoted yours. Were my worth greater, my duety would shew greater, meane time, as it is, it is bound to your Lordship, to whom I wish long life still lengthned with all happinesse. Your Lordships in all duety, William Shakespeare.

Shakespeare's second dedication to his patron (see above) appears to show progress in their cordial relationship, and it has been suggested that Shakespeare may well have spent the plague year of 1593–4 at Wriothesley's home at Titchfield, Hampshire, possibly writing the first draft of *Love's Labour's Lost* there. The reference to a 'pamphlet without beginning' is thought to refer to the fact that the opening stanzas of *Lucrece* say nothing about the 'test', mentioned in the prefatory Argument to the work, by which Collatine, Lucrece's husband, proved his wife's virtue. (During the siege of Ardea, the army leaders had met in the king's son's tent one evening after supper and in the course of a lively conversation each had defended his wife's virtue. Collatine, however, had claimed that his wife was the only one that was genuinely chaste. To put this to the test, all the men went to Rome, where, although it was late at night, Lucrece was found spinning among her maids, whereas the other wives were discovered 'revelling and dancing'.)

William **Shakespeare**, *Sonnets*, 1609

~ TO THE. ONLIE. BEGETTER. OF. THESE. INSUING. SONNETS, MR. W.H., ALL HAPPINESSE. AND. THAT. ETERNITIE. PROMISED. BY. OUR EVER- LIVING   POET. WISHETH. THE. WELL-WISHING. ADVENTURER. IN. SETTING. FORTH. T.T.

Little could Thomas Thorpe ('T.T.'), who published the *Sonnets*, have realised what a web of literary intrigues he was spinning when he wrote this really rather trite dedication. The identification of 'Mr. W.H.' has thus engaged literary detectives for centuries now, and the truth is still uncertain. Much seems to depend on the word 'begetter'. If this means 'inspirer', the dedicatee may have been the famous 'Fair Young Man' who features in the work, the 'opposite number' to the equally mysterious 'Dark Lady' who is the other main character. In the *Sonnets* Shakespeare urges the 'Fair Young Man' to marry, and it is known that in 1595 there were abortive negotiations for William Herbert (later Earl of Pembroke), whose initials certainly fill the bill, to marry. He is, too, one of the dedicatees in the posthumous collected edition of Shakespeare's works (see below). But a stronger claim has been made for Henry Wriothesley, Earl of Southampton, to whom Shakespeare himself dedicated two earlier works (see above) and for whom he seems to have expressed a particular affection.

Even if his initials are the wrong way round (part of the riddle?), they are still 'W.H.'. On the other hand, if 'begetter' simply means 'getter', 'obtainer', then the person indicated could simply have been a friend of Thomas Thorpe, and the man who procured the manuscript for him. But his identity is unknown. On balance, Henry Wriothesley is the favourite, although evidence for the 'W' standing for 'William' is additionally claimed by those who point to the wording of the so called 'Will Sonnets' (135 and 136), in which the word 'will' occurs eighteen times! Compare THOMAS THORPE's other dedication.

William **Shakespeare**, *Comedies, Histories, & Tragedies*, 1623
~ To the Most Noble and Incomparable Paire of Brethren, William Earl of Pembroke, &c. Lord Chamberlaine to the Kings most Excellent Majesty. And Philip Earle of Montgomery, &c. Gentleman of his Majesties Bed-Chamber. Both Knights of the most Noble Order of the Garter, and our singular good Lords. Right Honourable, Whilst we studie to be thankful in our particular, for the many favors we have received from your L.L. we are falne upon the ill fortune, to mingle two the most diverse things that can bee, feare, and rashnesse; rashnesse in the enterprize, and fear of the successe. For, when we valew the places your H.H. sustaine, we cannot but know their dignity greater, then to descend to the reading of these trifles: and, while we name them trifles, we have depriv'd our selves of the defence of our Dedication. But since your L.L. have beene pleas'd to thinke these trifles some-thing heeretofore; and have prosequuted both them, and their Authour living, with so much favour: we hope, that (they out-living him, and he not having the fate, common with some, to be exequutor to his owne writings) you will use the like indulgence toward them, you have done unto their parent. There is a great difference, whether any Booke choose his Patrones, or finde them; this hath done both. For, so much were your L.L. likings of the severall parts, when they were acted, as before they were published, the Volume ask'd to be yours. We have but collected them, and done an office to the dead, to procure his Orphanes, Guardians; without ambition either of selfe-profit, or fame: onely to keepe the memory of so worthy a Friend, & Fellow alive, as was our Shakespeare, by humble offer of his playes, to your most noble patronage. [...] In that name therefore, we most humbly consecrate to your H.H. these remaines of your servant Shakespeare, that what delight is in them, may be ever your L.L. the reputation his, & the faults ours, if any be committed, by a payre so carefull to shew their gratitude both to the living, and the dead, as is Your Lordshippes most bounden, John Heminge. Henry Condell.

This is the famous posthumous collection of Shakespeare's plays, twenty in number, known as the First Folio, saved for posterity by two of his fellow actors, John Heminge and Henry Condell, both churchwardens of St Mary's, Aldermanbury. The dedicatees are the 'Incomparable Paire of Brethren' William Herbert, 3rd Earl of Pembroke, identified by some with the 'Mr. W.H.' of the dedication to the *Sonnets* (see above) and Philip Herbert, 4th Earl of Pembroke and 1st Earl of Montgomery, favourite of James I.

Dell **Shannon**, *Felony at Random*, 1979
~ For Mary Allison, old friends gold, new friends silver, all much worth having.

Lionel **Shapiro**, *The Sixth of June*, 1957

~ There is a land blest with the heritage of knowing intimately her British kinsmen and her American neighbours and of loving and in a sense uniting both. The land is Canada, and it is to this precious heritage that I gratefully dedicate this book.

A historical novel based on the Second World War and the allied operations in Western Europe that culminated in Operation Overlord, the Normandy landings of 1942. Canada was an important ally in the war, with many of her men active in occupied France.

John **Sheffield**, 1st Duke of Buckingham, *Works*, 1722

~ To the memory of John Sheffield, Duke of Buckingham. These his more lasting remains (the monuments of his mind, and more perfect image of himself) are here collected by the direction of Catherine his Duchesse: Desirous that his ashes may be honoured and his fame and merit committed to the test of time, truth, and posterity.

The works of Sheffield, who had died the previous year, were published at the request of his widow, who was his third wife and herself the illegitimate daughter of James II by Catharine Sedley. She is thus the author of this dedication. Sheffield was a generous patron to DRYDEN, who dedicated his *Aureng-Zebe* (1676) to him.

Patricia Fox **Sheinwold**, *Too Young to Die: The Stars the World Tragically Lost*, 1980

~ Friend is a six-letter word, for Teresa.

Percy Bysshe **Shelley**, *Queen Mab*, 1813

TO HARRIET *****

Whose is the love that gleaming through the world,
Wards off the poisonous arrow of its scorn?
   Whose is the warm and partial praise,
   Virtue's most sweet reward?

Beneath whose looks did my reviving soul
Riper in truth and virtuous daring grow?
   Whose eyes have I gazed fondly on,
   And love mankind the more?

Harriet! on thine: – thou wert my purer mind;
Thou wert the inspiration of my song;
   Thine are these early wilding flowers,
   Thou garlanded by me.

Then press into thy breast this pledge of love;
And know, though time may change and years may roll,
   Each floweret gathered in my heart
   It consecrates to thine.

This, probably the best-known of Shelley's works, was believed by some to have been dedicated to Harriet Grove, the poet's cousin, if only because the five stars fitted her name. But it is now known the dedicatee was actually Harriet Westbrook, the daughter of a London retired tavern keeper, whom Shelley met through his sisters Mary and Ellen. They fell in love, and married in 1811, when she was sixteen, eloping to Scotland. But the marriage was not a success, and the following year Shelley fell in love with Mary Godwin, also sixteen, and the daughter of the philosopher and novelist William Godwin. They in turn eloped to Europe, but lived together in England on their return. Harriet tragically drowned herself in 1816, after which Shelley and Mary married and went to live in Italy for the rest of Shelley's short life. He died, himself also drowned, although accidentally, in 1822. He was twenty-nine.

Percy Bysshe **Shelley**, *The Cenci*, 1820

~ To Leigh Hunt, Esq. My dear Friend – I inscribe with your name, from a distant country, and after an absence whose months have seemed years, this the latest of my literary efforts. [...] Had I know a person more highly endowed than yourself with all that become a man to possess, I had solicited for this work the ornament of his name. One more gentle, honourable, innocent, and brave; one of more exalted toleration for all who do and think evil, and yet himself more free from evil; one who knows better how to receive and how to confer a benefit, though he must ever confer far more than he can receive; one of simpler and, in the highest sense of the word, of purer life and manners I never knew: and I had already been fortunate in friendships when your name was added to the list. [...] All happiness attend you! Your affectionate friend, Percy B. Shelley.

Leigh Hunt, poet, journalist and critic, was editor of the radical weekly, *The Examiner*, in which he introduced the work of Keats and Shelley to the public. In 1822 he travelled to Italy ('a distant country') to join Byron and Shelley in launching a perdiodical called *The Liberal*, but this came to an abrupt end after Shelley's early tragic death and the departure of Byron for Greece. The year before *The Cenci* was published, Shelley had written to Hunt from Italy as follows: 'I have written something and finished it, different from anything else, and a new attempt for me; and I mean to dedicate it to you. I should not have done so without your approbation, but I asked your picture last night and it smiled assent. If I did not think it in some degree worthy of you, I would not make you a public offering of it.' See also KEATS's dedication to Leigh Hunt (above).

Percy Bysshe **Shelley**, *Hellas*, 1822

~ To His Excellency Prince Alexander Mavrocordato, Late Secretary for Foreign Affairs to the Hospodar of Wallachia, the Drama of Hellas is inscribed as an imperfect token of the admiration, sympathy, and friendship of the author.

This was the last of Shelley's works to be published in his lifetime, inspired by news of the Greek War of Independence against the Turkish empire, and dedicated to their national hero, Alexandros Mavrokordatos, later Prime Minister of Greece, whom the poet had known in Pisa.

Jane de Forest **Shelton**, *The Salt Box House*, 1900

~ In honor of the long ago, and to those who, passing an old highway, see the signs written on moss-covered fences, in traces of old door yards, by lone-standing chimneys, and would know the interpretation thereof, to those whose pulses are stirred as they stand beneath the long sloping roofs, and whose hearts bow reverently as they read the records on the gravestones of the seventeen hundreds, this book is inscribed.

A nostalgic historical dedication. The gravestones would have been those of the original settlers in America.

Louise **Shelton**, *The Seasons in a Flower Garden*, 1906

~ To the memory of my little spaniel, 'Idol', for twelve years my shadow in my garden.

Thomas **Shelton**, *The History of the Valorous and Witty Knight-Errant Don Quixote of the Mancha, The First Part*, 1612–20

~ To the Right Honourable His Verie Good Lord, The Lord of Walden, &C. Mine Honourable Lord; having Translated some five or sixe yeares agoe, the Historie of *Don Quixote*, out of the Spanish tongue into English, in the space of forty daies; being therunto more than halfe enforced, through the importunitie of a very deere friend, that was desirous to understand the subject: After I had given him once a view thereof, I cast it aside, where it lay long time neglected in a corner, and so little regarded by me, as I never once set hand to review or correct the same. Since when, at the intreatie of others my friends, I was content to let it come to light, conditionally, that some one or other, would peruse and amend the errours escaped; my many affaires hindering mee from undergoing that labour. Now I understand by the Printer, that the Copie was presented to your Honour: which did at the first somewhat disgust mee, because as it must passe, I feare much, it will prove farre unworthy, either of your Noble view or protection. Yet since it is mine, though abortive, I doe humbly intreate, that your Honour will lend it a favourable countenance, thereby to animate the parent thereof to produce in time some worthier subject, in your Honourable name, whose many rare vertues have already rendred me so highly devoted to your service, as I will some day give very evident tokens of the same, and till then I rest, Your Honours most affectionate servitor, Thomas Shelton.

Shelton was the earliest translator of *Don Quixote* into English, and despite his misgivings and anxiety regarding the standard of the translation, it won great popularity, and references to Don Quixote in English literature were frequent from then on. Hardly anything is known about Shelton's life, and if he had not told us in his agreeably straightforward way about the origins of the translation, we would not have known even that much.

Eugenia **Sheppard** and Earl **Blackwell**, *Skyrocket*, 1980

~ To New York, the city that adopted a girl from the Midwest and a boy from the South, and helped them, as well as thousands of others, launch their skyrockets.

A novel of romance and fame, with the hero, Schuyler ('Sky') Madison, rocketing to acclaim and power.

Stephen **Sheppard**, *For All the Tea in China*, 1988
~ For the three mothers in my life, ladies without whom ... Ellen Mary who had to suffer me; Winky who chooses to; Annie who will ... one from the heart.

Richard Brinsley **Sheridan**, *The Critic*, 1779
~ To Mrs. Greville. Madam, In requesting your permission to address the following pages to you, which as they aim themselves to be critical, require every protection and allowance that approving taste or friendly prejudice can give them, I yet ventured to mention no other motive than the gratification of private friendship and esteem. I suggested a hope that your implied approbation would give a sanction to their defects, your particular reserve, and dislike to the reputation of critical taste, as well as of poetical talent, would have made you refuse the protection of your name to such a purpose. [...] Enough of what you have written, has stolen into full public notice to answer my purpose; and you will, perhaps, be the only person, conversant in elegant literature, who shall read this address and not perceive that by publishing your particular approbation of the following drama, I have a more interested object than to boast the true respect and regard with which I have the honour to be, MADAM, Your very sincere, And obedient humble servant, R.B. Sheridan.

The dedicatee, Frances Greville, née Macartney, was the wife of Richard Fulke Greville, of Wilbury House, Wiltshire (the family home of the better-known Charles Cavendish Fulke Greville, politician, whose brother, Algernon Sidney Greville, was Wellington's private secretary) and the mother of Sheridan's friend, Lady Frances Crewe, one of the most beautiful women of her time, to whom he dedicated *The School for Scandal* (1777).

Richard Brinsley **Sheridan**, *Pizarro*, 1799
~ To Her, whose approbation of this Drama, and whose peculiar delight in the applause it has received from the Public, have been to me the highest gratification its success has produced – I dedicate this Play. Richard Brinsley Sheridan.

To Sheridan's second wife, Esther Ogle, daughter of the Dean of Winchester, whom he had married three years before, after the death of his first wife. The mysterious 'To Her' caused much speculation and fanciful comment among his literary contemporaries, and the following appeared in the periodical *The Oracle* for 5 July 1799: 'A good deal of wit is sported on Mr. Sheridan's Dedication of his Play; some say it is inscribed to the Queen, others to Mrs. Sheridan, others to Mrs. Siddons, and why not – Mrs. Jordan? Perhaps the fact is, that it is dedicated to no *earthly power*, but to Melpomene, who has rendered no small assistance on the occasion.' Mrs Jordan, although famous for her 'breeches parts', had actually played leading female roles in Sheridan's plays, among them Lydia Languish in *The Rivals* (1775) and Lady Teazle in *The School for Scandal* (1777).

Fredrick W. Short, *The Ploughman*, 1977

~ To all those who walk upon the soil, hand in hand with God, that man may live.

J. Henry Shorthouse, *John Inglesant*, 1881

~ To Rawdon Levett, Esq. My dear Levett, I dedicate this volume to you, that I may have an opportunity of calling myself your friend. J. Henry Shorthouse.

This was the writer's best known book, a historical novel of religious intrigue, based on seventeenth-century fact.

Ebenezer Sibley, *A New and Complete Illustration of the Celestial Science of Astrology*, 1784–8

~ To the ancient and honourable Fraternity of Free and Accepted Masons. Gentlemen and Brethren, The Antiquity of your excellent Fraternity, the universality of its plan and the moral rectitude and purity of its design, claim a decided pre-eminence over every other Bond of Society into which mankind have ever formed themselves for the mutual welfare and happiness of each other. [...] To you, therefore, as the promoters of liberal sentiment, and the guardians of every useful science, I commit this venerable pile of ancient Astrology; a fabric obviously constructed by the Great Architect of the World, primeval with the Ordination of Nature, and inseparable from one of the grand subjects of your official contemplation. [...] I have the honour to profess myself, with unequivocal attachment and esteem, Gentlemen, Your Accepted Brother, And Faithful Servant, E. Sibley.

Professionally qualifying as a doctor, Sibley made his reputation as an astrologer with works such as this. He dated the dedication 'In the Year of Masonry, 5784' and followed it with a second, individual dedication three pages long 'to the young student in astrology'.

Walter Sichel, *Types and Characters*, 1925

~ To every one in these pages this book is dimly dedicated.

The book is subtitled 'A Kaleidoscope' and is a journalistic study of individuals and social groups in the mid-1920s, when the buzz word was 'new' ('the new poet', 'the new society', 'the new workman', and so on). Sichel is best remembered not for this, however, but as a historical biographer of such writers as Sheridan, Sterne and Disraeli.

Sir Philip Sidney, *Arcadia*, 1590

~ To my Deare Ladie and Sister, the Countesse of Pembroke. Here now have you (most deare, and most worthy to be most deare Lady) this idle worke of mine: which I fear (like the Spiders webbe) will be thought fitter to be swept away, then worn to any other purpose. For my part, in very trueth (as the cruell fathers among the Greekes, were woont to doo to the babes they would not foster) I could well find in my harte, to cast out in some desert of forgetfulness this child which I am loath to father. But you desired me to doo it, and your desire to my hart is an absolute commandement. Now, it is done onelie for you, onely to you; if you keepe it to your selfe, or to such friendes, who will weigh errors in the ballaunce of good will, I hope, for the fathers sake, it will be pardoned, perchance made much of, though in it selfe it have deformities. [...] Read it then at your idle tymes, and the follyes your good judgement wil finde in it, blame me not, but laugh at. And so, looking for no better stuffe, then, as in an Haberdashers shoppe, glasses, or feathers, you will continue to love the writer, who doth excedinglie love you, and most hartelie praies you may long live to be a principall ornament to the familie of the Sidneis. Your loving Brother, Philip Sidnei.

A dedication that is rightly singled out as one of the most attractive of its age. The work itself was a prose romance, interspersed with poems, written by Philip Sidney expressly for his sister while staying with her at Wilton House, Wiltshire. As was then common, it was not originally written to be published, but to be circulated in manuscript form. It, or extracts from it, would then have been copied more than once into commonplace books. It was thus only in 1593 that *The Countess of Pembroke's Arcadia* was published in revised form as the third and final version of the original. The Countess of Pembroke, now twenty-nine, was Mary Herbert, having married Henry Herbert, 2nd Earl of Pembroke, twice married previously and over twice her age (he was forty-four, she sixteen) in 1577. She was the dedicatee not simply of her brother's offering but of many other noted literary works, such as SPENSER's *Ruines of Time* (see below), NICOLAS BRETON's *Pilgrimage to Paradise* (see above) and Thomas Morley's musical *Canzonets* (1593). She was also a generous patroness, and a noted translator in her own right.

Arnold **Silcock,** *Verse and Worse: A Private Collection,* 1952

> To Those who Gave me Most I Give my Thanks;
> You Helped to Make This Book. – Oh, Generous Ranks:
> My Friends and Family! – Here Find your Roll
> Of Names – in Order Alphabetical! ...

A list of forty-two names follows, including Miss Diana Silcock (Mrs Christie) and Miss Ruth Silcock, the author-editor's daughters. Silcock, best known as an architect, himself died the following year, aged sixty-four.

Robert **Silverberg,** *Nightwings,* 1968

~ For Harlan, to remind him of open windows, the currents of the Delaware River, quarters with two heads, and other pitfalls.

Robert **Silverberg,** *Majipoor Chronicles,* 1981

~ For Kirby, who may not have been driven all the way to despair by this one, but who certainly got as far as the outlying suburbs.

Just two of the novels by the prolific American science fiction writer.

Mrs Frances **Simpson,** *Cats for Pleasure and Profit,* 1905

~ To the many kind friends, known and unknown, that I have made in Pussydom.

This feline manual had originally been published three years previously as *Cats and All About Them*.

J.A. **Simpson** and E.S.C. **Weiner**, preps, *The Oxford English Dictionary*, 2nd edn., 1989

~ This second edition of the Oxford English Dictionary is respectfully dedicated to HER MAJESTY THE QUEEN by her gracious permission.

Compare the dedications for the original *Oxford English Dictionary* (under the name of JAMES MURRAY) and for its *Supplement* (under R.W. BURCHFIELD). It is interesting that neither the dedication for the *Supplement* nor this one for the second edition of the *OED* actually gives the *name* of the royal dedicatee. This was doubtless to conform with the style of the original dedication of 1897 to Queen Victoria, who was also addressed anonymously.

Upton **Sinclair**, *The Industrial Republic*, 1907

~ To H.G. Wells, 'the next most hopeful'.

An earlyish tribute from the American novelist to the English writer and didact.

Rosemary Anne **Sisson**, *Beneath the Visiting Moon*, 1986

~ This novel is dedicated to the memory of Richard Burton and to his wife Sybil, who, long ago at the Old Vic, were both so kind to an aspiring playwright, and also to the memory of Alan Badel whose first might *Hamlet* at Stratford was a disaster, but who later in the run, unattended by the critics, became one of the finest Hamlets of our time.

A love story set in the 1950s, when the author, best known for her children's books, first began writing plays.

Joshua **Slocum**, *Sailing Alone Around the World*, 1900

~ To the one who said: 'The Spray will come back'.

She did, after taking the writer on his momentous single-handed voyage, narrated here.

Anthony **Smith**, *Smith & Son: An Expedition into Africa*, 1984

~ This book is for Adam, supreme companion (who had all of the fun, and some of the anxiety), for Barbara, his mother (who had none of the fun, but all of the anxiety), for Polly and Laura, his sisters (who had none of the anxiety, but also none of the fun, and whose turn must come).

An account of a north-to-south journey through Africa by motorcycle, made by the author and his nineteen-year-old son.

Elizabeth Thomasina Meade **Smith**, *The Children of Wilton Chase*, 1891

~ This story is dedicated with affection to Marjory, a child who, possessing a spirit of love and service, has inspired the idea of that other Marjory who appears in these pages.

This is just one of the literally hundreds of stories for girls written by the Irish-born children's author better known as L.T. Meade (the L standing for 'Lillie', a pet form of her first name).

F. Hopkinson **Smith**, *A White Umbrella in Mexico*, 1889

~ I dedicate this book to the most charming of all the Senoritas I know: the one whose face lingers longest in my memory while I am away, and whose arms open widest when I return; the most patient of my listeners, the most generous of my critics, my little daughter Marion.

Smith was an American writer, painter and engineer who illustrated his own travel sketches in the different countries he visited, which included Spain, Italy and Mexico. The book is not specifically one for children, despite the dedication. Compare his title below.

F. Hopkinson **Smith**, *A Day at Laguerre's and Other Days*, 1892

~ To my out-door friends everywhere: My good Espero, whom I love: Manual and his sweetheart: little Lucette with the velvet eyes, big-hearted captain Joe, and even Isaacs – Isaacs, the unfaithful, who is watching to fleece me again when next I visit Constantinople.

The book contains stories set in a variety of places, from the Bronx to Constantinople. The dedications are to characters in these places.

John **Smith**, *A Description of New England*, 1616

~ To the High Hopeful Charles, Prince of Great Britaine. Sir: So favourable was your most renowned and memorable Brother, Prince Henry, to all generous designes; that in my discovery of Virginia, I presumed to call two namelesse Headlands after my Soveraignes heires, Cape Henry, and Cape Charles. Since then, it beeing my chance to range some other parts of America, whereof I heere present your Highnesse the description in a Map; my humble sute is, you would please to change their Barbarous names, for such English, as Posterity may say, Prince Charles was their God-father. What here in this relation I promise my Countrey, let mee live or die the slave of scorne & infamy, if (having meanes) I make it not apparent; please God to blesse me but from such accidents as are beyond my power and reason to prevent. For my labours, I desire but such conditions as were promised men out of the gaines; and that your Highnesse would daigne to grace this Work, by your Princely and favourable respect unto it, and know mee to be Your Highnesse true and faithfull servant, John Smith.

The title of this book is said to be the earliest record of the name New England. John Smith, with his archetypical English name, was one of the first colonists to visit and explore America, in the process being captured by the Indians, sentenced to death, but rescued (according to his account) by the Indian princess Pocahontas. His wrote much on his travels and experiences, and here in his dedication to the sixteen-year-old Prince Charles, the future Charles I, is concerned to confirm his keenness to give patriotic English names to the places he discovered. (Charles approved of this, and always favoured the giving of

English names where there were 'barbarous' Indian ones.) Cape Charles and Cape Henry, both named by Smith, are still there today at the entrance to Chesapeake Bay, Virginia.

Henry **Somerset**, 8th Duke of Beaufort, *The Poetry of Sport*, 1885

~ Having received permission to dedicate these volumes, the Badminton Library of Sports and Pastimes, to His Royal Highness, the Prince of Wales, I do so, feeling that I am dedicating them to one of the best and keenest sportsmen of our time. I can say, from personal observation, that there is no man who can extricate himself from a bustling and pushing crowd of horsemen, when a fox breaks covert, more dexterously and quickly than H.R.H.; and that when hounds run hard over a big country, no man can take a line of his own and live with them better. Also, when the wind has been blowing hard, often have I seen H.R.H. knocking over driven grouse and partridges and high-rocketing pleasants in first-rate workmanlike style. I consider it a great privilege to be allowed to dedicate these volumes to so eminent a sportsman as H.R.H. the Prince of Wales, and I do so with sincere feelings of respect and esteem and loyal affection. Beaufort.

A paeon of praise and plaudits for the future Edward VII, known for his enthusiastic participation in the 'sporting life' in all its variety. The Duke was one of the editors of the Badminton Library, named after the ancestral home of the Dukes of Somerset, in Somerset, which also gave the name of a humbler but much more accessible sport than those described here, badminton.

Fred J. **Speakman**, *A Forest Night*, 1965

~ In memory of my father who led my first childhood steps among green trees, to my wife and children, who bring me the happiness I know, and to all who love the quiet places.

A soothing, contented dedication.

Spedding, *The Road and the Hills*, 1986

~ This book is dedicated to Alexander (356–23 BC) without whom, nothing.

A science fiction tale, Book One of *A Walk in the Dark*, set in a distant era, with its dedication to Alexander the Great. The author, who writes simply under her surname, is actually Alison Spedding.

Peter **Spence**, *Some of Our Best Friends are Animals*, 1976

~ To Jill, Without whom, Whose, Who has been my constant, Who has always, Who ...

In the original, all the words between the second and last are deleted, perhaps with the author's light-hearted implication that, for his dedication, mere routine words are not enough. The book itself is a factual one on wildlife and its conservation.

Stephen **Spender**, *Life and the Poet*, 1942

~ Dedicated to the Young Writers in the Armed Forces, Civil Defence and the

Pacifist Organisations of Democracy: in the hope that this tribute may encourage them to write.

An educative guide for budding poets written while the author, himself a poet of distinction, was serving as an A.R.P. warden (firewatcher) in London.

Edmund **Spenser**, *The Shepheardes Calender*, 1579
~ Entitled to the Noble and Vertuous Gentleman most worthy of all titles both of learning and cheualrie M. Philip Sidney.

Otherwise the famous Sir Philip Sidney, courtier, poet, critic, author (in possibly that order), to whom many works by contemporary writers were dedicated, this being one of the best known.

Edmund **Spenser**, *The Faerie Queene*, 1590, 1596
~ To the Most High, Mightie And Magnificent Empresse Renowmed for Pietie, Vertue, and All Gratious Government Elizabeth by the Grace of God Queene of England France and Ireland and of Virginia, Defendour of the Faith, &c. Her Most Humble Servant Edmund Spenser Doth in All Humilitie Dedicate, Present and Consecrate These His Labours to Live With the Eternitie of Her Fame.

Books I to III of this famous work were published in 1590, and Books IV to VI (as well as a second edition of I to III) appeared in 1596. Hence the two dates. The last eight words of the well-known dedication to Queen Elizabeth were added in the latter year. The style of the tribute is typical of the Elizabethan dedication, with the lowly author making his humble offering to the lofty patron. But in its final form the work, Spenser's greatest, has not only this dedication but a set of commendatory verses and no less than seventeen separate dedicatory sonnets to various court officials and aristocrats, the first fourteen to different lords, including Sir Francis Walsingham and Sir Walter Raleigh (see below), the fifteenth and sixteenth respectively to 'the right honourable and most vertuous Lady, the Countesse of Pembroke' and 'the most vertuous, and beautifull Lady, the Lady Carew', and the last 'to all the gratious and beautifull Ladies in the Court', each sonnet consisting of just two stanzas.

Edmund **Spenser**, *The Ruines of Time*, 1591
~ Dedicated to the right Noble and beautifull Ladie, the La. Marie, Countess of Pembrooke. Most Honourable and bountifull Ladie, there bee long sithens deepe sowed in my brest, the seede of most entire loue and humble affection unto that most braue Knight your noble brother deceased; which taking roote began in his life somewhat to bud forth: and to shew themselues to him, as then in the weakenes of their first spring: And would in their riper strength (had it pleased high God till then to drawe out his daies) spired forth fruit of more perfection. [...] I haue conceiued this small Poeme, intituled by a generall name of the *worlds Ruines*: yet speciallie intended to the renowming of that noble race, from which both you and he sprong, and to the eternizing of some of the chiefe of them late deceased. The which I dedicate unto your La. as whome it most speciallie concerneth: and to whome I acknowledge my selfe bounden, by manie singular fauours and great

graces. I pray for your Honourable happinesse: and so humblie kisse your handes. Your Ladiships euer humblie at commaund. E.S.

The work is an allegorical elegy on the death of Sir Philip Sidney, which had occurred six years earlier, and is dedicated, as were many works by Spenser's contemporaries, to his sister, Mary Herbert, Countess of Pembroke. See also the dedication to her by SIDNEY himself.

Edmund **Spenser**, *Prosopopoia, or Mother Hubberds Tale*, 1591

~ To the right Honourable, the Ladie Compton and Mountegle. Most faire and vertuous Ladie; hauing often sought opportunitie by some good meanes to make known to your Ladiship, the humble affection and faithfull duetie, which I haue alwaies professed, and am bound to beare to that House, from whence yee spring, I haue at length found occasion to remember the same, by making a simple present to you of these my idel labours; which hauing long sithens composed in the raw conceipt of my youth, I lately amongst other papers lighted upon, and was by others, which liked the same, mooued to set them foorth. Simple is the deuice, and the composition meane, yet carrieth some delight, euen the rather because of the simplicitie and meenesse thus personated. The same I beseech your Ladiship take in good part, as a pledge of that profession which I haue made to you, and keepe with you untill with some other more worthie labour, I do redemme it out of your hands, and discharge my utmost dutie. Till then wishing your Ladiship all increase of honour and happinesse, I humblie take leaue. Your La: euer humbly; Ed. Sp.

The dedicatee was Spenser's cousin.

Edmund **Spenser**, *Daphnaïda*, 1591

~ To the Right Honorable and Vertuous Lady Helena Marquesse of North-hampton. I haue the rather presumed humbly to offer unto your Honour the dedication of this little Poëme, for that the noble and vertuous Gentlewoman of whom it is written, was by match neere alied, and in affection greatly deuoted unto your Ladiship. The occasion why I wrote the same, was as well the great good fame which I heard of her deceased, as the particular goodwill which I beare unto her husband Master Arthur Gorges, a louer of learning and vertue, whose house, as your Ladiship by mariage hath honoured, so doe I find the name of them by many notable records, to be of great antiquitie in this Realme; and such as haue euer borne themselues with honourable reputation to the world, and unspotted loyaltie to their Prince and Countrey: besides so lineally are they descended from the Howards, as that the Lady Anne Howard, eldest daughter to Iohn Duke of Norfolke, was wife to Sir Edmund, mother to Sir Edward, and grandmother to Sir William and Sir Thomas Gorges Knightes. And therefore I doe assure my selfe, that no due honour done to the white Lyon but will be most gratefull to your Ladiship, whose husband and children do so neerely participate with the bloud of that noble family. So in all dutie I recommende this Pamphlet, and the good acceptance thereof, to your honourable fauour and protection. London this first of Ianuarie. 1591. Your Honours humble euer. Ed. Sp.

The work is an elegy on the death of the young wife of Sir Arthur Gorges. She was born Lady Douglas (*sic*) Howard, one of the great heiresses of the day, the only child of Henry Howard, Viscount Byndon. Spenser goes into genealogical detail to justify his dedication to the Marchioness of Northampton.

Edmund **Spenser**, *Colin Clouts Come Home Againe*, 1595

~ To the right worthy and noble Knight Sir Walter Raleigh, Captaine of her Maiesties Guard, Lord Wardein of the Stanneries, and Lieutenant of the Countie of Cornwall. Sir, that you may see that I am not alwaies ydle as yee thinke, though not greatly well occupied, not altogither undutifull, though not precisely officious, I make you present of this simple pastorall, unworthie of your higher conceipt for the meanesse of the stile, but agreeing with the truth in circumstance and matter. The which I humblie beseech you to accept in part of paiment of the infinite debt in which I acknowledge my selfe bounden unto you, for your singular fauours and sundrie good turnes shewed to me at my late being in England, and with your good countenance protect against the malice of euill mouthes, which are alwaies wide open to carpe at and misconstrue my simple meaning. I pray continually for your happinesse. From my house of Kilcolman the 27. of december. 1591. Yours euer humbly. Ed. Sp.

The dedicatee is the famous Sir Walter Raleigh, of course, the great courtier and adventurer, who actually features in the work as 'the Shepherd of the Ocean'. (Queen Elizabeth is complimented similarly as 'Cynthia', Sir Philip Sidney is 'Astrophel', and the Countess of Pembroke is 'Urania'.) Spenser, now living in Ireland, expresses his concern at the way some seem to have misinterpreted earlier works, especially those representing his contemporaries or the court. But in general he was now popularly acclaimed, and far more widely praised than criticised.

Edmund **Spenser**, *Astrophel*, 1595

~ Dedicated to the most beautifull and vertuous Ladie, the Countesse of Essex.

That is, to the widow of Sir Philip Sidney, Lady Frances Walsingham, who had married Francis Devereux, 2nd Earl of Essex, in 1590, four years after her husband's death.

Edmund **Spenser**, *Amoretti*, 1595

~ To the Right Worshipfull Sir Robart Needham Knight. Sir, to gratulate your safe return from Ireland, I had nothing so readie, nor thought any thing so meete, as these sweete conceited Sonets, the deede of that wel deseruing gentleman, maister Edmond Spenser: whose name sufficiently warranting the worthinesse of the work: I do more confidently presume to publish it in his absence, under your name to whom (in my poore opinion) the patronage therof, doth in some respectes properly appertaine. For, besides your iudgement and delighte in learned poesie: This gentle Muse for her former perfection long wished for in Englande, nowe at the length crossing the Seas in your happy companye, (though to your selfe unknowne) seemeth to make choyse of you, as meetest to giue her deserued countenaunce, after her retourne: entertaine her, then, (Right worshipfull) in sorte best beseeming your gentle minde, and her merite, and take in worth my good will herein, who seeke no more, but to shew my selfe yours in all dutifull affection. W.P.

Spenser's sonnets, inspired by his courtship of Elizabeth Boyle (the work's title means 'little loves'), are dedicated by their publisher, William Ponsonby, to Sir Robert Needham, as mentioned. The courtship resulted in marriage, and in the birth of Spenser's son, Peregrine.

Edmund **Spenser**, *Fowre Hymnes*, 1596

~ To the right honorable and most vertuous Ladies, the Ladie Margaret, Countesse of Cumberland, and the Lady Marie, Countesse of Warwick. Having in the greener times of my youth, composed these former two Hymnes in the praise of Love and beautie, and finding that the same too much pleased those of like age and disposition, which being too vehemently caried with that kind of affection, do rather sucke out poyson to their strong passion, then honey to their honest delight, I was moved by the one of you two most excellent Ladies, to call in the same. But being unable to doe so, by reason that many copies thereof were formerly scattered abroad, I resolved at least to amend, and by way of retraction to reform them, making in stead of those two Hymnes of earthly or naturall love and beautie, two others of heavenly and celestiall. The which I doe dedicate joyntly unto you two honorable sisters, as to the most excellent and rare ornaments of all true love and beautie, both in the one and the other kinde, humbly beseeching you to vouchsafe the patronage of them, and to accept this my humble service, in lieu of the great graces and honourable favours which ye dayly shew unto me, untill such time as I may by better meanes yeeld you some more notable testimonie of my thankfull mind and dutifull devotion. And even so I pray for your happinesse. Greenwich this first of September, 1596. Your Honors most bounden ever in all humble service, Ed. Sp.

The two sister dedicatees were the daughters of Francis Russell, 3rd Earl of Bedford, with Margaret Clifford, wife of George Clifford, 3rd Earl of Cumberland, then in her mid-thirties, the better-known. As Spenser explains, he was dissatisfied with his two original poems on 'earthly' love and beauty, but being unable to trace and withdraw them, decided to add two more 'heavenly' ones on the same themes, 'by way of retraction to reform them'.

Fritz **Spiegl**, *MediaSpeak/MediaWrite*, 1989

~ This book is dedicated to wife, petite blonde vivacious artist, stunning Ingrid Spiegl (39) with all my love [...].

Musician, writer, broadcaster, gifted columnist and language watcher Fritz Spiegl (63) has written several witty and perceptive books on the abuse and misuse of standard or grammatical English by the media, especially the popular press, radio and television. This book is really two in one: read *MediaSpeak*, subtitled 'basically, yer-know-what-I-mean, a book in terms of spoken English-if-you-like: radio, television, eck-settera', then turn it round and read its other half: *MediaWrite*, 'A hilarious tongue lashing expose speling out the highl-ights of journalists prose'n'cons'. The dedication is the same for both. Spiegl married his first wife, Bridget Fry, in 1952, and his second, Ingrid Frances Romnes, the dedicatee here, in 1976. The dedication itself is a pastiche of typical journalistic style, with its runs of adjectives, use of vogue superlatives ('stunning' meaning simply 'pretty') and irrelevant insertion of a person's age after his or her name.

Howard **Spring**, *Heaven Lies About Us*, 1939
~ Without permission, but with sincere affection, to J.C. Fox, a mentor of my infancy.

A childhood autobiography, as the title implies (although, to be pedantic, the original Wordsworth quotation was 'Heaven lies *around* us in our infancy').

Arthur Penrhyn **Stanley**, *Lectures on the History of the Jewish Church*, 1864
~ To the dear memory of Her, by whose firm faith, calm wisdom, and tender sympathy, these and all other labours have for years been sustained and cheered; TO MY MOTHER this work, which shared her latest care, is now dedicated in sacred and everlasting remembrance.

Stanley, who had just been installed as Dean of Westminster when this was published, was an indefatigable poet and sightseer. The previous year, aged forty-eight, he had married Lady Augusta Bruce, whom he had met five years previously.

Freya **Stark**, *Traveller's Prelude*, 1950
~ My dear Sydney, This is your book, written at your request in Arabia and in the pine woods of Cyprus. It was written during the war, and tried to render, in a small way, a war of its own, the clash and contrast of a human struggle, against a European background so different from ours as to seem aleady remote in time. This made it hard to write. Yet I hope that in its particular there is enough of the universal to make it interesting; in any case it has given me the pleasure of dedicating it to you. Freya.

The dedicatee was Sydney Cockerell, museum director and bibliophile, who had many famous friends in the literary world, and who (rather inconsequently) was father of Christopher Cockerell, inventor of the hovercraft. Freya Stark, an intrepid lifelong traveller, wrote several vivid accounts of her journeyings, and this was just one of them. Many of her excursions were in the east, and in 1976, for example, aged eighty-three, she made her indomitable way down the Euphrates.

Frances Patton **Statham**, *Phoenix Rising*, 1982
~ To the memory of the three hundred American nurses who died while on duty overseas during World War I.

A love story set in the First World War.

Danielle **Steele**, *Wanderlust*, 1986

~ To my most beloved wanderers, both of whom would infinitely prefer the Amazon, or Manchuria, and certainly the Orient Express, to a stroll in Central Park ... Both of whom began my life, in different ways ... the one to whom I gave the very beginning of my life ... and the other all the rest: My father, John, and my husband, John ... And to a very, very special little girl, Victoria, precious, precious child. May you not wander too far away from me as time goes on, but just far enough to satisfy your soul. With all my love, d.s.

A romantic dedication by the American author of many romantic novels.

Marguerite **Steen**, *They That Go Down*, 1952

~ To the memory of the late Rear-Admiral Robert Edmund Ross Benson, C.B., and to all those men of the old navy who gave their blood and their tears, their freedom and their manhood, that we might live in peace at home, this book is dedicated.

A historical novel set in the eighteenth century.

John **Steinbeck**, *The Moon is Down*, 1942

~ To Pat Covici, a great editor and a great friend.

See below.

John **Steinbeck**, *East of Eden*, 1952

~ PASCAL COVICI. Dear Pat, You came upon me carving some kind of little figure out of wood and you said, 'Why don't you make something for me?' I asked what you wanted, and you said, 'A box.' 'What for?' 'To put things in.' 'What things?' 'Whatever you have,' you said. Well, here's your box. Nearly everything I have is in it, and it is not full. Pain and excitement are in it, and feeling good or bad and evil thoughts and good thoughts – the pleasure of design and some despair and the indescribable joy of creation. And on top of these are all the gratitude and love I have for you. And still the box is not full. JOHN.

Steinbeck was married three times, but Pascal Covici was not one of the three wives.

John **Steinbeck**, *Travels with Charley in Search of America*, 1961

~ This book is dedicated to Harold Guinzberg with respect born of an association and affection that just growed.

Stendhal, *Scarlet and Black*, 1830

~ To O.H.H., who had every word of both volumes read to her when she was powerless to resist. C.K.S.M.

Original French title: *Le Rouge et le Noir*. This is not the French writer's dedication, but the Scottish translator's. He was Charles Kenneth Scott-Moncreiff, the author of several studies of Stendhal and translator of most of his works. He died in 1930, aged forty-one, the year before this English translation was published.

Sir Frank **Stenton**, *Anglo-Saxon England*, 1943

~ [...] That the book ever reached the stage of proof is due entirely to my wife. I owe to her the conditions which have permitted so long drawn out an undertaking, and I have discussed with her every page of typescript as it was produced. The index to the book, which she compiled, is no more than her final contribution to a volume which she had made possible. In all but formal dedication, this book is hers.

The work has no formal or indeed any other kind of dedication, and these closing words of the Preface serve instead as a virtual dedicatory tribute. Stenton's wife was Doris Mary Stenton, a noted historian in her own right, who with the help of professional colleagues, produced the (incomplete) third edition of the work in 1971, four years after her husband's death. She herself died later that same year, aged seventy-seven.

Thomas **Stephens**, *The Literature of the Kymry*, 1849

~ To His Royal Highness Albert Edward Prince of Wales, is respectfully dedicated, by permission of Her Majesty the Queen, the following record of literary and intellectual labours among the Ancient and Illustrious Race whose representative he is; in the hope, that when future years have extended his experience and ripened his judgment, he may feel a regard for the inhabitants of the Principality, as strong as is their affection for the Heir Apparent to the throne of Britain.

A royal dedication that almost makes the dedicatee sound inexperienced and of immature judgment. But the future Edward VII was only eight years old at the time! His mother, Queen Victoria, was now thirty.

Laurence **Sterne**, *Tristram Shandy*, 1759–67

~ To the Right Honourable MR. PITT. Sir, – Never poor Wight of a Dedicator had less hopes from his Dedication, than I have from this of mine; for it is written in a bye corner of the kingdom, and in a retir'd thatched house, where I live in a constant endeavour to fence against the infirmities of ill health, and other evils of life, by mirth; being firmly persuaded that every time a man smiles, – but much more so, when he laughs, it adds something to this Fragment of Life. I humbly beg, Sir, that you will honour this book, by taking it – (not under your Protection, – it must protect itself, but) into the country with you; where, if I am ever told, it has made you smile; or can conceive it has beguiled you of one moment's pain, – I shall think myself as happy as a minister of state; – perhaps much happier than any one (one only excepted) that I have read or heard of. I am, GREAT SIR (and what is more to your Honour) I am, GOOD SIR, Your Well-wisher, and most humble Fellow-subject, THE AUTHOR.

Typically of Sterne, the matter of a dedication was not straightforward. The famous eccentric novel was published in instalments as follows: volumes I and II in 1760, III and

IV in 1761, V and VI in 1762, VII and VIII in 1765, and IX in 1767. The dedication here, to Pitt, was not added until the second edition of volumes I and II, three months after the first, and also in 1760. A second dedication then appeared between volumes V and VI, and ran as follows: 'To the Right Honourable John, Lord Viscount Spencer. My Lord, I humbly beg leave to offer you these two volumes; they are the best my talents, with such bad health as I have, could produce: had Providence granted me a larger stock of either, they had been a much more proper present to your Lordship. I beg your Lordship will forgive me, if, at the same time I dedicate this work to you, I join LADY SPENCER in the liberty I take of inscribing the story of *Le Fever* to her name; for which I have no other motive, which my heart has informed me of, but that the story is a humane one. I am, MY LORD, Your Lordship's most devoted and most humble Servant, LAUR. STERNE.' Finally, a third dedication was prefixed to volume IX. It began thus: 'A DEDICATION TO A GREAT MAN. Having, *a priori*, intended to dedicate *The Amours of my Uncle Toby* to Mr. ***, I see more reasons, *a posteriori*, for doing it to Lord *******. [...] My opinion of Lord ******* is neither better nor worse, than it was of Mr. ***. Honours, like impressions upon coin, may give an ideal and local value to a bit of base metal; but Gold and Silver will pass all the world over without any other recommendation than their own weight. [...]' In later editions, these three dedications were sometimes included between other volumes of the complete work, thus making nonsense of Sterne's joke about '*a priori*' in the case of the third one. And as if that were not enough, Sterne puts a further (bogus) dedication into the mouth of the book's narrator-hero in Book I, at the end of chapter VIII. It runs as follows: 'My Lord, I maintain this to be a dedication, notwithstanding its singularity in the three great essentials of matter, form, and place: I beg, therefore, you will accept it as such, and that you will permit me to lay it, with the most respectful humility, at your Lordship's feet, when you are upon them, which you can be when you please, and that is, my Lord, whenever there is occasion for it, and I will add, to the best purposes too. I have the honour to be, My Lord, Your Lordship's most obedient, and most devoted, and most humble servant, TRISTRAM SHANDY.' Chapter IX then opens thus: 'I solemnly declare to all mankind, that the above dedication was made for no one Prince, Prelate, Pope, or Potentate, Duke, Marquis, Earl, Viscount, or Baron, of this, or any other realm in Christendom; nor has it yet been hawked about, or offered publicly or privately, directly or indirectly, to any one person or personage, great or small; but is honestly a true Virgin-Dedication untried on, upon any soul living.' (Sterne, or Shandy, then goes on to offer the dedication to any aristocrat who wants it for fifty guineas.) In the dedication to Pitt (i.e., William Pitt the Elder, then Britain's virtual prime minister), the 'retir'd thatched cottage' was Sterne's home, 'Shandy Hall', in the village of Coxwold, near Easingwold in Yorkshire, where he had a living as a clergyman. The third dedication, with its cryptic asterisks, was actually intended for William Pitt (the seven asterisks represent the letters of 'Chatham', of which he was 1st Earl). Thus Sterne dedicated the last book of his unique masterpiece to the patron of the first.

Robert Louis Stevenson, *An Inland Voyage*, 1878

~ To Sir Walter Grindlay Simpson, Bart. My dear 'Cigarette', It was enough that you should have shared so liberally in the rains and portages of our voyage; that you should have had so hard a paddle to recover the derelict *Arethusa* on the flooded Oise; and that you should thenceforth have piloted a mere wreck of mankind to Origny Sainte-Benoite and a supper so eagerly desired. It was perhaps more than enough, as you once somewhat piteously complained, that I should have set down all the strong language to you, and kept the appropriate reflections for myself. I could not in decency expose you to share the disgrace of another and more public shipwreck. But now that this voyage of ours is going into a cheap edition, that peril, we shall hope, is at an end, and I may put your name on the burgee. [...] R.L.S.

Stevenson and Simpson had toured the canals of France and Belgium in two sail-powered skiffs called *Cigarette* and *Arethusa*, with Stevenson in the latter. Hence his friend's nickname in this account of their travels and mishaps.

Robert Louis **Stevenson**, *Travels with a Donkey in the Cevennes*, 1879

~ My dear Sidney Colvin, The journey which this little book is to describe was very agreeable and fortunate for me. After an uncouth beginning, I had the best of luck to the end. But we are all travellers in what John Bunyan calls the wilderness of this world – all, too, travellers with a donkey; and the best that we find in our travels is an honest friend. [...] Every book is, in an intimate sense, a circular letter to the friends of him who writes it. They alone take his meaning; they find private messages, assurances of love, and expressions of gratitude dropped for them in every corner. The public is but a generous patron who defrays the postage. Yet though the letter is directed to all, we have an old and kindly custom of addressing it on the outside to one. Of what shall a man be proud, if he is not proud of his friends? And so, my dear Sidney Colvin, it is with pride that I sign myself affectionately yours, R.L.S.

Sir Sidney Colvin, a distinguished art and literary critic, was Director of the Fitzwilliam Museum, Cambridge, before becoming Keeper of the Department of Prints and Drawings at the British Museum in 1883. Ten years earlier he had made the acquaintance of Stevenson, and the two men would be close friends until the latter's death in 1894. When Stevenson was living in Samoa in his final years, Colvin kept regularly in touch by letter, advising him on the best way to complete his writings and get them published. After Stevenson's death, he published editions of his friend's correspondence and also brought out a posthumous complete edition of his works.

Robert Louis **Stevenson**, *The Amateur Emigrant*, 1879

~ To Robert Alan Mowbray Stevenson. Our friendship was not only founded before we were born by a community of blood, but is in itself as old as my life. It began with our early ages, and, like a history, has been continued to the present time. Although we may not be old in the world, we are old to each other, having so long been intimates. We are now widely separated, a great sea and continent intervening; but memory, like care, mounts into iron ships and rides post behind the horseman. Neither time nor space nor enmity can conquer old affection; and as I dedicate these sketches, it is not to you only, but to all in the old country, that I send the greeting of my heart. R.L.S.

Stevenson had travelled to California by emigrant ship in pursuit of Mrs Fanny Osbourne, the American lady ten years his senior with whom he had fallen in love. (She was married, with children, but was virtually estranged from her husband. He had met her three years earlier and would marry her the following year. See also *Treasure Island*, below.) The dedicatee here is his cousin, his uncle Alan's son, three years younger than Stevenson himself, who was now twenty-nine.

Robert Louis **Stevenson**, *Virginbus Puerisque*, 1881

~ My dear William Ernest Henley, We are all busy in the world building Towers of Babel; and the child of our imaginations is always a changeling when it comes from nurse. This is not only true in the greatest, as of wars and folios, but in the least also, like the trifling volume in your hand. [...] These papers are like milestones on the wayside of my life; and as I look back in memory, there is hardly a stage of that distance but I see you present with advice, reproof, or, praise. Meanwhile, many things have changed, you and I among the rest: but I hope that our sympathy, founded on the love of our art, and nourished by mutual assistance, shall survive these little revolutions undiminished, and, with God's help, unite us to the end. R.L.S.

Henley, poet, critic and editor, had met Stevenson in Edinburgh, and would serve as the model for Long John Silver in *Treasure Island*. The two were long close friends and co-wrote four plays. Their friendship, however, ended in a bitter quarrel. Compare HENLEY's own dedication, above.

Robert Louis **Stevenson**, *Familiar Studies of Men and Books*, 1882

~ To Thomas Stevenson, civil engineer, by whose devices the great sea lights in every quarter of the world now shine more brightly, this volume is in love and gratitude dedicated by his son, the author.

Stevenson's father was an engineer specialising in lighthouse construction, and was the inventor of the 'azimuthal condensing system' used in the process.

Robert Louis **Stevenson**, *The Silverado Squatters*, 1883

~ To Virgil Williams and Dora Norton Williams, these sketches are affectionately dedicated by their friend, the author.

Robert Louis **Stevenson**, *Treasure Island*, 1883

~ To S.L.O., an American gentleman, in accordance with whose classic taste the following narrative has been designed, it is now, in return for numerous delightful hours, and with the kindest wishes, dedicated by his affectionate friend, the Author.

A mock-serious tribute to Stevenson's thirteen-year-old stepson, Samuel Lloyd Osbourne, the child of his American wife Fanny Osbourne (see *The Amateur Emigrant*, above). Stevenson had been staying in Scotland two years earlier with a family party that included the boy, and with him planned a 'hidden treasure map' that proved to be the inspiration for the famous story itself. It first appeared as a serial in the children's magazine *Young Folks* that same year (by 'Captain George North'). Lloyd Osbourne became a novelist and playwright of some note, and collaborated with Stevenson in such works as *The Wrong Box* (1889), *The Wrecker* (1892) and *The Ebb-Tide* (1894).

Robert Louis **Stevenson,** *Kidnapped,* 1886

~ My dear Charles Baxter, If you ever read this tale, you will likely as yourself more questions than I should care to answer. [...] My dear Charles, I do not even ask you to like this tale. But perhaps when he is older your son will; he may then be pleased to find his father's name on the fly-leaf; and in the meantime it pleases me to set it there, in memory of many days that were happy and some (now perhaps as pleasant to remember) that were sad. [...] How, in the intervals of present business, the past must echo in your memory! Let it not echo often without some kind thoughts of your friend, R.L.S.

Much of this dedicatory letter is taken up with a historical justification of its subject, 'memoirs of the adventures of David Balfour in 1751', as part of the famous story's subtitle runs. It is dedicated to Stevenson's business adviser and lifelong friend, who in the writer's final years planned with him a limited de luxe edition of his works.

Robert Louis **Stevenson,** *The Strange Case of Dr Jekyll and Mr Hyde,* 1886

~ To Katherine de Mattos:

> It's ill to loose the bands that God decreed to bind;
> Still will we be the children of the heather and the wind.
> Far away from home, O it's still for you and me
> That the broom is blowing bonnie in the north countrie.

Stevenson's verse was rarely as good as his prose, with perhaps the exception of his verse dedications, such as this one and, especially, the last one below, to his wife. Mrs Katherine de Mattos was Stevenson's cousin, the sister of Robert Alan Mowbray Stevenson (to whom *The Amateur Emigrant*, above, was dedicated), and she and her baby daughter accompanied him on several of his travels in France, and were with him when he began the journey that he retold in *Travels with a Donkey* (see above).

Robert Louis **Stevenson,** *The Merry Men and Other Tales and Fables,* 1886

~ My dear Lady Taylor: To your name, if I wrote on brass, I could add nothing; it has been already written higher than I could dream to reach, by a strong and a dear hand. And if I now dedicate to you these tales, it is not as the writer who brings you his work, but as the friend who would remind you of his affection. Robert Louis Stevenson.

Stevenson was now living in Bournemouth, as were his friends there, Sir Henry Taylor and his wife, the latter née Theodosia Alice Spring-Rice. Taylor, a civil servant in the colonial department, was the author of a number of verse dramas, now almost all forgotten. He did, however, move in fairly elevated literary circles, and apart from Stevenson was also a personal friend of Southey and Tennyson.

Robert Louis **Stevenson,** *Memories and Portraits,* 1887

~ To my mother, in the name of past joys and present sorrow, I dedicate these memories and portraits.

Stevenson's father had died in May this year.

Robert Louis **Stevenson**, *Underwoods*, 1887

~ There are men and classes of men that stand above the common herd: the soldier, the sailor, and the shepherd not unfrequently; the artist rarely; rarelier still, the clergyman; the physician almost as a rule. He is the flower (such as it is) of our civilisation. [...] Gratitude is but a lame sentiment; thanks, when they are expressed, are often more embarrassing than welcome; and yet I must set forth mine to a few out of the many doctors who have brought me comfort and help. [...] One name I have kept on purpose to the last, because it is a household word with me, and because if I had not received favours from so many hands in so many quarters of the world, it should have stood upon this page alone: that of my friend Thomas Bodley Scott of Bournemouth. Will he accept this, although shared among so many, for a dedication to himself? And when next my ill-fortune (which has thus its pleasant side) brings him hurrying to me when he would fain sit down to meat or lie down to rest, will he care to remember that he takes this trouble for one who is not fool enough to be ungrateful? R.L.S.

Stevenson was in constant ill health, frequently moving his residence because of it. This dedication also names ten other doctors who had treated him in various parts of the world. Stevenson was now thirty-seven, and would die when only forty-four, of a brain haemorrhage.

Robert Louis **Stevenson**, *The Master of Ballantrae*, 1889

~ To Sir Percy Florence and Lady Shelley. Here is a tale which extends over many years and travels into many countries. By a peculiar fitness of circumstance the writer began, continued it, and concluded it among distant and diverse scenes. Above all, he was much upon the sea. [...] It is my hope that these surroundings of its manufacture may to some degree find favour for my story with seafarers and sea-lovers like yourselves. And at least here is a dedication from a great way off: written by the loud shores of a subtropical island near upon ten thousand miles from Boscombe Chine and Manor: scenes which rise before me as I write, along with the faces and voices of my friends. Well, I am for the sea once more, no doubt Sir Percy also. Let us make the signal B.R.D.! R.L.S. Waikiki, May 17, 1889.

Stevenson had left England the previous year in search of a place good for his health, and would never return. He was now in Hawaii. Sir Percy Florence Shelley was the son of the poet Shelley and his second wife Mary Godwin. But his sea-going days were now very limited, for he died in the same year that Stevenson's novel was published, aged seventy. 'B.R.D.' is the signal to board or 'be ready to depart'.

Robert Louis **Stevenson**, *Across the Plains*, 1892

~ To Paul Bourget. Traveller and student and curious as you are, you will never have heard the name of Vailima, most likely not even that of Upolu, and Samoa itself may be strange to your ears. To these barbaric seats there came the other day a yellow book with your name on the title, and filled in every page with the exquisite gifts of your art. Let me take and change your own words: *J'ai beau admirer les autres de toutes mes forces, c'est avec vous que je me complais à vivre.* R.L.S.

Bourget was a French novelist and critic who made his name with novels of psychological analysis in the 1880s, after beginning his writing career as a poet. He would certainly not have heard of Vailima, as this name, Polynesian for 'five rivers', was the one given by Stevenson to his estate above the town of Apia on Samoa, more precisely on its eastern island of Upolu. It was while living in Samoa, where he would end his days, that Stevenson became known as 'Tusitala', a Polynesian nickname meaning 'Teller of Tales'. The French words addressed to Bourget translate: 'It is in vain that I have made every effort to admire others, it is with you that I am pleased to live'.

Robert Louis **Stevenson**, *A Child's Garden of Verses*, 1895

TO ALISON CUNNINGHAM – FROM HER BOY

For the long nights you lay awake,
And watched for my unworthy sake,
For your most comfortable hand
That led me through the uneven land:
For all the story books you read:
And all the pains you comforted:
For all you pitied, all you bore
In sad and happy days of yore,
My second Mother, my first Wife,
The angel of my infant life, –
For the sick child now well and old,
Take, nurse, the little book you hold! [...]

Six more lines complete the dedication to Stevenson's childhood nurse, nicknamed by him 'Cummie', who looked after him from the age of eighteen months and remained devoted to him for life.

Robert Louis **Stevenson**, *Weir of Hermiston*, 1896

TO MY WIFE

I saw rain falling and the rainbow drawn
On Lammermuir. Hearkening I heard again
In my precipitous city beaten bells
Winnow the keen sea wind. And here afar,
Intent on my own race and place, I wrote.

Take thou the writing: thine it is. For who
Burnished the sword, blew on the drowsy coal,
Held still the target higher, chary of praise
And prodigal counsel, – who but thou?
So now, in the end, if this the least be good,
If any deed be done, if any fire

Burn in the imperfect page, the praise be thine.

This was Stevenson's last novel, left unfinished at his death, but regarded as a potential masterpiece. The dedication, one of his finest poems, was found by his wife one morning pinned on the curtains of her bed.

Jean **Stibbs,** *The Northern Correspondent*, 1984
~ To first impressions and final proofs.

A nineteenth-century historical romance set in a newspaper office. Hence the two rather nice puns in the dedication.

Sir William **Stirling-Maxwell,** *Annals of the Artists of Spain*, 1848
~ These pages, which I had hoped to dedicate to my Father, are now inscribed in affectionate homage to his memory.

The writer's father had died the previous year.

Bram **Stoker,** *Dracula*, 1897
~ To my dear friend, Hommy-Beg.

This was the Manx nickname, 'Little Tommy', of the famous author's friend, the half-Manx writer Sir Thomas Henry Hall Caine, whose first novel, *The Shadow of a Crime* (1885) was written with Stoker's encouragement. See HALL CAINE'S own dedication above.

Irving **Stone,** *The Passions of the Mind*, 1971
~ To my wife Jean Stone, who has been Editor in residence through twenty-five published books, and in her spare time runs a beautiful home, manages our business affairs, reared two children, maintains an exciting social life, helps in the causes of her community, keeps a difficult husband happy. With gratitude and love.

A tribute to a paragon by the famous American fictional biographer (born Irving Tennenbaum), who died in 1989 aged eighty-six.

Patsy **Stoneman,** *Elizabeth Gaskell*, 1987
~ This book is dedicated to the person who made me feel able to write it.

Mary **Storr,** *Before I Go ...*, 1985
~ I dedicate this book to my friends.

An alphabetical listing of (mainly) female names follows, from Alison to Zoe, with a small selection of male names at the end, exactly 200 names in all. The famous feminist and journalist undoubtedly included some of her well-known media colleagues in their number, such as Bea Campbell, Anna Coote, Margaret Howard, Mary Kenny, Bel Mooney, Serena Wadham, and so on, although she gives first names only.

Richard S. **Storrs,** *Bernard of Clairvaux*, 1892
~ To the Church of the Pilgrims, Brooklyn, New York. Trained by God's grace,

in its own happy work, till its freedom has become the helper of faith, its devoutness the teacher of catholic sympathy, the beauty of holiness its commanding ideal, the victory of Christ its supreme expectation, – long service which has been rich in reward, – these lectures, written in its library, and sketching a life of singular lustre, are affectionately inscribed.

Storrs was one of a family of American Congregational clergymen, and pastor of the church named here for more than fifty years.

Jack Trevor Story, *The Wind in the Snottygobble Tree*, 1971
~ To whom it may concern.

A phrasal formula that is bound to appeal to some dedicators.

Harriet Beecher Stowe, *Little Pussy Willow*, 1898
~ To Mary, Emily, Nellie and Charlotte, and all my little girl friends. Here is Pussy Willow in a book, just as I have promised you she should be. I send her to you as a Christmas and New Year's present, and I hope that you will all grow up to be nice good girls like her, with bright healthy faces and cheerful hearts, and the gift of always seeing 'The Bright Side of Everything'.

This book, by the famous author of *Uncle Tom's Cabin* (1851–2), was published after her death in 1896, and was presumably dedicated to her grandchildren.

Joyce Stranger, *Three's a Pack*, 1980
~ This book can only be dedicated to Chita, the fiendish puppy that exhausted me, gave me the challenge of my life, and now repays me, beyond measure, for all that I suffered on her behalf.

A book about three dogs, one of whom is the German shepherd pup named in the dedication.

Gene Stratton-Porter, *Freckles*, 1904
~ To all good Irishmen in general, and one Charles Darwin Porter in particular.

Otherwise to the author's husband. Gene Stratton-Porter was American-born as Geneva Stratton, marrying when she was eighteen. 'Freckles', the hero of the story, is the nickname of the waif Terence O'More who believes he is an orphan but who is eventually claimed by his rich father.

Gene Stratton-Porter, *A Girl of the Limberlost*, 1909
~ To all girls of the Limberlost in general and one Jeannette Helen Porter in particular.

Dedicated to the author's daughter. The book tells the story of Elnora, the companion of Freckles (see above), who pays for her own education by selling moths which she catches in the Limberlost Swamp. The latter is the real name of the area of Indiana where the American author grew up and where she lived after her marriage.

Gene **Stratton-Porter**, *The Harvester*, 1912

~ This portion of the life of a man of to-day is offered in the hope that in cleanliness, poetic temperament and mental force, a likeness will be seen to Henry David Thoreau.

A further Limberlost narrative (see above), dedicated to the famous author of *Walden* (1854). Thoreau had become something of an inspirational hero in the eyes of many Americans by his poetic account of his simple life in a lakeside hut. He died in 1862, the year before Stratton-Porter was born.

Gene **Stratton-Porter**, *Laddie*, 1913

~ To Leander Elliot Stratton. 'The way to be happy is to be good'.

Presumably to a member of the author's family. Perhaps a nephew?

William **Streat**, *The Dividing of the Hooff: or, Seeming-Contradictions throughout Sacred Scripture, Distinguish'd, Resolved, and Apply'd*, 1654

~ To God.

Whom else? The clergyman author, who graduated from Exeter College, Oxford, became rector of a church in the city of Exeter. As author of this work he describes himself on the title page as 'Master of Arts, Preacher of the Word, in the County of Devon', while the already lengthy title has the added note: 'Helpfull to every Household of Faith'.

A.G. **Street**, *The Gentleman of the Party*, 1936

~ To the agricultural labourer, the salt of England's earth.

One of the many rural books by the popular Wiltshire farmer, author and broadcaster, who made his name with *Farmer's Glory* in 1932. He died in 1966 at the age of seventy-four.

Whitley **Strieber** and James W. Kunetka, *Warday and the Journey Onward*, 1984

~ This book is respectfully dedicated to October 27, 1988, the last full day of the old world.

That is, to the day when, in the fictional account, nuclear war was unleashed by the superpowers. But as we now know ...

Whitley **Strieber** and James W. Kunetka, *Nature's End*, 1986

~ This book is dedicated to the human future.

Rather more realistically than the authors' earlier book above, this one is devoted to such planetary problems as overpopulation, possible ecological disaster, and other pressing topics.

Alice Crary **Sutcliffe**, *Robert Fulton and the Clermont*, 1909

~ This volume is affectionately dedicated to my father, the Reverend Robert Fulton Crary, D.D. (eldest grandson of Robert Fulton), for forty years rector of the Church of the Holy Comforter, Poughkeepsie, New York, whose services throughout life, no less than those of his illustrious ancestor, have been in the great navy of the Church of God.

Robert Fulton was the famous American engineer who invented the submarine and who built the steamboat *Clermont*. This last was not the first steamboat to be built, but she was the first to operate at a profit to her owners and the first of a 'line' of commercially operated steamboats.

Jonathan Swift, *A Tale of a Tub*, 1704

~ To His Royal Highness Prince Posterity. Sir, I here present your highness with the fruits of a very few leisure hours, stolen from the short intervals of a world of business, and of an employment quite alien from such amusements as this the poor production of that refuse of time, which has laid heavy upon my hands during a long prorogation of parliament, a great dearth of foreign news, and a tedious fit of rainy weather; for which, and other reasons, it cannot choose extremely to deserve such a patronage as that of your highness, whose numberless virtues, in so few years, make the world look upon you as the future example to all princes; for although your highness is hardly got clear of infancy, yet has the universal learned world already resolved upon appealing to your future dictates, with the lowest and most resigned submission; fate having decreed you sole arbiter of the productions of human wit, in this polite and most accomplished age. [...] In the meantime I do here make bold to present your highness with a faithful abstract, drawn from the universal body of all arts and sciences, intended wholly for your service and instruction: nor do I doubt in the least, but your highness will peruse it as carefully, and make as considerable improvements, as other young princes have already done, by the many volumes of late years written for a help to their studies. That your highness may advance in wisdom and virtue, as well as years, and at last outshine all your royal ancestors, shall be the daily prayer of, Sir, your highness's most devoted, etc.

This famous satire, Swift's first major work, was in part a parody of a bad book, and the mock dedication here is the fourth item, 'The Epistle Dedicatory', in an introductory section whose first three items are an 'Analytical Table' (outlined the nature and content of the work), 'The Bookseller's Dedication', and 'The Bookseller to the Reader'. This last purports to explain how the original manuscript was found and has now come to be published without the author's knowledge. The 'Bookseller's Dedication' proceeds (in part) as follows: 'To the Right Honourable John Lord Somers. My Lord, Although the author has written a large dedication, yet that being addressed to a prince, whom I am never likely to have the honour of being known to; a person besides, as far as I can observe, not at all regarded, or thought on by any of our present writers; and being wholly free from that slavery which booksellers usually lie under, to the caprice of authors, I think it a wise piece of presumption to inscribe these papers to your lordship and to implore your lordship's protection of them. [...] I should now, in right of a dedicator, give your lordship a list of your own virtues, and at the same time, be very unwilling to offend your modesty; but chiefly, I should celebrate your liberality towards men of great parts and small fortunes, and give you broad hints that I mean myself. And I was just going on, in the usual method, to peruse a hundred or two of dedications, and transcribe an abstract to be applied to your lordship; but I was diverted by a certain accident: for upon the covers of these papers I casually observed written in large letters the two following words, DETUR DIGNISSIMO; which, for aught I knew, might contain some important meaning. But it unluckily fell out, that none of the authors I employ understood Latin; (though I have them often in pay to translate out of that language); I was therefore compelled to have recourse to the curate of our parish, who englished it thus, "Let it be given to the worthiest": and his comment was, that the author meant his work should be dedicated to the sublimest genius of the age for wit, learning, judgment, eloquence, and wisdom.[...]' And so on, in playful mood. In other words, this is the dedication proper, made to Lord Somers when he was Lord Chancellor, and seeking promotion to an influential public post. Swift did not get it, however, and, transferring his political and social allegiance from the Whigs (Somers' party) to the Tories, became his deadly enemy.

Algernon Charles **Swinburne**, *Tristram of Lyonesse, and other poems*, 1882
~ To my best friend, Theodore Watts, I dedicate in this book the best I have to give him. [...]

Two stanzas follow. Theodore Watts was the writer Theodore Watts-Dunton, who had rescued Swinburne from alcoholism three years earlier and taken him to live with him in his home in Putney, where he would become his legal and financial adviser and intimate friend. Compare BARONESS ORCZY's dedication to the same writer.

Charles **Symmons**, *Life of Milton*, 1806
~ To the memory of my most dear and accomplished Son, CHARLES SYMMONS, by the co-operation of whose fine mind and perfect taste I have been largely benefited as a writer, and to the contemplation of whose piety and virtues, the sources of much of my past happiness, I am indebted for all my present consolation, I inscribe this Life of Milton; which as it grew under his eye, and was favoured with his regard, cannot be without value in my partial estimation. On the 23rd of May, 1805, before he had completed his twenty-second year, he was torn from my affection and my hopes, experiencing from his God in requital of a pure life the mercy of an early death. CHARLES SYMMONS

A moving tribute from a father to a son whose promise and hopes remained unfulfilled. Symmons was a Welsh clergyman and scholar who published several sermons and poems as well as a *Life of Shakespeare* which, like this of Milton, was prefixed to an edition of the writer's works.

❧ T ❧

Hippolyte **Taine**, *The Origins of Contemporary France*, 1875–93
~ To the archivists and librarians of the National Library and National Archives as a token of gratitude and respect.

Translated from the French by AR; original title: *Les Origines de la France Contemporaine*. A tribute from the great French historian to the professionals who helped in his researches in the famous Paris library.

Booth **Tarkington**, *Cherry*, 1903
~ To the diligent and industrious members of the class of '93 at Nassau Hall, also to the idler spirits who wasted Golden Hours of Youth in profitless playing of toss-the-ball; and even to those more dissolute ones who risked the tutor's detection at pitch-the-penny and carved their names on Adam's table – in brief, to all of that happy class is dedicated this heroic tale of the days when Commencement came in September.

A dedication by the prolific American novelist and playwright to his fellow students at Princeton in 1893, when he was twenty-four.

Bert Leston **Taylor** and W.C. Gibson, *The Log of the Water Wagon, or the Cruise of the Good Ship Lithia*, 1905
~ To all surviving saloon passengers of the good ship Lithia, who have rounded the Horn and passed through perilous Bering Straits, and suffered shipwreck, shock, and sudden thirst; to those intrepid souls who have clung to the slippery hull of the Water Wagon when it seemed the gallant craft could not live another hour; who, lashed to the sprinkler, have ridden out many a choking dust storm; who have heard the café Lorelei sing, and still hung on, deaf to her seductive song; and – to the memory of countless thousands lost at sea, swept into the seething drink without a word of warning, cut off in the blossoms of their resolutions and sent to their slate accounts with all their imperfections on their heads –, this little volume is affectionately dedicated.

Taylor was an American journalist who contributed a regular column called 'A Line o' Type or Two' to the Chicago *Daily Tribune*. The vivid descriptive style of the dedication is true to journalistic tradition.

Francis Taylor, *Grapes from Canaan*, 1658

~ To the Right Honourable FRANCIS ROUS, Esq., Provost of Eaton, and one of the Council to his Highness the Lord Protector. When I first design'd within my self the composure of this ensuing Poem, my thoughts were not in the least tendency for a publication, yet through the perswasion of some friends (whose better judgements I could not but value above mine own private opinion) I have sent my unfledg'd muse abroad into the world humbly assuming the boldness to shrowd it under the wing of your honour's protection, assuring myself it will find the better welcome for the name of the Patron. [...]

Francis Rous was not only a noted Puritan Provost of Eton but a writer of several religious works, from poems and hymns to hortatory addresses and tracts. He died a few months after Taylor's work appeared, aged eighty.

John Taylor, *Three weekes, three daies, and three houres Observations and Travel from London to Hamburgh in Germanie*, 1617

~ To the Cosmographicall, Geographicall describer, Geometricall measurer, Historiographicall, Calligraphicall Relater and Writer; enigmaticall, pragmaticall, dogmaticall observer; ingrosser, surveyer, and eloquent Brittish-Græcian Latinist, or Latine Græcian orator; the odcombyan Deambulator Perambulator, Ambler, Trotter, or un-tyred Traveller Sir Thomas Coryat, Knight of Troy, and one of the deerest darlings to the blinde goddesse Fortune. [...]

A whimsical dedication by the 'Water Poet', as he became known, from his original employment as a Thames waterman. He hit on the idea of inviting celebrities of the day to sponsor various journeys which he made either on foot or by water, writing up a lively verse account of his travels afterwards. This one is dedicated to a fellow eccentric and traveller, THOMAS CORYATE. 'Odcombyan' is a reference to Coryate's verse miscellany, *The Odcombian Banquet* (1611), named after his birthplace, Odcombe, Somerset. See also TAYLOR's dedications below.

John Taylor, *Taylor's Motto: Et Habeo, et Careo, et Curo, a Poem*, 1621

TO EVERYBODY

Yet not to every Reader, doe I write
But onely unto such as can Read right;
And with impartial censures can declare
As they find things to judge them as they are.

The Latin title of Taylor's poem translates: 'I both have, and have not, and care for'. The original edition of this had an engraving on the title-page showing Taylor standing on a rock.

John Taylor, *The Praise of Antiquity and the Commodity of Beggery*, 1621

~ To the bright eye-dazeling Mirrour of Mirth, Adelantado of alacrity, the Pump of pastime, spout of sport, and Regent of ridiculous confabulations Archibald Armestrong, *alias* the Court Archy.

Otherwise the Scottish court jester to James I and Charles I, Archie Armstrong, famous for his wit and infamous for his arrogance, who died in 1672, of uncertain age.

Alfred, Lord **Tennyson**, *Poems*, 1851

TO THE QUEEN

> Revered, beloved – O you that hold
>   A nobler office upon earth
>   Than arms, or power of brain, or birth
> Could give the warrior kings of old,
>
> Victoria, – since your Royal grace
>   To one of less desert allows
>   This laurel greener from the brows
> Of him the utter'd nothing base; [...]
>
> Take, Madam, this poor book of song;
>   For tho' the faults were thick as dust
>   In vacant chambers, I could trust
> Your kindness. May you rule us long, [...]

The first, second and fifth stanzas of the nine-stanza dedication of the first Laureate edition of Tennyson's poems to Queen Victoria. Tennyson had been appointed Poet Laureate the previous year, largely because Prince Albert had greatly admired his *In Memoriam* (1850); hence the title of the edition and the poem's reference to the laurel that he had inherited from Wordsworth ('him that utter'd nothing base'). Tennyson would not meet Victoria in person until 1862, however.

Alfred, Lord **Tennyson**, *Idylls of the King*, 1862

> These to His Memory – since he held them dear,
> Perchance as finding there unconsciously
> Some image of himself – I dedicate,
> I dedicate, I consecrate with tears –
> These Idylls. [...]

The opening lines of the famous memorial dedication to Prince Albert, Queen Victoria's husband, who had died the previous year. The dedication, which concludes with an effective prayer for the bereaved Queen, was prefixed to the second edition of the work, the first having appeared in 1859.

Alfred, Lord **Tennyson**, *Harold*, 1876

~ To his Excellency THE RIGHT HON. LORD LYTTON, Viceroy and Governor-General of India. My dear Lord Lytton, – After old-world records – such as the Bayeux tapestry and the Roman de Rou, – Edward Freeman's History of the Norman Conquest, and your father's Historical Romance treating of the same times, have been mainly helpful to me in writing this Drama. Your father dedicated his 'Harold' to my father's brother; allow me to dedicate my 'Harold' to yourself. A. Tennyson.

Tennyson's historical play was based on the life of Harold II, who died in 1066 in the Battle of Hastings. The dedicatee here is not Edward Bulwer Lytton, 1st Baron Lytton, the author of *The Last Days of Pompeii* (1834), who had anyway died three years earlier, but his son (who is still sometimes confused with him), the diplomat and poet Edward Robert Bulwer Lytton, 1st Earl of Lytton, now aged forty-five. Bulwer Lytton Sr's *Harold* had appeared in 1848. The son wrote a warmly appreciative letter (19 January 1877) thanking Tennyson for the dedication and the way it linked him with his father.

Alfred, Lord **Tennyson**, *Ballads, and Other Poems*, 1880

> TO ALFRED TENNYSON, MY GRANDSON
> Golden-hair'd Ally, whose name is one with mine,
> Crazy with laughter and babble and earth's new wine,
> Now that the flower of a year and a half is thine,
> O little blossom, O mine, and mine of mine,
> Glorious poet who never hast written a line,
> Laugh, for the name at the head of my verse is thine.
> May'st thou never be wrong'd by the name that is mine!

Aged just eighteen months at the time of this dedication, Alfred Tennyson Jr lived to be seventy-three, dying in 1952.

Alfred, Lord **Tennyson**, *Becket*, 1884

~ To the Lord Chancellor, THE RIGHT HONOURABLE EARL OF SELBOURNE. My dear Selbourne, To you, the honoured Chancellor of our own day, I dedicate this dramatic memorial of your great predecessor; – which, altho' not intended in its present form to meet the exigencies of our modern theatre, has nevertheless – for so you have assured me – won your approbation. Ever yours, Tennyson.

Tennyson's tragedy, based on the quarrel between Henry II and his chancellor, Thomas à Becket, resulting in the murder of the latter in Canterbury Cathedral for his antimonarchic stance in defending the rights of the Church, was dedicated to Roundell Palmer, 1st Earl of Selbourne, who was now in his second term of office as Lord Chancellor (the chief legal officer in England).

Alfred, Lord **Tennyson**, *Tiresias and Other Poems*, 1885

~ To my good friend, Robert Browning, whose genius and geniality will best appreciate what may be best and make most allowance for what may be worst, this volume is affectionately dedicated.

'It is characteristic of a certain shyness in Tennyson that he never told Browning of the dedication, and it was not until the book was in the hands of the public, that the latter learned the circumstance from a friend' (Arthur Waugh, *Alfred, Lord Tennyson*, 1893).

Hallam **Tennyson**, *Alfred Lord Tennyson: A Memoir – By His Son*, 1898

~ These volumes are dedicated by permission to the Queen.

That is, Queen Victoria. Compare Tennyson's own first dedication above. Hallam Tennyson was named after his father's close friend, the poet Arthur Henry Hallam, whose sudden and untimely death in 1833 at the age of twenty-one prompted the famous elegiac poem *In Memoriam A.H.H.* (1850).

W.M. Thackeray, *Pendennis*, 1848–50

~ To Dr. John Elliotson. My dear Doctor: Thirteen months ago, when it seemed likely that this story had come to a close, a kind friend brought you to my bedside, whence, in all probability, I should never have risen but for your constant watchfulness and skill. I like to recall your great goodness and kindness (as well as acts of others, showing quite a surprising friendship and sympathy) at that time, when kindness and friendship were most needed and welcome. And as you would take no other fee but thanks, let me record them here in behalf of me and mine, and subscribe myself, Yours most sincerely and gratefully, W.M. Thackeray.

Thackeray died in 1863, having been in indifferent health for some years. Here, he thanks his doctor for treating him in a severe illness in 1849, which set back work on the novel he was drafting. Elliotson was a famous London doctor who founded University College Hospital and who was keen on mesmerism. Dickens was also one of his patients.

W.M. Thackeray, *Henry Esmond*, 1852

~ To the Right Honourable William Bingham, Lord Ashburton: My dear Lord, The writer of a book which copies the manners and language of Queen Anne's time, must not omit the Dedication to the Patron; and I ask leave to inscribe these volumes to your Lordship for the sake of the great kindness and friendship which I owe to you and yours. My volumes will reach you when the Author is on his voyage to a country where your name is as well known as here. Wherever I am, I shall gratefully regard you, and shall not be less welcomed in America because I am, Your obliged friend and servant, W.M. Thackeray.

William Bingham Baring, 2nd Baron Ashburton, had many noted literary friends, including Carlyle (who developed a close interest in Lady Ashburton, much to Mrs Carlyle's displeasure). Thackeray made the first of two lecture tours of the United States in the year his famous three-volume historical novel was published.

St Theresa of Lisieux, *The Story of a Soul*, 1897

~ For Mother Agnes of Jesus. My dearest Mother, it is to you, to you who are in fact a mother twice over to me, that I now confide the Story of my Soul.

Translated from the French by Michael Day, 1951; original title: *L'Histoire d'une Ame*. St Theresa of Lisieux, whom the French know better as Thérèse de l'Enfant-Jésus (et de la Sainte Face), and who was born Thérèse Martin, was a Carmelite nun who entered the nunnery at Lisieux in 1888, at the age of fifteen, and who died there in 1897, aged twenty-four. *The Story of a Soul* is her autobiography, which she originally wrote in three parts, each requested by a different person. The first, completed in 1896 as a 170-page manuscript, was entitled 'The Springtime Story of a Little White Flower, written by herself and dedicated to the Rev. Mother Agnes of Jesus'. The second, only ten pages in length, was also written in 1896, and was called 'Letter to Sister Marie of the Sacred Heart, written at Sister Marie's request'. The third, finished in 1897, and 74 pages long, was entitled 'Notebook written for the Rev. Mother Marie de Gonzague'. Each part was dedicated to the person who had asked her to write it. Mother Agnes, the Prioress, was Theresa's own sister Pauline; Sister Marie of the Sacred Heart was her eldest sister; Mother Marie de Gonzague was Mother Agnes's successor as Prioress. After Theresa's death, the manuscripts were edited by Mother Agnes and rearranged into a single book, with an injunction from her sister that all three were to be dedicated to herself personally. However, the names of the individual requestors remain at the head of the respective sections, so that chapters I to VIII are 'For Mother Agnes of Jesus', chapters IX and X are 'For Mother Marie de Gonzague' and chapter XI is 'For Sister Marie of the Sacred Heart', with the opening words of the narrative addressed to the person named. Theresa was canonised in 1925.

Paul **Theroux,** *The Great Railway Bazaar*, 1975

~ 'To the legion of the lost ones, to the cohorts of the damned, To my brethren in their sorrow overseas ...' And to my brothers and sisters, namely Eugene, Alexander, Ann-Marie, Mary, Joseph, and Peter, with love.

The American train-odysseist and travel-writer quotes from Kipling's *Gentlemen Rankers* for the first part of his dedication.

Paul **Theroux,** *The Mosquito Coast*, 1981

~ To 'Charlie Fox', whose story this is, and whose courage showed me that the brave cannot be killed. With grateful thanks for many hours of patient explanation and good humour in the face of my ignorant questioning. May he find the peace he deserves on this safer coast. *Naksaa*. P.T.

The hero of the story, Allie Fox, takes his family from the civilised world to live in the Honduran jungle, with tragic but also farcical results. The novel is a study of the essential incompatibility between civilization and savagery, and of what happens when the former tries to master the latter on its own terms.

Leslie **Thomas,** *This Time Next Week*, 1964

~ Dedicated to my mother and father wherever they may be in the hope that, by this time, they have made it up.

The autobiography of the former Barnados boy whose parents had died when he was young.

Lowell J. **Thomas,** *With Lawrence in Arabia*, 1924

~ To Eighteen Gentlemen of Chicago: this narrative of a modern Arabian Knight is gratefully dedicated.

The American journalist, together with a photographer and two assistants, had been commissioned by President Wilson in 1917 to prepare a historical record of the First World War by visiting those parts of the world, notably the Middle East, where it was being waged. During his travels, Thomas had met T.E. Lawrence ('Lawrence of Arabia') and made him famous with this book. The four men's expedition was funded by 'eighteen distinguished private citizens', who however remained nameless in Taylor's account. In the event, their world tour took three years, not one year only, as originally planned.

Maurice **Thompson**, *Alice of Old Vincennes*, 1900

~ [...] Accept then this book. In my mind and yours, I hope, it will always be connected with a breezy summer house on a headland of the Louisiana gulf coast, the rustling of palmetto leaves, the fine flash of roses, a tumult of mocking-bird voices, the soft lilt of creole patois, and the endless dash and roar of a fragrant sea over which gulls and pelicans never ceased their flight, and besides which you smoked while I dreamed. [...]

The book is a romantic historical novel of the North West territory and the exploits of the Virginian soldier George Rogers Clark. The dedicatee was the Frenchman Placide Valcour. This extract is just part of the heady whole.

Phyllis **Thompson**, *Mr Leprosy*, 1980

~ To Mary and Vicky, whose friendship I have treasured since the time the three of us lived together, and to Flora, whose open heart and open home have enriched my life, I dedicate this book.

A biography of Dr Stanley Browne, the famous leprosy specialist and missionary and, in his later years, head of the Leprosy Study Centre in London.

Winfield M. **Thompson** and Thomas W. Lawson, *The Lawson History of the America's Cup; a Record of Fifty Years*, 1902

~ To Sportsmen – manly men, men of gentle mind and simple heart, brave men, fair men; to men who say to the weak, 'may I?' and to the strong, 'I will!' – to men to whom sham is dishonor and truth a guiding star; to men who look upon the sea, the plain, the forest, the mountains, the rising and the setting sun, and the immutable Heavens, with a deep sense of their own littleness in the great scheme of things, – I dedicate this book. Thomas W. Lawson.

And how about sportswomen – womanly women? But that was then, and we are now nearly a century on. The America's Cup, the famous international yachting contest, was first raced in 1851, when the winner was the New York schooner *America*. The trophy, originally the Hundred Guinea Cup, offered by the Royal Yacht Squadron of Britain, was subsequently named after this ship.

James **Thomson**, *Liberty, a Poem*, 1738

~ To his royal highness, Frederick, Prince of Wales. Sir, When I reflect upon that ready Condescension, that preventing Generosity, with which Your Royal Highness received the following Poem under your Protection; I can alone ascribe it to the Recommendation, and Influence of the Subject. In you the Cause and Concerns of Liberty have so zealous a Patron, as entitles whatever may have the least Tendency to promote them, to the Distinction of your Favour. [...] If the following Attempt to trace Liberty, from the first Ages down to her excellent Establishment in Great Britain, can at all merit your Approbation, and prove an entertainment to your Royal Highness; if it can in any degree answer the Dignity of the Subject, and of the name under which I presume to shelter it; I have my best reward: particularly, as it affords me an Opportunity of declaring that I am, with the greatest Zeal and Respect, Sir, Your Royal Highness's most obedient and devoted servant, James Thomson.

The royal dedicatee was thus Frederick Louis, son of George II and father of George III. He was hardly an obvious champion of liberty, however, and most of his zeal was directed towards opposing the measures introduced by his father and his father's prime minister, Walpole. But he was a generous patron of literature, unlike the indifferent Walpole, and had several famous literary supporters, including Fielding and George Lyttelton, as well as Thomson.

George Walter **Thornbury**, *Songs of the Cavaliers and Roundheads*, 1857

~ To DOUGLAS JERROLD, the Dramatist, Satirist, and Novelist, these verses are dedicated by the author, from one who is struggling and hopes to win, to one who has struggled and won.

Jerrold is best remembered as a writer of comedies and farces, one of the best known being *Black-eyed Susan* (1829). Thornbury, despite his strenuous struggles, is hardly remembered at all. He died of overwork in 1876, aged forty-seven.

Thomas **Thorpe**, *St Augustine, of the Citie of God*, 1610

~ To the Honorablest Patron of Muses and good mindes, LORD WILLIAM, EARL OF PEMBROKE, Knight of the Honourable Order, etc. Right gracious and gracefull Lord, your late imaginary, but now actuall Travailer, then to most-conceited Viraginia, now to almost-concealed Virginia; then a light, but not lewde, now a sage and allowed translator; then of a scarce knowne novice, now a famous Father; then of a devised Country scarse on earth, now of a desired citie sure in heaven, then of Utopia, now of Eutopia; not as by testament, but as a testimonie of gratitude, observance, and hearts honour to your Honor, bequeathed at hence-parting (thereby scarse perfecting) this his translation at the imprinting to your Lordship's protecting. [...] Wherefore his legacie laid at your Honour's humbly thrise kissed hands by his poore delegate, Your Lordship's true devoted TH. TH.

This is the same Thomas Thorpe as the writer of the famous dedication to SHAKESPEARE'S *Sonnets*, which he had published the previous year. His language is even more contrived than in the earlier dedication, but there seems little doubting his sincerity. He was not of course the translator of St Augustine's *City of God*, which had been 'Englished by J.H.' (who was the little known author John Heaney). Thorpe almost certainly chose William Herbert, 3rd Earl of Pembroke, as his dedicatee because Heaney had earlier dedicated to him his translation of Bishop Hall's *Discoverie of a New World*, although this had been issued by another publisher.

Jon **Thurley**, *The Burning Lake*, 1985

~ To my androgynous friend Duma Malva Dijen Tobad, whose help and support have been equivalent to that of at least eight people.

E. Temple **Thurston**, *The Garden of Resurrection*, 1911

~ My dear Dakin, Partly because you have a love of gardens, partly because together we have seen Ballysheen when the gorse was in its full blast of yellow, but most of all because I feel I owe you a debt of gratitude for a great friendship, I am asking you to accept this book of mine. It was after a talk with you one night that I went straight home and wrote Chapter I on a clean sheet of paper, therefore the book is doubly yours and I ask you to accept it in proof of the fact that, not only am I grateful, but also that I am Your sincere friend, E. Temple Thurston.

The first page of this novel – about romance rather than religion, despite the title – reveals that the dedicatee is a doctor, one W.R. Dakin. Thurston was the author of similar stories published in Newnes' Sevenpenny Series about this time, such as *The Greatest Wish in the World*, *The City of Beautiful Nonsense* and *Sally Bishop*. But who reads any of them now?

William **Thynne**, *The Workes of Geffroy Chaucer*, 1532

~ […] I thought it in maner appertenant unto my dewtie, and that of very honesty and love to my countrey I ought no lesse to do, than to put my helpyng hande to the restauracion and bringynge agayne to lyght of the said workes, after the trewe copies and exemplaries aforesaid. And devisyng with my selfe who of all other were most worthy to whom a thyng so excellent and notable shulde be dedicate, which to my conceite semeth for the admiracion, noveltie and strangnesse that it myght be reputed to be of in the tyme of the author in comparison as a pur and fyne tryed precious or polyced jewell out of a rude or ingest masse or mater, none coulde to my thynkyng occurre, that syns, or in the tyme of Chaucer, was or is suffycient, but onely your maiestie royall, whiche by discrecyon and jugement, as moost absolute in wysedome and all kyndes of doctryne coulde, and of his innate clemence and goodnesse wolde, adde or gyve any authorite herunto. […]

He gets there in the end, and all we need to know is that the royal dedicatee was none other than Henry VIII himself. This was the first collected edition of Chaucer's works, and although incomplete, and containing writings later found to be not by Chaucer at all, it formed the basis for all subsequent scholarly editions. It is quite possible, however, that the dedication was not written by Thynne after all, but by his colleague, Sir Bryan Tuke, secretary to Henry VIII.

George **Ticknor**, *Life of William Hickling Prescott*, 1864

~ To William Howard Gardiner and William Amory. We are more than once mentioned together in the last testamentary dispositions of our friend, as persons for whom he felt a true regard, and to whose affection and fidelity he, in some respects, intrusted the welfare of those who were dearest to him in life. Permit me, then, to associate your names with mine in this tribute to his memory.

Ticknor was an American historian and educator. Prescott, the subject of his biography, was a noted Spanish historian who had died five years earlier.

Count Nikolai **Tolstoy**, *The Half-Mad Lord*, 1978

~ This book is dedicated with permission to my fellow Brothers, past and present, of the Sublime Society of Beef Steaks.

George **Tooke**, *The History of Cales Passion*, 1652

~ My worthy good Cousin, Having thus transplanted this little Lean-to from the calmnesse of my private Nursery into the bleak and open champion; and not knowing how much it there may suffer by the stormy gusts of censure without some extraordinary stake supporting it, I thus betake me to your own good self for protection, and if you please to passe it under the value of your name, misdoubt not the successe, and shall with much cheerfulnesse intercept all further opportunities of acknowledging myn selfe, Your most affectionate Cousin, to love and honour you, G.T.

Tooke was a soldier as well as a writer, and this work was an account of the unsuccessful expedition led by Sir Edward Cecil to Cadiz in 1625, in which Tooke had commanded a group of volunteers. The full title of the work continues: 'or as some will by-name it, the Miss-taking of Cales presented in Vindication of the Sufferers, and to forewarne the future'. ('Cales' is Cadiz.) Tooke's cousin was the mathematician and astronomer John Greaves, who died that year, aged fifty. *Champion* is really 'champaign', otherwise 'country', 'plain'.

John Horne **Tooke**, *The Diversions of Purley*, 1786

~ To the University of Cambridge, One of her grateful sons – who always considers acts of voluntary justice towards himself as favours, – dedicates this humble offering. And particularly to her chief ornament for virtue and talents, the reverend doctor Beadon, master of Jesus college.

Horne Tooke was a radical politician and philologist, with this work a treatise on the etymology of English words, with witty asides on metaphysics and politics. (Its main title, printed in Greek, was *Epea pteroenta*, 'Winged Words'. Many of the etymologies are purely speculative, but the work laid the basis of the linguistic discipline later known as comparative philology.) Richard Beadon, elected Master of Jesus College in 1781, was a contemporary of Tooke's at St John's College, Cambridge.

Paul **Tortelier**, *A Self-Portrait: In Conversation with David Blum*, 1984

~ To my friends, the young, who carry our hope for tomorrow.

The autobiography of the famous cellist.

Calvin **Trillin**, *American Fried*, 1974

~ For Alice and Sarah and Abigail (who, when she was four, reacted to polishing off a particularly satisfying dish of chocolate ice cream by saying, 'My tongue is smiling').

Calvin **Trillin**, *Alice, Let's Eat*, 1978

~ To Alice, of course.

Calvin **Trillin**, *Third Helpings*, 1983
~ To Alice and Abigail and Sarah – the same old crowd.

Three books by the popular American writer on food. It is fairly easy to work out who's who in his family.

Flora **Tristan**, *London Journal*, 1982
~ Men and women of the working class, I dedicate my book *to all of you*; I wrote it so that you might understand your plight, therefore it belongs to you. [...]

Translated from the French by Jean Hawkes; original title: *Promenades dans Londres*, published in two parts in 1840 and 1842.

Barbara **Tufty**, *1001 Questions Answered About Earthquakes, Avalanches, Floods and Other Natural Disasters*, 1969
~ To those enduring scientists who take valuable time to help explain their theories and observations to a layman. To Watson Davis, who believed that any scientific event, no matter how complex, could be described accurately in nonscientific language.

Davis, who died in 1967, was the Director of Science Service in the United States.

George **Turberville**, *The Eglogs of the Poet B. Mantuan Carmelitan*, 1567
~ Worshipful, as desire not altogither to be idle and waste the golden Time (the rarest of all Jewels) procurde me to undertake the translation of this Poet; so Nature with your sundrie curtesies bestowed on me without hope of recompence at any time, enforced me (for want of better way to shewe my goode meaning) to dedicate to you this rude and slender Booke, translated into our mother tongue. Hoping that as I have not wronged the Poet in any poynt in my translation, or impairde his credite with the Latins, in forcing him to speake with an English mouth contrary to his nature and kinde: so neyther that I have ministred you occasion to myslike with me for dedication of the same to you: a man whose benefits I may and will endevour to requite, but shall never be able to rid my score of his good turnes, or cancell the obligation of hys many and infinite curtesies. [...] Wherfore (Uncle) as I shal crave you to accept this my slender gift, undertaking the Patronage and Defence of the same: So shall I request the Gods to allowe you the aged Nestors yeares, with no mysseadventure in al your life. Your nephewe and daylie orator, George Turberville.

The *Eclogues* of the fifteenth-century Italian Carmelite writer Giovanni Battista Spagnoli were 'Turned into English Verse and set forth with the argument to every Eglog by George Turbervile, Gent.', a noted poet, anthologist (as we would now call him) and translator of his day, and were dedicated to his uncle, 'Maister Hugh Bamfild', of whom little is otherwise known. Turberville is conscientiously concerned to be faithful to his original on the one hand, while making a worthy offering to his uncle on the other, thus properly honouring both.

Ivan Turgenev, *A Song of Triumphant Love,* 1881
~ Dedicated to the memory of Gustave Flaubert.

Translated from the Russian by AR; original title: *Pesn' torzhestvuyushchey lyubvi.* A brief dedication, but a significant one in Russian literature. The famous French novelist had died the previous year, and Turgenev and he had been personal friends, meeting frequently when the Russian writer was living in Paris in his latter years. The work itself is unusual for Turgenev, and is a purely visionary tale, unlike most of his descriptive, realistic writing. The dedication is followed by a short quotation from Schiller: *Wage Du zu irren und zu träumen!* ('Dare to go astray and to dream!'). Not that Flaubert, a rigidly realistic writer, served as an example in this respect, although he certainly turned to historical themes for his novels, as Turgenev was now doing for his own story, set in sixteenth-century Italy.

William Turner, *The First and Seconde Partes of the Herbal,* 1568
~ To the most noble and learned Princesse in all kindes of good lerninge, Queene Elizabeth. The printer had geven me warninge there wanted nothinge to the settinge our of my hole Herbal, saving only a Preface, wherein I might require some both mighty and learned Patron to defend my laboures against spitefull and envious enemies to all mennis doyinges saving their owne, and declare my good minde to him that I am bound unto by dedicating and geving these poore labours unto him. I did seeke out everye where in my mind, howe that I could come by such a Patron as had both learning and sufficient autoritie, joyned therewith to defend my poore laboures against their adversaries, and in the same person suche friendshippe and good will towards me, by reason whereof I were most bound unto above all other. After long turninge this matter over in my mind, it came to my memorye that in all the hole realme of England, that there were none more fit to be Patronesse of my Booke, and none had deserved so muche, to whom I shuld dedicate and geve the same as your most excellent sublimitie hath done: I have dedicated it therefore unto your most excellent sublimitie, and do geve it for the avoydinge of all suspicion of ingratitude or unkindnes unto you as a token and a witnes of the acknowledginge of the great benefites that I have receyved of your princely liberalitie of late years. [...]

The lengthy dedication goes on to expand on the writer's reasons for being grateful to the Queen and to make a detailed case for the worthiness of the book and thus for her acceptance of it. This was a new edition of the original *Herbal* of 1551, which itself was the first botanical treatise in England presented in anything like a scientific manner. But Turner's almost conversational account of how he came to hit on the right person and patron for his work is still worth reading 400 years on.

Mark Twain, *The Innocents Abroad,* 1869
~ To my most patient reader and most charitable critic, my aged mother, this volume is affectionately inscribed.

Mark Twain, *Roughing It,* 1872
~ To Calvin H. Higbie of California, an honest man, a genial comrade, and a

steadfast friend, this book is inscribed by the author in memory of the curious time when we two were millionaires for ten days.

The book tells how a supposed 'lucky strike' had made Twain and his friend prospective (but not actual) millionaires. In point of fact Twain was more worried about an unpaid $6 butcher's bill than any possible fortune. The account is autobiographical.

Mark Twain, *The Prince and the Pauper*, 1882
~ To those good-mannered and agreeable children, Susy and Clara Clemens, this book is affectionately inscribed by their father.

A playfully worded dedication by Mark Twain (whose real name was Samuel Langhorne Clemens) to two of his daughters.

Mark Twain, *Personal Recollections of Joan of Arc*, 1895
~ To my wife, Olivia Langdon Clemens, this book is tendered on our wedding anniversary, in grateful recognition of her twenty-fifth year of valued service as my literary adviser and editor. The author.

Mark Twain, *Following the Equator*, 1897
~ This book is affectionately inscribed to my young friend Harry Rogers with recognition of what he is, and apprehension of what he may become unless he form himself a little more closely upon the model of The Author.

The book is an autobiographical narrative.

Joseph Hopkins Twichell, *John Winthrop*, 1891
~ To the City of Hartford, where John Winthrop's priceless Journal was first printed, the Capital of the Commonwealth of which his oldest son was eighteen times chosen governor, this volume is affectionately dedicated.

Twichell, a Congregational clergyman, was a member of the literary circle to which Harriet Beecher Stowe and Mark Twain also belonged. (In the latter's *A Tramp Abroad*, he features as Harris.) John Winthrop, first governor of the Massachusetts Bay Colony, had written an important historical account of the colonising of the territory, where he himself had come from England in 1630, as his *Journal* (1790), with this work later republished in expanded form as *The History of New England from 1630 to 1649* (1825–6). Twichell had edited his letters. Winthrop's son, the dedicatee here, and Suffolk-born, like his father, was Governor of Connecticut more or less continuously from 1657 to 1676. John Winthrop Sr died in 1649; his son in 1676.

❧ V ❧

H.A. **Vachell**, *The Hill*, 1905

~ To George W.E. Russell. I dedicate this Romance of Friendship to you with the sincerest pleasure and affection. You were the first to suggest I should write a book about contemporary life at Harrow; you gave me the principal idea; you have furnished me with notes innumerable; you have revised every page of the manuscript; and you are a peculiarly keen Harrovian. [...] That there are such boys as Verney and Scaife, nobody knows better than yourself. Believe me, Yours most gratefully, Horace Annesley Vachell.

A novel about schoolboys, but not really for them. The title of the book, of course, refers to Harrow-on-the-Hill, where the famous public school is. The book was the author's first popular success, and was partly based on his own life at Harrow, where Russell had also been (although earlier than Vachell). George William Erskine Russell, not to be confused with George William Russell ('Æ'), was a politician and literary biographer, for example of Matthew Arnold. Russell died in 1919, aged only fifty-six, but Vachell died in 1955, aged ninety-three, and was still publishing in his late eighties. See just one more of his dedications below.

H.A. **Vachell**, *This Was England*, 1933

~ To all who think sometimes of the yesterdays, to all who are loth to forget what is passing away so swiftly, to those to whom folk-lore, ancient customs, and the still untrodden ways are dear, to those who can still smile at the myths connected with our common flowers and the legends concerning our saints, I dedicate this book.

A nostalgic journey, with the subtitle of the book telling all: 'A pilgrimage through the by-ways of yesterday, through the England that used to be, with its flowers and fields and trees and birds, with its legends, stories and fables, its quaint customs and folk-lore'. Books like this are still popular today, and there will doubtless always be a market in rural-cum-literary reminiscences of this type.

Laurens **van der Post**, *Venture to the Interior*, 1952

~ For Ingaret Giffard, in order to defeat the latest of many separations.

See below.

Laurens **van der Post**, *The Lost World of the Kalahari*, 1958

~ To the memory of Klara who had a Bushman mother and nursed me from birth; and to my wife Ingaret Giffard, for saying without hesitation when I mentioned the journey to her: 'but you must go and do it at once'.

Just two of the books by the well-known South African writer and explorer. Ingaret Giffard was his second wife, whom he married in 1949.

Henry **Van Dyke**, *Little Rivers*, 1895

> To one who wanders by my side
> As cheerfully as waters glide,
> Whose eyes are brown as woodland streams,
> And very fair and full of dreams;
> Whose heart is like a mountain spring,
> Whose thoughts like merry rivers sing,
> To her – My little daughter Brooke,
> I dedicate this little book.

This book, with its title to match the name of the dedicatee, was one of the earliest by the American Presbyterian minister and poet, who became Professor of English Literature at Princeton. He was now forty-three.

Henry **Van Dyke**, *Fisherman's Luck*, 1899

~ To my Lady Graygown: here is the basket; I bring it home to you. There is no great fish in it. But perhaps there may be a little one here and there to your taste. And there are a few shining pebbles from the bed of the brook, and a few ferns from the cool green woods, and a few wild flowers from the places that you remember. I would fain console you, if I could, for the hardship of having married an angler: a man who relapses into his mania with the return of every spring, and never sees a little river without wishing to fish in it. But after all, we have had good times together, as we have followed the stream of life to the sea. And we have passed through dark days without losing heart, because we were comrades. So, let this book tell you one thing that is certain: in all the life of your fisherman, the best piece of luck is just YOU.

Henry **Van Dyke**, *The Poetry of Tennyson*, 1905

~ To a young woman of an old fashion, who loves art not for its own sake, but because it ennobles life; who reads poetry, not to kill time, but to fill it with beautiful thoughts; and who still believes in God and duty and immortal love – I dedicate this book.

Perhaps to the poet's daughter. The book was now in its tenth edition.

Henry **Van Dyke**, *Days Off*, 1907

~ To my friend and neighbour, Grover Cleveland, whose years of great work as a statesman have been cheered by days of good play as a fisherman, this book is dedicated with warm and deep regards.

Stephen Grover Cleveland was twice president of the USA, and lived in Princeton, where Van Dyke lived, for the last ten years of his life. Van Dyke has been described as a 'melodious but facile' poet (*Oxford Companion to American Literature*), but he is still quoted in the anthologies. He died in 1933, aged eighty-one.

Eric **van Lustbader**, *Dai-San*, 1978
~ For the little boy who lived down the lane – Welcome home.

Mrs C.M. **Van Wagenen**, *A Catagraph*, nd (*c.* 1885)
~ Dedicated to the memory of Satinella, my cat.

The work is a humorous poem playing on words that begin 'cat-', such as 'catacomb', 'cataract', 'catafalque', and so on, a particular pun that has frequently appealed to cat-owners over the years. Mrs Van Wagenen was the American author of a number of twee poems, mostly dedicated, like this one, to various people and objects. Examples: *The Story of Helen* ('To my Mother and Father'); *My Lady's Chamber* ('To Friendship'); *Little Thatcher's Fourth Birthday* ('To the Four-leafed Clover'); *The Joys of Childhood* ('To Betty, to my Doll'). Not all of her writings were published.

Henry **Vaughan**, *Silex Scintillans: or Sacred Poems and Private Ejaculations*, 1650

> My God! Thou that didst die for me,
> These Thy death's fruits I offer Thee:
> Death that to me was life and light,
> But dark and deep pangs to Thy sight.
> Some drops of Thy all-quick'ning blood
> Fell on my heart; those made it bud,
> And put forth thus, though, Lord, before
> The Ground was curs'd and void of store.
> Indeed I had some here to hire,
> Which long resisted Thy desire,
> That ston'd Thy servants, and did move
> To have Thee murder'd for Thy love;
> But Lord, I have expell'd them and so bent,
> Beg Thou wouldst take Thy tenant's rent.

The dedication is for the poet's famous book of meditative verse, with its Latin title translating 'The Flashing Flint'. The metaphor is that of a hardened heart struck by affliction until it yields a spark. Vaughan styled himself as 'Silurist', in allusion to his homeland, the border country of Wales, once inhabited by the British tribe known as the Silures (who gave the Roman name of their capital, Venta Silurum, now Caerwent). In a later (1655) edition of the volume, Vaughan added two more stanzas, and introduced the poem thus: 'To my merciful, my most loving, and dearly loved Redeemer, the ever blessed, the only Holy and Just One, Jesus Christ'.

Lope de Vega, *A Tragic Crown*, 1627

~ To our Most Holy Pope Urban VIII, Pont. Max. The History of Mary Stuart, Queen of Scotland, an extraordinary victim of all that mortals call Fortune, in whose life adversity and patience competed equally from the cradle to the axe, I dedicated to Your Holiness first, befittingly, in the Latin tongue, not only because of the greatness and authority of the subject as because of Your Holiness having in your tender years honoured her tomb with such excellent Praise that it was as beatifying her in prophecy: in that today Your Holiness occupies the Apostolic chair with the general commendation of the Church. This time, Most Holy Father, it is in the common language of Spain. [...] May Your Holiness receive it benignly, adjusting the infinite distance of my rudeness to the splendour of your superior understanding, as so well employed boldness expects of your bountiful magnificence. May Our Lord keep Your Holiness many years, for the universal Church has the need, and it is the desire of your servants. Most Holy Father, Humble servant of Your Holiness, Lope Felix de Vega Carpio.

Translated from the Spanish; original title: *Corona trágica*. This must suffice for just one of the literally hundreds of plays by the prolific Spanish dramatist, most of which have substantial dedications to persons prominent in the church or the court.

Peter Verstappen, *The Book of Surnames*, 1980

~ To Margaret Evans Thomas Kilroy Verstappen and Henri Verstappen, proof positive that surnames combine with improbable results.

The book, subtitled 'Origins and Oddities of Popular Names' is about British names, but its author is American-born. He had, however, been living in Britain for thirteen years at the time of publication.

Voltaire, *Brutus*, 1730

TO LORD BOLINGBROKE

If I dedicate to an Englishman a work made known in Paris, it is not, my Lord, that there are not also most enlightened judges in my own country, and excellent men of wit to whom I could have paid this homage; but you will know that the tragedy of *Brutus* was born in England. You will recall that when I retired to Wandsworth, to stay with my friend Mr Falkener, that worthy and virtuous citizen, I busied myself in his house by writing the first act of this play in English prose, more or less as it is today in French verse. I spoke to you of it sometimes, and we were surprised that no English writer had taken up this subject, which, of all subjects, is perhaps the best suited to your theatre. You encouraged me to continue writing a work that was capable of expressing such great sentiments. Allow me, then, to present *Brutus* to you, although written in another language, *docte sermones utriusque linguæ*, you who gave me lessons in French as well as in English, you who would teach me at least to give my language that strength and energy which the noble liberty of thinking inspires: for the vigorous sentiments of the soul constantly pass through language; and whoever thinks strongly, speaks in the same way. I confess to you, my Lord, that on my return from England, where I had passed almost two years in a continual study of your language, I encountered difficulties when I wished to compose a French tragedy. I had almost become accustomed to thinking in English: I felt that the phrases of my own language would not offer themselves to my imagination in the same abundance as before: it was like a stream whose source has been diverted; I needed time and care to make it flow in its former course. I then realised all too well that to succeed in an art, one must cultivate it all one's life. [...]

Translated from the French by AR; original title as in English. Henry St John, 1st Viscount Bolingbroke, statesman, orator, philosopher, writer, was a personal friend of Voltaire and had laid down the precepts endorsed by the French dramatist in *Letters on the Study of History* (1752). The two men later quarrelled, however. Voltaire's play, on the life and death of Brutus, was not a success. (This was the sixth-century Roman who liberated Rome from the Tarquins, not the first-century conspirator who assassinated Caesar.) In saying that no previous author had chosen the subject as the basis for a play, Voltaire was not strictly correct, for Nathaniel Lee's play *Lucius Junus Brutus* had appeared in 1680. The extract quoted here is just the first page of Voltaire's sixteen-page dedication, most of which is given up to discussing his tragedy and the state of contemporary French theatre. The Latin phrase quoted by Voltaire is from Horace, meaning 'discourses learnedly in each of two languages'.

Voltaire, *Fanaticism, or Mahomet the Prophet*, 1741

DEDICATED TO POPE BENEDICT XIV

Most Holy Father, Your Holiness will pardon the liberty taken by one of the humblest of men, but one of the greatest admirers of virtue, in dedicating to the head of the true religion a work directed against the founder of a false and barbarous religion. To whom could I more appropriately address the satire upon the cruelty and the errors of a false prophet than to the Vicar and imitator of a God of peace and truth? May your Holiness deign to permit me to lay at your feet both book and author. I dare ask of you protection for the one, and a blessing for the other. It is with these sentiments of profound veneration that I bow and kiss your sacred feet.

Translated from the French; original title: *Le Fanatisme, ou Mahomet le Prophète*. Voltaire's enemies had been horrified at the impieties of this tragedy when it was first staged, and it was withdrawn after only three performances. Voltaire then decided to dedicate it to the Pope, as here. Flattered, and fancying himself as a literary expert, Benedict XIV wrote back warmly approving. Voltaire was quick to point out that in literary judgments, as in other matters, the Pope was infallible!

Victor W. Von Hagen, *Search for the Maya: The Story of Stephens and Catherwood*, 1973

~ For Alberto Beltran, 'My Catherwood', who travelled with me through Mexico, Yucatan and Peru, and who illustrated ten of my books so marvellously. With affection and gratitude.

The original dedication, here translated by AR, is in Spanish. The book tells the story of the two Victorian explorers, one American, one English, who discovered the Maya civilisation in Mexico.

Kurt Vonnegut, *Jailbird*, 1979

~ For Benjamin D. Hitz, close friend of my youth, best man at my wedding. Ben, you used to tell me about wonderful books you had just read, and then I would imagine that I had read them, too. You read nothing but the best, Ben, while I studied chemistry. Long time no see.

❧ W ❧

Charles **Wagner**, *The Better Way*, 1903

~ To Pierce Wagner, Paris, Feb. 24, 1884. Montana-sur-Seine, August 20, 1899. My child, I began this book by your bed of pain and in my lonely walks on the mountain. Many a time I interrupted the writing to go and do for you one of thos innumerable little services 'at once so sad and so sweet'; and away from you in the Alpine pathways, in the high pastures and solitary midlands, my aching heart was filled with your image. To you, then, I dedicate these pages. May they be offered you not as sad tokens of what no longer is, but as an eternal pledge between our inseparable souls and as an act of homage, that I would were purer and fuller of consolation, rendered from the midst of a transitory world to that which never dies.

A sad memorial to a son who died when only fifteen. In view of the locations mentioned, he was presumably a victim of tuberculosis.

Bishop Jonathan **Wainwright**, *Women of the Bible*, nd (*c*. 1852)

~ To thoughtful readers, men as well as women, the one being interested equally with the other in what constitutes the character of mother, wife, daughter, sister, this book of female portraits drawn from the highest and holiest record of life is dedicated. J.M. Wainwright.

Wainwright was an English-born American Protestant Episcopal clergyman, consecrated Bishop of New York in the year this was probably published. A 'Who's Who' of biblical women is of course nothing original in itself.

J. Bernard **Walker**, *An Unsinkable Titanic*, 1912

~ To the memory of the chief engineer of the *Titanic*, John Bell, and his staff of thirty-three assistants, who stood at their posts in the engine and boiler rooms to the very last and went down with the ship, this book is dedicated.

The book, published in the year the great passenger liner, on her maiden voyage, struck an iceberg and sank with the loss of 1,500 lives, is subtitled 'Every Ship its Own Lifeboat' and is a practical proposal for constructing a ship in such a way that it can serve as a rescue vessel for its passengers and crew if holed.

Lew **Wallace**, *Ben Hur*, 1880

~ To the wife of my youth, who still abides with me.

The American soldier and writer, author of the famous novel of Roman times, had married Susan Arnold, also a writer. She outlived him by two years, dying in 1907.

Lew **Wallace**, *The Prince of India*, 1893

~ To my father, David Wallace. He loved literature for the pleasure it brought him, and could I have had his counsel while composing this work, the critics would not be so terrible to me now that it is about going to press.

The book is a somewhat turgid novel based on the story of the Wandering Jew.

Horace **Walpole**, *The Castle of Otranto*, 1765

SONNET TO THE RIGHT HONOURABLE LADY MARY COKE

> The gentle maid, whose hapless tale
>   These melancholy pages speak;
> Say, gracious lady, shall she fail
>   To draw the tear adown thy cheek?
>
> No; never was thy pitying breast
>   Insensible to human woes;
> Tender, tho' firm, it melts distrest
>   For weaknesses it never knows.
>
> Oh! guard the marvels I relate
> Of fell ambition scourg'd by fate,
>   From reason's peevish blame.
> Blest with thy smile, my dauntless sail
> I dare expand to Fancy's gale,
>   For sure thy smiles are Fame.
>
>   H.W.

The famous 'Gothic' novel had this dedicatory sonnet in its second edition as an address to Lady Mary Coke, daughter of the Duke of Argyll. She was a friend of Walpole and the (rather reluctant) wife of Edward Viscount Coke.

Horace **Walpole**, ed., *The Life of Edward, Lord Herbert of Cherbury: Written by Himself*, 1771

~ To the most noble Henry Arthur Herbert, Earl of Powis, Viscount Ludlow, Lord Herbert of Cherbury, Baron Powis and Ludlow, and Treasurer of his Majesty's household. My Lord, Permit me to offer to your Lordship, in this more durable manner, the very valuable present I received from your hands. To your Lordship your great ancestor owes his revival; and suffer me, my Lord, to tell the world what does you so much honour, you have given him and me leave to speak the truth: an indulgence which, I am sorry to say, few descendants of heroes have minds noble enough to allow. Hitherto, Lord Herbert has been little known as an

Author. I much mistake, if hereafter he is not considered as one of the most extraordinary characters which this country has produced. Men of the proudest blood shall not blush to distinguish themselves in letters as well as arms, when they learn what excellence Lord Herbert attained in both. Your Lordship's lineage at least will have a pattern before their eyes to excite their emulation; and while they admire the piety with which you have done justice to your common Ancestor, they cannot be forgetfull of the obligation they will have to your Lordship's memory for transmitting to them this record of his glory. I have the honour to be, my Lord, Your Lordship's most obedient and most obliged servant, Horace Walpole.

In a letter to George Montague of 26 July 1764, Walpole wrote that he and the poet Gray had read Lord Herbert's *Life* aloud to amuse Lady Walgrave, and that they 'could not get on for laughing and screaming'. Walpole had found the manuscript in the house of Lady Hertford, to whom Lady Powis had lent it. At first, Lord Powis refused to allow it to be printed, so Walpole wrote this flattering dedication to him, 'which I knew he would swallow; he did, and gave up his ancestor'. Lord Herbert's *Life* had been written in 1624, and covered the time from his birth to that year. It is now frequently referred to as his *Autobiography* and is a unique original record of his times.

Hugh **Walpole**, *Mr Perrin and Mr Traill*, 1911

~ To Punch. My dear Punch, There are a thousand and one reasons why I should dedicate this book to you. It would take a very long time and much good paper to give you them all; but here, at any rate, is one of them. Do you remember a summer day last year that we spent together? The place was a little French town, and we climbed its high, crooked street, and had tea in an inn at the top – an inn with a square courtyard, bad, impossible tea, and a large black cat. It was on that afternoon that I introduced you for a little time to Mr. Perrin, and you, because you have more understanding and sympathy than any one I have ever met, understood him and sympathised. For the good things that you have done for me I can never repay you, but for the good things that you did on that afternoon for Mr. Perrin I give you this book. Yours affectionately, Hugh Walpole.

This was the novel that began the fashion for school stories and that was based on the author's own experiences as a teacher at Epsom College. The dedicatee was Walpole's close friend Percy Anderson, an artist and stage costume designer, then aged fifty-nine as against Walpole's twenty-seven. Henry James, who also knew Walpole well, admired the novel but found the dedication effusive, and teased him about it. Perhaps he was jealous? In fact Walpole did dedicate two later novels posthumously to James: *The Apple Trees* (1932) and *The Killer and the Slain* (1942).

Hugh **Walpole**, *Rogue Herries*, 1933

~ For a trusted friend and in love of Cumberland.

Where the story is set in the eighteenth century.

Izaak **Walton**, *The Compleat Angler*, 1653

~ To the Right Worshipful John Offley, of Madeley Manor, in the County of Stafford, Esquire, My most honoured Friend. Sir, – I have made so ill use of your former favours, as by them to be encouraged to entreat, that they may be enlarged to the patronage and protection of this Book: and I have put on a modest confidence, that I shall not be denied, because it is a discourse of Fish and Fishing, which you know so well, and both love and practise so much. […] And lest a longer epistle may diminish your pleasure, I shall make this no longer than to add the following truth, that I am really, Sir, your most affectionate Friend, and most humble Servant, Iz. Wa.

Walton's well-known work, published when he was sixty and subtitled 'The Contemplative Man's Recreation; Being a Discourse of Fish and Fishing, not unworthy the perusal of most Anglers', was dedicated to his close friend John Offley, who lived not far away at Madeley Manor, west of Newcastle-under-Lyme. Walton was a frequent visitor there, though his book was about fishing in the River Lea, between Tottenham and Ware, to the north of London.

Mrs Humphry **Ward**, *Robert Ellesmere*, 1888

~ Dedicated to the memory of my two friends, separated in my thought of them by much diversity of circumstances and opinion; linked in my faith about them to each other, and to all the shining ones of the past, by the love of God and the service of man; Thomas Hill Green (late professor of moral philosophy in the University of Oxford), died 26th March, 1882, and Laura Octavia Mary Littleton, died Easter Eve, 1886.

For once a dedication that helpfully spells out the identity of the dedicatee, or dedicatees, in this case. Still popularly known by her husband's name, the author, Mary Augusta Ward, was the daughter of Thomas Arnold, younger brother of the poet and educationist Matthew Arnold. In 1872, when she was twenty-one, she married Thomas Humphry Ward, an Oxford don and later art critic for *The Times*. Her novel here charts her spiritual pilgrimage from orthodox Christianity to a faith free from historical beliefs, in which her practical idealism could be expressed.

Mrs Humphry **Ward**, *Eleanor*, 1900

~ To Italy, the beloved and beautiful, instructress of our past, delight of our present, comrade of our future: – The heart of an Englishwoman offers this book.

Charles Dudley **Warner**, *Baddeck*, 1874

~ To my comrade, Joseph H. Twichell, Summer and Winter Friend, whose companionship would make any journey a delightful memory, these notes of a sunny fortnight in the Provinces are inscribed.

Warner was an American writer who wrote familiar essays, travel sketches, novels and the like. Twichell had been his travel companion on more than one occasion, just he had been that of Mark TWAIN (whose own dedication to him see above).

William **Warner**, *Albions England*, 1586–1612

~ To the right Honorable, my very good Lord and Maister, Henrie Carey, Baron of Hunsdon: Knight of the most noble Order of the Garter: Lord Chamberlaine of her Majesties most Honorable Houshold: Lord Governour of Barwicke: Lord Warden of the East Marches for and anempst Scotland: Lord Lieftennant of Suffolke and Norfolke: Captaine of her Majesties Gentlemen Pencioners: and one of her Highnes most Honorable Privie Councell. This our whole Iland, anciently called Brutaine, but more anciently Albion, presently containing two Kingdomes, England and Scotland, is cause (right Honorable) that to distinguish the former, whose only Occurrents I abridge, from the other, remote from our Historie, I intitle this my Booke *Albions England*; a Subject, in troth (if self conceit work not me a partial Judge) worthie your Honorable Patronage, howbeit basely passed under so badd an Author. [...] I, therefore, [...] having dedicated a former Booke to him that from your Honor deriveth his Birth, now secondly present the like to your Lordship: with so much the lesse doubt, and so much the more dutie, by how much the more I esteeme this my latter labour of more valew, and (omitting your high Titles) I owe, and your Lordship expecteth especiall duetie at the hands of your Servaunt. And thus (right Honorable) hoping better than I can performe, and yet fearing lesser than I may offend, desirous to please, desperate of praise, & destitute of a better Present, I make tender only of good will: more I have not, for your Honors good worde, lesse I hope not. Your Lordships most humble and duetifull Servant, W. Warner.

A rather anxious but naturally modest address by the author to his patron, whose 'high Titles' he enumerates in full. Henry Carey, 1st Lord Hunsdon, was Governor of Berwick (i.e., Berwick-upon-Tweed) and Chamberlain of Queen Elizabeth's Household, and was born as the son of William Carey, an official of Henry VIII's court, and Mary Carey, the sister of Anne Boleyn, Henry's ill-fated second wife, who herself was the mother of Queen Elizabeth. Warner's work, which went into several editions, was enormously popular and was a kind of episodic verse narrative mingling history and legend. *Anempst* is a form of 'anent', so means 'regarding'.

Booker T. **Washington**, *Up from Slavery: An Autobiography*, 1901

~ This volume is dedicated to my wife, Mrs Margaret James Washington, and to my brother, Mr John Washington, whose patience, fidelity, and hard work have gone far to make this work at Tuskegee successful.

The famous black American leader, son of a slave mother and a white father, founded (in 1881) and ran the Tuskegee Institute at Tuskegee, Alabama, for the practical training of blacks in various trades and professions.

William **Watson**, *The Dream of Man*, 1893

TO LONDON, MY HOSTESS
City that waitest to be sung, –
For whom no hand

> To mighty strains the lyre hath strung
>   In all this land,
> Though mightier theme the mightiest ones
>   Sang not of old,
> The thrice three sisters' Godlike sons
>   With lips of gold, –
> Till greater voice thy greatness sing
>   In loftier times,
> Suffer an alien muse to bring
>   Her votive rhymes. [...]

The first of five strained stanzas in the same vein, concluding 'Take thou my song!' Watson's verses are now all virtually forgotten, except, perhaps, for just one: 'April, April, Laugh thy girlish laughter; Then, the moment after, Weep thy girlish tears!' Love it or leave it, it is nonetheless a valid poetic concept, even if hackneyed, and much more memorable than the contrived composition above.

Isaac **Watts**, *The Knowledge of the Heavens and the Earth Made Easy*, 1725

~ To my learned friend, Mr. John Eames, Fellow of the Royal Society. Dear Sir, It would be trifling to say anything to you of the Excellency and great Advantage of these Sciences, whose first Rudiments I have here drawn up. Your Acquaintance with these Matters hath given you a just relish of the Pleasure of them, and well informed you of their solid Use. [...] Farewell, dear Sir, and forgive the Trouble that you have partly devolv'd on yourself by the too favourable Opinion you have conceived both of these Sheets and of the Writer of them, who takes a pleasure to tell the World that he is with great Sincerity, Sir, Your most obedient Servant, Isaac Watts.

The long dedication is in essence a treatise on the need for the 'unlearned' to become 'learned', or familiar with the sciences set forth in the work, otherwise 'The First Principles of Astronomy and Geography', as the subtitle explains. Today Watts is perhaps best remembered not for his scientific writings, however, but for his hymns, such as the well-known 'O God, our help in ages past' and 'When I survey the wondrous cross'. He was, after all, basically a theologian. Eames, who died in 1744, was a (dissenting) tutor in natural science, and edited this work, as the dedication implies. He published nothing of his own, but was involved in the production of several academic works written by others. Watts called him 'the most learned man I ever knew'.

Theodore **Watts-Dunton**, *Aylwin*, 1898

~ To C.J.R., in remembrance of sunny days and starlit nights when we rambled together on crumbling cliffs that are now at the bottom of the sea, this edition of a story which has been a link between us is inscribed.

The dedicatee was the author's future wife, Clara Jane Reich, whom he did not marry, however, until 1905, when he was seventy-three. Watts-Dunton (who was Theodore Watts until 1897, when he added his mother's maiden name of Dunton) is best remembered for being a close friend of Rossetti, who is portrayed in fictional form in his novel here, and for looking after the poet Swinburne in his own home for thirty years when the latter was in abject circumstances. See SWINBURNE's own dedication, and also that of BARONESS ORCZY.

Auberon **Waugh**, *Country Topics*, 1974

~ For My Children, Sophia, Alexander, Daisy, and Nathaniel, all honour and glory through the ages.

A dedication to his two sons and two daughters for one of his many books by the writer, columnist and reviewer who is the son of EVELYN WAUGH.

Evelyn **Waugh**, *Put Out More Flags*, 1942

~ To Major Randolph Churchill, 4th Hussars, Member of Parliament. Dear Randolph, I am afraid that these pages may not be altogether acceptable to your ardent and sanguine nature. They deal, mostly, with a race of ghosts, the survivors of the world we both knew ten years ago, which you have outflown in the empyrean of strenuous politics, but where my imagination still fondly lingers. [...] These characters are no longer contemporary in sympathy; they were forgotten even before the war; but they live on delightfully in holes and corners and, like everyone else, they have been disturbed by the rough intrusion of current history. Here they are in that odd, dead period before the Churchillian renaissance, which people called at the time the Great Bore War. So please accept them with the sincere regards of Your affectionate friend, The Author.

Waugh wrote this novel in the Second World War while serving in the Royal Marines. His dedicatee, Randolph Churchill, was the colourful son of Winston Churchill and the writer of biographies of Lord Derby and Anthony Eden. He and Waugh were close friends, and were together on a military mission in Yugoslavia in 1944, with Churchill acting as an intelligence officer. Both men died when still middle-aged: Waugh in 1966, aged sixty-three, and Churchill two years later, aged fifty-seven.

Alice **Weber**, *When I'm a Man*, nd (*c.* 1880)

~ To Ethel and Maimie, and a certain arm-chair.

B.L. Putnam **Weale**, *The Unknown God*, 1911

~ To a pair of bright eyes, laughing under a green hat.

The author, whose real name was Bertram Lenox Simpson, was an English journalist who wrote many books on the Far East, such as *Indiscreet Letters from Peking* (1911), *The Truth about China and Japan* (1919), and the like. He died in 1930, aged fifty-three.

John **Webster**, *The Duchess of Malfi*, 1623

~ To the Right Honourable George Harding, Baron Berkeley, of Berkeley Castle, and Knight of the Order of the Bath to the Illustrious Prince Charles. My noble lord, That I may present my excuse why, being a stranger to your lordship, I offer this poem to your patronage, I plead this warrant: men who never saw the sea yet desire to behold that regiment of waters, choose some eminent river to guide them thither, and make that, as it were, their conduct or postilion: by the like ingenious means has your fame arrived at my knowledge, receiving it from some of worth, who both in contemplation and practice owe to your honour their clearest service. [...] I am confident this work is not unworthy your honour's perusal; for by such poems as this poets have kissed the hands of great princes, and drawn their gentle eyes to look down upon their sheets of paper when the poets themselves were bound up in their winding-sheets. The like courtesy from your lordship shall make you live in your grave, and laurel spring out of it, when the ignorant scorners of the Muses, that like worms in libraries seem to live only to destroy learning, shall wither neglected and forgotten. This work and myself I humbly present to your approved censure, it being the utmost of my wishes to have your honourable self my weighty and perspicuous comment; which grace so done me shall ever be acknowledged, by your lordship's in all duty and observance, John Webster.

A version in modern spelling of the dedication by the fine Jacobean tragedian to the 8th Baron Berkeley, aged only twenty-two at the time, who two years earlier had been the dedicatee of Burton's *Anatomy of Melancholy*.

Noah **Webster**, Jun., *Dissertations on the English Language*, 1789
~ To His Excellency Benjamin Franklin, Esq., LL.D., F.R.S., Late President of the Commonwealth of Pennsylvania, the following Dissertations are most respectfully inscribed by His Excellency's most obliged and most obedient servant, The Author.

A supporting essay follows, saying that the writer has chosen Franklin not because he is a great man, but because he is 'great in common things'. He died the following year, aged eighty-four. Noah Webster was the author of the famous *Webster's Dictionary*, first published in 1828, and the American equivalent of the *Oxford English Dictionary*.

John **Weever**, *Ancient Funerall Monuments*, 1631
~ To the Sacred and Imperiall Majestie of our dread Soveraigne, the most magnificent, illustrious, and puissant Monarch, CHARLES, by the divine Providence, of Great Britaine, France, Ireland and many Ilands, King, the most powerfull protector of the Faith, the most royal patron, preserver, and fosterer of the undoubted religion of Jesus Christ, the Patterne of true pietie and Justice and the President of all Princely vertues, His Highnesse most lowly and most loyall subject John Weever in all humility consecrateth these his labours, though farre unworthy the view of so resplendent a greatnesse.

In the original, this florid tribute is displayed in the form of a multifold cross in thirty-three lines, with 'To' by itself as the top line and 'greatnesse' as the 'base'. Weever was obviously a believer in the grandiose, and the full title of his work here almost matches the dedication to Charles I: 'Ancient Funerall Monuments within the United Monarchie of Great Britaine, Ireland, and the Islands adjacent, with the dissolved monasteries therein contained, their Founders and what Eminent Persons have been in the same interred'. However, lengthy titles were not uncommon in his day. This work, and its dedication, contrast completely with a minuscule book produced earlier by Weever. This was a tiny 'thumb-book', 1½ inches high, giving a poetical account of the life of Christ. Its title was simply *Agnus Dei* (1606), and its dedication was just 'To Prince Henry. Your humble servant. Jo. Weever'. Not, of course, that he had much room for more. The dedicatee was also of limited size: James I's son, Prince Henry Frederick, then aged twelve.

Molly **Weir**, *Best Foot Forward*, 1972

~ To my mother, and to all of that gallant band who were sojer-clad, but major-minded.

A volume of autobiography by the popular Scottish actress.

H.G. **Wells**, *Meanwhile, The Picture of a Lady*, 1933

~ One day about the time of the general strike in England I visited the celebrated garden of La Mortola near Ventimiglia. As I wandered about that lovely place, I passed by an unknown little lady sitting and reading in a shady corner. Her pose reminded me of another little lady who has always been very dear to me. [...] I went my way to the beach and sat there and as I mused on things that were happening in England and Italy and the world at large, that remembered and reinforced personality mingled with my thoughts, became a sort of frame for my thoughts, and this story very much as I have shaped it here presented itself suddenly to my imagination. [...] I went home and began to write. The garden of this book is by no means a replica of the garden of La Mortola, which was merely the inspiring point of departure for this fantasia of ideas, this picture of a mind and of a world in a phase of expectation. Gorge and Caatinga you will seek at La Mortola in vain. But all sorts of things grow upon that wonderful corner of sunlit soil, and this novel, which I dedicate very gratefully to the real owners of the garden, gratefully and a little apologetically because of the freedoms I have taken with their home, is only the least and latest product of its catholic fertility. H.G. Wells.

The substance of a slightly longer 'Preface Dedicatory', explaining the rather romantic genesis of this particular novel, one of Wells's lesser works, dealing with issues topical at the time, such as the General Strike, but now very dated and mostly polemic in the form of 'meaningful conversations'.

Carol **Wensby-Scott**, *Lion Invincible*, 1984

~ To the memory of Richard Plantagenet, King of England; neither saint nor devil but merely human.

The book is a study of the king and his times.

Morris **West**, *The Navigator*, 1976

~ This book is for those of us, children still, who, even at the gates of midnight, dream of sunrise.

A story of mystery and adventure on board ship.

Sir George Wharton, *Calendarium Ecclesiasticum*, 1660
~ To the truly honourable that signal embleme of Englands Pristine Gallantry, John Lewkener, of Hungerford Parke, Esq., the author (out of gratitude for civilities received) humbly offereth these his this yeares observations.

The work is one of the annual almanacs published by the famous astrologer and royalist. For a dedication to another year's issue he broke into second-rate verse, with the following tribute to Charles II:

'Some Princes have been surnamed Red, some Black,
Some Tall, some Crooked (as well in Mind as) Back;
Some for their Learning, some for valour stand,
Admired by this learned and warlike land;
Our gracious King's both Black and Tall of stature,
Learned, valiant, wise and liberal too, by nature.
But that adorns Him more than all the Rest,
Is mercy in his most Religious Breast;
Which mixed with Justice, makes him thus to shine,
The increasing glory of the Regal line.'

Dennis Wheatley, *Such Power is Dangerous*, 1933
~ To J.G.L., in memory of an expedition across a marsh and of a thousand hospitalities. D.W.

Dennis Wheatley, *The Fabulous Valley*, 1934
~ To Peggy and Bino, together with those many South African friends in London and the Union whose kindness enabled me to enjoy every moment of my stay in their wonderful country.

Dennis Wheatley, *Contraband*, 1936
~ To my old friend, Frank van Zwanenberg, in memory of many kindnesses, and because he likes 'straight' thrillers.

Dennis Wheatley, *The Quest of Julian Day*, 1939
~ For His Excellency Russell pacha, in friendship, admiration, and gratitude for the central theme of this story which he gave me by telling me about the lost legions of the Cambyses one night in Cairo.

Dennis Wheatley, *The Rising Storm*, 1949
~ I dedicate this book to my mother, with love and in grateful memory of my first visits with her to Paris, Versailles and Fontainebleau.

The story is set in 1789, at the time of the French Revolution. See also the next dedication below.

Dennis Wheatley, *The Man who Killed the King*, 1951
~ For my grand-daughter, Antonia, and my step-grand-children, Caroline,

Maxine, Christopher, Julian and James, this story which, with its predecessor *The Rising Storm*, will give them, when they are old enough, the whole true picture of the French Revolution in 'history without tears'.

See above.

Dennis **Wheatley**, *Traitors' Gate*, 1958

~ For my friend and war-time colleague, Colonel Sir Ronald Wingate, C.I.E., O.B.E., who was so often ahead of official 'Intelligence' in correctly appreciating future enemy intentions, and whose humour, unruffled calm and wisdom were in time of stress a tonic to all.

Dennis **Wheatley**, *The Satanist*, 1960

~ To the memory of that most illustrious story-teller, Alexandre Dumas Père, whose books gave me enormous pleasure when I was a boy. [...]

Dennis **Wheatley**, *Vendetta in Spain*, 1961

~ For Shelagh, *still,* 'the dazzling young Duchess of Westminster', *who knew and loved Spain at the period of the story.*

A footnote attributes the quotation to Robert Sencourt in *King Alfonso* (Faber & Faber, 1942).

Dennis **Wheatley**, *Mayhem in Greece*, 1962

~ For Helen, a long overdue 'thank you' for securing me my first review in the *Sunday Times*, and for many years of friendship. And for my good friend, John.

Dennis **Wheatley**, *The Sultan's Daughter*, 1963

~ For Derrick Morley, Ambassador Extraordinary and 'Most Secret' during the years we spent together in the Offices of the War Cabinet, and for Marie Jose, this tale of great days in France. With my love to you both, Dennis.

Dennis **Wheatley**, *Bill for the Use of a Body*, 1964

~ For Sheila, and for all those who showed such gracious hospitality to my wife and myself while we were in the Far East.

Dennis **Wheatley**, *Unholy Crusade*, 1967

~ With love, for 'Smallest Daughter' Sheilakin, with whom my wife and I spent our happiest days in Mexico.

Dennis **Wheatley**, *The Ravishing of Lady Mary Ware*, 1971

~ As several chapters of this book concern Marshal Bernadotte, the founder of the present Royal House of Sweden, I take great pleasure in dedicating it to my friend Iwan Hedman, who has done so much to popularise the Swedish translations of my books.

Dennis **Wheatley**, *The Strange Story of Linda Lee*, 1972

~ For Jim and Helen Phillipson, at whose home, the Manor House, Everton, the plot of this story was thought out early in the mornings of a Saturday and a Sunday.

Dennis **Wheatley**, *Desperate Measures*, 1974

~ In 1940 I dedicated a book to 'My soldier stepson, with deep affection and the wish that crossed swords and batons may one day grace the shoulders of his tunic'. Jack Younger had then just left Sandhurst and I watched him as an ensign in the Coldstream Guards march off from Chelsea Barracks to the war in North Africa. Now he wears those crossed swords of a Major General on the shoulders of his tunic and I am so happy to dedicate this book to him.

The story is set in the Napoleonic Wars. Major General Sir John William Younger, now retired (he was sixty-nine in 1989), was Commissioner-in-Chief of the St John Ambulance Brigade for the last five years of his working life. And something of Dennis Wheatley's working life is represented by the selection of dedications above. He died in 1977, aged eighty, the author of seventy-five books.

George **Whetstone**, *Promos and Cassandra*, 1578

~ To his worshipfull friende and Kinseman, William Fleetewoode Esquier, Recorder of London. Syr, (desirous to acquite your tryed frendships with some token of good will) of late I perused divers of my unperfect workes, fully minded to bestowe on you the travell of some of my forepassed time. But (resolved to accompanye the adventurous Captaine Syr Humfrey Gylbert in his honorable voiadge) I found my leysure too littel to correct the errors in my sayd workes. So that (inforced) I lefte them disparsed amonge my learned freendes, at theyr leasure to polish, if I faild to returne: spoyling (by this meanes) my studdy of his necessarye furnyture. Amonge other unregarded papers, I fownde this Discource of Promos and Cassandra; which for the rarenesse (& the needeful knowledge) of the necessary matter contained therein (to make the actions appeare more lively) I devided the whole history into two Commedies, for that, decorum used, it would not be convayed in one. [...] Although the worke (because of evel handlinge) be unworthy your learned Censure, allowe (I beseeche you) of my good wyll, untyl leasure serves me to perfect some labour of more worthe. No more, but that almightye God be your protector, and preserve me from dainger in this voiadge, the xxix of July, 1578. Your Kinsman to use, George Whetstone.

Whetstone had taken his story of Promos and Cassandra from a tale by the sixteenth-century Italian writer Cinthio, and his version of it, although never acted as a play, in turn served as the basis for Shakespeare's *Measure for Measure*. The story concerns a heroine who sacrifices her virtue (to put it in the manner of the day) in order to save her brother from death. (In Shakespeare's play, Promos is Claudio, and Cassandra Isabella.) Much of Whetstone's dedication to Fleetwood is taken up with a criticism of the contemporary theatre.

William **Whewell**, *Philosophy of the Inductive Sciences*, 1847

~ To the Rev. Adam Sedgwick: When I showed you the last sheet of my *History of the Inductive Sciences* in its transit through the press, you told me that I ought to add a paragraph or two at the end, by way of Moral to the story; and I replied that the Moral would be as long as the story itself. The present work, the Moral which you then desired, I have, with some effort, reduced within a somewhat smaller compass than I then spoke of; and I cannot dedicate it to anyone with so much pleasure as to you. It has always been my wish that, as far and as long as men might known anything of me by my writing, they should hear of me along with the friends with whom I have lived, whom I have loved, and by whose conversation I have been animated to hope that I too might add something to the literature of our country. [...]

The dedication concludes with a reference to the college to which both men belonged, 'and in which we have lived together so long and so happily': Whewell was Master of Trinity College, Cambridge and twice Vice Chancellor of the University, while Sedgwick was Professor of Geology there.

Alan **Whicker**, *Whicker's World Down Under*, 1988

~ For the pertinently named Dorothy Fremantle (as was – before she collected a hyphen), with love.

An account by the well-known television broadcaster of the ten programmes he had made in Australia as one of his *Whicker's World* series ('Living with Waltzing Matilda') over the previous twelve months.

John D. **Whidden**, *Ocean Life in the Old Sailing-Ship Days*, 1908

~ To Captain Joseph W. Clapp of Nantucket: Dear Old Boy: – Although nearly fourscore years have silvered your head, yet you retain your mirth and sense of humor, as evidenced by your frequent letters, which have been to me a source of inspiration. To you, then, in memory of the pleasant days passed in genial companionship in old Montevideo, S.A., upwards of forty years ago, this work is affectionately dedicated by the author.

'S.A' is of course South America.

James McNeill **Whistler**, *The Gentle Art of Making Enemies*, 1890

~ To the rare Few, who, early in life, have rid themselves of the Friendship of the Many, these pathetic Papers are inscribed.

A witty, sophisticated work by the famous American painter.

Frederick **White**, *Good and Bad Cats*, 1911

~ To Fuzzy-Wuzzy – a perfectly good cat except when she is bad or (as is usually the case) utterly indifferent.

Katherine **Whitehorn**, *View from a Column*, 1981

~ To Margaret Grat, Aunt of Aunts, who not content with being the sanest woman I know goes about recklessly saving the sanity of other people including me.

Katherine Whitehorn, wife of the writer Gavin Lyall, has been a regular columnist for various British publications since 1960, and, since 1980, assistant editor of *The Observer*.

John Greenleaf **Whittier**, *Snow-Bound*, 1866

~ To the memory of the household it describes, this poem is dedicated by the Author.

The poem, one of the American poet's best, is subtitled 'A Winter Idyll' and recalls his boyhood, when a sudden snowstorm would frequently transform his parents' Massachusetts farm, causing normal routine to be disrupted. A note to the poem says: 'The inmates of the family at the Whittier homestead who are referred to in the poem were my father, mother, my brother and two sisters, and my uncle and aunt, both unmarried. In addition there was the district schoolmaster who boarded with us'.

Jeremiah H. **Wiffen**, *Jerusalem Delivered: Translated into English Spenserian Verse from the Italian of Torquato Tasso*, 1826

> TO GEORGIANA, DUCHESS OF BEDFORD
> Years have flown o'er since first my soul aspired
>   In song the sacred Missal to repeat,
> Which sainted Tasso write with pen inspired –
>   Told is my rosary, and the task complete:
> And now, 'twixt hope and fear, with toil untired,
>   I cast the ambrosial relique at thy feet;
> Not without faith that in thy goodness thou
> Wilt deign one smile to my accomplish'd vow. [...]
>
> Thus then, O Lady, with thy name I grace
>   The glorious fable; fitly, since to thee
> And thine the thanks are due, that in the face
>   Of time and toil, the Poets' devotee
> Has raised the enchanted structure on its base,
>   And to thy hand now yields th' unclosing key, –
> Blest, if in one bright intellect like thine,
> He wins regard, and build himself a shrine!

The first and last stanzas of the six-stanza dedication to the second wife of John Russell, 6th Duke of Bedford, for whom Wiffen worked as librarian at Woburn Abbey, and to whom he dedicated his translation of *Garcia Lasso de la Vega* (1823). Wiffen's translation of the fourth book of *Jerusalem Delivered* was published in 1821, with the complete work, delayed by a fire in the printing office, appearing in 1824. The edition here was the second.

Kate Douglas **Wiggin**, *Kindergarten Chimes*, 1890

~ To the hundreds of little children who have clustered round my knee, this book is lovingly dedicated, in the hope that when their yellow hair shall have changed to silver, and the dimples give place to wrinkles, there will still be an echo in their hearts of the rhymes and songs of their childhood days.

Kate Wiggin, née Smith, was an American author and kindergarten teacher, whose husband, Samuel B. Wiggin, had died unexpectedly the previous year, when she was still only thirty-three. Her best-known book is almost certainly *Rebecca of Sunnybrook Farm* (1903), about a lovable but precocious little girl. In 1878 she had founded the first kindergarten west of the Rockies, in a San Francisco slum. Compare her dedication below.

Kate Douglas **Wiggin**, *The Village Watch-Tower*, 1895

~ Dear Old Apple-Tree, under whose gnarled branches these stories were written, to you I dedicate the book. My head was so close to you, who can tell from whence the thoughts came. I only know that when all the other trees in the orchard were barren, there were always stories to be found under your branches, and so it is our joint book, dear apple-tree. [...] It should be a lovely book, dear apple-tree, but alas, it is not altogether that, because I am not so simple as you, and because I have strayed farther away from the heart of Mother Nature.

Written in Hollis, Maine, on 12 August 1895, when she was thirty-nine. She died, aged sixty-seven, in 1923.

Maurice **Wiggin**, *Fishing for Beginners*, 1962

~ To Farmer Tom Jones of Bramshott Chase in the County of Hampshire, keenest and kindest (and ever a boy at heart) this book is affectionately dedicated.

Wiggin, fifty when this was published, was a noted journalist and writer on books and country matters. Compare his dedication below.

Maurice **Wiggin**, *My Life on Wheels*, 1963

~ The bit I like best about writing a book is the dedication, though I sometimes wonder who reads it, apart from me. I always read it. Well, however that may be, this one I inscribe with unequivocal and unabashed affection TO THE GOOD COMPANIONS of many a hilarious, adventurous, ludicrous, perilous or plain laborious session, on the road or in the workshop or simply at the fireside living it all over again. [...] Namely, Eddie Dawson, Alistair Bartlett, John Pézare, Tim Solly, and Bill Smith. Not forgetting for a moment the green memory of Hardy, so gallant and so gay.

A journalist's loving account of the various new and second-hand cars he has owned and driven over the years. This was Wiggin's ninth book, written when he was television critic of the *Sunday Times Weekly Review*. Compare his dedication above.

Oscar **Wilde,** *The Ballad of Reading Gaol*, 1898
~ In memoriam C.T.W., sometime Trooper of the Royal Horse Guards, obiit H.M. Prison, Reading, Berkshire, July 7, 1896.

Wilde's famous poem was entirely inspired by the arrival at Reading Gaol, where he himself was interned, of Trooper C.T. Wooldridge, who had been charged with, and was in prison executed for, the murder of his young wife in a fit of rage. The poem was first published under Wilde's prison number, 'C3.3'.

Eric **Williams,** *Dragoman*, 1959
~ In the summer of 1956 my wife and I were, as every Party member we met told us, 'privileged' to be the first Westerners to wander alone and camp like gypsies through Communist Hungary, Rumania and Bulgaria. Wherever we went we were made welcome by those whom the same Party members called 'the masses'; and it is to the people, the individual men and women, of those three beautiful East European countries, that I dedicate this story in the hope and belief that they will, one day, break free.

A novel set in Eastern Europe, telling how Roger Starte and his wife agree to smuggle an agent out to the West. Today, thirty years and more on, his hope looks like being fulfilled.

Philip **Williams,** *Hugh Gaitskell: A Political Biography*, 1979
~ To the memory of Charles Anthony Raven Crosland, admired and beloved friend for forty years.

The Labour Foreign Secretary, Anthony Crosland, who died in 1977 when only fifty-nine, was often confused in the public mind with Hugh Gaitskell, the Labour party leader, who also died young, in 1963 when fifty-seven.

Henry **Williamson,** *Tarka the Otter*, 1927
~ Dedicated to the memory of William Henry Rogers, Esquire, late Tutor in college at Eton, and sometime Master of the Cheriton Hunt.

Henry **Williamson,** *Salar the Salmon*, 1935
~ To T.E. Lawrence of *Seven Pillars of Wisdom* and V.M. Yeates of *Winged Victory*.

Williamson, who died in 1977, was a close friend of 'Lawrence of Arabia' and wrote a biography of him, published in 1941. The two books here are among his best known, as moving tales of animal life.

J. Tuzo **Wilson,** *One Chinese Moon*, 1959
~ Indulgent reader, be warned that an altogether worthless fellow who has written no books now essays to be an author. Only a weakness of understanding and an excess of conceit allow him to offer his services as a guide on a journey along the labyrinthine paths of China, concerning which he should be the first to plead

ignorance and to admit but a passing acquaintance. The results of his labours would indeed be unworthy of consideration by your discerning eye and spacious intellect if it had not been smoothed by the skill and lightened by the wit of that fountain of tranquil comprehension to whom this book is fondly dedicated, MY NUMBER ONE WIFE.

The Canadian author, John Tuzo Wilson, was fifty when his first book here was published and in academic life Professor of Physics at Toronto University. His 'Number One Wife' was Isabela Jean Dickson, whom he had married in 1938. A Sinophile, his hobbies included sailing a Hong Kong junk.

Steve **Wilson**, *Dealer's Move*, 1978
~ This here's for Shrap, Frankie, Mrs. and the Piglet. They know who they are.

They *sound* like family.

Woodrow **Wilson**, *The New Freedom*, 1913
~ To every man or woman who may derive from it, in however small a degree, the impulse of unselfish public service.

By the 28th United States President who was a noted liberal reformer.

John **Wingate**, *Frigate*, 1980
~ This book is dedicated to the single biggest factor in war: the man.

A former naval officer and schoolmaster, Wingate is the author of a number of nautical tales for boys, of which this is one. It appeared, the first of a trilogy, when he was sixty.

Helen M. **Winslow**, *Concerning Cats: My Own and Some Others*, 1900
~ To the 'Pretty Lady', who never betrayed a secret, broke a promise, or proved an unfaithful friend; who had all the virtues and none of the failings of her sex, I dedicate this volume.

Shelley **Winters**, *Shelley: Also Known as Shirley*, 1981
~ For Blanche, who has always made my reach exceed my grasp.

The autobiography of the famous film actress, whose original name was Shirley Schrift.

Owen **Wister**, *The Virginian*, 1904
~ To Theodore Roosevelt: Some of these pages you have seen, some you have praised, one stands new-written because you blamed it; and all, my dear critic, beg leave to remind you of their author's changeless admiration.

Wister, an American novelist, famous for his Westerns, was a friend of the United States president, and in 1930 published *Roosevelt: The Story of a Friendship, 1880–1919*, the latter year being that of Roosevelt's death. Wister himself was a grandson of the English actress Fanny Kemble.

George **Wither,** *Abuses Stript and Whipt*, 1613

~ To himself G.W. wisheth all happinesse. [...] But because I begin to grow tedious to my owne selfe, since therfore I shall have opportunitie enough to consider with thee what is further needful without an epistle: with my Prayers for my prince, my country, my friends, and my owne prosperitie, without any leave-taking or commendations of my Selfe, I hartily wish my owne soul to fare-well. Thy princes, thy Countries, thy friends, thine owne, whilst reason masters affection, Geo. Wither.

The collection of satirical essays (which got him into trouble) is dedicated by the poet to himself, with most of his dedication devoted to giving seven reasons why he should choose to do so in preference to appealing to a patron.

P.G. **Wodehouse,** *The Adventures of Sally*, 1923

DEDICATION TO GEORGE GROSSMITH

Dear George, The production of our mutual effort, The Cabaret Girl, is a week distant as I write this; and who shall say what the harvest will be? But, whether a week from now we are slapping each other on the back or shivering in the frost, nothing can alter the fact that we had a lot of fun writing the thing together. Not a reproach or a nasty look from start to finish. Because of this, and because you and I were side by side through the Adventure of the Ship's Bore, the Episode of the Concert In Aid of the Seamen's Orphans and Widows, and The Sinister Affair of the Rose of Stamboul, I dedicate this book to you. P.G. Wodehouse.

The dedicatee was the actor-manager and playwright son of the identically named author (with his brother Weedon) of the classic comic novel, *The Diary of a Nobody* (1894). With some justification, *The Times* obituary of Wodehouse (died 1975) claimed that his own novels were the finest examples of English humour since the publication of that very book.

P.G. **Wodehouse,** *The Heart of a Goof*, 1926

~ To my daughter Leonora without whose never-failing sympathy and encouragement this book would have been finished in half the time.

A traditional humorous dedication that has occurred many times since, and which may not have been original to Wodehouse in the first place. The dedicatee was actually his step-daughter, the child of Ethel Rowley, née Newton, the widow that he married in 1914. Leonora herself later married (in 1932) the racehorse trainer Peter Cazalet, but died while undergoing a minor operation in 1944.

P.G. **Wodehouse,** *The Gold Bat*, 1974

~ To that Prince of Slackers, Herbert Westbrook.

One of 'Plum's' last books.

Thomas **Wolfe,** *Of Time and the River*, 1935

~ To Maxwell Evarts Perkins, a great editor and a brave and honest man, who stuck to the writer of the book through times of bitter hopelessness and doubt and would not let him give in to his own despair, a work to be known as 'Of Time and the River' is dedicated with the hope that all of it may be in some way worthy of the loyal devotion and the patient care which a dauntless and unshaken friend has give to each part of it, and without which none of it could have been written.

A generous tribute by the American novelist. But Wolfe was as impetuous as he was impassioned, and shortly after writing this dedication, he left both Perkins and his publisher in a huff. He died three years later, still only thirty-eight, after two operations for a brain infection. The novel itself continues the story of Eugene Gant, the hero of Wolfe's earlier bestseller, *Look Homeward, Angel* (1929), which was strongly autobiographical.

Henry **Wood**, *Ideal Suggestion through Mental Photography*, 1893
~ Fraternally dedicated to all seekers for Truth, with whom it stands above Sect, System or Conventionality.

James **Woodforde**, *The Diary of a Country Parson. 1758–1802*, 1924–31
~ To Lord Fitzmaurice of Leigh, In Memory of many Good Talks of HISTORY, BOOKS, and MEN in a Wiltshire Garden.

The highly readable record of the daily life of a rural clergyman in Somerset and Norfolk, published long posthumously. Despite the wording of the dedication, the *Diary* itself is quite devoid of any intellectual content, and merely records the details of local events, from household remedies to cricket matches. Example: 'I wore my largest gouty Shoes to Church today.'

George Frederick **Wright**, *The Ice Age in North America*, 1911
~ To Elisha Gray, Chevalier de la légion d'honneur, inventor of the harmonic telegraph, the telephone and the telautograph, whose intelligent interest in glacial geology and whose generous appreciation of my work has been a constant inspiration, this volume is affectionately dedicated.

Gray *claimed* to have invented the telephone, true, but after a long and bitter legal battle, the US Supreme Court found in favour of Alexander Graham Bell. The telautograph was a sort of primitive fax machine, transmitting facsimiles by telegraph.

Harold Bell **Wright**, *That Printer of Udell's*, 1903
~ To that friend whose life has taught me many beautiful truths; whose words have strengthened and encouraged me to live more true to my God, my fellows and myself; who hoped for me when others lost hope; who believed in me when others could not; who saw good when others looked for evil; to that friend, whoever he is, wherever he may be, I affectionately dedicate this story. H.B.W.

Presumably an ideal friend rather than an actual one. This was an early novel by the popular American writer whose stories were almost all set in the open spaces of the American Southwest or, like this one, Midwest, and that combined human love with a love for adventure and wholesome, manly morality.

Mabel Osgood **Wright**, *Flowers and Ferns in their Haunts*, 1901

~ This book is dedicated to Nell Gwyn my pony – by whose name there hangs a tale – in recognition of our friendship, and of her intelligence in knowing where to stand still.

The American writer was well known for her nature books, such as this one. Maybe her pony was partial to oranges? Or formed a meaningful relationship with a pony called Charles?

William **Wycherley**, *The Plain-Dealer*, 1677

~ To My Lady B——. Madam, Though I never had the honour to receive a favour from you, nay, or be known to you, I take the confidence of an author to write to you a *billet-doux* dedicatory; – which is no new thing. For by most dedications it appears that authors, though they praise their patrons from top to toe, and seem to turn 'em inside out, know 'em as little as sometimes their patrons their books, though they read them out; and if the poetical daubers did not write the name of the man or woman on top of the picture, 'twere impossible to guess whose it were. But you, madam, without the help of a poet, have made yourself known and famous in the world; and because you do not want it, are therefore most worthy of an epistle dedicatory. And this play claims naturally your protection, since it has lost its reputation with the ladies of stricter lives in the playhouse; and, you know, when men's endeavours are discountenanced and refused by the nice coy women of honour, they come to you. [...] And of you, madam, I ought to say no more here, for your virtues deserve a poem rather than an epistle, or a volume entire to give the world your memoirs, or life at large; and which (upon the word of an author that has a mind to make an end of his dedication) I promise to do, when I write the annals of our British love, which shall be dedicated to the ladies concerned, if they will not think them something too obscene too; when your life, compared with many that are thought innocent, I doubt not, may vindicate you, and me, to the world, for the confidence I have taken in this address to you; which then may be thought neither impertinent nor immodest; and whatsoever your amorous misfortunes have been, none can charge you with that heinous, and worst of women's crimes, hypocrisy. [...] But you, in fine, madam, are not more a hypocrite than I am when I praise you; therefore I doubt not will be thought (even by yours and the play's enemies, the nicest ladies) to be the fittest patroness for, madam, your Ladyship's most obedient, faithful, humble servant, and the PLAIN DEALER.

Wycherley addressed his mock fulsome dedication to the noted Covent Garden procuress, 'Mother Bennett', using it as a 'counterblast' to dedications of this type to Nell Gwyn, such as those by APHRA BEHN and THOMAS DUFFETT (above). The play, Wycherley's fourth and last, is a robustly satirical version of Molière's much gentler *Le Misanthrope*. Like his earlier and more obviously indecent comedy, *The Country Wife* (1675), it had shocked the sensibilities of many of those who saw it, as he here indicates. The play's dedication, however, was admired by many of Wycherley's literary contemporaries, such as Steele, who in No 266 of his *Spectator* wrote: 'The ironical commendation of the industry and charity of these antiquated ladies, these directors of Sin, after they can no longer commit it, makes up the beauty of the inimitable dedication to *The Plain Dealer*, and is a masterpiece of raillery on this vice.' The original is at least four times as long as the extracts quoted here, much of it outspoken ('You have been a constant scourge to the old lecher and often a terror to the young', and the like).

John Allan Wyeth, *Life of General Nathan Bedford Forrest*, 1901

~ To Emma Sanson. A woman worthy of being remembered by her countrymen as long as courage is deemed a virtue, who rode with General Forrest in the engagement at Black Creek, May 2, 1863, and by guiding his men to an unguarded ford, enabled him to capture Colonel A.D. Streight and his entire command, – this volume is dedicated as a token of admiration and respect.

General Forrest was a Confederate leader in the American Civil War who after a succession of defeats and victories, like the one outlined here, was finally obliged to surrender at Selma, Alabama, in 1865.

❦ Y ❦

Chelsea Quinn **Yarbro**, *False Dawn*, 1978
~ For Bonnie Dalzell, Jane Robinson, and Diana Thatcher, who remember what happened to the dinosaur.

A science fiction novel.

Dornford **Yates**, *Lower than Vermin*, 1950
~ To the Gentlemen of the Old School, who, whether they were peers or ploughmen, masters or servants, shop-assistants or statesmen – whatever walk of life they adorned, justly commanded the respect of their fellow men.

Frank **Yerby**, *Tobias and the Angel*, 1975
~ For my sons, Jac and Jan, who being of this generation, dwell quite comfortably in vast aqueous dreamscapes, very similar to the ones evoked in this book, whose shores are but obliquely tangential to what *mine* thought of as reality, swimming through them as easily, as gracefully as fish do through water. Or – as do lemmings, in certain cycles of what men call time ...

Yerby is a black American novelist who gained overnight fame with his historical bestseller *The Foxes of Harrow* (1947), set in the pre-Civil War South. Most of his novels since then have been similarly historical. This one, published when he was sixty, is set in 1922, that is, if time has any meaning for the hero, Tobias Tobit, who has just come out of a psychiatric hospital.

Francis Brett **Young**, *The Island*, 1944
FOR JESSICA, 1904–1944
Dearest, in all my life I have known but two
Unwavering loves: for England, and for you:
What then more just than that this tribute paid
To one should at the other's feet be laid?

Jessica Hankinson was a school gym teacher who first met Young when he was twenty, in 1904. They married four years later, and she subsequently became a concert singer. The year 1944 was not only that of the book's publication but their fortieth wedding anniversary. The book itself, which took four years to write, was Young's most ambitious work, inspired by the Battle of Britain, and giving a poetic narration of Britain's island history from the beginnings to 1940, using a verse form appropriate to each period. The strain of writing it broke Young's health, and on medical advice he and his wife moved to South Africa, where he died ten years later, aged seventy.

❦ Z ❦

Adam **Zameenzad**, *The Thirteenth House*, 1987

~ For Hilary. When the world shut its door, she came in through the cat-flap and helped me to live. It was hard to write with her sitting on my typewriter; it is harder now, without. With gratitude, love and grief.

The account of one person's oppressed life in Pakistan.

Israel **Zangwill**, *The Melting Pot*, 1908

~ To Theodore Roosevelt, in respectful recognition of his strenuous struggle against forces that threaten to shipwreck the Great Republic, which carried mankind and its Fortunes, this play is, by his kind permission, cordially dedicated.

This was Zangwill's most popular play, describing immigrant Jewish life in the United States, and expressing his own views as a campaigner for Jewish rights. He himself was born in London, of Russian-Jewish descent. He died in 1926, aged sixty-two.

BIBLIOGRAPHY

Source material on dedications divides quite neatly into books and articles. Of the *books*, the following are the most comprehensive:

Mary Elizabeth Brown, *Dedications: An Anthology of the Forms Used From the Earliest Days of Book-making to the Present Time*, G.P. Putnam's Sons, New York and London, 1913.

Clara Gebert, ed., *An Anthology of Elizabethan Dedications*, Philadelphia University Press, Philadelphia 1933.

William F. Hazlitt, *Prefaces, Dedications, Epistles, Selected from Early English Books, 1540–1701*, privately printed, 1874.

Henry B. Wheatley, *The Dedication of Books to Patron and Friend: A Chapter in Literary History*, Elliot Stock, London, 1887.

When it comes to *articles*, the field is more diffuse. Learned literary journals such as *Notes and Queries* constantly contribute to the subject, and readers can consult their indexes. Certain individual articles in more accessible publications deserve a mention here, as do more popular pieces on the subject in general magazines and newspapers. So the reader anxious for more could try one or more of the following:

Cleveland Amory, 'Trade Winds', in *Saturday Review*, 27 November 1971.

Anonymous, 'Dedications', in *All The Year Round*, 26 September 1891.

Anonymous, 'To Irma, Who Will Know Why', in *The Christian Century*, 25 January 1961.

J. Sydney Boot, 'Some Curious Dedications', in *The Gentleman's Magazine*, June 1907.

István Csicsery-Rónay, 'The Art of Book Dedication', in *Library Journal*, June 1957.

Edmund Gosse, 'Elizabethan Dedications of Books', in *Harper's Monthly Magazine*, July 1902.

John Grigg, 'Their Words Their Bond', in *The Times*, 2 January 1988.

John Gross, 'The Fine Art of Dedicating', in *New York Times Book Review*, 29 April 1984.

Christopher Hawtree, 'To Lalage, Without Whom ...', in *Daily Telegraph*, 5 August 1989.

Tony Kellen, 'Bücherwidmungen', in *Zeitschrift für Bücherfreunde*, volume 5, 1901–2.

Edna Kenton, 'The New Order of Dedication', in *The Bookman*, December 1912.

Letters to the Editor, 'Credit where due', in *The Times*, 8, 11, 12, 16, 21 January 1988. (Correspondence after John Grigg's article, above.)

William Dunn Macray, 'Early Dedications to Englishmen by Foreign Authors and Editors', in *Bibliographica*, volume 1, 1895.

J. Rogers Rees, 'The Romance and Reality of Dedications', in *The Bibliographer*, October 1884.

Fran R. Schumer, 'Lovers, Enemies and Other Dedicatees', in *New York Times Book Review*, 28 September 1986.

W.M. Thackeray, 'Prefaces and Dedications', in *Living Age*, April 1859.